THE
LANGUAGE OF
LANDSCAPE

The Granite Garden: Urban Nature and Human Design

THE
LANGUAGE OF
LANDSCAPE

Anne Whiston Spirn

Photographs by
Anne Whiston Spirn

Yale University Press
New Haven and London

Designed by Mary M. Mayer
Set in Minion type by Amy Storm

Printed in the United States of America by Thomson-Shore, Inc.

Library of Congress Cataloguing-in-Publication Data
Spirn, Anne Whiston, 1947-
     The language of landscape / Anne Whiston Spirn.
          p.   cm.
     Includes bibliographical references and index.
     ISBN 0-300-07745-9
     1. Landscape architecture. 2. Landscape. 3. Landscape assessment.
4. Human ecology. I. Title.
SB472.S685 1998   98-7487
712—dc21   CIP

A catalogue record for this book is available from the British Library.

The paper in this book meets the guidelines for permanence and durability of
the Committee on Production Guidelines for Book Longevity of the Council on
Library Resources.

10 9 8 7 6 5 4 3 2 1

For
My Mother and Father
and My Danish Parents

Contents

THE LANGUAGE OF LANDSCAPE

Why the language of *landscape?* The language you describe is about so much more than landscape, it includes buildings and cities.

—*An architect*

Why not the language of *environment,* or *place*? Landscape is so ambiguous.

—*An environmental historian*

Landscape can't be *language!* You mean landscape is representation.

—*A scholar of literature*

Landscape. (Alex S. MacLean/Landslides)

Introduction

"But where's the art?" I was startled by this reaction, of some readers, to my first book, *The Granite Garden: Urban Nature and Human Design*. If the book was about sustaining health, safety, and welfare, was it, therefore, not about aesthetics? Their impulse to see the pragmatic and poetic as separate, or even contradictory, troubled me greatly, for it was my motivation to connect the two that had inspired and driven me to write the book. I was also surprised to learn how deep-seated was the resistance of some readers to considering cities part of the natural world; they were not persuaded that natural processes of air, earth, water, and life shape cities. I had failed to take account of how ideas of nature and what is "natural" stem from strongly held feelings and beliefs, how highly personal and varied these views are, and how persuasion is not simply a matter of marshaling compelling verbal arguments, but of reaching both mind and heart.

In response, I was determined to write an entire book about the *poetics* of city and nature, one that would fuse function, feeling, and meaning. I planned to derive this theory from places that exemplified it, and I hoped the new book would inspire the creation of many more, similarly successful places where people could feel, as well as reflect on, connections, and find them useful. But why propose a theory if argument alone fails to persuade many readers? Because the places I know about are so few and far apart and, further, are seldom perceived as linked. And because theory gives fresh meaning to old places, connects the seemingly unrelated, and guides action. Few people, even if they have seen both Glenn Murcutt's design for the house in Bingie, Australia, and my proposals for West Philadelphia, would regard the two as analogues, but they are, even though one is built, the home of a single family, the other a plan that may never be built, for a neighborhood of thousands of families. The design for Bingie and the plan for West Philadelphia are connected by the designers' kindred way of thinking and working.

But, in the process of looking, thinking, and writing the book on poetics, I came to realize that the poetics applies to all landscapes, not urban landscapes alone, and to buildings, too, and that defining such an aesthetic theory demanded, first, the description and codification of a *language* of landscape. But, just as some readers earlier objected to the idea that city and nature are of a piece and that art and function are related, so now I encountered considerable resistance to the concept of landscape as language. Arguments put to me forced me to confront many difficult questions, to reconsider certain proposals, and to respond. This book has, in consequence, taken far longer to write than I ever imagined.

The language of landscape is the principal language in which I think and act; my conviction that there is such a language arises first from that fact. It is also the language used skillfully by designers whose work I most admire. My own work has been a laboratory, theirs a library for me, in exploring and defining the language of landscape. Visual thinking—photography and drawing—my primary mode of thought, was extended through response to other senses, then recorded in my journals. Writing, for me, requires a translation of images and experiences into words and phrases, then a converting of weblike (landscapelike) writing into prose in which sentences follow sentences, constructing a line of reasoning that others can follow. Personally, I find digital web-authoring, with its linked, embedded structure and display of color images a more natural medium of expression than any other. My lectures are always composed of two parallel essays: one spoken, one seen, with the visual essay structuring the verbal.

Landscape architecture has been my sphere of action and service, just as photography is my touchstone and way of knowing. The landscapes I help shape are collective projects most successful when others assume ownership. The landscape architect's experience helps me see significance; the photographer's disciplined, feeling way of seeing leads me to deeper insights. I try to see things fresh by ranging broadly, then gradually zeroing in, often drawn to a detail without knowing yet what the whole is, then coming to understand the whole through many significant details. Photographs prompt and push my thinking: I let them speak, work on my feelings and mind, and sort them as images first, seeking connections. *The Language of Landscape* began this way.

Places are my primary data, and photographs and travel journals with written and drawn notes of sights, sounds, smells, and reflections are primary source material. For this reason I write primarily about places where I have been. Once, in the space of seven weeks, I traveled from a Philadelphia summer to an Australian winter, then back, in August, to San Francisco, Philadelphia, and Cape Cod, and then to Amelia Island, off the coast of Georgia, in September. The transect across climates heightened my sense of air's weight, wetness, light, and earth's texture, from Sydney's hard, dry ground to Philadelphia's soaked, soft, spongy soil to the grainy give of sandy beaches in Truro and Amelia. I appreciated why explorers like Lewis and Clark recorded their impressions of an unfamiliar world in vividly sensual terms, slogging through deep mud, the crunch of prickly cactus underfoot.

In an unfamiliar place, senses sharpen, a survival instinct; in familiar territory, senses dull, and it takes an effort to refresh them. Trying to read a foreign landscape is, for me, like reading Dutch, with English as my native language, Danish my fluent second, German limited: I may not understand everything, but I get the gist. Still, missing the meaning of a single key word or landscape feature can mislead. The language of landscape makes significant details stand out and helps me frame questions, but reading landscape deeply requires local knowledge. On foreign ground, one needs an interpreter.

I believe that we are imprinted with the landscape of our early childhood. I am a creature of the Eastern Deciduous Forest. Except for brief excursions into desert, prairie, and dry woodland, I have spent my life in the temperate forest of North America and Western Europe. I feel a sense of coming home every time I return to northwestern Connecticut, though my family moved away when I was two years old, first to Massachusetts, then to Ohio. Memories of my first place are layered: brief visits separated by long absence. I remember a landscape of steeply rolling hills and valleys, big rocks, swiftly flowing streams, thickly growing second-growth woods, houses and barns of weathered wood, stone walls, and white churches where my father and grandfather were ministers. The summer when I was eight and we drove from Cincinnati to stay for a month in Connecticut, I studied drawing with a local painter, sketching outdoors, in a nearby town, on a farm. A few years later, I was photographing river, rocks, and woods there. The light in those photographs is the low, weak light of November, and it is this light that I associate with the place, for in college and after Connecticut became, for my family, the landscape of Thanksgiving.

When I was six, we moved from Massachusetts to a suburb of Cincinnati, where we lived for the next twelve years. There my landscape broadened, progressively, from yard and street to neighborhood, town, city, and region. What I now know makes sense of what were mysteries then. There was a large vacant lot down the street with a meadow, a grove of trees, and a little stream—The Wilderness. I once dug a big hole there; as I dug, the dirt changed from dry, dark brown, to dense, yellowish brown, to sticky bluish-grey. One year, I drew charts of clouds. A bike ride away there was a forest with a creek whose bed was filled with tiny stone twigs and shells—fossils. Downtown Cincinnati was a twenty-minute bus ride away. There, green hills framed the Ohio, a broad, brown river that flooded the sloping stone landing where the *Delta Queen*, a steamboat like the one Twain piloted, was moored.

This book's philosophical foundations, like its landscape roots, were imprinted in childhood. Dialogues—with people, places, and self, between thinking and doing—were how I learned to learn. I was raised by the Socratic method, led by questions through response to insight, taught to frame questions, in turn, and listen to the answers. When I read John Dewey's *Art as Experience* in college and William James many years later, it was with a start of recognition, for I had absorbed the ideas, unattributed, as part of my family's atmosphere. My relationship to Emerson and the Transcendentalists is also cultural rather than scholarly; the texts I read in Unitarian Sunday school, and the hymns we sang, were steeped in their ideas.

At seventeen, I lived for a year with a family on a small farm in Denmark and attended school, a gymnasium, in a nearby town. There I learned landscape as livelihood, following my Danish father around, helping to feed and talk to the pigs, milk the cows, hoe sugar beets, polish eggs. I watched sows giving birth, made them roll over when they lay on their babies, loaded grown pigs onto the truck from the slaughterhouse, pulled a calf out of its mother's womb when its time came. The only hot water was in the barn where it was needed to sterilize milk cans. There was none in the house, except in winter in a room off the kitchen. Mornings began with a cold shower; a hot bath meant hauling in water from the barn. I learned the difference between standard of living and quality of life, between nature as poetic idea and natural phenomena as complex, unreliable reality.

I went to college expecting to major in art only to find that in Harvard's Fine Arts Department one studied the history of art not its making. In sophomore tutorial, I learned to *see*, to read works of art—drawings, prints, paintings, sculptures, buildings (but not landscapes!)—without the aid of written texts. Original drawings, prints, and paintings hung in pairs on the wall, confronted me each time I walked into the classroom in the Fogg Art Museum: landscapes by Rembrandt and Van Gogh, portraits by Rubens and Ingres, others by Picasso, Klee, as well as by their students and forgers. I had ten minutes to examine one pair of works, five to present my findings and reasoning: What artist, time, and place? Both by the same artist, or not: study and finished work? master's work and student's copy? or forgery? The culmination of the year was a thirty-page essay on a single work of art: mine was on El Greco's portrait of Fray Hortensio Felix Paravicino y Arteaga in Boston's Museum of Fine Arts. Many short papers led to that final product: on materials and techniques, formal analysis, style, subject, iconography, relation to other works, provenance, significance. I found a book of Paravicino's poetry in Widener Library, published in Spanish in 1650, and held my breath as the librarian checked it out to me; as I remember, the last borrower had been in the 1800s. I fell in love with scholarship that year and often wandered among the stacks of Widener, surrounded by books in so many different languages, feeling the condensed knowledge contained there, taking books off the shelves and paging through them. I feel the same way, now, in landscapes layered with deep, varied history. There is no Widener, no British Library of landscape literature, though; the texts are dispersed in places, in landscapes, around the world.

Ian McHarg's book *Design with Nature* introduced me to landscape architecture. His manifesto in the catalogue of the University of Pennsylvania, where he was chairman of the department of landscape architecture, promised a career of action bridging the arts and sciences. It stirred, then lured me. In graduate school at Penn there were no textbooks or reading lists for most courses, but rather field trips within the physiographic regions of the Delaware River Basin—from Coastal Plain to Piedmont, Ridge and Valley, to Appalachian Plateau—where we dug soil pits, collected rocks and leaves, interviewed people, and learned to read landscape. It was a surprisingly small step from discerning differences of style and quality in the lines of Old Master drawings to reading line, shape, and structure in trees, rivers, and gardens, and then a longer leap to using this knowledge to design new landscapes. Understanding relationships between process and material, form, and space was the key. I knew little landscape when I started graduate school and found it difficult, at first, to understand professors who taught with images more than with words. I learned to think and speak in drawings, diagrams, maps, and photographs.

McHarg was both professor at Penn and partner at Wallace, McHarg, Roberts, and Todd (WMRT), an office of landscape architects, architects, urban designers, and city planners. I worked in this office for five years on projects ranging from a study of an entire metropolitan region to portions of cities, from plans for new communities to park designs. On every project, he challenged us to reframe problems, take risks, break new ground, even as we drew from past experience, adapting that knowledge to new situations. Lessons learned in practice prompted refinements in the university curriculum. In the 1960s and 1970s, successive dialogues between theory developed at Penn and its application in practice advanced the field of landscape architecture: Penn's curriculum was a model imitated by universities around the world; one after another of McHarg's professional projects were, and still are, landmarks. Long before I read Donald Schon's description of professional thinking as reflection-in-action, I learned its power firsthand.

From private practice I moved to Harvard to teach, then to Penn, but the years in practice still influence the kinds of questions I ask, the methods I use, and what I write. Even in a successful, reflective practice like McHarg's there are avenues one has neither time nor funds to pursue. So I created a "research practice" in which grants and a university salary enable me to set my own agenda and support action-research projects for some clients, like community gardeners and children, who cannot afford a designer, and others who do not know they need one, like community development corporations, city agencies, and public schools. What began, in 1984, as a study of how vacant urban land could be exploited as a resource to restore the city's natural environment and rebuild inner-city neighborhoods, grew into an investigation of how to combine a comprehensive, "top-down" approach with an incremental, "bottom-up" approach to urban design and community development. Starting in inner-city neighborhoods of Boston's Roxbury and Dorchester and continuing in West Philadelphia, students and I met with community residents and politicians, planners, and engineers. We designed and built community gardens, playgrounds, and small parks on vacant lots and proposed strategic improvements to the urban infrastructure of streets, sewers, and open space as a framework for renewal that would stimulate investment and improve air and water quality. We surveyed vacant lots, plotted old floodplains, gathered census data, searched archives for historic maps, photographs, and newspaper articles, mapped land use and other features, and created a digital database with which to compare and overlay this information. The dedicated adults and bright, earnest children I met led me to reevaluate and reinterpret the dismal picture painted by statistics alone; we found rich resources and models of success in even the poorest communities. Contrary to professional wisdom and my own expectations, I discovered that many community gardeners are astute critics who recognize and value design that serves their needs and expresses their dreams. Furthermore, they are often quicker to grasp the devastating impact and potential value of natural features like buried streams than are the professionals responsible for planning the city. If community gardens are indeed communities, could the gardeners not apply their understanding of successful design and respect for natural processes to help plan the larger neighborhood and region? Watching, listening, talking, photographing, drawing, writing, I searched for a common language with which to shape and share visions for the future.

All my work—photography, writing, teaching, design, and planning—is devoted to helping people recognize the good and beautiful that exist in the world, to bolster and build from them, and to recognize the ugly and the dangerous, to avoid them. I want to demonstrate the commonalities among landscapes of natural beauty, those designed by trained designers and artists and those crafted by ordinary people, and to inspire the making of new places with extraordinary qualities and significance. And I want to trace the legacy of others who have built and written in this tradition.

This book is written out of my life as author and reader, performer and critic, artist and scholar of landscape, out of fieldwork and archival research. I use practice to develop and test theory, and theory to critique practice, alternating between engagement and detachment, passion and dispassion.[1] Making things happen is a messy process full of unforeseen obstacles and opportunities, disappointments and joys. Unexpected events challenge theory, demand revision; refined, theory holds. As actor and author, I have both a pragmatic and a poetic sensibility. When I look at a designed landscape, I calculate the difficulty of the task, judge the intentions implicit in others' deeds, applaud or condemn the risks they take, and admire the grace with which multiple demands are fulfilled.[2] As an artist, I respond to light, detail, and presence with the empathy for living and nonliving things that landscape photography demands.[3] As a scholar, I document the tradition within which I think and act, compare what other authors do to what they say, study the context of their actions and writings.[4] Art and action push me at times to take poetic license or to venture beyond the point where the scholar might stop.

My conviction that landscape is language has startled some people and outraged others, but it seems natural to many landscape architects, for landscape is a language derived from the core activity of landscape architecture: artful shaping, from garden to region, to fulfill function and express meaning. The roots of this theory are strong, deep, and varied, grounded in many fields—anthropology, geography, geology, ecology, history, art history, literature, linguistics, and landscape architecture, among others. It is a radical theory: in the sense of being rooted in the basic elements of nature and human nature; in the sense of offering a fundamentally different perspective than from any one individual root; and in demanding and enabling radical change in how we choose to think and act.

Landscape architecture is a profession I discovered by chance soon after college. Most of my students come to it much later in life, often after other careers. Despite its scope and the significance of the discipline, it is, in many respects, an invisible profession compared to the related fields of architecture and engineering, and this reflects the greater problems described in this book. If this book inspires others to enter and contribute to this wonderful, crucial profession, I will be happy.

Prologue: The Yellowwood and the Forgotten Creek

Once a yellowwood stood by an old library, leafing, flowering, fruiting, setting seed; roots grabbed hold, sucked air and water from beneath a plaza of brick. Its skin-smooth silver trunk bore knobby limbs. Floppy leaves clung to long stems, catching wind, moving green shadows across red bricks. Students sat each spring under the yellowwood, listening to names named, glad for green shade, walked under it to the library, breathed musky June flowers, kicked yellow leaves of October across red bricks.

For many years the yellowwood grew; red stone blackened, the building decayed. Then men came one day to fix the library, piled stacks of tools, tiles, and sacks around the tree, sealing soil under bricks. Two years later, the library reopened, leaded glass gleaming, blackened stone brightened, furnace fixed. How elegant, people said. That fall the tree lost its leaves in September.

Next May, the yellowwood flowered early and profusely. Thousands of fragrant white blooms hung in long clusters; petals covered bricks, blew across grass. How beautiful, people said. How sad, though. Several years' bud scars bunched up against each twig's growing tip. Abundant flowers signaled a dying, and seeds found no purchase in the plaza. People admired the tree and walked on; they had lost the language that gives tongue to its tale. Once a yellowwood stood. No more. And few knew why.

One day a street caved in. Sidewalks collapsed into a block-long chasm. People looked down, shocked to see a strong, brown, rushing river. A truck fell into a hole like that years back, someone said. A whole block of homes collapsed into a hole one night a long time ago, said someone else. They weren't sure where. Six months later, the hole was filled, street patched, sidewalks rebuilt. Years went by, new folks moved in, water seeped, streets dipped, walls cracked.

Once a creek flowed—long before there was anyone to give it a name—coursing down, carving, plunging, pooling, thousands of years before dams harnessed its power, before people buried it in a sewer and built houses on top. Now, swollen with rain and sewage, the buried creek bursts pipes, soaks soil, floods basements, undermines buildings. During storms, brown water gushes from inlets and manholes into streets and, downstream, overwhelms the sewage treatment plant, overflowing into the river from which the city draws its water.

Vacant lots overgrown by meadows and shrubby thickets near boarded-up homes and community gardens filled with flowers and vegetables follow a meandering line no one seems to see. In a school that stands on this unseen line, the gym floods every time it rains. Once a year, teachers take students on buses to a place outside the city to see and study "nature."

On a once vacant lot, brand new houses—red brick, yellow siding, green sliver of lawn out front, gates open—rise in contrast to nearby older, shattered houses and land laid waste: "First Time Buyers, own this home for less than you pay in rent," a sign urges. The houses have been built by churches from coins and foundation funds, the land a gift from the city. How beautiful, people say. No one wonders why the land was free, why water puddles there, why the name of the place is Mill Creek.

Signs of hope, signs of warning are all around, unseen, unheard, undetected. Most people can no longer read the signs: whether they live in a floodplain, whether they are rebuilding an urban neighborhood or planting the seeds of its destruction, whether they are protecting or polluting the water they drink, caring for or killing a tree. Most have forgotten the language and cannot read the stories the wildflowers and saplings on vacant lots tell of life's regenerative power; many do not understand the beauty of a community garden's messy order. They cannot hear or see the language of landscape.

Architects' drawings show no roots, no growing, just green lollipops and buildings floating on a page, as if ground were flat and blank, the tree an object not a life. Planners' maps show no buried rivers, no flowing, just streets, lines of ownership, and proposals for future use, as if past were not present, as if the city were merely a human construct not a living, changing landscape. Children's textbooks, from science to history, show no nearby scenes, suggest or demand no firsthand knowing, just formulas and far-off people and places, as if numbers and language had no local meaning, as if their present had no past, no future, the student a vessel not an actor.

The yellowwood was the first yellowwood I ever saw, its perfumed flowers an amazing surprise my first year as a graduate student, the same year the hole and the river emerged near my apartment. The yellowwood, gone, is still on my daily path; the forgotten creek is now the heart of my work. Back then I knew nothing of dying trees or buried rivers. Now I have learned to read what sloping valleys and sinking streets tell, what bud scars say. Landscapes are rich with complex language, spoken and written in land, air, and water. Humans are storytelling animals, thinking in metaphors steeped in landscape: putting down roots means commitment, uprooting a traumatic event. Like a living tree rooted in place, language is rooted in landscape.

The meanings landscapes hold are not just metaphorical and metaphysical, but real, their messages practical; understanding may spell survival or extinction. Losing, or failing to hear and read, the language of landscape threatens body and spirit, for the pragmatic and the imaginative aspects of landscape language have always coexisted. Relearning the language that holds life in place is an urgent task. This book is dedicated to its recovery and renewal.

One

"Nature's Infinite Book": The Language of Landscape

The face of the water, in time, became a wonderful book—a book that was a dead language to the uneducated passenger, but which told its mind to me without reserve, delivering its most cherished secrets as clearly as if it uttered them with a voice. And it was not a book to be read once and thrown aside, for it had a new story to tell every day.

—Mark Twain, *Life on the Mississippi*

In nature's infinite book of secrecy
A little I can read.

—Shakespeare, *Antony and Cleopatra*

Landscape as text: The Ridgeway. Avebury, England.

1
Dwelling and Tongue:
The Language of Landscape

LANDSCAPE IS LANGUAGE

The language of landscape is our native language. Landscape was the original
dwelling; humans evolved among plants and animals, under the sky, upon the
earth, near water. Everyone carries that legacy in body and mind. Humans
touched, saw, heard, smelled, tasted, lived in, and shaped landscapes before the
species had words to describe what it did. Landscapes were the first human texts,
read before the invention of other signs and symbols. Clouds, wind, and sun were
clues to weather, ripples and eddies signs of rocks and life under water, caves and
ledges promise of shelter, leaves guides to food; birdcalls warnings of predators.
Early writing resembled landscape; other languages—verbal, mathematical,
graphic—derive from the language of landscape.[1]

The language of landscape can be spoken, written, read, and imagined. Speaking and reading landscape are by-products of living—of moving, mating, eating—
and strategies of survival—creating refuge, providing prospect, growing food. To
read and write landscape is to learn and teach: to know the world, to express ideas
and to influence others. Landscape, as language, makes thought tangible and
imagination possible. Through it humans share experience with future generations, just as ancestors inscribed their values and beliefs in the landscapes they left
as a legacy, "a treasure deposited by the practice of speech," a rich lode of literature:
natural and cultural histories, landscapes of purpose, poetry, power, and prayer.[2]

Landscape has all the features of language. It contains the equivalent of
words and parts of speech—patterns of shape, structure, material, formation,
and function. All landscapes are combinations of these. Like the meanings
of words, the meanings of landscape elements (water, for example) are only
potential until context shapes them. Rules of grammar govern and guide how
landscapes are formed, some specific to places and their local dialects, others universal. Landscape is pragmatic, poetic, rhetorical, polemical. Landscape is scene of
life, cultivated construction, carrier of meaning. It is language.

Verbal language reflects landscape. Up and down, in and out—the most
basic metaphors of verbal language—stem from experience of landscape, like
bodily movement through landscape.[3] Verbs, nouns, adverbs, adjectives, and their
contexts—parts of speech and the structure of verbal language—mirror landscape processes, products, and their modifiers, material, formal, and spatial. Just
as a river combines water, flowing, and eroded banks, sentences combine actions and
actors, objects and modifiers. The context of a word or sentence, like that of hill or

Landscape legacy: avenue of stones. Avebury, England.

valley, defines it. Verbal texts and landscapes are nested: word within sentence within paragraph within chapter, leaf within branch within tree within forest. Words reflect observation and experience; dialects are rich in terms specific to landscape of place, like "estuary English," described so vividly by John Stilgoe.[4] Shakespeare, Mark Twain, T. S. Eliot, Anthony Hecht, and Adrienne Rich, like verbal poets of every literature, mine landscape for structure, rhythm, and fresh metaphors of human experience; so do poets of landscape itself, "Capability" Brown, Frederick Law Olmsted, Frank Lloyd Wright, Lawrence Halprin, Martha Schwartz.[5]

Landscape is the material home, the language of landscape is a habitat of mind. Heidegger called language the house of being, but the language of landscape truly is the *house* of being; we dwell within it. To dwell—to make and care for a place—is self-expression. Heidegger traced that verb in High German and Old English; in both, the root for "to dwell" means "to build." In German, the roots for building and dwelling and "I am" are the same. I am because I dwell; I dwell because I build. *Bauen*—building, dwelling, and being—means "to build," "to construct," but also to "cherish and protect, to preserve and care for, specifically to till the soil, to cultivate the mind."[6]

Landscape associates people and place. Danish *landskab*, German *landschaft*, Dutch *landschap*, and Old English *landscipe* combine two roots. "Land" means both a place and the people living there. *Skabe* and *schaffen* mean "to shape"; suffixes *-skab* and *-schaft* as in the English "-ship," also mean association, partnership.[7] Though no longer used in ordinary speech, the Dutch *schappen* conveys a magisterial sense of shaping, as in the biblical Creation. Still strong in Scandinavian and German languages, these original meanings have all but disappeared from English. *Webster's Dictionary* defines *landscape* as static, "a picture representing a section of natural, inland scenery, as of prairie, woodland, mountains . . . an expanse of natural scenery seen by the eye in one view"; the *Oxford English Dictionary* traces the word to a Dutch painting term (*landskip*).[8] But landscape is not a mere visible surface, static composition, or passive backdrop to human theater; therefore dictionaries must be revised, and the older meanings revived. The words *environment* and *place*, commonly used to replace *landscape* in twentieth-century English, are inadequate substitutes, for they refer to locale or surroundings and omit people. In midcentury, the declining use of *landscape* was in part a reaction to the Nazis' adoption of "blood and soil," a linking of native landscape and racial identity. *Environment* and *place* seem more neutral, but they are abstract, disembodied, sacrificing meaning, concealing tensions and conflicts, ignoring the assumptions *landscape* reveals. *Landscape* connotes a sense of the purposefully shaped, the sensual and aesthetic, the embeddedness in culture. The language of landscape recovers the dynamic connection between place and those who dwell there.

Landscape is loud with dialogues, with story lines that connect a place and its dwellers. The shape and structure of a tree record an evolutionary dialogue between species and environment: eucalypt leaves that turn their edge to bright sun, deciduous leaves that fall off during seasonal heat or cold. And they record dialogues between a tree and its habitat. Tree rings thick and thin tell the water and food of each growing season of the tree's life. Size, shape, and structure—low-branched or high, densely branched or spare—reflect dialogues between a tree and a group of trees in open field or dense forest. Each species has a characteristic form from which individuals deviate, as true of human body shape—muscled or fat, short or tall—as of trees. A coherence of human vernacular landscapes emerges from dialogues between builders and place, fine-tuned over time. They tell of a congruence between snowfall and roof pitch, between seasonal sun angles and roof overhang, wind direction and alignment of hedgerows, cultivation practices and dimensions of fields, family structure and patterns of settlement. Dialogues make up the context of individual, group, and place. The context of life is a woven fabric of dialogues, enduring and ephemeral.

Humans are not the sole authors of landscape. Volcanoes spew lava, remaking land; rain falls, carving valleys. Mountains, gardens, and cities are shaped by volcanoes and rain, plants and animals, human hands and minds. Trees shade ground and shed leaves, produce a more hospitable place for life with similar needs. Beavers cut trees and dam streams to make ponds: a dwelling place. People mold landscape with hands, tools, and machines, through law, public policy, and actions undertaken hundreds, even thousands, of miles away. All living things share the same space, all make landscape, and all landscapes, wild or domesticated, have coauthors, all are phenomena of nature and culture. Others share the language, but only humans (as far as we yet know) reflect, worship, make art, and design landscapes like the gardens of the Villa d'Este that "set the formal strictures" within a natural context "where the tension lectures us on our mortal state."[9]

Landscape Is Meaningful and Expressive

Landscape has meaning. Rivers reflect, clouds portend. Wilderness, for many now a sacred symbol of undefiled nature, was once a terrifying symbol of chaos. Some meanings are human inventions, and yet significance does not depend on human perception or imagination alone. Significance is there to be discovered, inherent and ascribed, shaped by what senses perceive, what instinct and experience read as significant, what minds know. Any organism with senses has the potential to read and understand landscape. To a deaf man, a rustling bush cannot signal an approaching animal, but moving leaves or vibrating ground may. To a canoer a river is a path, waves and eddy lines are signs to steer by. To a fish a river is a watery world of light and shadow, surface movement is sign of prey. Fly fishermen try to read rivers as fish do in order to trick them, picking then flicking the fly at line's end, mimicking real flies abroad on the stream to convince the fish the fly is real. Norman Maclean describes a master fly-tier who lay under a glass tank filled with water to study the insect he planned to imitate.[10] The best fly fishermen think like fish, become the fish, in an intimate bonding of hunter and hunted.

Landscapes are as small as a garden, as large as a planet. To a person the garden is a landscape, to a people the nation is, to the human species, a planet. A pond is a landscape to a beaver, a tree to a bird, a forest to a tree. Ice floes on a river, lake, or arctic sea, inhabited by birds and seals, are a landscape. Ice crystals on a winter window look like ice floes seen from the air, are uninhabited, yet to a poet a landscape of the imagination. Landscape may be inhabited in imagination alone.

There are landscapes within landscapes within landscapes. Every landscape feature is both a whole and part of one or more larger wholes: leaf and twig, twig and tree, tree and forest; garden and house, house and street, street and town, town and region. Every phenomenon, thing, event, and feeling has a context. A valley is not a valley if it has no ridge or plateau, no up and down. Motion is imperceptible without rest, sound without stillness. Without sense of past and future, there can be no present, without threat no refuge. The same material, form, or action may have different meanings in different settings—water in a desert, water in a sea.

Anomalies are clues to what the wider context is. A "wolf" tree is a tree within a woods, its size and form, large trunk and horizontal branches, anomalous to the environs of slim-trunked trees with upright branches. It is a clue to the open field in which it once grew alone, branches reaching laterally to the light and up. With that field unmowed, unplowed, or ungrazed, younger woodland trees grew thickly

In wolf tree, see the former field. Amherst, Massachusetts.

together around the older tree, their branches finding light by reaching up. The older tree, engulfed by a dense woodland of younger trees, no longer able to find light horizontally, sends new branches upward. Landscape is dynamic, present context includes the past; the story of the wolf tree is part of the human story.

When valley and river, path and user fail to correspond—when, for example, a valley is vast but a river small, a path broad and well-worn, but those who pass that way infrequent—valley and path may have been shaped by context not now visible or no longer relevant: valley by a great flood, path by an earlier surging crowd. Also, context may be actual or latent—every landscape has both real and potential form—what is, what has been, what will, what might be.

Metaphors grounded in landscape guide how humans think and act. George Lakoff and Mark Johnson demonstrate what Emerson observed: that humans understand and experience one kind of thing in terms of another, projecting bodies and minds onto the surrounding world: trees and clouds seen as bounded, a river seen as having a mouth, a mountain as having a foot, front, back, and side.[11] One might just as easily see things as continuous and undifferentiated; viewing them as separate is more a function of individual consciousness than an inherent quality of landscape. Many metaphors are grounded in fundamental relationships with landscape—moving, making, eating, wasting. The most common refer to space and direction: in and out, up and down. In American culture, high and in are good, down and out are bad; central is important, marginal is not. Landscape imagery conveys feelings and ideas: emotions churning like a stormy sea, rivers of time, clouds where gods live, sacred mountains, Father Sky impregnating Mother Earth with rain as the seed, Zeus and Thor hurling thunderbolts in anger, Siva flashing lightning from his Third Eye, a flare of cosmic intelligence, the god of Jews and Christians dispatching plagues of locusts and disease to punish the wicked. Personification, the attribution of human feelings like intention, anger, love to natural forms and phenomena, is the foundation of myth and religion.

Landscapes are the world itself and may also be metaphors of the world. A tree can be both a tree and The Tree, a path both a path and The Path. A tree in the Garden of Eden represents the Tree of Life, the Tree of Knowledge. It becomes the archetype of Tree. When a path represents the Path of Enlightenment of Buddhism or the Stations of the Cross of Christianity it is no longer a mere path, but The Path. The yellow brick road in *The Wizard of Oz* is both path and Path. The similar is the stuff of metaphor, simile, and personification; contrasts are the stuff of paradox and oxymoron. Landscape actors, objects, and modifiers may enhance meaning without rhetoric: rivers reflect and run, but they do not pun.

Built landscapes may be rhetorical. Landscape features, like hill and street, may be emphasized or embellished for effect, slope steepened to make climb difficult, street broadened and lined with trees to impress the viewer. Gardens of allusion reflect oral and written literature: Shakespeare gardens allude to the bard's plays and poetry, their herbs and blooms references to his works; eighteenth-century English gardens, with their buildings in classical style and pastoral landscape, refer to classical literature. When Mussolini built a monument in 1938 to those who died in a battle of the First World War in Redipuglia, near Italy's northwestern boundary, he used the language of rhetoric. More than one hundred thousand soldiers are buried there in twenty-two terraces of tombs, arranged from bottom to top in alphabetical order, sixty thousand buried at the top of the hill in a common grave surmounted by three crosses, like Calvary. Words engraved in the pavement tell how these soldiers died for the glory of Italy, immortal in memory. Facing the hill of tombs is the grave of their general, as if addressing his entombed soldiers. Their inscriptions answer, *"Presente."* "I am here."

The language of landscape can be spoken and read even though never codified, without recourse to rules. People follow paths and make them, plant gardens, are awed by the scale of mountains and cathedrals; great designers use landscape

Landscape of power and rhetoric: World War One cemetery. Redipuglia, Italy.

fluently, all without dictionaries or grammars. Thomas Jefferson linked landscape and learning at the University of Virginia where he designed and sited the original buildings. Sigurd Lewerentz and Gunnar Asplund comforted the bereaved in the Hill of Remembrance and Woodland Chapel at Forest Cemetery in Stockholm. Glenn Murcutt associated people, sun, wind, and water in a house at Bingie on the coast of Australia. Even those who exploit landscape cynically may do so masterfully, as Mussolini did when, at Redipuglia, he fostered feelings of heroic nationalism to promote fascism, or as Disney has exploited it, for profit, at Disneyland and Disney World.

Landscapes are a vast library of literature. The myths of Japan's Fuji and Australia's Uluru, the folksy tales of trolls and pink flamingos on American lawns, the classical works of earth, water, and wind at Yosemite and the Grand Canyon, the high art of the Alhambra and Manhattan's Central Park, and countless other places, ordinary and extraordinary, record the language of landscape. The library ranges from wild and vernacular landscape, tales shaped by everyday phenomena, to classic landscapes of artful expression, like the relationship of ordinary spoken language to great works of literature. Worship, memory, play, movement, meeting, exchange, power, production, home, and community are pervasive landscape genre. To be fully felt and known landscape literature must be experienced in situ; words, drawings, paintings, or photographs cannot replace the experience of the place itself, though they may enhance and intensify it.

Landscape literature is a resource to be treasured. Several decades ago, archeologists in Israel discovered ancient water-gathering systems in the Negev Desert that employed simple channels, check dams, and broad depressions. These techniques, lost for many centuries, have inspired the landscape architect Shlomo Aronson and others to reshape whole landscapes to gather water; they planted groves and grassy meadows in the desert, all sustained by dewfall and rain. The water engineer Ken Wright is working with archeologists to study the water systems of the Incas in Peru, not just to understand, but to use their knowledge. I have studied dozens of community gardens in Philadelphia as landscape expressions. The literature of landscape contains a vast repertoire of similar examples, adaptations to a wide range of circumstances, not just in the diversity of genes and behavior, but in ideas and cultures. Some are cherished and cared for, others are being rediscovered, but entire volumes of landscape literature are being lost and forgotten, whole libraries destroyed.

LANDSCAPE HAS CONSEQUENCES

The language of landscape is a powerful tool. A person literate in landscape sees significance where an illiterate person notes nothing. Past and future fires, floods, landslides, welcome or warning are visible to those who can read them in tree and slope, boundary and gate. Knowing how to tell what one wants to express—pragmatics—makes landscape authors more adept; making landscapes appeal to emotion and reason depends on understanding rhetoric. To know landscape poetics is to see, smell, taste, hear, and feel landscape as a symphony of complex harmonies. Natural processes establish the base rhythm that is expressed in the initial form of the land, to which culture, in turn, responds with new and changing themes that weave an intricate pattern, punctuated here and there by high points of nature and art. Landscape symphonies evolve continually in time, in predictable and unpredictable ways, responding to process and to human purpose, and, in landscape symphonies, all dwellers are composers and players.

The language of landscape humans have always known but now use piecemeal, with much forgotten. People still read paths and create them, identify boundaries and define territory, delight in a flowering tree comparing it to a lover, but most people read landscape shallowly or narrowly and tell it stupidly or inadequately. Oblivious to dialogue and story line, they misread or miss meaning entirely, blind to connections among intimately related phenomena, oblivious to poetry, then fail to act or act wrongly. Absent, false, or partial readings lead to inarticulate expression: landscape silence, gibberish, incoherent rambling, dysfunctional, fragmented dialogues, broken story lines. The consequences are comical, dumb, dire, tragic. Those who admired the yellowwood's excessive, early flowering on the campus in Philadelphia were blind to what the bud scars told, failed to read the flowers' poignant message, were unable to imagine the tree's connection to soil, plaza, and contractor. When I tried to convince the dean, himself an architect, to find another site for the contractors' trailer and tools, he refused, unconvinced or not caring that the yellowwood would die as a consequence. Those who first built houses over the buried creek in West Philadelphia and those who rebuilt in the same place were illiterate in the language of landscape and so could not read the creek's presence. I tried and failed, at first, to convince planners at the City Planning Commission and engineers at the Philadelphia Water Department that the buried creek was a resource to be exploited and a force to be reckoned with. The yellowwood is dead, but it is not too late to restore Mill Creek—the water, the people, the place.

Ironically, the professionals who specialize, reading certain parts of landscape more deeply than other parts and shaping them more powerfully, often fail to understand landscape as a continuous whole. Once those who transformed landscapes were generalists: naturalist, humanist, artist, engineer, even priest, all combined. Now pieces of landscape are shaped by those whose narrowness of knowledge, experience, values, and concerns leads them to read and tell only fragments of the story. To an ecologist, landscape is habitat, but not construction or metaphor. To a lawyer, landscape may be property to regulate, to a developer, a commodity to exploit, to an architect, a site to build on, to a planner, a zone for recreation or residence or commerce or transportation, or "nature preservation." As in the story of the blind men who each touch a different part of the elephant— trunk or tusk or tail alone—then arrive at a false description of the whole animal, so each discipline and each interest group reads and tells landscape through its own tunnel vision of perception, value, tool, and action. And as each shouts its own fragment, landscapes of cities, suburbs, and regions are severed, become impoverished, dysfunctional. It is even fashionable now to design buildings, gardens, and cities deliberately as dislocated and unconnected fragments to emphasize the erosion of common ground, a misanthropic view of cultural differences.

Loss of fluency in the language of landscape, in turn, impoverishes verbal language. Words like *bore* and *guzzle* refer to features and processes many no longer perceive—and which can injure or even kill. To know the meaning (and location) of bore and guzzle is to be safe, to survive: a bore is the "noisy rush of the tides against the current in a narrow channel"; a guzzle, the low place in the dunes where water drains and the sea comes crashing through in a "century storm."[12] To know bore is to avoid it at high tide; to know guzzle is to decide not to build and settle there. Such nuances, preserved in specialized, professional language, are now lost to common verbal language. Aboriginal peoples become more "civilized" and less attuned to landscape; young Papua-New Guineans, for example, no longer learn to sing with waterfalls and birds. A loss of language and loss of knowledge limits the celebration of landscape as a partnership between people, place, and other life and further reduces the capacity to understand and imagine possible human relationships with nonhuman nature.

We shape landscape and language; they shape us. To know landscape is to read in Boston's Fens and Riverway artful reconstructions of places laid waste by human occupation. Not to know is to fail to discern what merely grew and what was planted, and thus, for example, to mistake the Fens and Riverway as "preserved" wetland and floodplain forest; they were, rather, the product of human purpose mindful of natural processes of regeneration. Failure to recognize the Fens and Riverway as being *designed* and *built*, not happenstance, blinds us to the possibility of designing and building similar transformations elsewhere.

Landscape metaphors modify perceptions, prompt ideas and actions, molding landscape, in turn. To see wilderness as chaos provokes fear and prompts flight, perhaps even the urge to destroy; to believe it sacred fosters appeal, reverence, and the desire to cherish. To know nature as a set of ideas not a place, and landscape as the expression of actions and ideas in place not as an abstraction or as mere scenery promotes an understanding of landscape as a continuum of meaning.[13] Not to know, and to confuse landscape and nature, is to equate landscape with mountain, meadow, farm, and country road, but not highway or town. Yet a designed urban park is no less a landscape than a planted cornfield, the island of Manhattan no less a landscape than its Central Park. Notions of landscape as countryside, but not city, falsely fragment intimate connections and produce such ironies as inner-city schoolchildren bused out of town to study old-field meadows, ignoring the same plants growing on vacant lots next door.[14] To see landscape as mere scenery gives precedence to appearance at the expense of habitability and risks trivializing landscape as decoration—landscaping—concealing the significance of senses other than sight and of parts hidden from view, the deep context underlying the surface. To call some landscapes natural and others artificial or cultural misses the truth that landscapes are never wholly one or the other.

Once most of life was lived outdoors, in constant dialogue with wind, water, soil, plants, and animals; now most livelihoods no longer depend upon literacy in landscape. Or so we imagine. Our most intimate relationships with nature (finding food and water, disposing of waste) are now negotiated by large, distant institutions. Schools and popular media train children to experience the world many steps removed, through textbooks, calculations, and secondhand images and sounds in film, video, and computer. People work in offices with windows that do not open, or with no windows at all. Meanwhile naturalists, gardeners, and fly fishermen, like modern shamans, preserve and pass on bits of the language— knowledge of bird and insect, soil and seed, water and fish—and write books to reflect on and communicate the meanings of human life and relations with non-human nature, inheritors of Thoreau's *Walden* like Annie Dillard's *Pilgrim at Tinker Creek*, Michael Pollan's *Second Nature*, and Norman Maclean's *A River Runs Through It.*

Even farming and fishing are now high-tech, capital-intensive industries whose owners may never touch soil or sea. In 1990, for the first time in American history, the category "farmer" was eliminated from the U.S. Census. "Agricultural laborer" took its place. Laborers, those in most intimate contact with earth and plants, water and fish, now perform work dictated in distant offices by people who may never see the consequences of their policies and plans. At Disney's EPCOT (Experimental Prototypical Community of Tomorrow), an elaborate exhibit called "The Land," sponsored by Kraft Foods, shows a soil-less, factorylike future for American agriculture: plants hang from wires, move as products in an assembly line, roots exposed, sprayed by aerosols of water and fertilizers, divorced from dirt. This is a perilous vision because the sense of control it conveys is false, an illusion. The plants are fragile, dependent upon the sprayers' continued function; lives hang, literally, by a thread. If the sprayers fail plants shrivel rapidly, for their roots are not held in soil's reservoir of moisture and nutrients.

The power to read, tell, and design landscape is one of the greatest human talents; it enabled our ancestors to spread from warm savannas to cool, shady forests and even to cold, open tundra. But, now, the ability to transform landscape beyond the capacity to comprehend it threatens human existence. Having altered virtually every spot on the planet, humans have triggered perturbations that threaten to change it irrevocably and dangerously. Many, as a consequence, feel control slipping, exposed for the illusion it always was. Our lives are like the plants hanging from wires at EPCOT, roots exposed, dependent upon technologies which, should they fail, will spell disaster. Some speak of the end of nature, but it is nature as *we* know it that is threatened, not the planet itself, not the universe.

To recover and renew the language of landscape is to discover and imagine new metaphors, to tell new stories, and to create new landscapes. John Berger describes, and the photographer Jean Mohr illustrates, a language of lived experience with which to interpret the common and the particular across the gulf of different cultures.[15] Gregory Bateson says that humans must learn to speak the language "in terms of which living things are organized," in order to read the world not as discrete things, but as dynamic relations, and to practice the art of managing complex, living systems.[16] Aldo Leopold writes of the need for humans to "think like a mountain," to escape the short-sightedness that threatens the larger habitats of which humans are part.[17] Berger, Bateson, Leopold, and others have envisioned or implied the need for such a language; none have elaborated or codified it. The language of landscape is such a language: in terms of it the world is organized and living things behave, humans can think like a mountain, can shape landscapes that sustain human lives and the lives of other creatures as well, can foster identity and celebrate diversity.

The language of landscape prompts us to perceive and shape the landscape *whole*. Reading and speaking it fluently is a way to recognize the dialogues ongoing in a place, to appreciate other speakers' stories, to distinguish enduring dialogues from ephemeral ones, and to join the conversation. The language of landscape reminds us that nothing stays the same, that catastrophic shifts and cumulative changes shape the present. It permits us to perceive pasts we cannot otherwise experience, to anticipate the possible, to envision, choose, and shape the future. We can see what is not immediate, a forest in a meadow, the yellowwood dying of starved and suffocated roots, and seeing, we can choose to save or snuff it. Or we can see water underground in the tree along a dry creek bed, in the cracks of a building's foundation, the slumps in pavement in a city; or see the connections between buried, sewered stream, vacant land, and polluted river, and imagine rebuilding communities while purifying water. And we can imagine poetry.

Humans' survival as a species depends upon adapting ourselves and our landscapes—settlements, buildings, rivers, fields, forests—in new, life-sustaining ways, shaping contexts that acknowledge connections to air, earth, water, life, and to each other, and that help us feel and understand these connections, landscapes that are functional, sustainable, meaningful, and artful. Not everyone will be farmers or fishermen for whom landscape is livelihood, but all can learn to read landscape, to understand those readings, and to speak new wisdom into life in city, suburb, and countryside, to cultivate the power of landscape expression as if our life depends upon it. For it does.

2

Survival and Imagination: Reading and Telling the Meanings of Landscape

The surface of the Mississippi River, Mark Twain wrote, is "a wonderful book" that "told its mind . . . without reserve, delivering its most cherished secrets as clearly as if it uttered them with a voice."[1] Riverboat pilots read the river to steer safely around snags and sandbars, following the deep main channel. A pilot taught Twain to read the river's depth and shape from patterns on the water's surface: "Now look out—look out! Don't you crowd that slick, greasy-looking place; there ain't nine feet there." The "long slanting line on the face of the water" revealed a bluff reef below that would "knock the boat's brains out"; how at the head of the reef "where the line fringes out at the upper end and begins to fade away," it was safe to cross. Beneath "fine lines . . . that branch out like the ribs of a fan" lay smaller reefs: "miss the ends of them, but run them pretty close." The Mississippi tested even the experienced pilots, for it changes day by day, season by season, year by year: "It was not a book to be read once and thrown aside, for it had a new story to tell every day." From one year to the next, the river, altered, became an unfamiliar text, landmarks gone, submerged, displaced. The river had moved across the land.

Reading landscape reveals the past and foretells the future: history can be deciphered in shape of valley and hill, field and fence; tomorrow's weather can be told from evening sun and clouds. Verbal and mathematical languages, the word and the formula, merely describe and interpret the world for they are not the things they describe, but always one or more steps removed. In landscape, representation and reality fuse when a tree, path, or gate is invested with larger significance. In a sacred landscape, a path is seldom only a path, but the Path, where pilgrims climb to reach a hilltop shrine and, within a church, traverse the path between portal and altar, tracing a metaphorical and an actual journey. Ambiguity—layers of landscape meanings—and the metaphors and paradoxes it engenders are a source of rich material for reading and telling.

LANDSCAPE CONTESTED, CELEBRATED, RECLAIMED: SLESVIG AND THE DANISH HEATH

A tall stone column rises from Skamlingsbanke, the highest point in southern Jutland, Denmark's western peninsula. Up close, it looks like a stack of broken blocks, corners chipped. Its significance can be read even without understanding the Danish words cut into stone: "Raised 1863. Blown up by the Prussians March 21, 1864. Raised again May 1, 1866. Memorial to the Champions of the Danish

Cause in Slesvig." There is no broad river or high ridge between Denmark and Germany, and Danevirk, the ancient Viking earthwork, proved a puny obstacle to Prussian armies. The provinces of Slesvig-Holstein were a broad zone of contested terrain for more than seventy years from 1848 to 1920.[2] After a devastating defeat by Germany in 1864, Denmark was reduced to its smallest land area ever. From 1864 to 1920, the border between Denmark and Germany was just south of Skamlings-banke, and the Danish-speaking population of Slesvig-Holstein were forbidden to speak their own language. Between 1865 and 1905, some 55,000 Danes emigrated from Slesvig to the United States. When, in 1920, Slesvig became Danish once again by popular vote mandated by the Treaty of Versailles, there were only 165,000 people left.[3] On April 9, 1940, German troops marched across Slesvig once again to begin a new occupation, and, in 1945, more than 80,000 people gathered at Skamlingsbanke after liberation for a *folkfest* sponsored by the Danish Resistance.

Skamlingsbanke is both prospect and refuge. The hilltop, a landmark visible from afar, affords a distant view over farm fields to the south and west and over the water to the east. From the base of the monument, a narrow dale slopes steeply down to form a natural amphitheater. In 1843, some farmers bought the hill as a place to celebrate Danish culture. Skamlingsbanke soon became a spiritual Danevirk where Danish leaders spoke to large crowds in the amphitheater; here is where N. F. S. Grundtvig, founder of the Danish folk high schools, announced his plans. Memorial stones set up over the years link land, language, and motherhood.

In the eighteenth century, western Jutland was a remote part of Denmark, poor neighbor to more fertile lands in eastern and southern Jutland. Mostly heath, it was sparsely inhabited by people who eked out a meager living from graz-ing sheep and cutting sod for fuel. After the loss of Slesvig in 1864, reclaiming the heath became a patriotic cause. "What is lost without, must be won within," was the motto of the Heath Society, founded in 1866 to promote the process.[4] The transformation from heath to farm was achieved with great difficulty, for heather produces a tough, water-resistant hardpan in the dry, sandy soil of the outwash plain. Today only remnants of heath remain, the low, leathery heather replaced by hard-won wheat fields and conifer plantations.

Roaring in the windbreaks, bending trees so they lean permanently eastward, pruning them into arcs, the west wind blows from the North Sea across the open farmland and heath of western Jutland. Dense hedges enclose each farmstead like a snug collar, hemming in a compact cluster of house, barn, garden, and grove of fruit and shade trees. Out on the heath, there is nothing to stop the wind. It pushes against your body, sometimes so hard that standing upright is a struggle. One is grateful for the occasional dales and the refuge they offer.

Kongenshus Memorial Park is a large heath preserve, so large one can look out over the heather and imagine the landscape of western Jutland as it once was, as Danish authors and artists described the heath in the nineteenth century. At the heart of the park is a dale, its hillsides covered with purplish, greenish-brown

Landscape of instruction. Skamlingsbanke. Denmark.

heather, stiff, moving in clusters; for there is a breeze, even down in the vale. Tall, upright stones, like menhirs, line a long path leading down, their faces inscribed with text and symbols. Standing before one stone, reading the letters cut into the rock, I recognized the words of Hans Christian Andersen's "Jutland Between Two Seas" and recalled the weight of the thick, blue Folk High School Songbook with its thin pages and the melody, sung so often during morning song, the period which marked the beginning of every Danish school day.[5] The poem, written in 1859, urges Danes to go see the heath before it becomes wheat fields. Two circular graphs cut into the stone compare the extent of cultivated fields, forest, and heath in the district in 1850 (57 percent, 3 percent, 40 percent) and 1950 (80 percent, 13 percent, 7 percent). Each large, upright stone bears a text, each recording a different proportional change from heath to field and forest. The tall stones, thirty-nine in all, represent districts; smaller stones, lying prone, like headstones in Danish

Paradoxical memorial: the heath reclaimed, restored. Kongenshus Memorial Park. Denmark.

Recording the conquest: district stone. Kongenshus Memorial Park. Denmark.

churchyards, accompany each tall stone, one for every parish, bearing the names of farmers who tilled the heath. At the end of the path, at the bottom of the dale, is a circle of more than seventy stones, each inscribed with the name of a man whose words celebrate the heath or whose deeds reclaimed it. Past the circle, the dale opens out, the ridges framing a distant view of green pasture, wheat fields, and forest plantations. At the bottom of the little valley, heath, farm, and forest are juxtaposed in a single view. The park at Kongenshus is paradoxical—a memorial to the heath and a monument to the people who struggled to conquer it.

But the paradox is deeper still. The heath, reclaimed with such effort, must now be maintained, for without burning and grazing, trees will replace heather. Western Jutland was not always an open landscape; hundreds of years ago, it was covered with oak forest, as place-names like Agerskov (fieldforest), Egebjerg (oakhill), and Skovhus (foresthouse) testify.[6] Iron Age farmers burned and cut the forest, cultivated the soil, then grazed the land so intensively that they exhausted its fertility. Forced to abandon farming, many men from western Jutland joined the Germanic invasion of England in the fifth century, and heather invaded the fields and pastures they left behind. Like other Danish landscapes, this one has been worked over through the centuries since the last Ice Age; the heath is a hu- man artifact, a by-product of agriculture—or so many scholars think. There is some debate among those who read oak pollen in bogs and dig under Bronze Age barrows to find heather buried there.[7] How one chooses to tell the story depends, at least in part, on whether one wishes to see the heath as the product of human abuse or as ancient, wild, Danish nature. Probably it is both.

There is also deep irony at Kongenshus, for the heath there was first re- claimed in the mid-eighteenth century by immigrants from the German Rhineland lured by the Danish king with promises of being given their own land. This was one hundred years before the conquest recorded in the stones, before the impetus to reclaim the heath after Denmark's defeat by Prussian armies in 1864. Many people in this area spoke German even in the late nineteenth century.

Kongenshus Memorial Park is a political monument, with a subtext as strongly ideological as the patched column on Skamlingsbanke. The land for the park was purchased in 1942 during the Nazi Occupation, and plans were delayed until 1945, the year of Germany's defeat; the park was dedicated by the king and queen of Denmark in 1953. Fifty years later, it is nature that seems endangered, not culture; the heath has taken on new meaning, and the Heath Society is villain, not hero. Kongenshus is a polemical landscape layered with complex, paradoxical meanings. "So very Danish," my Danish friends and family tell me.

These details are Danish, but the stories told are old and common: there is always a tension in landscape between the human impulse to wonder at the wild and the compulsion to use, manage, and control. And every nation has its "native" nature, worked by physical and mental labor into landscapes, with which its peo- ple identify. To authors from Cicero to Marx, "first nature" represents a nature unaltered by the human labor that yields "second nature." The Latin words *natura*, *naturans* refer to the given—naturally occurring materials, forms, and phenomena —*natura / naturata* to those reworked by human hands. Cicero wrote, "We sow corn, we plant trees, we fertilize the soil by irrigation, we confine the rivers and straighten or divert their courses. In short, by means of our hands we try to create . . . a second nature within the natural world."[8] To John Dixon Hunt and the sixteenth-century humanists whom he cites, gardens are yet a "third nature," a self-conscious re-presentation of first and second natures, an artful interpretation "of a specific place . . . for specific people."[9] As are other kinds of *designed* landscapes.

Meanings: Inherent, Invented, Ambiguous

Rivers reflect, clouds conceal. Water and fire purify and destroy. Circles have centers, paths have direction. These meanings are inherent in the qualities of landscape elements; they are grasped by humans and other life-forms as bodies and minds permit. Meanings of a landscape feature—a tree, for example—depend upon what it is in itself, its seed, its root, its growth and decaying, its networks of relationships, its setting, whether standing alone on a heath or surrounded by forest. They depend also on what it has come to mean in a human culture—a person, refuge from a storm, or the Tree of Knowledge. Trees, in some cultures, stand for humans, as long-lived individuals that grow from roots, stand upright, bear fruit, and die. Or a tree represents a family descended from a single ancestral pair, each branch a new pair or generation. A Tree of Knowledge may derive from trees' long life span and the association of age with wisdom.

Inherent qualities of landscape features and phenomena account for similar meanings across time and place: flowing rivers and growing trees, wet water and solid earth, round circles and angular squares, solid walls and open gates. Humans interpret landscape signs and elaborate upon them, reading meanings in to tell stories. The closer invented meanings are to significant, inherent qualities the more they draw from embodied knowledge rather than disembodied, abstract ideas, and the more likely those meanings are to be shared broadly; the further removed the less likely that meanings will be shared. Meanings and associations experienced directly are universal among human cultures or nearly so: water and purity, path and journey. Meanings not experienced bodily, as a sensation, even when strongly suggested by inherent qualities are not universal; not all cultures regard rivers as signifying time, air and light as intangible spirit, a circle as a cycle. Invented meanings remote from experience depend entirely on the mind's imagining: a circle as heaven, a square as earth.

Clouds and birds convey information and become ancestors: to the Hopi, clouds are signs of rain in a dry land; to the Kaluli tribe of New Guinea, birds surround their descendants with chatter and comment. Willows, with their weeping shape and ability to regenerate, are signs of resurrection; even cut branches of a willow planted as fence posts will sprout, and many nineteenth-century Christian cemeteries are planted with willows. Garden and paradise have strong associations in Christian and Islamic cultures, a connection renewed through centuries of dialogue between literature and architecture. Cloistered gardens with a central fountain (representing the Virgin Mary) have been set in monasteries and convents since medieval times and before. Light animates the world; many cultures link light to life, to knowledge, and to the sacred. Such meanings build upon inherent qualities—of clouds, birds, willows, gardens, water, springs, light—arising from landscape and cycling back through myth.

Some landscapes are sacred, some are homelands, others are cherished or abhorred for what once happened there. Plymouth Rock is particularly significant to descendants of Pilgrims who came from England on the *Mayflower*. A vacant lot at Prinz-Albrecht-Strasse 8 in Berlin is a place of horror to most who know it once was the site of Gestapo headquarters. As links to personal and collective pasts, such landscapes may inspire pilgrimage.

New ideas, new events bring fresh meanings. The ha-ha, widely invoked by landscape designers in eighteenth-century England, is a sunken fence or ditch to confine grazing sheep to pasture, so the larger landscape can be seen, unbounded, from the owner's garden. During the Iran hostage-taking crisis of 1979–81 and the 1991 war in the Persian Gulf, Americans tied yellow ribbons to doors, cars, and trees to express their support of American hostages and troops. Red poppies sold on Armistice Day (now Veterans' Day) recall the dead of Flanders fields in the First World War, and there was surely once a time when Englishmen could not see a field of flowering poppies without hearing, "In Flanders fields the poppies blow / Between the crosses row on row."[10] To Christians the cross is a symbol of the sacrifice of Jesus. Some meanings, like the yellow ribbons, are fleeting; others become embedded and endure.

If sky is associated with deity, then clouds and mountains are divine domains. If a square is earth and a circle heaven, square within circle is earth within heaven. In sacred landscapes, movement, path, and portal often overlap, with spiritual transformation at the threshold where they meet. Put two or more elements together and potential meanings and associations grow. Elements may overlap, coincide, or be a mere analogue, their relation immediate or mental. Mazes and mountaintops become sacred landscapes, the maze a puzzle-path whose destination is hard to reach, the mountaintop shrine with steep steps a difficult journey of commitment.

Ambiguity: Meaning as Complex

Landscape meaning is complex, layered, ambiguous, never simple or linear. A river flows, provides, creates, destroys, simultaneously a path and a boundary, even a gateway. Fire consumes, transforms, and renews. A circle is hierarchical— it has a center, after all—yet nonhierarchical—all points along the circumference are equidistant from the center. Landscape elements have, as I. A. Richards said of words, "equally and simultaneously, vastly different" meanings that weave a rich fabric. Meanings of elements, like those of words, are not stable, and multiple meanings are a source of metaphor and other tropes, as well.[11] Metaphor and irony juxtapose meanings: harmonious, contrasting, or conflicting. Figures and tropes are rarely isolated in landscape; combined, overlapped, juxtaposed, they introduce correspondences, prompt reflection, invite investment of meaning.

To many Danes, the landscape of Lejre is the ideal Danish landscape. Its features—low rolling hills and valleys, small villages, farms, groves of beech and linden, and ancient barrows—echo the words of songs sung at morning song from the Folk High School Songbook by every Danish child for the past century. Parts of this landscape are protected by law: as scenery, history, resource, nature, and wildlife habitat. Landscape records stories of continuous human settlement over thousands of years; to a historian, Stone Age burial mounds and ancient roads, old cottages with thatched roofs, tiny medieval churches, and baroque manor surrounded by gardens reveal glimpses of past lives. To an art historian, rolling terrain, brooks, barrows, farms, and groves were models for paintings from Denmark's Golden Age in the first half of the nineteenth century; modern windmills of white metal now intrude there. To residents of the new crop of homes built on soil deemed marginally productive by planners, the farmhouses and open fields they overlook are native Danish scenery, the windmills a source of electric power and symbol of green politics. Lejre is now more bedroom community than farm village. To a planner, highways, railroad, and underground water pipes all point to Copenhagen, more than twenty miles to the east, where one-quarter of Denmark's population now lives. The pipes are invisible, but the waterworks that pump groundwater to Copenhagen are housed in monuments of neoclassical modernism. To a hydrologist, these pipes and pumps reveal what is not present: there is no water in the low-lying meadows. The five-kilometer allée of centuries-old lindens that leads to and from the baroque manor, runs past the waterworks, pointing toward Copenhagen, perhaps a deferential gesture from a loyal subject to his king.[12]

This landscape was my home more than thirty years ago when I was seventeen and lived for a year with a Danish family. How it was then, how it is now, are juxtaposed in my mind. From a distance, the house and barn, tucked behind a windbreak of trees, look just as they did. Then, close up, I see the hedges are gone from under the trees, opening up a view out to the fields, but exposing the house to wind. The barns, once filled with pigs, cows, and chickens, are empty. The farmer, my Danish father, now retired, lives in a new housing development on a hill above the farm, his armchair turned to face out the window over the fields. There is no farmer in the farmhouse; the doctor and businessman who live there work in the city. By law, the fields must be plowed, planted, and harvested by a farmer, so the retired farmer is now a "gardener" hired by the new owner to cultivate the fields.

Danish nature, Danish culture: Åvangsgården. Lejre, Denmark.

A few summers ago, the green fields were full of red poppies, like Monet's paintings of the fields near Giverny, crimson dots so bright they sear photographic film, from a distance, red patterns in the fields. People said they had never seen so many poppies. But the farmer pointed out how poppies were concentrated in fields where rape grew thin, indicating a poor crop. He had watched as every year rape was planted, though rape ought not to be planted more often than once a decade. As I walked through the fields, I saw his meaning; where the poppies grew most densely, the rape stalks were sparse, the dry dirt exposed. As in many other places, decisions about what to plant and how to cultivate are increasingly made by those who have never worked the soil themselves or even seen the places their policies shape. There is imbalance between local knowledge and expert's overview, between the passionate provincialism of local residents and the indifference or ignorance of distant owners or bureaucrats.[13]

Readers and Readings

I once found a grove of dogwoods on a hillside in eastern Pennsylvania: slender, corky trunks, lacey branches, clouds of delicate, white blossoms. I remarked on its beauty to the owner, a farmer, and was surprised that he did not see the grove at all, only the field he had been forced to leave fallow a decade before. My beautiful grove was the farmer's abandoned field.

"You have to find more beautiful examples of community gardens if you expect me to get excited about them," an architecture student once told me. Community gardens have a messy vitality that some find appealing; and, like an occasional flower growing in a rocky field, they exist against all odds, especially in inner-city neighborhoods, where they are expressions of collective vision, artful inventiveness, sustained effort, an investment of hard-won resources. They may not always be Art, but, in the eyes of their authors, they are beautiful.

Never do all people have the same response or read identical stories in the same landscape through the lens of the same metaphor, and few recognize the picture whole. To naturalists, forests may be habitats for animals that deserve preservation for their own sake; naturalists read in a forest the diversity of plant and animal life and the size of their populations. To foresters, woods are a crop to be managed for human consumption; they read how hard the wood is, how straight the timber, how long till the next harvest and the next replanting. To a hiker, the forest may be a refuge from urban life and labor, to the lumberman a living. To a bird, high branches are refuge from predators, bark a source of bugs; to a beaver, a tree is material for dam and dwelling. Whether landscape is habitat, nature, system, artifact, historical record, ideology, wealth, site, or scenery depends on one's perspective, as visitor, resident, actor, or student.[14] Jarvis also... and Relph

In *Touching the Rock*, John Hull, who is blind, describes relying on his hearing for spatial perception and orientation. The sound of rain reveals the surrounding landscape: "Rain has a way of bringing out the contours of everything. . . . Here and there is a light cascade as it drips from step to step. . . . I can even make out the contours of the lawn, which rises to the right in a little hill. The sound of the rain is different and shapes out the curvature for me. . . . everywhere are little breaks in the patterns, obstructions, projections, where some slight interruption or difference of texture or of echo gives an additional detail or dimension to the scene."[15]

Blindness transcends the eyes. Culture can prevent eyes from seeing and ears from hearing. Those who see nature and city as opposites or deserts and forests as disordered are blind to the natural processes in cities and the order in wilderness. I was shocked when an Australian architect told me she had no desire to visit her country's Red Center because it was a desert "chaos"; to me it was one of the most clearly ordered landscapes I had ever seen, organized by extremes of light, heat, and water. Landscape as chaos or order depends largely upon expectation and knowledge. During a five-month stay in suburban southern California a few years ago, a place foreign to my customary urban, temperate-forest habitat, I was reminded of how essential knowledge is to reading landscape. I could read only the most obvious stories and not the subtleties. I did not know the plants that grew there, their seasonal patterns, their preferences for soil and water. I felt blinded and disoriented.

With knowledge, one sees what is invisible to the unaided eye. The Walbiri, desert dwellers of Australia, find underground water by signs on the surface. A geologist sees notches lining opposite hillsides as shoreline terraces cut by waves into the slopes and sees the glacial lake that once filled the valley. Mark Twain, after years' experience, learned to read the Mississippi. Microscopes and telescopes, microphones and amplifiers, cameras and satellites extend human ability to look and listen; they reveal landscape patterns and contexts we otherwise would not see or hear. But sophisticated tools do not bring understanding, necessarily. Without knowledge, a person notes nothing, like the passengers on Twain's steamboat who were oblivious to the river's text, like those who walked past the yellowwood with no eyes for its distress.

"The land offers us good reading, outdoors, from a lively, unfinished manuscript," writes May Theilgaard Watts. "Records, prophesies, mysteries are inscribed there, and changes—always changes. Even as we read from some selected page, whether mountaintop, forest, furrow, schoolyard, dune, bog, we see changes: in stirrings and silences, flavors and textures, spacing, tolerances, and confrontations and tensions at the edges."[16] Novice readers, moving from Watts's guidebooks to the landscapes of North America and Europe to the texts outside their doors, will find that the more they know, the more they can read. And the more they read the more they can tell.

Landscape Dialogues: Reading and Responding

We see, hear, smell, touch, and taste what our human eyes, ears, nose, skin, tongue, and tools permit and our cultures condition. The sense of up and down, forward and backward, left and right is determined by the form of the body that perceives them: by head and feet, face and back, by the distinction between one eye, one arm, one breast, one leg, and the other. Our human bodies predispose us to recognize symmetrical patterns. Had humans different bodies and minds we would sense different qualities and read and respond to different meanings.

Humans are not alone in reading and responding; animals read landscape, too, and they also are limited by their bodies and brains. Birds, baboons, and people hear a bird's alarm call as a signal of danger, cows follow the beaten track from barn to field and back again. Frogs' vision, quite different from birds' or primates', is geared to "detecting an accessible bug" by an object's size and how it moves, but "a frog will starve to death surrounded by food if it is not moving."[17] What is significant to a person is not relevant to a frog. Other life-forms participate in the language of landscape; to the extent that their senses, memories, or social behavior resemble ours they read and inscribe it similarly. Ethologists describe how bees, birds, beavers, and baboons interpret their landscapes, build, and even transform them; zoosemioticians codify signs by which animals communicate.[18] Plants, animals, rivers, and mountains create landscape, and some use the language, but in their own, nonhuman, terms.

Nineteenth-century artists and poets like Caspar David Friedrich and William Wordsworth believed there was a language of nature manifest in landscape that spoke directly to human emotions independent of culture. They sought to return to inherent "meanings" of landscape features as vehicles for expressing their own emotions as artists and to jettison meanings traditionally associated with such features.[19] John Ruskin objected to the tendency of some authors to personify nonhuman organisms, inanimate objects, and abstract ideas, to attribute human emotions and intentions to them, and coined the term *pathetic fallacy* to describe it.[20]

To say that landscape elements have inherent qualities to which humans (and others) attribute significance is not to insist, necessarily, that meaning, for humans, can exist outside of culture; to say that animals, plants, and other features of landscape participate in the language is not to personify them, necessarily. They participate on their own terms. Neither mountains nor bacteria *decide* to create form (though people of some cultures might say they do), but even the most primitive living organisms reproduce and may even make architectural shells to protect themselves. Initiation and intention mark the difference between the animate, inanimate, and inorganic, whether an entity reads and responds to its landscape involuntarily or deliberately, by instinct or learning, or is merely an unwitting respondent to forces of gravity and water flow. Many animals are social; they experience community, dominance, kinship, exchange, and mark and make territory for those activities, but apparently none reflect or imagine. Humans initiate, consider, remember, imagine; only human life, as far as we know, reflects on its past and invents possible futures. The ability to imagine and create what is not yet, *to design*, is human; so are art and worship. Landscape literature, though it may include the works of nonhuman nature, is a phenomenon of the human imagination.

Dialogues: Unconscious, Deliberate, Extroverted, Introverted

Landscapes are a cacophony until sorted into individual dialogues by focusing on a primary signal to which many elements respond, by tracing a single set of dialogues. The sun sends a pervasive signal. All landscape elements respond to its light and heat: sunflowers track the sun, turning faces east to west from morning to evening; earth dries out on west-facing hillsides so only drought- and heat-tolerant plants grow there; desert plants develop a thick skin to buffer temperature extremes from day to night; desert people build houses with thick walls. In summer, desert dwellers fall into a rhythm, rising early when the light is low and air is cool, sweating, seeking shade by late morning—even the narrow shadow cast by a palm trunk or saguaro cactus—staying inside during the afternoon, craving water to replace the moisture sucked out of body, drinking water, glass after glass, going out again in the evening after sunset. Animals do the same; there is no birdsong at midday, the desert landscape comes alive with the noises of evening. Sunflowers' tracking, soil's drying, plants' thick skin, people's sweating are unconscious dialogues with the sun; building thick walls is deliberate.

The common garden bean, *Phaseolus vulgaris*, in its thousands of varieties, is the product of dialogues between humans and beans over millennia. As we shaped the bean, it shaped us, notes William Cronon: "It will not sprout, it will not grow, it will not thrive or yield seed unless we treat it in the ways it demands."[21] In *Nature's Metropolis*, Cronon traced how Chicago's commodity markets shaped the American West: from fields to silos to pigs, to market, from cows to pastures to barns; from corn to fields to silos to grain elevators to railroads.[22]

Landslides are dialogues among rain, rock, soil, building, and living. John McPhee tells such stories in "Los Angeles Against the Mountains."[23] On landslide-prone slopes, falling rain soaks soil, weighs it down, and sends it slipping—an unconscious, involuntary dialogue. People cut into such slopes to make level ground, then build streets and houses, weighing down soil; rain falling and sprinklers spraying lawn soak soil, and send it slipping. Cutting, building, and watering are deliberate acts, but often not recognized as dialogues with slope and soil. Failure to recognize the resulting landslide as part of ongoing dialogues, misreading dialogues as fate or Mother Nature's revenge, leads to rebuilding in the same place and in the same way despite repeated disasters.

Some dialogues are extroverted and physical. People plant hedgerows to block strong winds, build steep roofs where snowfall is heavy; then wind blows up and over, snow slides off. Similar dialogues take place between cultivation practices and field dimensions, family structure and settlement patterns. The vernacular landscapes that emerge from such dialogues have a coherence, like that of the Illinois corn belt, which Robert Riley describes as governed by two laws: "square to the road, hogs to the east."[24] For more than thirty years, the Swedish landscape architect Sven-Ingvar Andersson has engaged in dialogues with his garden. He describes how four privet shrubs, left over after planting the hedges of his garden, were set in a serendipitous group, then a few years later "developed a sudden desire to become long-necked birds." "We helped them," he said, "with pruning and clipping."[25] His garden is full of such dialogues—a single rose stem "decides" to grow through the privet hedge and blooms alone against clipped green. The autonomy of nonhuman actors and the impulse to interpret their stories underlie garden design, inform the dialogue of clipped and unclipped, of control, serendipity, and response.

Some dialogues are introspective, like the dialogue between Claude Monet and his garden: between artist and landscape; practices of designing, gardening, and painting; the actual and the virtual. Monet started by observing and representing landscape through painting, then created a garden that was planted, painted, and altered repeatedly from 1883 until his death in 1926. Like Monet at Giverny, the Zen monks at the Japanese Buddhist monasteries Saihoji and Shisendo, Pliny in his country villa, and many others used their gardens to reflect on nature. So too, not only poetry and painting, but scientific experiments and the forms of human settlements record such introspective dialogues. In *Fish Magic* (1925), Paul Klee painted flowers growing in a vaselike vessel, fish swimming, moon shining, a clock, and a person with two faces poised between realms of nature and culture.[26] "For the artist," observed Klee, "dialogue with nature remains

Garden dialogues. Marnas. Sweden.

a *conditio sine qua non*. The artist is a man, himself nature and part of nature in natural space."[27]

Joining the Conversation

Landscape is the sum of countless dialogues. It has no silence to be filled, no blank page; in landscape, dialogues have already begun before a new author enters the conversation. Some designers do not understand the ongoing dialogues and offer irrelevant responses, even rude interruptions. While one may welcome abrupt interruptions from genius, when every designer presumes genius the result is merely confusing and annoying.

Designers and planners of landscapes must try to read a place through their clients' eyes, as well as their own, to read and respond to the ongoing dialogues. The task is easiest for a single designer working with a single client. With many clients, in a political arena, the task is difficult, even with good intentions, especially since many professionals now commonly work outside their own regions and cultures; the best-known practitioners travel back and forth across oceans and continents to work in other countries. Sven-Ingvar Andersson, though Swedish, practices in Denmark and was chosen by the Dutch, after a year-long international search, to prepare a plan for the Museumplein, one of Amsterdam's most important public spaces. "It is difficult to work in foreign countries," he writes, reflecting on his seven years' work on another project, Vienna's Karlsplatz, not so much because of language or lack of a professional network, as because "one is outside one's professional and social tradition."[28] A sense of one's own place in time, space, and culture helps one navigate the shoals of foreign customs, but things can easily go awry. Misunderstandings and misreadings can also occur closer to home.

Many years ago I sat in a public meeting in Boston's Roxbury, listening first to a landscape architect present proposals for a new park design, then to the heated, hostile discussion that followed. The audience was primarily African American, many of them residents of the public housing project nearby; the designers were all Caucasian and lived elsewhere. The site of the park-to-be was at the heart of the community on vacant land; once filled with homes and businesses, it had been condemned and cleared for a highway. Some at the meeting were among those who had opposed and halted the roadway's construction; to them the site and its history had personal and political significance. Many objected to the proposed design because its bland lawns and groves reflected neither their own needs nor their interests; it told no stories they found meaningful. Others opposed the entire idea of a park; they wanted a supermarket, a laundromat, a bank, places to work. Furthermore, they were insulted by the designer's presentation. Following common practice, he had offered three schemes: one design that required minimal investment, a second unattractive for some other reason, and a third that the designer preferred. His presentation was intended to steer the choice to the third; the audience, like Goldilocks tasting the bears' porridge, was expected to find his own scheme to be "just right." His strategy failed; this audience saw through the sham, was outraged at the failure to offer genuine options, and rejected the designer's plan. He had failed to read the landscape through their eyes, failed to see, hear, and respond to their landscape dialogues.

A few years before that Roxbury meeting, I experienced a similar failure as a graduate student in landscape architecture at the University of Pennsylvania. The occasion was an experimental course meant to teach us students sensitivity to local dialogues; landscape architecture and anthropology students worked in teams to study and plan for a real place. My team's assignment was Alloway, a small town and farming community on the coastal plain of southern New Jersey. We conducted field surveys and interviews to elicit people's needs and desires, attended local events like the Volunteer Firemen's Pancake Supper, and developed plans and designs based on our readings of the landscape. Curious about our proposals, residents invited us to present our plans at a potluck supper at the Grange Hall in May. Midway through our presentation, I showed a slide of a vacant lot in the middle of town where we were proposing that new apartments be built. "That's no vacant lot, that's Elmer's potato patch!" shouted someone in the audience. The crowd laughed. So did I, though mortified; there had been no sign of potatoes, or Elmer, when we surveyed the town that winter.

Some dialogues continue for years before anyone knows whether they are successes or failures. My dialogue with Mill Creek in West Philadelphia is one such. It began in 1971 when I was a student, and the street caved in. The sight of the big, hidden, brown river was so startling, it changed forever how I look at depressions and valleys in urban landscapes, and it compelled me to seek to track the history not only of this, but of other, buried streams in other places. On my return to Philadelphia in 1986, after nine years' practicing and teaching in Boston, I resumed my dialogue with the forgotten creek, tracing its course in cracks and dips and vacant lots, plotting its restoration and the rebuilding of the neighborhood through which it flowed. I began more than a decade of conversations with community gardeners, city planners, engineers, teachers, and with schoolchildren and parents whose basements flooded after rains. Some of these dialogues have yielded tangible results: gardens in the creek's floodplain, a Mill Creek curriculum in the local middle school where the community itself has become the classroom. Other of my dialogues with the landscape are still dreams.

My dialogue with Mill Creek, like any other, must be read alongside others, large and small, plain and obscure, predictable and unforeseen, enduring and ephemeral, concluded and open-ended. Together, they form the context of Mill Creek, the place. Some of those other dialogues have extended over thousands of years: the erosion of mountains and building of plains, the growth and decline of forests, the rise and fall of cultures. Every place embodies enduring stories that are deeply embedded in the shape and structure of landscape.

Building public landscapes can be accomplished successfully only by close collaborators who care to define and agree on what ideas will guide the project, especially ideas about special qualities of the place, how the place will be used and experienced. The larger the project, especially if it is a public project, the more numerous and diverse the clients to get to know, the agencies to confer with, the colleagues in other disciplines to consult, the contractors in construction and maintenance to meet with. The essence of a project can easily be lost in a welter of confusing misunderstandings or competing interests, or be sacrificed to tight funding or bland common denominators. Andersson has evolved a simple strategy to draw all the actors involved in a project together. After initial meetings, he composes a brief, lyrical statement of the special qualities of the site, the clients' hopes, and the intent of the design, which blends the sensual and ecological, the poetic and pragmatic.[29] His text is integral to the act of design and forms an implicit compact between himself and his clients. The ideas in his texts are elemental, simple, stated with charm, but, unexpressed, they would readily be lost. These touchstone texts serve as a standard against which to measure results, a reminder that the material product must hold the dream.

Lawrence Halprin also frequently works on complex and often controversial public projects with diverse clients who are in actual or potential conflict, but he has a different strategy. He was hired by Orange County, California, for example, to propose alternative alignments for a new highway to cut through the Laguna

Canyon Wilderness Park. He was expected to engage many participants in the process: elected officials, public employees, developers, and interested citizens, including those altogether opposed to the highway. Halprin's method is to conduct workshops that bring the various actors into a public conversation; he employs techniques that he calls "RSVP cycles": "R" for the resources in a place; "S" for scores, the means by which activities are carried out; "V" for "valuaction," evaluation leading to decisions on actions to take; "P" for performance, the acting out of a score; cycles, to emphasize that the process is interactive and nonlinear.[30] Halprin uses this method in undertaking projects for highways and downtowns, in designs for new transit malls, main streets, and parks. It has succeeded in facilitating public dialogue and often results in a consensus that amounts to collective speech. In the Laguna Canyon Wilderness Park project, he "scored" a series of "awareness" tours designed to give all participants a common experience of the place, to stimulate their ideas, and to establish a common language. Their responses formed the basis for beginning to work together and they guided his work. Then he led several workshops in which small groups of participants sketched proposals, presented them to the larger group, and discussed and debated the issues they raised. Halprin's own proposals, presented at the very end of the process, after several workshops, incorporated many ideas that emanated from the workshops.

"Designing with the Bloody Invisible": Murcutt's Ball and Bingie

The architect Glenn Murcutt, who has invested a lifetime in reading and responding to local landscape, does not accept commissions outside Australia. "Did you see the structure on those buildings? It takes your breath away . . . how does he dare?" "He's designing with the bloody invisible!" Two experienced architects looking at Murcutt's work were referring to its spare structure and the way his buildings capture and play with breezes and winds. To Murcutt, these phenomena are not invisible, but rather felt, embodied knowledge. He grew up along Sydney Harbor, swimming the currents, sailing with winds "by the seat of his pants," literally, by feeling the shifts and bumps in air and water. He learned to use his body like a fine-tuned instrument, to rely upon observation and experience when a learning disability made reading difficult. He learned winds by building model airplanes, watching them glide, then by refining shape and set of wings, and he learned the flood of water by diving once into a river in flood, as Loren Eiseley had floated down the Platte River, letting himself go, feeling part of the flow.[31] Murcutt swam to the bottom, felt the speed of water flow change with depth, the increased friction near the bottom, the mass of water above, like boundary layer winds slower at earth's surface, in response to friction. His dialogues with wind, water, light, plants, and animals are deliberate and habitual. He is like Norman Maclean's brother, a master fly fisherman who tried to explain his own success: "All there is to thinking, is seeing something noticeable which makes you see something you

Embodied knowledge: wind, rain, sun, shelter. Bingie, Australia. (Glenn Murcutt)

weren't noticing which makes you see something that isn't even visible."[32]

Murcutt studies his clients' patterns of living as closely as he studies the processes of sun shining, plants growing, water flowing, and wind blowing, and he designs rooms and rooms' arrangement to correspond to the patterns of clients' lives. When the artist Sydney Ball requested a place of meditation, Murcutt designed an elevated verandah enclosed on three sides, on a wooded slope, facing downslope, with a view of blue, distant mountains. The elevation and the sloping ground beneath bring tree branches to eye-level, an unusual perspective that lifts one out of the everyday to a transcendent view.

Murcutt works alone; because he is in great demand, clients must wait two to three years for a design of their home, office, or museum. But the period is not fallow; Murcutt meets with them, from time to time, to talk about their lives, habits, likes, dislikes, hopes, and dreams, and, in turn, shares with them his ideas of an ecologically responsible approach to design. He addresses the dimensions of production, construction, and maintenance and relates how materials, site layout, and the design itself conserve environmental resources. He and his clients come to consensus about basic aims, or, if not, he suggests another architect. The product of these dialogues, like the house for Ball and a vacation home for the Magnie family at Bingie, along the Pacific coast in southeastern Australia, express the daily and seasonal rhythms of the place and the people who live, work, or come there. The Magnies camped out on the site in tents on weekends and holidays for years

Empathetic imagination: water, light, and life, aligned. Bingie, Australia. (Glenn Murcutt)

before they built the house. Murcutt designed a building like a spacious, sunny tent, with two bedrooms and a verandah facing the water, with windows, doors, and vents that can be opened or closed, and with kitchen, bathroom, and corridor along the back. The roofline echoes the silhouette of a gull in flight, wings spread; the gutter is in the middle of the inward-sloping roof, instead of at the edge, and two downspouts are columns at either end. The shape of the ceiling inside the house and the corridor along which people move reflect the path along which the water flows. Rain drums on the roof, streams into the gutter, swirls down the cylindrical downspouts, visible through glass doors at either end of the hall, and falls into an underground tank—the only water supply for the house. Water is linked to its source in rain and sky and to a reservoir in the ground, necessary dialogues made poetic, everyday experience made aesthetic. Elegant spareness, a hallmark of Murcutt's work, expresses his environmental ethics.

Murcutt's skill in the language of landscape brings his clients in deliberate dialogue with processes that sustain their lives, and that are often taken for granted. People adjust windows and walls to admit, intensify, or block light and air flow, as one adjusts sails on a boat to catch or avoid the wind, and, in the process, they *learn.* For those who live in such houses, light changing, wind blowing, rain falling, and reservoir filling become visible, audible, and tangible. Imagine an entire neighborhood or town—buildings, streets, sewers, parks—as at Ball and Bingie, that engage residents in dialogues with natural processes.

Living in such places, one learns to read and tell landscape, to understand connections among seemingly unrelated phenomena, to phrase an appropriate response. Such dwelling invokes a sense of empathy, prompts reflection on the continuity of human lives with other living things and with the places we all inhabit. Empathy, the imaginative projection of one's own consciousness into another being, especially the sympathetic understanding of other than human beings—is surely one of the most important human abilities.[33] Fluency and literacy in landscape are aids not only to survival, but also to the empathetic imagination.

3
Artful Telling, Deep Reading:
The Literature of Landscape

The Poetry of Worship, Conquest, and Defense: Mont-Saint-Michel

Even before the silhouette of the Mount appears in the distance across the coastal plains of Normandy, the traveler anticipates the mythic isle shrouded in mist, shining in sun, surrounded by sea, by vast tidal flats. The real matches the image. The abbey's spire, wrapped by ramparts, looks like (and is) both cathedral and fort; it is dedicated to St. Michael, captain-general of the hosts of heaven, protector of the church militant. When "there was war in heaven" St. Michael took up the sword and cast Satan out.[1]

In the *Chanson de Roland*, at the climax of Roland's death, the Mount appears as "Saint Michael in Peril from the Sea." The Mount rises off the northern coast of France in a bay leading to the English Channel. The four main piers of the abbey were built in 1058, eight years before William of Normandy launched the Norman conquest of England. During the Hundred Years War when English armies occupied Normandy, the Mount remained French. The Bayeux Tapestry (ca. 1095) shows Harold of England pulling soldiers out of quicksand near the Mount.[2]

The bay has the strongest tides in Europe, with a swing between low and high tides of up to forty-five feet, and many unwary pilgrims (and numerous tourists) crossing at low tide on the nine miles of exposed sands have been sucked down or trapped and drowned on the sand flats by a rushing high tide. When the tide runs up narrow channels, it produces a bore, a wave up to three feet high. For pilgrims, the trip across the bay was once a risky allegorical journey, tides, currents, and sands like the menace of Satan, yet undertaken with the protection of the Archangel Michael. Once an island out in the middle of the bay, a mile from shore, accessible only by boat at high tide, by foot, horse, or carriage at low tide, the bay around the Mount has silted in and, since 1856, has been deliberately filled. A causeway was constructed in 1879; it is an island no more.[3] The modern pilgrim risks neither life nor limb to reach it.

From mean sea level to the original peak, which lies under the center where nave and transept cross between the original piers, the Mount rises 240 feet. The church, large western terrace, cloister garden, and refectory all perch on a huge platform in the sky, supported by crypts and other buildings rising from lower slopes in a sheer wall pierced by narrow windows. The Mount is hierarchical: secular town at the bottom, church and monastery at the top; vernacular buildings in the town, classic structures in the abbey and its church. The church is visible from miles away; close-up, from below, one first sees only the town and its street after entering the outer gate—the only breach in the ramparts—into a fortified courtyard, then under a portcullis through the King's Gate. Just beyond, the abbot's soldiers lived on the Grande-Rue, the only real street of the town. Narrow, lined with restaurants and shops catering to pilgrims and tourists for hundreds of years, the street ramps steeply up, curving around the hillside to several steep flights of steps, through a gate into the abbey's domain and up another long flight. At the top is a large terrace, facing west over bay and mainland. At low tide, the rivers' and bay's channels can be seen etched in sand, a huge brown sandpainting of braided, branching, meandering channels with pools of water trapped here and there, reflecting sky and clouds.

Inside the abbey is an interior landscape of darkened stairs and corridors, faintly lit by slitted windows, leading to room after room, one, a forest of great round pillars, its trunks lit softly on one side, in deep shadow on the other. Seen through the forest is a large, luminous room, its stone floor and walls awash in a blue-green light as if under the sea. Here and there, narrow rays of sunlight shine through the pale glass, moving patterns on the window's deeply recessed stone reveal. In all these rooms, the blue-green panes are translucent not transparent, telling a story of those who chose an inward focus over the panoramic view of the world beyond the walls.

LANDSCAPE STORIES

When the stone marker inscribed with the words Taliesin West was set up near the entrance to his home in Arizona, Frank Lloyd Wright pointed to the name Taliesin molded into the wall of the parking area opposite: "That's the book," he said; then to the new marker, "And that's the chapter."[4] As with Taliesin North, in Wisconsin, he saw his homes as texts with the same plot. Taliesin North, rooted in the first half of Wright's career, was built as "a garden and a farm behind a workshop and a home," and Taliesin West was a new chapter in his work, both of them built versions of his utopian texts, *Disappearing City* and *The Living City*, his ideas of a world made better by design.[5] The Taliesins, as villas, belong to a landscape literature thousands of years old, rooted in the contrast between city and country, integrating the genres of home, production, and power.[6]

In landscape, each rock, each river, each tree has its individual history. A river's history, a tree's, is the sum of all its dialogues, nothing less but nothing more; they contain no emotion, no moral. Human cultures embellish these stories in gardens, buildings, and towns. Stories humans tell have a plot, often with beginning, middle, and end, a deliberate narrative: stories of survival, identity, power, success, and failure. Like myths and laws, landscape narratives organize reality, justify actions, instruct, persuade, even compel people to perform in certain ways. Landscapes are literature in the broadest sense, texts that can be read on many levels.

Landscape stories have common themes across cultures: struggle for survival; the character of human society (the relations of individuals to family, deities, state, or corporation); the nature of nature and the place of humans within it; where things came from, and how specific places came to be (stories of origins and creation—of mountains and rivers, of flowers and humans). How you read a scene, the patterns you see there and the context you see them in, influences the story you will tell. The opposite is also true. The story you want to tell influences how and what you read. Some narrators see the world as getting better, others as getting worse. William Cronon describes how two historians, Paul Bonnifield and Donald Worster, read the same scene, the Dust Bowl, in quite different ways, a reminder that story is at the heart of *history*.[7] To Bonnifield the Dust Bowl is a story of human triumph in the face of natural disaster; he concluded that the landscape of the Great Plains was ultimately improved as a result of the Dust Bowl. Worster saw the Dust Bowl as a story of human failure to adapt to nature and concluded that the landscape was getting worse. Stories have consequences. If cities are seen as treasures of civilization, they will be made treasures through cultivation. If cities are seen as degraded, they will be made so through neglect.

Bonnifield and Worster told their stories through words; landscape authors tell similar stories by shaping landscape directly: siting the paths along which others experience landscape, choosing what people will see (and what they will not see), and in what order, framing the view. Telling a story by designing a path and the elements along it is a common narrative technique, particularly in religious and political landscapes in which path represents "the way." Kongenshus Memorial Park, in Denmark, was deliberately, artfully composed as landscape literature. The Danish heath was shaped without conscious intent of self-expression, but its story can, and has been, read as literature. The Mississippi River and Yosemite Valley did not compose themselves as literature but become literature when we read our own stories into them. Vernacular landscapes may acquire the status of folklore, as they are retold, reproduced, and adapted over time. Extraordinary places crafted to express ideas and evoke feeling, ordinary places of everyday activities, all are connected to each other. Landscape literature is the product of life not a mere representation of it.

Folklore, Myth, Tragedy, Comedy, Epic, Poetry

Landscape literature, like all literatures, has multiple modes: prosaic homilies, folklore, myths, drama—tragic and comic, satires, parodies, epics, oratory, and poetry. Mont-Saint-Michel is mythic and poetic, part classical (gates, cathedral, cloister), part folk (the hodgepodge of shops and houses lining the single, rising street). Vernacular landscapes, such as memorials to persons killed in automobile accidents along the side of a highway, are expressed in everyday language, usually in the dialect or common mode of expression of a particular place. Built usually by amateurs who work unself-consciously with local materials and in a folk tradition, they tend to reflect their ethnic origins and religious traditions. Classical landscapes, which employ more formal language drawn from precedents or models from the past, are more likely to be designed by trained artists or professionals. The Vietnam Veterans Memorial is such a work, an elegy, a lamentation for the dead. It begins in a descent, arousing feelings of mourning, then, as one moves up to ground level again, it ends in a mood of calm and consolation.[8] Going down instead of up, using black stone instead of white, it goes against convention for monuments in Washington, D.C.

Memorials to the famous (Pantheon, Lincoln Memorial) or to horrific events (Dachau, Mont Valérien outside Paris and Ryvangen in Copenhagen where members of the French and Danish Resistance, respectively, were executed during the Second World War), and monuments of wars and battles (Verdun, Gettysburg) may also be forms of elegy. They are often composed with deliberate allusions to other literary works, written or built: Stowe, in England, with its sculptural monuments to "Ancient Virtue" and the "British Worthies," set within a pastoral landscape of lawn and groves, is a self-conscious landscape version of classical elegy.

Kongenshus Memorial Park and the St. Louis Arch (its official title, the Thomas Jefferson Memorial to Westward Expansion) are epics, landscapes designed to tell heroic tales about deeds and events of great cultural significance. Other landscapes are full of lighthearted comedy, like the jokes and tricks in Italian gardens—fountains that spray unexpectedly. The garden of stones at Ryoanji is poetry, its language condensed and figurative: metaphor—rocks as mountains, gravel raked in wavy lines as sea, the whole as Japan; paradox—dry stones as water. The rocks are placed with rhythmic precision, and though the garden is small, not all the elements can be seen at once. One has to read and reread.

To the architect Steen Eiler Rasmussen a garden is a slow play, an art of time, space, and story.[9] Landscape's evolving play is never finished; to design landscape is to come on stage during a performance already long under way and to engage and extend ongoing dialogues. Landscape is a play with many actors—flowers, people, trees, rocks—who come and go across the stage, some staying a day, a week, a season, others remaining for eighty or two hundred or a thousand years. Beatrix Ferrand designed the garden for Abby Rockefeller's summer home on Mount Desert Island in Maine so the actors—the flowers—would bloom in June when the owners were in residence. Landscape can also be the stage, with living figures acting a role. Marie Antoinette and her guests dressed up as shepherdess and shepherds to play at the Hameau, an ornamental farm at Versailles. Eighteenth-century English landowners created pastoral landscapes linked to classical tradition with replicas of classical buildings, incorporating whole villages, and they sometimes employed "hermits" and shepherds to inhabit the gardens. At Williamsburg in Virginia, Sturbridge Village in Massachusetts, and many other reconstructed places, people in period costume act and cook and shoe horses. "Hosts" at Disney's Magic Kingdom dress as Mickey Mouse, Donald Duck, Goofy, and at EPCOT's World Showcase, Germans, Norwegians, Mexicans, Japanese, and Frenchmen wear native costume to wait on customers in themed restaurants and shops. The inhabitants of France's Regional Cultural Parks act themselves for tourists by practicing their traditional lives and crafts. "All the world's a stage / And all the men and women merely players."[10]

Author's Voice: Provocative, Dignified, Disguised

Twenty buried automobiles push up out of the asphalt in the parking lot of Hamden Plaza, a shopping mall in Connecticut, some almost fully emerged, others only a bulge in the pavement the shape of a car roof. Plenty of spaces remain for customers' cars, some of them right next to cars covered with asphalt. It is Ghost Parking Lot (1978), a project by SITE (Sculpture in the Environment), an environmental design firm based in New York City. The work of SITE's designers makes one laugh first, then think, for their humor often depends on an inversion, in this case, of asphalt and cars, whimsical yet black, extending beyond a one-line joke to gentle social critique. In the ghost lot they bury the automobile, producing an artwork that, in contrast to more conventional public sculpture plopped down on a location, cannot be separated from its site. SITE is perhaps most famous, or infamous, for a series of shopping mall showrooms for the Best Company that poke fun at contemporary architectural theory. The facade peels off one building in Richmond, Virginia, and tilts (seemingly) precariously off a second in Towson, Maryland, while forest invades a third, also in Richmond. The authors' voice that imbues SITE's landscapes is simultaneously hilarious and dead serious. As James Wines, SITE's creative director, says of humor, "It's the last plateau between oneself and the apocalypse. One cannot possibly accept the serious world as being truly serious."[11]

Bryant Park, behind the New York Public Library on East 42nd Street, has a new authors' voice, heard in the recent revision of the park (1980s) that had been rebuilt once before (1935) in a Beaux Arts style in tune with the massive neoclassical library building (on the site of the city's old waterworks). The park has now been opened up to surrounding streets and sidewalks: iron fences removed, openings cut in stone balustrades, ramps and steps installed to provide access in and out, shrubs and trees removed and other trees planted.[12] Because the comprehensive rebuilding matches the tone of the building and the former park so well, many will mistake the new park for part of the original composition. Others may believe the same of the promenade along the Hudson River in Battery Park, also in Manhattan; the stone pavement, solid metal rail, and traditional lampposts and benches recall the best of the city's older public places. The voice of the landscape authors Robert Hanna and Laurie Olin, who designed Bryant Park and the Battery Park Promenade, is serious, dignified, elegant, formal, polite, like their urbane

Provocative and irreverent: Ghost Parking Lot. Hamden, Connecticut (SITE)

public and their corporate clients. Literate in classical landscape literature, their works allude principally to English, French, Italian, and nineteenth-century American gardens and urban places. Their voice is distinctive, though subtle, their landscapes well crafted, with painstaking attention to details of material and form. They have been attacked by professional peers for not being more provocative at Battery Park City, for example, but their intention was "to produce an environment so quintessentially 'New York' that it would unconsciously become part of people's lives . . . that would not call attention to itself, but rather direct one's consideration elsewhere."[13]

Aldo Leopold struggled for twelve years (1935–48) to restore soil fertility and native plants and wildlife to an old farm along the Wisconsin River not far from the one where John Muir grew up a century before. Twenty years after Leopold died helping neighbors fight a grass fire, at least half of the 16,000 pines he and his family planted were thriving; more than sixty years after they began, the sandy, once depleted soil of a worked-out farm sustains prairie grasses, stands of pine, oak, and hickory.[14] Leopold's daughter Nina recalls how they "gathered seeds of native grasses, planted them among the old corn stubble, planted native hardwoods and forest wildflowers and shrubs, carried pails of water. We learned how to nurture, how to care."[15] There is little sign of design on the Leopold Memorial Reserve; plants seem to sow their own seed, blown on the wind, carried by birds, and so they do, helped then and now by the Leopold family, a nursery of native

Urbane and polite: Bryant Park. New York City. (Hanna/Olin)

prairie plants the only overt clue to their role. The voice of its human authors is modest and disguised; the voice of its nonhuman authors is prominent. The reserve and also Leopold's book, *Sand County Almanac,* are classics of environmental literature; in the book, he describes the place and reflects on the ethical issues the process of its transformation prompted. The shack he built, in which he wrote the book, has become an icon, a place of pilgrimage for environmentalists. How ironic it is that the shack, the simple human shelter, is taken as the symbol and not the landscape itself, the focus of his efforts: the soil, water, plants, and animals.

This is an old paradox: the works of those human landscape authors who are most deferential to nonhuman landscape authors are often not appreciated at all as the literary constructions they are. Frederick Law Olmsted (1822–1903) left a legacy of wonderful places, from New York's Central Park to Boston's Emerald Necklace, from Niagara Falls to Yosemite, but few recognize these now as built landscapes.[16] Many people are startled to learn that Central Park was constructed, that even the Ramble is an "artful wilderness," and that Boston's Fens and River-way were molded out of polluted mudflats and carefully planted to grow into tidal marsh and floodplain forest. Even those who do recognize Central Park and the Fens as constructions are surprised at how extensively the experiences of Niagara Falls and Yosemite are also shaped by design, for both have come to stand, incorrectly, as monuments of nature untouched by human artifice. Olmsted's contemporaries certainly recognized that landscapes like Central Park and the Fens were

Deferential and disguised: Leopold Memorial Reserve. Sand County, Wisconsin.

designed and built—after all, they were familiar with what those sites had looked like before and also, with the lengthy and ambitious process of transformation. However, this realization soon faded with time. Olmsted was so skilled at concealing his artifice that the projects he so brilliantly constructed as well as the profession he had worked so hard to establish—landscape architecture—became largely invisible. Today the works of the profession of landscape architecture are often not seen, even by contemporaries, not understood as having been designed and deliberately constructed, even when the landscape has been radically reshaped. Thus, many landmarks of landscape architecture are assumed to be either works of nature or felicitous, serendipitous products of culture. Their very success prevents appreciation of their triumphs as artful answers to knotty problems of conflicting environmental values or competing purposes.

Landscape Genres

Landscape genres correspond to archetypal activities like movement, play, or worship that share patterns of function and form from culture to culture yet are adapted to a certain people, a certain place, a certain period.[17] Genres relate and often combine; so, Mont-Saint-Michel was (and to varying degrees still is) a locus of worship, conflict, defense, commerce, and community. Ancient trade routes were landscapes of movement and meeting, boulevards and main streets still are.

Danish farms were built as units of home and production, house and barn enclosing an interior courtyard. Villas, from ancient Rome and Renaissance Veneto to eighteenth-century England and nineteenth-century America, were landscapes of home, production, power, and play. In cities of Western Europe, home, movement, commerce, production, power, and play often occupy the same space, an integration of landscape genres. In North American metropolitan regions of the twentieth century, home and production tend to be in separate domains.

Wilderness—now enshrined in national parks and world biosphere reserves—is sacred ground to many, as it was to Muir, who invited Ralph Waldo Emerson to join him "in a month's worship with Nature in the high temples of the great Sierra Crown beyond our holy Yosemite."[18] But what is sacred to some is a place to play for others or even a place of production. Multiple genres often appear in one landscape, and there is tension when they conflict. To Gifford Pinchot, Yosemite's water and timber were resources to conserve and use; to his contemporary Muir, grazing the meadows and cutting the trees was sacrilege, a plunder of paradise. And millions of people come yearly to play in Yosemite.[19] Design can reconcile conflict, as Olmsted's did. He could speak of the sacred qualities of Yosemite, the "reverent mood" it evoked, yet condone cutting and planting trees and shaping the scene, envisioning future groves and glades still sublime.

Landscapes of Worship

The forest at Ise, ancestral shrine of the Japanese emperor and Shinto gods, is ancient, dark, and dense. Most of the broad, towering cypress and cryptomeria trees are hundreds, some more than a thousand years old. The trunks of the largest trees soar upward, veiled by layered foliage of smaller trees, saplings, seedlings. The trees germinate, grow, reproduce, and die, yet the forest endures. By ritual the huge forest of ordinary trees is transmuted into a sacred precinct, set off from the profane world by distinctive boundaries; only priests and those engaged in ritual may leave the path and walk within it. Uncut for thirteen hundred years, except for a few trees felled to construct the shrines, the forest embodies both the enduring and the ephemeral.

Naiku, the Inner Shrine of Ise, is a building complex within a sacred precinct in the forest atop a huge platform of stone and earth. The principal shrines, and also the bridges and gates within the huge forest domain, are taken down and rebuilt deliberately every twenty years; these artifacts, like the individual trees of the forest, do not endure, though the ritual of rebuilding has continued for more than a millennium.[20]

At Ise the crowds are subdued. Before I reached Naiku itself, I had entered a special domain, passed through torii (gates) and crossed a bridge over the river into the forest reserve. I had cleansed my mouth and hands in the river, then walked some distance through the forest on a broad, ceremonial path.

Here and there, huge trees rise from the path, their trunks embraced by protective armor of bamboo slats to prevent people from peeling off bits of bark as mementos of this sacred place. The branches of these trees, isolated from the forest by the gravel path at their base, join the canopy far above the ground. I approach Naiku obliquely. A wall of massive boulders, covered in lichens and moss, looms behind the trees—the foundation for the monumental platform. I walk up the worn stone steps and beneath the first gate through the outermost fence and encounter another gate, its opening covered by a white silk cloth through which only ghostly outlines of the buildings within are visible. Beyond the fence are two other wooden fences, each different, each delimiting a progressively more sacred precinct. I watch as people approach the white silk screen, throw coins into a broad box, bow deeply two times, clap twice, bow again, and back away. For the millions of pilgrims who journey to Ise each year, this is their destination. They may go no further.

But I did. As I wait to be led, by special permission, into the precinct beyond the second fence, I hear the background murmur of people talking softly, punctuated by the clink, pause, clap clap of each person's praying, like phrases overlaid but distinct, the interval between clink and clap marking the depth of each bow (and, thus, reverence). And encompassing it all is the roaring buzz of cicadas.

I follow the priest down the narrow alley between the two outer fences, walking on rough, grey river cobbles that clatter underfoot. The priest's large, black wooden shoes amplify the sound, emphasizing passage across the rocks, up the wooden steps of the gate and down again into a large, open area: clatter clatter, clomp clomp, clatter clatter. We cross the clearing, pass under three trees, step onto a broad path of white rocks, and stop. We face a torii, and through that a fence and gate, and beyond that another fence and gate—the two innermost precincts we would not penetrate. The noise of our walking underscores the stillness of our immobility. Now, no sound of people, only the cicadas.

Within three years all of these artifacts will vanish, to be replaced by new construction on the adjoining vacant plot. Twenty years later this site will be reoccupied in turn. Ise is a celebration of cultural continuity; ritual reconstruction of the shrines has endured for more than a thousand years. The bridge of raw wood at the entrance to Naiku's domain, recently reconstructed, presages the coming reconstruction and destruction of Naiku. I feel both the presence of these constructions and their absence. We bow twice, clap twice, bow again, and return.

Ise is also a political landscape, for the authority of the Japanese emperor is vested in his divine descent from Amaterasu, the sun goddess; Ise is her shrine, and only the emperor may enter the innermost precinct. But Ise also speaks to fundamental conditions of human existence within nature and community, the forest and its long-lived trees a contrast to the transience of a human life.

Sacred landscapes are shaped by ritual, usually progressing from secular to sacred: a series of nested enclosures at the Japanese shrine in Ise, the innermost the most sacred; a climb from low to high at Mont-Saint-Michel, from shops selling

Landscape of worship. Ise shrine. Japan.

Carp. Ise shrine. Japan.

souvenirs below to the church at the top, from outside the town to inside the abbey. There are thresholds or gateways that mark progressive passage and, often, an inner domain that only initiates may enter, as at the sacred places of Australian Aborigines. The destination may require an arduous journey—a long pilgrimage, dangerous passage, or steep climb—a metaphor for the difficulty of reaching the desired goal, be it enlightenment, virtue, or strength. There is often a place of prayer or reflection.

In worship one transcends separate, individual consciousness and becomes a part of something beyond oneself. Movement, offering, reflection, transformation are part of religious rituals, prescribed and repetitive acts reenacting the creation of the world, inducing a sense of transport from the material world to a world of the spirit or an altered state of consciousness.[21]

The setting of worship at Gothic cathedrals like Chartres and Notre Dame of Paris contrasts with the settings of daily life: there are portals decorated with sculptures, stained-glass windows shining like jewels, soaring ceilings. The Ise shrines of Japan offer no such lavish display of precious metals or jewels or monumental structures, but are rather modest buildings of human scale, built from plain, unadorned, weathered wood, decorated with white rice paper and small branches from a particular tree, the *sakaki* (meaning, literally, plant-god).[22] The ground of the shrine's most sacred precincts is covered with white river cobbles, elevated from the ordinary to the extraordinary by the uniformity of their color and size. The gods honored at Ise are gods of everyday phenomena: the sun, the harvest, the wind. The most extraordinary places in Japan are often a simple, subtle transformation of the everyday.

Light is used significantly in most sacred landscapes, for emphasis or, figuratively, for divinity, enlightenment, or spirit. Light filters dimly through densely layered leaves of the forest at Ise, shines brightly in the clearings around important shrines. The cathedral of Notre Dame in Paris is like a sacred grove, its aisles dark, enclosed, arches forming a low canopy, but the brighter nave is lined with columns like tall trees; the cross's center, where nave, apse, and transepts meet, is brightest, like a forest clearing. Afternoon sun shines through a Rose Window—red, magenta, blue glass brilliant like backlit leaves at a clearing's edge seen against black, branching tracery. The light cast on the stone floor, filtered through all those colors, seems as green as forest light. At Mariebjerg Cemetery, north of Copenhagen, two parallel, long dark avenues, lined by four rows of elms, culminate, like a church's nave, in a bright clearing formed by a circle of trees.

Sacred landscapes are revered for qualities associated with the divine, found (as in mountaintops, springs, and forest clearings) or built (as in Mariebjerg and Notre Dame). Some remain sacred to successive cultures: springs and hilltops in England were used by Druids, later by Christians. Ordinary landscapes can become sacred for what happened there—real or mythic—as the farm fields and woods at Gettysburg had for Lincoln: "We cannot dedicate, we cannot consecrate, we cannot hallow this ground. The great men, living and dead, who struggled here, have consecrated it far above our poor power to add or detract." Many people are compelled to make a *place* in which to remember a death or traumatic event. Memorials and cemeteries become sacred ground.

Landscapes of Memory

Verdun is a sacred landscape to many French. Thousands of soldiers lost their lives in the siege of that city during the First World War. The sole lifeline by which Verdun was supplied—the Sacred Way, or Voie Sacrée—is lined with mileposts decorated with stars and laurel branch and topped with a soldier's helmet along its entire fifty-eight-kilometer length. Battles had raged across cropland, pasture, homes, and villages; whole villages outside Verdun were destroyed, pummeled into muddy, metaled craters by tons of mortar, their fertile soil rendered untillable. "Mort pour la France" reads a memorial stone to the town of Fleury, set up on its former site. Villages and forts are now overgrown within a great forest preserve and military reservation, but beneath the trees the ground is still hummocky, cratered. The streets of Fleury are laid out where they once were, marked by street signs in German, French, and English, sites of shops and homes identified by their former use (bakery) or by the owners' occupation (street worker). The only building is a tiny chapel, Our Lady of Europe. Up the road from Fleury is the huge cemetery for soldiers killed in the Battle of Verdun: 15,000 graves in rows of identical white stone crosses set in green grass, a red rose planted at the base of each—Frenchmen all. Above the long, sloping lawn stands a monumental stone ossiary, shaped like an upright missile, or a phallus, tomb for the remains of 130,000 unknown soldiers.

On Mont Valérien, a hill outside Paris, long straight rows of white marble crosses set in clipped green grass march under trees and up, down, and along the slopes at the cemetery for American soldiers who died in the First World War. Except for those who came from the same family (who may be buried next to one another), the dead are buried at random, without regard to rank or date of death. Crosses have name, rank, batallion, division, date of death, and the state each was from; the only variation, here and there, are posts with a Star of David. Further up Mont Valérien, on the Rue Calvare (Calvary), is a wall against which the Nazis executed 4,500 prisoners during the German Occupation in the Second World War. Were the Nazis aware that this had been a sacred site for hundreds of years, a place where pilgrims once climbed the hill on their knees?[23] The old wall, part of the fortifications of the Mount (the military still occupies the hilltop fort), pitted with bullet holes, is now the National French Resistance Memorial. The memorial, set against the wall-hill, is flanked by stepped terraces of asphalt and stone and faced by a large open plaza. It is a place made for a throng to come together, not for the solitary visitor.

A First World War cemetery at Redipuglia existed before Mussolini, in 1938, built the largest Italian war memorial to remember that war in a very different way; he had the bodies in the first cemetery disinterred and moved across the road to the new monument. The former one was on the Hill of St. Elia, where the graves in concentric circles around the hill bore simple markers with lines of poetry and the rows were marked by relics representing the roles of the dead as soldiers: infantry with weapons and helmets, signal corps with radio, and so on. At Mussolini's monument, the soldiers are buried in alphabetical order, in tombs set into gigantic terraces. IN GLORIA PATRIA say huge words cut into the stone. Crowds are visiting when I am there, small children with parents and grandparents. This is a landscape of instruction.

What comfort can the individual who grieves the loss of a friend or relative find in these places? In the American cemetery at Mont Valérien the loved one is one of a vast army of dead, the place, the marker undifferentiated; at the Resistance memorial, at Redipuglia, one is reminded that the cause—defense against an oppressive force, or for national honor and glory—was considered greater than the individual, and that one should salute the cause and not mourn the loss.

The Vietnam Veterans Memorial in Washington, D.C., in contrast, is about loss and grieving; it honors the memory of the soldiers not the war itself. The sponsors wanted the memorial to be "conciliatory," "reflective and contemplative in character," and stipulated that it must make no political statement about a war still a source of national rift. Although it is on the Mall, it was built with private, not public, funds. By March 31, 1981, the deadline, 1,421 entries were received, making this the largest design competition ever held in America or Europe. Maya Lin, then a student at Yale, won the competition with a design submitted as an assignment in a class on funerary architecture: two two-hundred-foot-long retaining walls of polished black granite. The walls form a right-angled V set into the ground facing a grassy slope. At the point of convergence, the walls are ten feet high, at their tips, flush with the ground. On each wall are seventy panels inscribed with the names of the more than fifty-seven thousand Americans killed in Vietnam and of the several thousands still missing.

The Vietnam Veterans Memorial is now the most-visited site in a city of memorials and monuments. Many who come are moved to tears, many touch or kiss a name or take a rubbing of it; many leave flowers, messages for the dead and missing named on the wall. Mementos are taped to the wall or laid at its base; photographs, boots, medals, letters from kids who never knew their dad. They personalize memory and promote empathy, as did the original cemetery at Redipuglia; Mussolini's monumental memorial made the dead a faceless mass. Psychotherapists who specialize in the treatment of Vietnam veterans have brought therapy groups to the memorial. Yet at the time of its construction, critics called the design "a shameful degrading ditch, a black gash of sorrow," and a group of congressmen sent a letter of protest to President Ronald Reagan: "The Black Hole of Calcutta needs no re-creation on the Washington Mall . . . this

Hill of Remembrance. Forest Cemetery. Stockholm.

design makes a political statement of shame and dishonor." They demanded that "the color be changed to white, the wall be raised above the ground, and the scheme include an American flag." In 1982, the sponsors agreed to erect a flagpole near the memorial and commissioned the sculptor Frederick Hart to design an eight-foot-high bronze sculpture, *Three Fighting Men*. People pause by that statue for a photograph, but it is the wall that draws and holds them.

The crosses, row on row, and destroyed towns around Verdun still evoke feeling. Will the Vietnam Veterans Memorial do so once the friends and families who experienced loss are themselves dead? When the names erode, what will the memorial mean in one hundred years, or five hundred? The war in Vietnam divided the American nation; like the Civil War it prompted violence within, set brother against brother, father against son. It was a national trauma with far-reaching consequences for American society, when many Americans felt betrayed by their government, lost faith in and gained a cynical distrust of those who professed to lead them. Will the sense of pathos evoked by the memorial endure?

In Stockholm's Forest Cemetery, another starkly simple landscape that focuses and amplifies emotion, the Hill of Remembrance was designed "to give form to a sorrow that cannot be told." [24] As I walk through the passage into the cemetery, enclosed between two stone retaining walls that start high overhead and end much lower, creating an effect of distance through "forced perspective," I see it in the distance: a rounded, grassy hill, rising out of undulating land, with a grove of

Enfolded ascent. Hill of Remembrance. Forest Cemetery. Stockholm.

elms at the top—the trees catch the wind and move—and under the trees, a low wall. To reach the top, I climb a path up stairs set within grassy berms, enfolded by the hill. The steps rise, then gradually level out, carrying me through an opening in the low stone wall. I come to rest in a little clearing under the trees, within the precinct of the walls. There is a progressive sense of threshold, gateway, refuge. The trees are small, a species selected for their dwarfed habit to make the hill seem bigger.[25] Enclosed by the low wall of stone, the hilltop provides a prospect over meadow, graves, a large cross, a chapel and crematorium, the city. The Hill of Remembrance is a classic place of reflection, where a sense of overview and refuge engenders a special kind of remembering in which past and present are compared and integrated.

Later, I sit on the bench just inside the cemetery entrance on an overcast summer evening. A man cycles by. A woman leaves. A huge hare lopes across the grass. The birds are in full song—many different songs. Then, black smoke rises from the crematorium chimney for a few, brief moments, and is gone, dissipating, floating off into the sky. A bird flies in and perches on the top of the cross. And then, at last, the light comes; a low, golden light bringing the landscape alive.

Landscapes affirm or negate the memory of a personal past, record a collective, cultural past, even a past beyond individual experience or human memory. They transmit memories from one generation to another, as adults teach children at Verdun, Redipuglia, and Washington, D.C., a prompting to remember a person or event in a particular way. "To know what we were confirms what we are," David

Lowenthal says in *The Past Is a Foreign Country*.[26] Memory is central to identity. When American cities like Boston and Dallas razed entire districts as part of urban renewal programs, substituting new office buildings, cultural enclaves, governmental and convention centers, they erased parts of their identity. Forgetting the past can be foolish, and attempts to reinvent it may even be dangerous: in Berlin, traces of the wall are being rapidly and systematically expunged, denying and forfeiting an opportunity to come to terms with a tragic past.

Landscapes of Play

Johan Huizinga calls humans *Homo ludens*, describing places of play as "temporary worlds within the ordinary world, dedicated to the performance of an act apart."[27] Sports fields are places apart, for recreation (from the Latin word for "restore" or "refresh") and entertainment (from the French word for "hold"): players engage in action, and are restored; spectators are entertained, held in thrall, but are passive bystanders who may neither participate, except by cheers or catcalls, nor invade the field. Many games, such as basketball, soccer, baseball, and tennis, require movement within a fixed frame of rules and landscape geometry; golf is a marked-off ground. Places designed for play alone have multiplied in the twentieth century, from the first urban playgrounds at the turn of the century to the sports fields and large recreation areas of midcentury, to the elaborate end-of-the-century theme parks like Disney World and Sea World. A broader spectrum of society than ever before has sought out seaside resorts and ski lodges, and new towns of second homes are booming.

Down the street from our house in Belmont, Massachusetts, when my son was two to five years old, was a playground with a small sandbox, swings, a stage coach of metal pipes painted red, yellow, and blue, ducks that bounced on metal springs, two concrete benches, and an open lawn. The assumption was that adults would stand and watch, not play. Parents tried to sit on the ducks or swings, and failed, then shifted uncomfortably on the hard, backless benches. No one stayed very long. Nor did any of the expensive play "equipment" hold children's attention for long; they ran from place to place, trying one thing then another; the sandbox was the exception. The playground made me angry, not just because it was so boring but because it demonstrated such ignorance of the importance of play. My own most vivid memories of play before the age of five are of climbing huge rocks in the woods and exploring a thicket of sumac. I don't remember playing in playgrounds except during school recess. At six, I hid under a huge rosebush so dense no one could see in and I built dams in a gutter in the street when it rained. I swung in a swing suspended on long ropes from a tree branch from the time I was six, through my teens. From seven to nine, the most magical places were vacant lots, construction sites, remnant woods, and storm sewers.

When I asked my graduate students in landscape architecture to design a playground, the designs they produced were unimaginative. They had forgotten what it was like to be a child, so I invited my son's day-care class of four-year-olds to visit as consultants. First they told the students what they liked to do best: "Dig for dinosaur bones!" "Trap wild animals!" We unrolled a long sheet of paper on the floor, and each child drew an ideal playground; one drew a "bottomless pit," another a "ladder to the sky." Digging or unearthing was central to many, the idea of discovery was in all. When it was time to leave, the four-year-olds lined up, and I led them out to the railing that looked out over three floors of open architectural studios, all under one roof, connected by a long series of stairs, filled with hundreds of students working at drawing tables.[28] The children looked down over the three floors below and realized instinctively the dramatic potential of the space: "Hello down there," yelled my son. Four hundred heads looked up from their desks to the small figures along the fourth-floor rail. The children waved, the students responded, waving and clapping, many climbed up on their drafting stools and stood there as the children paraded down four flights of open stairs and out the door. It was only the second time I had seen this space used theatrically in seven years. After the children left, my students were very quiet. "How did we lose that?" I could see them thinking. The results of such loss are everywhere.

Ever since that time, I have tried to help my students recapture their most vivid memories of childhood play. I have discovered that my own memories are not unique. Students remember exploring, hiding, and imagining; their special childhood places commonly include leftover bits of space between properties, on vacant land, often with some measure of danger, real or imagined, forts, hiding places, prospects or overviews. None mention playgrounds. Their remembered places were often destroyed by adults, and they report a sense of loss, and wonder why adults failed to appreciate what a special place it was. Kevin Lynch and Clare Cooper Marcus, who have studied children's play and adults' memories, have found many similar stories.[29] Lynch, writing in 1956, described one man's memory of Manhattan's Riverside Park along the Hudson River before and after it was "developed" with playgrounds: "I remember there being a lot more space to play in [before playgrounds were built]. [Afterwards] there simply wasn't enough space just to go and play in and do idiotic things in. You couldn't dig, for example."[30] Playgrounds, as Galen Cranz reminds us, are an artifact of the twentieth century.[31]

Tanner Fountain, just outside Harvard Yard in Cambridge, was not built as a playground yet it has become a place for play. Rocks form a field of circles, small jets in pavement emit steam in winter and intermittent, misty spray in summer, sparking rainbows. Many small children jump around the circles, from rock to rock, screech when water sprays, reach for rainbows. A fountain at Parc André Citroën in Paris is even more successful as a playground (whether or not it was meant to be one). Even when the water is not running, the fountain is still a place: a large, sloping plane of stone. When it is running, more than a hundred jets of water erupt from the pavement, transforming the space, their height changing at random intervals, their patterns unpredictable and seemingly never the same. One

Landscape of play: Parc Citroën. Paris.

moment all 120 jets are bubbling up a few inches above the surface, the next they are shooting twelve feet up then disappearing, rising again to one foot, or three, or six, or ten, then back down again. From the top of the slope to the bottom there are fifteen rows of spouts, each row eight spouts across; in each row, water spurts up to the same height, though height may vary from row to row. Sometimes the tops of the jets form a plane of water, level or tilted, high or low. When the jets are shooting high, over eight feet, the fountain is like a forest, the columns of water like trees; children dash up and down and across the spaces between them. Some people bring beach balls to balance on top of the spouting water. Children, singly and in groups, invent games, variations on water play, like playing in the shifting water's edge of a beach. When the water disappears, momentarily, a child sits on a nozzle, waiting for the water to blast up from below. On a hot Saturday afternoon in July, the place—like a beach itself—is filled with people: young, old, some playing in the water (in swimsuits, clothes, underwear, bare), others watching, some with children, some not.

Carl Theodore Sørensen watched children playing on construction sites with sand, bricks, and tree stumps, and proposed, in 1931, a new kind of playground—*skrammelejeplads*, or "junk playground"—of old cars, packing crates, and timber so children could build their own places.[32] He saw "nicely designed" play equipment and hopscotch lines painted on asphalt as evidence of adults' profound misunderstanding of children's play.[33] The first adventure playground, built in 1943 in

Landscape of play: West Philadelphia. (West Philadelphia Landscape Project)

Emdrup, just north of Copenhagen, was a flat, open area of dirt sunk below the level of the surrounding land and bounded by berms covered with dense, thorny shrubs; entry was through a small wooden building in one corner.[34] The whole created a frame for activity and for messy constructions. The dense boundary provided privacy and shielded the children's work from view. Photographs from the 1940s show an open space with piles of bricks, old boards, pipes, barrels, water, and other construction materials and children, in groups and alone, laying bricks and hammering nails, fixing a flagpole atop a shack. Photographs from the early 1960s depict neat rows of little houses. Adult play leaders had taken over as supervisors and regulators; Sørensen was very disappointed. Emdrup Adventure Playground, as it originally was, captured the imagination of many in other countries. Arvid Bengtsson was inspired to build adventure playgrounds in Sweden. Lady Allen of Hurtwood came from England to see it in 1945 just after the war was over: "Some caves are dug twelve feet down into the earth, look-out towers are built, and finally an artesian well to irrigate the cement channels which guide the water to the paddling pool built by the older children for their younger brothers and sisters."[35] From Denmark to Sweden and England, the idea spread farther to Switzerland, Israel, and the United States.

Sven-Ingvar Andersson regards adventure playgrounds as important for grown-ups as for children, a place to express themselves, to do something silly that does not count. Marnas, his own garden in Sweden, is a fantasy world, a personal playground of past projects and ongoing experiments: a man made of boards, a sculpture of branches, a pear growing in a brandy bottle.

Landscapes of Movement and Meeting

Lawrence Halprin calls freeways, with "their graceful, sinuous, patterns . . . like great free-flowing paintings," among the most beautiful and typical structures of the age. To him, they speak "in the language of a new scale," of the high-speed motion and the changes of everyday experience.[36] He considers freeways "a form of action calligraphy where the laws of motion generate a geometry which is part engineering, part painting, part sculpture, but mostly an exercise in choreography in the landscape."[37] In the early 1960s, he urged that freeways, so destructive to cities, be reconceived as works of art and as social opportunities; he invented choreographic techniques, called scoring, to understand and design motion and change in landscape, and applied them to designs for freeways and freeway parks, plazas, malls, gardens, and communities. At their best, his works are something to experience, not merely to look at, places where the whole is understood only through the process of movement, an overlapping of many viewpoints.

The destruction wreaked by highway building in many cities since the 1950s stems from the single-minded pursuit of efficient movement of cars and trucks. Two years after Halprin's book *Freeways* was published in 1966, the city of Seattle asked him to help them solve a problem: a freeway was a chasm between downtown and a nearby neighborhood, isolating two districts once closely related. Halprin proposed to bridge the freeway with an elevated park: "The trick," he explained, "is to perceive the old freeway as part of the city-scape and tame it, rather than complain about it."[38] Cars, trucks, and buses now whiz by on a highway through the heart of Seattle, then disappear beneath the hanging vines, trees, plazas, and gardens of Freeway Park, and reemerge moments later. From the park itself, the traffic is sometimes visible between branches of trees, but mostly it is hidden, the noise of its passing disguised by rushing water in the park's many waterfalls. Halprin's integration of the freeway into other aspects of urban life, such as walking, playing, and meeting, is part of a larger tradition of parkways and boulevards. Boston's Riverway, built in the 1890s, had walking and bridle paths, a stream for boating, a broad roadway for through traffic; it was a precursor to Freeway Park, as was New York's Bronx River Parkway, built in the 1920s. The Blue Ridge Parkway of Virginia and North Carolina celebrates the delights of movement; its designers, landscape architects, chose the route, shaped the scene, and directed the gaze. The Blue Ridge Parkway is a national park, a destination in itself, as Seattle's Freeway Park has become.

From trade routes to main streets to commercial strips, principal routes are not only thoroughfares but also places to meet and exchange goods and information. When Walt Disney made Main Street the primary route of Disneyland and a principal place of exchange, he was tapping a fundamental association. His Main

Street is the way in and out; behind its decorated facades are places to store belongings, to purchase film, cameras, and souvenirs, to learn about Disney.

The subways crisscrossing Japanese cities like Tokyo and Osaka are places of movement, meeting, and exchange. Subways stations are filled with people all day and late into the evening. In downtown Osaka and Tokyo, the principal subway stations are large, subterranean neighborhoods with restaurants and grocery stores, often connected to the interior of tall buildings by elevators that open out not only to offices, but also to stores and restaurant districts high in the sky. One hurtles along in a subway car, steps off and walks through subterranean corridors, then rises up in an elevator, each floor a different world.

I travel for half an hour through the subway to Osaka Center on a weekday evening, through a maze of corridors, filled with people traveling in groups. I board an elevator and ascend, reminded of a science fiction fantasy in which, by stepping through a portal, one is transported to a distant and exotic place. The elevator rises toward a restaurant district on floors 29 through 34; each floor is a neighborhood of restaurants of a similar cuisine from Oriental to Western. I step off on the thirty-fourth floor onto a street of small restaurants offering Japanese-style food, tempura, noodle shops, tearooms. Each has a different decor, its menu displayed as plastic models of food in cases along the corridor. It is my first day in Japan. As I go from point to point within the enclosed capsules of subway car and elevator, I become disoriented and long to go outside to get my bearings. Some days later, I would become accustomed to these interior worlds.

Landscapes of Production and Waste

Middleton Place, in South Carolina, the oldest landscape garden in the United States, was once a rice plantation, its ornamental ponds an integral part of a productive landscape, a system powered by water flow and slave labor. Gardens, house, and fields are oriented to the Ashley, a tidal river and the main route to Charleston, twenty miles downstream. The river was more easily traveled than the inland road, which was often impassable well into the early twentieth century. Tidewater rice cultivation, once prevalent in South Carolina and now defunct there, required an understanding of hydraulic engineering, for rice needs periodic flooding at specific times and cannot tolerate saltwater. Planters used slaves to carve out rice fields from tidewater swamps, to build dikes, ditches, and tidal gates along the river, and to clear and dam upland swamps for reservoirs, to dig canals leading to rice fields. Such extensive water systems buffered the fields at Middleton Place from effects of drought and flood. Upland reservoirs were a source of freshwater in drought and when coastal storms drove saltwater upriver; they protected fields from flooding by freshets—floods from inland. Tidal gates controlled drainage and permitted the river's upper layer of freshwater to enter at high water, blocking saltwater; dikes prevented flooding from the river. Water flow from a dammed millpond powered a mill that hulled the rice to be sent downriver to Charleston.[39]

Henry Middleton (1717–84) had laid out the garden in 1741 with a series of water canals and ponds on terraces that step down from high ground to rice fields and tidal river. The house on a bluff overlooks gardens, fields, and river, aligned on an axis with the river's course. Middleton plotted the gardens precisely within the structure of a 90 degree triangle. One side bisected the main house (now destroyed), principal terraces, and Butterfly Ponds, and points down the river; the other side still bisects a long reservoir that doubles as a reflection pool. It took one hundred slaves nearly ten years to build the gardens and pools.[40] In 1774, when Middleton was elected president of the Continental Congress, he was one of the largest landholders in Carolina, owning more than fifty thousand acres and about eight hundred slaves.[41] Sherman's army burned the main house in 1865 at the end of the Civil War; its shell was toppled by the earthquake of 1885. The gardens fell into ruin, overgrown and neglected until 1916, when their restoration began. Middleton is no longer a rice plantation, but grassy terraces still step down to the river, overlooking the ponds and sky mirrored in their surface, and the skeleton of the water system is still clear, a landscape shaped by power and production.

Like Middleton Place, the English patchwork landscape of small fields and hedgerows and of mill towns like Manchester is a landscape of production. Though the rural fields and industrial townscapes are different in form, they belong to the same landscape, linked by the process of growing sheep for wool and weaving cloth, a process no longer economically viable here. Fields and hedgerows, valued highly by the English for their scenic beauty and traditional associations, are still maintained despite their outmoded form; urban mills, not so valued, were left to ruin. Abandoned mills and factories, clear-cut forests, slag heaps, and derelict land have become wastelands, by-products of improvidence or outmoded production. Landscapes of production are shaped by demands of materials—rice and its cultivation, sheep grazing and shearing—and processes of their transformation into products—harvesting and milling, spinning and weaving—and they change with shifts in fashion, technology, capital, and labor.

Wastelands and wilderness, once synonymous, are now often seen as opposites. In contemporary North America, a wasteland generally refers to lands laid waste by humans: mined-out regions, clear-cut forests, garbage dumps, and abandoned factories and neighborhoods, no fit abode for man or beast. Wilderness, originally the space beyond the pale—the common boundary fence—a place where wild beasts roamed, a lawless region, a fearful place with no value to anyone but hermits and prophets, has been promoted to sacred place and city has been demoted to wasteland, revealing a belief that humans degrade what they touch, leading to failure to link landscapes of production, waste, and renewal. One kind of ignorance has replaced another, both examples of cultural blindness and environmental illiteracy.

The transformation of Boston's Fens and Riverway from urban wasteland into urban "wilderness" (in the modern sense of the terms) was the first attempt anywhere, so far as I know, to *construct* a wetland. It was built over nearly two decades, the 1880s and the 1890s, the Fens dredged out of the muddy flats of a former millpond, the Riverway shaped from floodplains fouled by sewage and industrial effluent. Both were designed to purify water and to protect adjacent land from flooding, to reclaim and reoccupy "lands laid waste by human improvidence or malice . . . [by becoming] a co-worker with nature in the reconstruction of the damaged fabric."[42] The marshes, meadows, and floodplain forests Olmsted conceived were built of materials both given and worked: earth, rock, water, and plants of the place; dredged mud, quarried stone, channeled water, and bred plants. His landscapes were constructed by human imagination and human labor, then by processes of nonhuman nature. His drawn plans and on-site adjustments guided the work of others—dredging, grading, planting, pruning, tending—to carry out his visions of how trees, shrubs, grasses, and flowers would grow, beget, and nurture other plants, live, and die, and how water, flowing through the channels he molded, would modify further the shorelines he shaped.

Everyone at the time was aware of the transformation of a filthy, stinking, muddy mess into the Fens and Riverway. Their awareness became part of the social meaning and aesthetic power of the Fens and Riverway. But today these works are widely, and falsely, assumed to be preserved bits of nature in the city, not the designed and built places they really are, daring experiments of engineering, ecology, landscape design, and city planning. The function and the appearance of the Fens and Riverway were also revolutionary; earlier, most urban parks were designed in formal or pastoral styles.[43] Olmsted introduced a "wild" landscape to bring the appearance of "natural scenery" of places like Yosemite to "those who cannot travel" to see them.[44]

Like the Fens, Werribee Farm in Melbourne, Australia, is a landscape of waste and renewal. Its canals, lagoons, marshes, and grasslands cover twenty-seven thousand acres and treat 60 percent of the sewage from a region of nearly three million people. Engineers and wildlife ecologists have designed lagoons for sewage treatment and wetland habitat. The farm is open to birdwatchers, who have sighted more than two hundred species: ground birds, arboreal birds, birds of prey, wetland and sea birds. Werribee Farm is also a landscape of production, one of the largest farms in southern Australia. Sewage irrigates and fertilizes pastures grazed by a herd of fifteen hundred cattle and a sheep flock of comparable size. The cattle and sheep are slaughtered and sold for meat, producing income that reduces the cost of sewage treatment. The landscape of Werribee Farm displays connections between wastes and resources, processes of production and renewal.

Landscapes of Home and Community

A garden was, in the biblical story, the first home. Garden is a potent and complex symbol; it embodies pleasure, fertility, sustenance, and renewal. Gardening is a life-embracing act, an act of faith and hope, an expression of commitment to the

Landscape of waste and renewal: Werribee Farm. Melbourne, Australia.

future; it can even be a political act. Community gardens are a place for planting, growing, and harvesting food, but they are also the locus for many other life processes: for sharing and trading, for meeting and play, for making and building, for dreaming and worship. They are the scene of both cooperation and conflict.

"This garden is a town, we have everything but a penal colony," says Hayward Ford, president of Aspen Farms, a community garden in Mill Creek, the inner-city neighborhood of West Philadelphia named after the forgotten creek buried beneath the surface. Aspen Farms looks like a miniature farm, but it is more like a town, with individual plots and common ground. The plots are laid out in a grid, divided by straight paths, much like Philadelphia's streets. Each plot is related to the community garden as a whole, just as each individual private property is to its surrounding neighborhood. Just as urban real estate changes hands, so owners of the gardens change, but the boundaries remain the same year to year. There are meeting places and shared resources, like the greenhouse, the compost pile, the water supply and irrigation system. Originally colonized in 1976 with parallel plots divided by small paths and one large, central path, the garden has continued to change, with individual initiatives, negotiations, and group decisions. The gardeners set the rules and elect officers, including a chaplain.

Aspen Farms' gardeners range in age from 12 years old to 103; most are over 60, all are African American. One or more of the fifty gardeners seem always to be there, digging, planting, cleaning, weeding, harvesting, building, talking, resting,

"This garden is a town": Aspen Farms, 1988. (West Philadelphia Landscape Project)

watching. "If you can't improve each year, why be here?" So Ford sums up the gardeners' philosophy. In 1975, the site was like much of the land nearby: vacant, weedy, full of trash; by 1980, gardeners had taken over half of the large vacant lot. The garden brought people together to improve their neighborhood. The houses in blocks around Aspen Farms are well maintained with small front gardens; none is vacant. Every year the gardeners take on new projects, host neighborhood parties, and give away much of their harvest. They tend flowers outside the garden's gate and have lured the pink hollyhocks growing along the interior of the fence to creep through and embellish the sidewalk.

I first met Ford and the other gardeners in 1988, when they asked my landscape architecture students at the University of Pennsylvania to design a new meeting place for the garden. It was a complex design problem. Not only were there fifty gardeners, but the garden community had already been in existence for twelve years. Carving out a place for meeting meant taking away space from one or more garden plots. The students began by getting to know their clients and the neighborhood; each stayed for a weekend with one of the gardeners. The students' designs turned out to be both similar to and different from each other. Most proposed a circular or square place for meeting, but some sited it in the middle of the garden, some at the corner nearest the street, some at the entrance. All offered good reasons for their decisions, based on what they had heard the gardeners say. One student, responding to a group who wanted a new fence, designed a fence in-

Main street: Aspen Farms, 1990.

stead, but because of a fixed budget, spending money on a fence would mean no meeting place. Two days before the presentation to the gardeners, one student, John Widrick, decided to revisit Aspen Farms and ask for comments on his design for a circular meeting place in a central location. He was unprepared for the reaction of polite horror. What we had idealized as one big community was actually several smaller groups, each with its singular territory and leaders. Widrick's original scheme not only displaced several garden plots, it disposed of most of one group's entire territory. He returned to class, distressed, threw out his drawings, and, with one day to go, began again by thinking how to use what he now knew about the garden's politics and turfs.

Widrick had been my research assistant for two years on the West Philadelphia Landscape Project, my laboratory for developing and testing ideas about the language of landscape. He reflected on that work and discarded the assumption that a meeting place had to be a broadly shaped space; a path is a meeting place, he realized. His new plan proposed that the central path become the common meeting place so each group's territory would border it and the space given up to create the common area could be evenly shared. When the students presented their designs to the gardeners at the Mill Creek Community Center the next day, the gardeners chose to build his.

Two gates lead into the wide meeting place–path that forms the main street of Aspen Farms. The path now resembles a small street with benches for people to sit, rest, watch, and talk. The benches and raised flower beds are boundaries between the public path and the adjacent, more private, garden plots. Small openings between benches and planters are gateways leading to the garden plots beyond. Groups of plots form small neighborhoods within the larger garden that compete with each other for the best flower beds along the main path outside the gate to their plots. The design for Aspen Farms' main street turned conflict and competition into common benefit.

Unlike a garden where plots of similar size and regular pattern are laid out prior to planting (like Aspen Farms), Powelton/Summer-Winter Community Garden, in another West Philadelphia neighborhood, has no regularity. Individual plots are carved out of a weedy meadow of grasses and wildflowers still thriving at the edges of the garden, on untended plots, and over the fence and sidewalks to form a border of spontaneous growth for the garden as a whole. Each plot merges into the next garden, with barely discernable borders. Plots of varying shapes and sizes are distinguished primarily through the types of plants each gardener grows and how they are cultivated, whether, for example, they are laid out in rows or mixed together. The seeming chaos reflects an anarchist political structure, in which gardeners act as free agents, governed not by set rules but by common values.

Form conveys meaning. Both the pattern of Aspen Farms with its regular boundaries and the seemingly amorphous plots and sprawling edges of the Powelton/Summer-Winter garden are eloquent expressions of different governance and different values. The Spruce Hill Garden, in yet another part of West Philadelphia, with lawn and flower beds that flow into one another to form a single, larger whole, marks one mind at work, and Aspen Farms, with its many, clearly divided plots, many minds and hands.

Nærum Garden Colony north of Copenhagen has dozens of separate gardens, each enclosed by an elliptical hedge, each with a tiny house and its own address; a numbered map is posted at the main gate. Most everyone has an apple tree, a small lawn, flowers near the house, a vegetable garden. The hedges are laid out in the same elliptical form, but of several different species, privet, hawthorn, and beech. And yet, each garden reflects its owner's taste. Each maintains an oval hedge, but at quite different heights. Some are only waist high, their owners being outgoing gardeners who want to see who walks by and want everyone to see in, perhaps to stop and talk. Some hedges are dense and over six feet high, their owners gaining more privacy. But the grassy common land between the hedges is uniformly clipped; each owner is responsible for maintaining the lawn outside their own hedge. Freestanding hedges were the designer C. Th. Sørensen's solution to the most common disputes between neighboring gardeners when hedge boundaries are shared: how high to clip the hedge. They leave odd-shaped, curving spaces between the gardens that echo and emphasize the curve of the hilly ground plane.

Nærum Garden Colony is like a little *landsby*, that is, a Danish country village. The fields have shrunk to a lawn between the house/gardens snug behind their boundary hedges, clipped short, revealing the roll of the land just as cropfields do in the rural landscape. On a fine day, the Danish flag flies over many of the gardens, for each has its own flagpole. How very Danish the place is, with its rolling landform, its cultivated landscape, its protected private life, its well-ordered public life, and its flags.

Living in Village Homes, in Davis, California, is something like living in a community garden such as Nærum year round. Here, much of the landscape is edible: pomegranate hedges and dwarf grapefruit, orange, and lemon trees line public walkways within; double rows of almond trees border the roadway outside. There are vegetable plots of various sizes on common land; surplus produce may be sold at the Davis Farmers' Market. In Village Homes, there are at least three levels of property ownership, each with fuzzy, often invisible boundaries: a private lot, a space common to small clusters of houses, and the larger public space shared by the entire community. Houses are small and close to one another, private gardens tiny. Decks and porches are the principal private outdoor space behind the houses; the private lot is almost entirely occupied by the house itself and extends only a few feet from the building line. It is difficult, even impossible, to tell where one person's private walk ends and where common land begins. Space owned in common by clusters of houses is maintained by the people who live there, in many places by extending their own garden into the common space. Community public space—drainage ways, roadways, greens, vegetable plots, vineyard, nut orchard, day care, swimming pool—is maintained by gardeners employed by the community association. The developer of Village Homes lives in the community himself. By not building underground storm drains, he saved enough money to pay for the landscaping of all the common property and to give new residents money to plant what they wanted. In one cluster, some residents built a dam in the stormwater channel to create a tiny pond stocked with mosquito fish. Village Homes has a village feel, largely because of the personalization of the landscape. The small, cluster-maintained common spaces keep the larger public space from seeming uniform and bland. This is different from other developments that try to establish a sense of village or community largely through architectural features constructed before anyone moves in.

When those of one culture mistake their own conventions for human universals, problems arise. Recent architectural history is full of such examples: in Australia, the government built new houses for Aborigines, but they chose not to live in them; instead they locked up their valuables in the house and continued to eat, meet, and sleep outdoors. Compared to those of many other cultures, American houses are extroverted. Windows and doors usually open out onto the street; front yards are rarely bounded by an opaque wall or fence, but are open to view of passersby. Americans' home landscapes emphasize identity over privacy. Japanese houses tend to be introverted, though sited directly upon the street; most have shuttered doors and windows. The garden, if there is one, is walled, a private precinct, part of the interior world, and there is seldom any hint of these gardens from the street. But within a traditional Japanese house is an open, fluid space with no locked doors, only sliding paper screens, or shoji; in an American house, rooms are divided by thick walls and doors. The nature of privacy is distinctly different: from the outside view in Japan; from the inside view in the United States. But the outward orientation of the American home seems to be changing, in response to fear of crime and perhaps to discomfort with diversity: new suburban homes are increasingly built within guarded enclaves; random shootings and street crime in inner-city neighborhoods are driving people indoors, older folks off their porches, children off the sidewalks.

Superficially, Tokyo, Osaka, and Kyoto appear much like their North American counterparts; streets provide access to blocks of single or multiple properties, doors or gates to buildings generally face the street, and each property has an identifying number. These similarities obscure a profound difference. Finding an address in a Japanese city can be a bewildering experience for a westerner. It is not just a matter of trying to decipher the Japanese characters, for often there are no street signs. American addresses are defined by their location along public property—the street; Japanese addresses refer to their position or chronology on privately owned property—the block. In American cities, an address denotes location along a street with numbers progressing consecutively, usually odd numbers on one side of the street, even numbers on the other. The numbers continue from one block of properties to another, marking and spanning the street's linear path across the city. A block is a group of properties facing each other across a street, and it receives its name from the segment of the larger street; thus, Americans refer to the 4400 block of Walnut Street, for example. In Japan, only major streets have names. Numbers on buildings refer to their location on the block itself; the numbers of houses facing each other across a street are unrelated. An address in a Japanese city is a nested series of locations: the position on the block (sometimes related to the order in which buildings were built rather than geographic location); the block itself; a named cluster of blocks; a city district; and the city. Thus, the address 3-1-1 Kasumigaseki, Chiyodaku, Tokyo, identifies building number one on block number one in ward three of the Kasumigaseki neighborhood of the Chiyoda district in Tokyo.

In an American city, the streets are figure and the blocks are ground. Streets form the spine of each block, and each block is a segment of a network linking all parts of the city. In the Japanese city, the blocks are figure and the street is ground; each block is self-contained. The American emphasis on the street, a segment of a line, underscores the importance of movement, the Japanese emphasis on the block underscores place, which implies repose. So, also, the contrast between the games of chess and go. In chess, you capture your opponent through direct, linear movement; in go, you capture your opponent through enclosure.

Western urban design traditionally has been concerned with public space, with avenues, plazas, and the relationship of buildings, particularly their facades, to these public places. Commonly axial, Western design is based on the street and the vista. Traditional Japanese urban design has an interior orientation, nested enclosures recurring in both everyday and sacred precincts, marking the progression from the public to the private, from the profane to the sacred.[45] Japanese subways are well suited to the high density and this nested, place-oriented urban space. Everywhere in Japan, I was aware of stepping across boundaries from one domain into another; gates are prominent features, so are bridges, channels, walls, and fences.

ARTFUL TELLING, DEEP READING

Landscape, like Twain's Mississippi, "is not a book to be read once and thrown aside," for not only does it have a new story to tell every day, but it has many stories. Rudolph Arnheim describes art as combining high order and high complexity, a work capable of inspiring and sustaining multiple readings versus a decorative "one-liner" that has no lasting effect. Artful authors craft many-layered landscapes with multiple meanings, overlapping functions and contexts. Deep readers decode these layers, view each element within the context of landscape features, each feature within place and region, the author's other work and life, country, period. Artful telling and deep reading demand knowledge of the vocabulary and of the grammar that governs their relationships, not for the purpose of following routine by rote rules, but to recognize when and why to break them.

Allusion: Origins, Authority, Sentiment

An allusion is a reference, usually indirect, to an event, person, place, or work. The Vietnam Veterans Memorial in Washington, D.C., alludes to the war, the deaths of individual soldiers, and other walls of mourning and memory. The heather at Kongenshus Memorial Park alludes to the heath, the tall stones lining the path to ancient menhirs (one of Sørensen's early sketches showed a dolmen instead). But landscape features like mountains and trees also allude to the processes and materials that shape them, when people read them as such. The wolf tree and the wind-pruned tree are allusions to past events, interpreted by humans in stories of science and myth. To geologists, the small holes in the flank of Uluru (Ayre's Rock) in Australia allude to erosion; to Aborigines who live nearby the marks are scars alluding to a mythic battle. Allusions may be taken for granted or go unperceived, like the bean which does not call attention to itself as something created or the flowers planted to bloom in June which the owners do not see as a deliberate allusion to their arrival and departure.

An allusion communicates shared understanding and relies upon common knowledge. Like Mussolini's monument at Redipuglia, it can remind one of collective identity, traditions, values, or heritage, establish authority or instruct, evoke mood or create a setting. An allusion can tap powerful personal and cultural memories and elicit strong emotions. A flower transplanted from a dead relative's garden and planted in one's own is an allusion with great personal significance.[46] The three crosses above the hill of crypts at Redipuglia evoke Calvary, thus portraying the Italian soldiers buried there as martyrs to a Christian cause.

By placing the glistening, golden fountain of Apollo and his horse-drawn chariot on axis with his bedroom at Versailles, Louis XIV, the Sun King, asserted his authority as kin of the god of the sun. Landscape architects may seek to establish the authority of their gardens and clients by using classical motifs or by echoing forms used in the gardens of French kings and Italian princes; architects do the same for houses. Chains of allusion connect American corporate headquarters, estates of American industrialists, eighteenth-century English landscape gardens, ancient Roman villas. Frank Lloyd Wright, Jens Jensen, and other members of the Prairie School eliminated or disguised allusions to European traditions in an effort to establish an American style. Wilhelm Miller spoke for them: "Let us not copy Europe and the East, but have something they can never have! The way for every new country to come into its own is to apply universal principles of design to the native materials."[47]

Parks and gardens often allude to or imitate other garden traditions. The perennial borders so popular now in American gardens imitate English borders developed by Gertrude Jekyll and others at the turn of the twentieth century, which referred in turn to the informal mix of plants in the traditional English cottage garden, a contrast to the fashionable, formal "carpet beds" of the Victorian era. Such choices may or may not be highly significant. In southern California developers of new housing establish an identity for their projects through a mixture of fashionable allusions: courtyard gardens with tile-lined fountains refer to Spanish gardens, irrigated lawns with groves of trees to English pastoral parks. But, when the English landscape garden displaced the formal garden in France after the French Revolution, not fashion alone but ideology had influenced both change and choice.

Disneyland's Main Street alludes, with deliberate intent and unmistakable message, to the American small town of the turn of the century. The rides in Fantasyland are designed as stories, with allusions to fairy tales and children's books as told in Disney feature cartoons like *Snow White*, *Peter Pan*, *The Wind in the Willows;* other areas, like Tom Sawyer's Island in Adventureland, embody similar allusions. Disneyland belongs to a long tradition of dialogues among the literatures of landscapes, words, and art. Classical Chinese gardens contain complex allusions to poetry, with clues inscribed on rocks, above or beside gateways and windows. According to Sun Xiaoxiang, Chinese scholars banished from the Imperial Court built gardens with subtle poetic references that were treasonous political statements concealed by the seeming innocence of the garden.[48] English landscape gardens, like Stowe and Stourhead, represented Arcadian landscapes described by Virgil and emulated paintings of classical motifs by Claude Lorrain; they also in-

Allusion. Aspen Farms. (Bilge Friedlander, West Philadelphia Landscape Project)

spired the novels of Jane Austen and the poetry of Alexander Pope. Ian Hamilton Finlay, a twentieth-century landscape designer and poet, continues this tradition. His garden Little Spartica in Scotland is full of words and scenes from poetry and art, like a stone inscribed with the words "See POUSSIN Hear LORRAIN," a reference to the seventeenth-century artists Nicholas Poussin and Claude Lorrain and their influence on landscape perception and design. Another scene, "The Great Piece of Turf," a stone carved with Albrecht Dürer's initials beneath a clump of grasses, is a garden version of a Dürer drawing. The density of allusions to classical literature in gardens like Stourhead and Little Spartica can be cloying, even euphuistic—affected, ornate, striving to be elegant and erudite.[49]

A landscape can even come to be, for some, an allusion to the story rather than the reverse: the English Lake District as an allusion to the poetry of Wordsworth, the "downs" to the novels of Thomas Hardy, the Danish heath to the poetry and prose of Steen Steensen Blicher and Jeppe Aakjær.[50] Many have read Aldo Leopold's book, *Sand County Almanac*, but few have read the restored landscape of the old farm to which much of the text alludes; most visitors undoubtedly perceive the place as an allusion to the book.

Inner-city community gardens in African-American neighborhoods frequently allude to the Bible. Gethsemane, a healing garden in West Philadelphia, is named for the place where Jesus prayed before being forsaken and betrayed by his disciples. The name of another Philadelphia community garden—The Garden of

Eatin'—is a punning allusion to the Bible's first garden. At Aspen Farms, the phrase "Deut. 24:19," hand-painted on a wooden sign, is an allusion to the values shared by those who garden here and live by these words: "When you reap your harvest in your field, and have forgotten a sheaf in the field, you shall not go back to get it; it shall be for the stranger, the fatherless, and the widow, that the Lord your God may bless you in all the work of your hands."

A Literature of Lived Life

The power of landscape literature lies in its potential not only to symbolize, represent, or project feelings and ideas, but also to be the very site where life and death take place. The Hill of Remembrance at Stockholm's Forest Cemetery gives "form to a sorrow that cannot be told"; it *is* also the cemetery where loved ones are buried or ashes scattered, where trees and flowers are fed by bodily decay, planted and tended by grieving friends and family. By the authors' design, visitors are made to feel close to earth and sky: earth enfolds those who climb the steps of the hill; sky is framed by trees at the summit. Suzanne Langer calls art "the creation of forms symbolic of human feeling," and works of art "congruent with the dynamic forms of our direct, sensuous, mental, and emotional life," projections of "felt life," as Henry James puts it, "into spatial, temporal, and poetic structures."[51] Forest Cemetery is art, a work that belongs to great landscape literature.

Literature endows common experience with significance. In the small provincial Danish town of Åbenrå, a walk to school or into town becomes a sacred passage through a secular cathedral. C. Th. Sørensen made this place at the edge of town by planting a long allée—four rows of poplars planted together, now fifty feet tall—a sheltered path from countryside to town, a transition from pasture and meadow to house, school, and street. A meandering brook enters one end of the allée and is transformed into a straight canal. From a distance, the tall line of trees stands as a landmark on the flat plain. A rushing noise, like the sound of running water in a stream, grows louder as you approach, but the wind on the sports fields, broken by the trees, grows calmer. A surprise, the stream is a placid canal, the noise is from millions of poplar leaves catching the wind, loudest as you walk down the path between the trees, softer beyond it. Within the allée, leaves flutter, making a magical, flickering light. The dark green canal reflects a white strip of light—the sky—its surface rippling with moving water, sparkling with leaf/shadow dancing. The air itself seems to shimmer. So simple, so ordinary, so extraordinary.

Overlapping functions, feelings, and meanings enrich the experience and reading of a place when expressed in material form. At the Hill of Remembrance, the fusion of walking, rising, enfolded by hill and trees, mourning, thinking, of associations with other hills, like Calvary, brings multiple feelings and meanings into play simultaneously. So does the allée at Åbenrå, as one walks through its cathedral-like space, to and from town, sheltered from wind. Feeling and meaning also merge in the experience of the St. Louis Arch, but the arch does not arch over anything; it is a freestanding monument, *only* a representation. Meaning, but not related feeling or function, is present in Philadelphia's Welcome Park, a plaza whose paving represents the original plan of the city, as drawn by Thomas Holmes in 1682: streets are bands of white marble, dark brown clay tiles are the blocks within. Meaning is expressed primarily through words rather than landscape: texts are inscribed in pavement, on walls, a decorated surface of words.[52] On a hot, sunny, summer day, reflected glare and radiated heat do not welcome but repel.

One can barely feel the wind's force through words and images, or appreciate its lull down in a dale, hear birds' song or silence, feel the contrast between hot, sunny plaza and cool, shady patio; far better to be there. Verbal texts can be printed and experienced by a reader directly; landscapes are like musical or choreographic scores that must be performed to be fully experienced. Every landscape has a distinctive set of sounds, smells, and textures: the Danish heath is windy, the soil dry and sandy; the air in Japan is humid, the light green; the desert soil of Arizona is hard, its plants prickly. Words, drawings, paintings, photographs, or video cannot replace the experience of the place itself, though they may enhance and intensify that experience and may even inspire construction of actual landscapes. No matter how many photographs I have seen of the Vietnam Veterans Memorial, I am unprepared, when I am there, for the ways in which it evokes feeling, even beyond the names on the wall, mementos left there, other people's actions, and what they mean. It is easy to control my feelings at the start when the wall is low, hard when scale changes and the wall is over my head; feelings well up and do not lighten again until your head is above ground again on the other side. The air is loud with chatter at the entry to the memorial; hushed down at the bottom where the wall is highest. Like many great works of tragedy, it arouses feelings of pity or grief then provides catharsis.

Landscape, as a literature of lived life, must be experienced in place to be fully felt and known. And skill in the language of landscape amplifies the experience. Those fully literate recognize stories, themes, and genres shared across cultures; they read regional landscapes as inscriptions of environmental and cultural history, values, and visions. The barely literate may read some significance in landscape, especially in their own region, but miss allusions and multiple layers of function, feeling, and meaning. They fail to recognize the ethical and aesthetic intentions in landscapes like those by Olmsted and Leopold, mistaking them for accidents. The illiterate compose crude, dysfunctional landscapes, full of gibberish. With literacy and fluency comes an appreciation of figurative and rhetorical landscapes and an awareness of how such landscapes evoke feeling and instill meaning; with them comes the ability to shape landscapes more knowledgeably and expressively. To be fluent is to master landscape composition—the elements of landscape language and the context and grammar that govern their meaning—and to grasp pragmatics, poetics, and polemics.

Two

"Without Form and Void" to "Heaven and Earth": Landscape Composition

In the beginning God created the heaven and the earth. And the earth was without form, and void; and darkness was upon the face of the deep. And the spirit of God moved upon the face of the waters. And God said, Let there be light: and there was light. And God called the light Day, and the darkness he called Night. And the evening and the morning were the first day.

—Genesis 1:1–5

Anatomy must contain an analogue of grammar because all anatomy is a transform of message material, which must be contextually shaped. And finally, contextual shaping is only another term for grammar.

—Gregory Bateson, *Mind and Nature*

Two paths, sea. Denmark.

4

Is a Leaf Like a Noun, Flowing Like a Verb?
Elements of Landscape and Language

Elements of landscape language are like parts of speech, each with separate functions and associations. Flowing, like a verb, is a pattern of events expressed in both water and path. Water and path, like nouns, are action's agents and objects; like adjectives or adverbs, their qualities of wetness or breadth extend meaning. Elements do not exist in isolation, but rather combine in significant ways, like words in a phrase, clause, or sentence, to make a tree, fountain, street, or a larger, more complex landscape story—garden, town, or forest. Every landscape feature, such as a mountain, embodies at least one complete expression—its own formation. Describing the elements is like looking at landscape—scanning the scene, then successively zooming in and out on significant details, letting the context blur but keeping it always in view.

The Vietnam wall of war, memory, and mourning conjures up boundary, blocked passage, executions against a wall, the Wailing Wall. The meaning of the memorial would be different were it white instead of black, or composed of rough, unpolished stone instead of polished granite, or of many small stones set in thick mortar, rather than large sheets set flush, almost seamless. Materials modified by form give landscapes presence and space. Processes—polishing of stone—like verbs, provide action and time. The meanings of the Vietnam Memorial come not just from the inherent qualities and traditional meanings of individual elements—stone, grass, wall, polished surface, path rising and falling—but from the ways they modify and amplify each other. The meaning would be different if the wall were freestanding rather than embedded in earth, if one could walk behind it, if it were a single straight line, rather than broken and angled. And the meaning would be different if no one left mementos there or traced the names of loved ones on the face of the stone. Process is perceived through the act of polishing in the surface of the granite, the act of remembering in the names cut into its surface, as well as the offerings people leave. Material influences shape and structure: the hard stone holds a smooth, sharp outline, can be cut into thick blocks to make an upright wall. Form affects material properties: the flat surface enhances the dark stone's ability to reflect. Process molds form, and form shapes process: the narrow path hugs the base of the wall, keeping the visitor close to the names that are listed in order of death, and all the messages left by mourners. As you leave, it rises, directing the gaze to the Washington Monument and the Lincoln Memorial.

The elements are so intimately linked—why, then, try to separate them? To read landscapes more deeply, as signifying wholes, and to tell other landscapes more artfully. To be literate and fluent, one must first have a vocabulary. Although some learn the language of landscape intuitively, through living and making, without studying vocabulary or grammar, many miss significance and connections and fail to see and make the landscape whole. Many designers compose formal arrangements, quoting the plan of a historic garden, borrowing a phrase here and there from a contemporary work. Many choose materials belatedly and consider processes rarely, if at all. This is like trying to compose a sentence entirely of nouns and adjectives, without verbs. In landscape, context supplies elements the author neglects or forgets. Incomplete utterances lead to unforeseen consequences: to buildings, parks, and playgrounds which fail to function or are unsustainable, destroyed by those who use them or by wildfires, floods, and landslides.

Process: Actions and Patterns of Events

Burning, Blowing, Raining, Slipping, Growing, Building: Orange County

October 1993, Irvine. Wildfires burn out of control along the California coast south of Los Angeles. Spicy, smoky smells of burning eucalypts and sage fill the air miles away. Flames flash and flicker on television screens, while reporters, in apocalyptic language, invoke images of heaven and hell, paradise and expulsion from paradise, Mother Nature's revenge. Scientists explain cause and effect: hot, high, Santa Ana winds; canyons shaped like chimneys; fire suppression; piled-up fuel; flammable plants and houses; lightning; arson; a homeless man, mentally ill, building a small fire to keep warm. Burned-out residents stand stunned, staring, speak of insurance, wonder if they will rebuild, tell reporters they do not recall other fires of several years before or never imagined it would happen here.

February 1994, Laguna Canyon. Four months later, the earth is still bare and brown, green gone. Coarse black skeletons—burned shrubs—stand out against a clear blue sky. The size of remaining branches tells how hot the fire burned: very hot, for the charred branches are thick as a finger, ending in stubby stumps, twigs vaporized.[1] Prickly pears—prostrate masses of blackened flesh, like deflated balloons—are the most grotesque of all, perhaps because their shriveled flesh is still visible. A prickly pear, just one, has sent forth tiny shoots of reddish new growth, and minute leaves are sprouting from the base of a few blackened skeletons. Down in the canyon all that remains of the houses are concrete slabs, fireplaces, and chimneys—the hearth; furniture, walls, roofs are gone. A few isolated homes are left, untouched by fire. Up on the ridge what look like black tree trunks stand against the sky: chimneys. The low afternoon sun rakes across the hillsides, lights up short, green shoots of new plants on the opposite and moister slope; another slope, hydro-seeded after the fire, looks like a greyish-white moonscape. The mulch has formed a crust that seeds cannot penetrate: the human urge to do something has been counterproductive. Winter rains cut deep gullies in soil stripped of plant cover, especially along the road. Heavy storms are forecast for the coming week; sandbags line the street. We speak in hushed voices. The scene is almost beyond imagining, so much life gone, no movement, no sound.

February 1994, Irvine. Thick, brown mud, flowing, slides down slopes, through doorways, out windows, carries houses down, flows onto Route 1—on the television screen. Reporters warn of roads closed and slides to come on burned slopes. Scientists speak of cause and effect: roads cut and houses built on unstable hillsides; watered gardens, leaky swimming pools; barren slopes stripped of plants by fire; heavy winter rains.

May 1994, Laguna Canyon. Flaming orange poppies and yellow goldfields bloom brightly along paths leading to concrete pads. Long, green grasses cover burned-over slopes. New street signs stand on each corner. A few houses are under construction.

May 1996, Laguna Canyon. The air is full of buzzing insects, birdsong, hammers, and workmen's distant voices: the process of regeneration. A huge prickly pear, once blackened and deflated, is overgrown by luxuriant new growth of other shrubs; the pear is gone except for a few branches with new sprouts. Up on Skyline Drive, two years' difference is dramatic and disorienting, the streets nearly unrecognizable. Most houses are rebuilt, though many lots remain empty, For Sale signs on some. The street down in the canyon is full of movement, cars and trucks coming and going, people bustling. Public money has been spent: a new bridge, road, and culvert. Most of the rebuilt homes are fancier than the houses that survived: insurance money? new owners? or residents had more money than their old, rather modest houses led one to think? Only a few concrete pads remain. On a house under construction a sign above the door, hand-lettered in white paint: "And the birds will sing again." Ready for the next fire, for it will surely come.

March 9, 1998, Philadelphia. "Dream houses are toppled," says the headline over a large color photograph on the front page of the morning newspaper; shattered debris, unrecognizable as a home, cascades down a steep slope: "Home gives way on a hillside in Laguna Beach." The story describes the many houses destroyed and the homeowners' astonished response: "It's a million cubic feet of mud that came down on my house. Who ever imagines that something like that's going to happen?"[2]

Transforming Events, Repeating: Order, Rhythm, Change

Burning is a process; flame and ashes, burning and burned substances that can be seen and touched. Wind is sensed through fanned flames, moving trees and clouds, rustling leaves, whipped waves, blown sand dunes, air pressed against body, evaporation through dry skin, chapped lips, and thirst. Falling rain and flowing, seeping water weather, color, crack, and crumble rock, cause it to slide. The idea of process shows landscape features as dynamic, as related markers of change, not discrete, not fixed objects. Mountains are thrusting up or eroding, not static; trees are growing, or not, evidence of invisible events.

Water flowing, like sun shining, shapes and structures landscape. The trail up Palm Canyon in the Anza Berega Desert of southern California starts out level, crosses a wide rubble-strewn wash fanning out onto the desert, winds among rocks brought down by water; the trail climbs up the alluvial fan in a narrow streambed cut between two mountain ridges. Higher up, the trail bends around boulders and crosses a small stream; the sound of water rare and soothing, brilliant green plants along the stream bank are shocking against the dusty desert plants below. As the trail rises, the cleft between knife-sharp, rocky ridges narrows, the boulders become huge—a claustrophobic space. One can sense the rushing torrent that has torn these boulders off the hillsides and tumbled them into the valley. It would be unimaginable but for the rocks and broad, sandy washes. At the head of the trail is an oasis of palms, fed by a spring.

Water flowing off the broad, red sandstone flanks of Uluru (Ayre's Rock) in Australia structures the desert landscape for a mile from its base. As one walks across the red sand, Uluru still miles away, the red rock rises in the distance. A thousand feet from the rock, plants are greener, mulga trees grow in slight hollows. Closer still, black marks appear, streaking down from notches in the orange-red rock, traces of water, streaming rarely, over thousands of years. At the bottom of each black streak is a pool and a grove of trees filled with brilliant birds, the air cooler, moister, filled with their song. The Aborigines' sacred places are not on Uluru's summit, but at its base.

Thousands of years ago, Persian engineers built *qanats*, underground tunnels to bring water from aquifers under mountain slopes to arid plateaus. Many are still used. Water flowing—tapped to irrigate crops, to drink, to carry wastes— orders human settlement. The drier the climate, the more elaborate the water system, the more pervasive and enduring the system's influence on the form and meaning of landscape. In Persian settlements, houses of the wealthy are uphill of fields and poorer districts; they receive water before others do; as water flows downhill it is used and reused. When the City of Los Angeles obtained the rights to water in the Owen River and transported it more than two hundred miles to the San Fernando Valley, Los Angeles bloomed and grew, the Owens Valley withered and declined. Water, the material, and the process by which it was bought, then brought, transformed these places.

When a single process or a single set of processes dominates—water flowing, wheat growing, wind blowing—or when contexts are relatively homogeneous, as in sandy seashores, arid deserts, and grassy prairies, then landscapes reveal process most clearly. Beaches and deserts are good landscape primers. Sandy beaches and silty tidal flats reveal patterns of water flow; sand dunes and wheat fields reveal wind. But landscapes are seldom the product of a single process or even a small set of dominant processes. As in Laguna Canyon, the processes they reflect are simultaneous and successive, congruent and conflicting, layers upon layers, overlain and overlapping, continuous and interrupted, contingent and independent, once acting or still acting.

Fires spread rapidly in Laguna, through canyons and up hillsides, turning vast areas to ashes within hours; muddy slopes after heavy rains brought down rocks, streets, homes also within hours. But fires and mudslides do not happen every year. Fire's fuel, houses and plants, accumulates over years of fire suppression; slopes may have slipped in the same place, from time to time for thousands of years. Tempos, durations, and rhythms differ, hence events recur, and parts of a landscape evolve, at divergent rates. Processes have speed (fast or slow), duration (long periods or brief spurts, seconds, days, years), and rhythm (character of repetition, constant or intermittent). Landscape composition must take speed, duration, and rhythm into account; it must acknowledge or adapt to change over time.

The rhythm of repeating events—order in time—is even or uneven, regular or irregular: periodic fires and mudslides, daily fluctuations of tides and the commute of cows and people, seasonal migration of nomads, snowbirds, and summer people, irregular occurrence of earthquakes. The pulse and periodicity of the sun coordinate and synchronize melting snow to rushing streams to rising sap, to plowing of fields, to budding plants, or the Rockefellers' visit to their blooming June Garden in Maine. Time is relative to the process that shapes it, the organism that experiences it. A sense of time depends upon perceptible change, patterns of recurring events, and culture. Rhythms differ from place to place. Aborigines in Australia's tropical northeastern Arnhem Land name at least six seasons, each associated with patterns of temperature, rain, wind, thunder, plant growth, and animal behavior: Dhuludur, the pre-wet season (October-November), Barramirri, the growth season (December-January), Mayaltha, the flowering season (February-March), Midawarr, the fruiting season (March-April), Dharratharramirri, the early dry season (May-July), Rarrandharr, the principal dry season (August-October).[3] The traditional four seasons of temperate climates seem gross in contrast. And, within them, there are nuances. Bostonians call March slush season, a month when ankle-deep, icy water fills street gutters, drains blocked by piles of snow. In Denmark, patterns of light change radically from summer to winter; there are traditions associated with each. In Danish mid-December, when dawn comes late and twilight early, one goes to school or work and back in the dark; in mid-June, when sun sets in late evening and rises a few hours later, night is never truly dark. Both winter and summer have a long twilight, "darkening" in the winter, "summerlight" in the summer. Candles, "living lights," flicker in windows, as beacons on winter afternoons; in the summer, twilight lingers for hours, dim, glowing.

Time controls much behavior, a process recognized in landscape itself. Certain landscapes are devoted to marking time: sundials convert sun's changing shadows into time of day; Stonehenge, some think, charted the position of sun and moon, permitting prediction and celebration of the equinox and solstice,

Water flowing: farm in floodplain. (Alex S. MacLean/Landslides)

when the rising sun shone directly through the pillars of the avenue leading to the inner circle of stones.[4] Most landscapes are designed to be sensed through movement, at a particular tempo, for a specific duration, in a rhythm. The vast scale of seventeenth-century French gardens, like Versailles, Vaux-le-Vicomte, and Chantilly, was calculated to impress at a walking pace. Nineteenth- and early twentieth-century American parkways, like Boston's Riverway and New York's Bronx River Parkway, were meant to be seen at the speed of a horse-drawn carriage, then by automobile. "New vistas unfold because of elevated freeways," writes Lawrence Halprin. "Vast panoramic views are disclosed which were never seen before. The great vivid skylines of the city can be seen, all of a sudden, not as a static picture, but as a series of constantly changing impressions which move by like the frames in a motion picture."[5] The landscape of the San Jose freeway was designed to be experienced at an even, high speed. The series of framed views of Rousham, an eighteenth-century English garden largely by William Kent, are seen from a path at a rhythm of long, leisurely movements in a single direction, punctuated by occasional stops. In Bowood, also in southwestern England, a garden of the same period by "Capability" Brown, with no single principal path, the rolling terrain, the rounded groves of trees with trunks silhouetted up to the height of browsing sheep, and the architectural monuments propel walkers through the landscape to the destinations. Bowood, cinematic, not photographic, is experienced through continuous movement, not static views.

Water flowing: buildings and vacant land in floodplain. Dudley Street neighborhood. Boston.
(Alex S. MacLean/Landslides)

Processes Connect: Making Sense of Events and Experience

When I first saw the Dudley Street neighborhood of Boston in November 1984, I was dismayed. I knew the statistics—twice the unemployment rate of Boston as a whole, 30 percent of the land abandoned—but they simply did not prepare me for the place itself: entire square blocks of vacant land, some heaped with big chunks of concrete, piles of tires, and trash; playgrounds with broken equipment, cracked pavement, and smashed glass; wooden houses with peeling paint, sagging porches, roofs with holes, both triple-decker apartments and large, single-family homes with fine architectural details. The waste was overwhelming. With me that day was Hans Kiemstedt, a German friend; he said he had not seen such destruction since Germany after the war; how could Americans permit such conditions in peacetime? Our guide, Charlotte Kahn, director of Boston Urban Gardeners, pointed to what was neither waste nor destruction, the many community gardens, not as visible in late fall as they would have been in summer, and also houses under repair, 40 percent of them owned by those who lived in them.

As I lay awake that night, sure I had missed something, I replayed what I had seen. The fifteen hundred vacant lots were not scattered evenly, but concentrated. Few were on hilltops and hillsides; houses there were substantial, most in good condition, some had sweeping views over the city. I got out of bed and pulled out the U.S. Geological Survey maps of Boston. With colored pencils of light to dark brown, I filled in the spaces between contours for a sense of the shape of the land-forms and the pattern of vacant lots. I discovered that we had been driving back and forth across a long valley between two hills; most of the abandoned land was in that valley. When my students plotted the vacant lots on aerial photographs of the area several months later, they calculated that 90 percent of the lowest parts of the valley was vacant, 95 percent of the hillside properties was inhabited. The reason had to be water, water flowing down from the hills into the valley, saturating the soil, puddling after rain. Water now not visible except by inference. A stream once flowed there—it was the old boundary between the towns of Roxbury and Dorchester—and it still does, flowing underground in a sewer, carrying the community's wastes and rainfall. Consulting old atlases, I tracked the changes in the neighborhood from 1876 to 1886, 1892, 1903, 1910, 1922, 1934, 1948, 1964. Houses in the valley were built later than houses on the hills, many as apartments for poorer people. The first vacant lots in the valley were recorded in the early twentieth century, within twenty years of construction there. By 1964, large areas in the valley bottom had been abandoned.

Water, flowing and pooling, was not the whole story; such conditions could not be simply a matter of poor drainage. Someone I knew whose basement flooded after every heavy rain had installed a sump pump and built a drain around the foundation. His house, originally a worker's cottage, was built on marshy ground, as were his neighbors', but all of those houses were well maintained and freshly painted in pastel colors with white trim; there were no signs of drainage problems underground. But then his street was in Cambridge, a ten-minute walk from the Harvard campus, not in one of the poorest neighborhoods in Boston.

Initial abandonment of Boston's Dudley Street neighborhood was the product of several related processes: water flowing downhill, pooling in the valley; a stream sewered and buried; housing built and rented for short-term profit. That process of abandonment continued until the 1980s, accelerated by processes of decay, subsidence, industrial decline, unemployment, red-lining (denial of insurance and loans for homes and businesses in areas with older homes and immigrant or nonwhite population), arson. City planners commonly recognize the last set of problems without appreciating the existence and contributing effects of buried streams. Corresponding patterns exist in similar neighborhoods throughout Boston, as in many other American cities. In fact, I found exactly the same situation in West Philadelphia's Mill Creek just a few years later. Patterns seemingly unrelated, yet highly coincident—like abandonment and topography—should prompt the questions: do they correspond? if so, how, and why?

Processes connect, literally, physically, and figuratively; if we can read them, they make sense of events apparently unrelated: blazing wildfire, whipping wind, fleeing people; pouring rain, oozing mud, slumping hillsides; burning tissue, dying, then sprouting, flowering, animals returning, people rebuilding. Connections between material, form, and territory, the elements of landscape and language.

Hydrologic cycle: Patio de la Reja. The Alhambra. Spain.

Processes connect the organic and inorganic, the animate and inanimate, the physical world and the organisms that inhabit it. Leaves transpire and roots suck, animals breathe, drink, and excrete, all exchanging air and water between atmosphere, earth, and life. As plants and animals die and decay, organic tissue mingles with minerals and microorganisms to make soil, a living medium.

Processes overlap: water wears away stone, rolls rounded river cobbles, and dumps them downstream; people gather the smooth stones and lay them to form patterned pavement; footsteps over time wear them away. Some processes (movement, exchange, growth, and decay) overlap the organic and inorganic, animate and inanimate. Others (sensing, sustenance, birth, and death) are common to animate and inanimate alike, to organisms with mind and those without, while many like making/building, learning, playing, fighting, dreaming are the province of animate organisms alone, human and nonhuman, though human cultures differ in what is considered animate. Australian Aborigines believe animate ancestors shaped their landscape, including many plants and animals.

Process as Metaphor and Means to an End

Processes, like poems, are full of metaphors, relationships among significant details, such as lines, cycles, and circles. The hydrologic cycle describes water moving from ocean to air, from air to earth, from earth to river and sea, an exchange between heaven and earth powered by the sun: "All the rivers run into the sea, yet the sea is

Braided rivers and star. Patio de la Reja. The Alhambra. Spain.

not full; unto the place from whence the rivers come, thither they return again."[6]

Water spills from source in the fountain onto pavement, its sound amplified by surrounding walls. It puddles on the stone floor, evaporates, and cools the air. In the Alhambra in Granada, Patio de la Reja, a small enclosed patio, is an economical, elegant, and powerful statement about the qualities of water, a poetic description of the hydrologic cycle. Small, river-worn pebbles, each embodying the action of water over time, are set in packed earth that permits water to seep beneath them to irrigate the roots of the cedar trees planted at each corner of the courtyard. In a tightly organized geometric pattern, elongated black stones form flowing, braided rivers, rounded whitish-grey stones, alternately ground and stars. The whole forms a deep congruence between function, feeling, and meaning.

The hydrologic cycle is an idea shared by many cultures. It is taken for granted by most Western scientists as a fundamental concept; every textbook in geology and physical geography describes it, and yet, as the geographer Yi-Fu Tuan points out, the standard version, combining processes that occur within moments and others that take place over thousands of years, is so general that it is almost meaningless.[7] Tuan traces the history of the concept from 1700 to 1850 in natural philosophy and theology as evidence of the wisdom of God, of the economy of means and ends.

In the moss garden at Saihoji, in Kyoto, no leaf lies on the moss; any leaf that drops is raked up promptly. A rake propped against a tree and a pile of leaves nearby make the garden seem contrived, separate from the real forest. Decay and regeneration are here, but the steps in between that make rebirth possible are not—no seeds, no decaying leaves that create soil and fertilize the trees. The garden exists in a perplexing, steady state, time suspended, a complex metaphor.

Moving, exchanging, reproducing, growing, dying, the processes of life are understood and celebrated in terms of what one knows and values. Is growth good and decay bad? What, if anything, is the ideal state: movement or stasis? Is birth-life-death cyclical or linear? Are processes, is time, linear or cyclical? It depends. It depends, for example, on one's worldview and religion, Hindu, Jewish, Christian, Buddhist. Stephen Jay Gould describes the tension between seeing time as progressive or cyclical as the assertion of the uniqueness and contingency of history, on the one hand, and as the immanence and timelessness of law, on the other.[8] He observes that most cultures have viewed time as being cyclical; Jewish and Christian religions are exceptional in their emphasis on time as being linear. There is ample support in the world for both views, in phenomena like day and night and seasonal change, in the fact that water flowing over varying rock materials and steepness of slope cuts different patterns, just as the process of worship yields different forms of ritual paths and shrines in dissimilar cultures.

Flood, fire, earthquake have been seen as expressions of God's punishment for human sins, as Nature's revenge for human abuse, as a natural process prompted by rainfall, lightning, or colliding continental plates. Causes differ in the perception of differing cultures. In Genesis, humans are at the center of the story, as both stewards and exploiters, admonished to "be fruitful, and multiply, and replenish the earth, and subdue it." To Gaians the purpose of natural processes is the maintaining of the planet as a whole, its land, seas, atmosphere, together with all its life. Many scientists, it is sobering to remember, until quite recently believed that natural processes left to themselves would maintain what they saw as the inherent stability, balance, and harmony of Nature.[9]

Process, as a deliberate act by a conscious being, is a means to an end. All human processes are cultural, deliberate means by which humans sustain themselves, adapt to their environment, and relate to one another. Most basic are those processes essential for survival of individual and species: physical—moving, exchanging, sensing, reproducing, growing, and decaying; social—identifying, communicating, making/building, trading, playing, learning, competing, and fighting; spiritual—dreaming and worship. Human habitats—buildings, gardens, neighborhoods, towns, and cities—must satisfy all three of these kinds of basic human processes. Design, the imagining, making, adapting of human artifacts and settlements, has this express purpose.

"This course goes against everything I have learned about design," a student once complained to me. Like many others of my students, he had a hard time seeing the design of a *process* as a legitimate and essential aspect of his art and craft. This is difficult; it demands the ability to envision and anticipate evolving form rather than a single, finished form. Recently, I asked students to design a nursery for street trees, a living laboratory for middle school students, to be planted and maintained as part of a new curriculum in environmental education. My students' task was to design not merely an attractive nursery but one that reflected a new middle school curriculum and stimulated the process of learning. Furthermore, they had to design the process by which sites for planting the new trees are selected and secured (vacant lots and blocks for future planting), by which a program is promoted, trees planted, cared for, transplanted, and cared for in their new site. This required conceiving of change and phasing over a period of ten years and beyond—from conception, initiation, selecting sites, planting, caring for, and transplanting. All but a few students produced lovely drawings of a nursery but failed to design the curriculum it served or the processes by which it would be created, attract support, and be sustained over time.

Architects and landscape architects tend to focus not on process, but on form and material; when designs fail to be sustained in the real world, it is often because designers ignore the processes that shape them during and after construction. When the audience at the public meeting in Roxbury attacked the landscape architect's design for a new park in their neighborhood, they were undoubtedly thinking of other playgrounds built a few years before but not maintained, playgrounds filled with smashed glass that became scenes of crime. Material, form, and space are sensed and shaped by processes, by touching, seeing, moving and by erosion, fire, vandalism, care. Processes provide action. Neglecting pertinent processes can lead not only to failure of function and expression but even to destruction and death.

Matter: Sensual and Dynamic

Medium of Seeing, Smelling, Hearing, Touching, Tasting

Rock, Water, Wood, Air, Fire: Finland. Flying to Helsinki over the archipelago—water and rock—tiny islands in a dark, blue-black sea; later, over the mainland—water and trees—thousands of long, narrow lakes, all aligned north-south, surrounded by a vast forest. Gradually forest gives way to small farms and scattered woodlots. Then the city. As I walk around Helsinki, I look down a street and see sky and sea. Rocks rise out of the water, push up from under the ground, the soil a thin skin. Late spring air is fresh and cool, light brilliant—a sharp, low, blinding light that backlights birch leaves and rakes across stone buildings. Motoring out on the water, I pass dozens of islands, many little sauna houses, painted red, lining the shores. Late-evening light turns long, flat islands into glowing lines along the horizon—yellow, then rose.

On an island in the archipelago wind is still, water ripples gently, a silky, pearly grey. The sauna is perched on rocks, facing water. Outside, the cold is bracing; inside, dry heat penetrates skin and lungs. Scent of hot rocks and wood walls, floors, and roof permeates air; lungs draw in wood and rocks with each breath. I emerge from dry heat, swat skin with freshly cut birch switches, air that had seemed cold despite shirt, sweater, down vest, and jacket now seems comfortable in bare skin. I walk barefoot over smooth, round rocks, diving into the archipelago, the water cool, but not cold. Returning to the sauna, I ladle water over rocks, and sit in steamy mist. Air, rock, water, fire, wood, and body are joined. No wonder Finns speak of sauna with reverence.

We see, smell, hear, touch, and taste landscapes through materials; they are sensual. Gravel crunches underfoot, grass swishes, a wooden bridge thumps hollow. To a blind person, snow may give a sense of walking through an endless, undifferentiated nothing, for it muffles sound.[10] In some times and places, sense of sound seems heightened, discrete sounds amplified: when air carries sound farther at night, and in early morning; where ambient noise is low, in a quiet cloister, where sounds bounce off walls. The courtyard of the Hotel de Sully in Paris is a garden cloistered between the raucous Rue de Saint Antoine and the stately Place des Vosges, quiet, protected from street noise by massive stone buildings. Birds bring the space alive, chirping from within ivy on the walls, hidden but for their sudden flitting and the moving leaves.

Farmers sense soil with their fingers: sand is grainy, falls loosely; clay is fine, swells with water, shrinks when dry, rolls between fingers; humus, sponge of decayed plants, is springy when damp. Soil is mineral, vegetal, and animal, a living medium for growth: eroded, dissolved, ground-up rock; organisms, decayed and alive; water, and air. Vintners taste soil—slatey, gravelly—in wine; the French have a name for it: *terroir*. Brown, black, red, yellow, grey, blue, glittering mica are colors of earth particular to place: red comes from iron; mottled, blue-grey gley from seasonal water; green from serpentine. Adobe, bricks, and tiles are the colors of local soil, gravel, the colors of local rocks, crushed; Black Earth, Wisconsin, is aptly named. I was shocked thirty years ago when I first saw the bright red soil of Oklahoma; I had always assumed that Thomas Hart Benton (1889–1975) painted his red hills with artistic license.

Air—medium of light—is seen as life and spirit, celestial and ethereal not material, not real in itself. Ironically, the more evident its actual materiality (the more water and dust it contains) the more immaterial the world seems. Air filled with water and dust is misty and hazy, blurring the edges, dissolving the seeming solidity of things. Airborne water and dust reveal the colors of light's spectrum in rainbows, sunsets, and haloes. Humidity and dust change light's quality—its color, clarity, and brilliance—variously from place to place. A low, raking light shining through clear, dry air accentuates the texture of things and heightens a sense of materiality. Add reflective surfaces of the sea and a special light results: the iridescent light of southern California, the brilliant bounciness of winter light in Sydney, of late spring and early summer in Denmark and the Helsinki Archipelago.

The contrast between desert and oasis makes one conscious of air: dry desert air parches nose, lips, mouth, and sucks moisture from skin; moist, cool air in an oasis is palpable, invisible, but not intangible. Walled gardens and narrow, shady streets aligned to capture cool evening breezes are typical of old districts in desert cities like Jeddah. Screens that filter air and light and rooftop wind-catchers that funnel breezes through moist cloth to cool the interiors of building are common to traditional desert architecture.[11] The International Style, imported to desert countries like Saudi Arabia, displaced traditional design, substituting urban districts of high-rise buildings surrounded by hot, glaring pavement and cooled by air conditioners. In twentieth-century Europe and North America, most planners, designers, and builders ignore air as a material to be skillfully shaped: the result is noisy, windswept streets and plazas, cold in winter and hot in summer, and sealed buildings requiring heating or cooling even on the most temperate days. Tanner Fountain at Harvard University is a delightful exception: in summer its nozzles produce a fine mist, cooling air; warm steam once emerged in winter from underground pipes that heat university buildings. Unfortunately, the steam was discontinued after some objected that it was wasteful of energy.[12]

Sensations shift easily into feelings and emotions; witness the description of the Laguna fire, laden with empathetic response to the fire and its aftermath: hard, barren, gullied slopes, stubby, blackened stumps, acrid odor of burnt tissue, silenced birds and insects, their absence once noted, keenly felt. Response has much to do with memory. George Eliot in *The Mill on the Floss* wrote, "Our delight in the sunshine on the deep-bladed grass today" would be no more than a "faint perception," were it not for the "sunshine and grass of far-off years, which still live in us and transform our perception into love."[13] One whiff and one is transported back across the years. Memories are sensual, personal, place-specific. Asked to describe his home landscape, a student from Saudi Arabia spoke of the special, seldom smell of rain. My memories of childhood landscape are of big rocks and stone walls in the woods, the sour smell of smashed Osage orange, lilacs in May, fresh-cut grass, burning leaves, moldy soil, the tart, sweet taste of raspberries, apples, and sour grass.

The light in Japan is often green. One day in Kyoto, as I walk up the entrance path to Shisendo, the air is so humid I can feel its weight pressing against my body, its moisture clinging to my skin. The sun is bright but does not penetrate directly into the bamboo grove through which the entrance path leads. Sunlight filters through layers of leaves, each leaf absorbs light, leaving the light passing through one shade darker. The surrounding surfaces have a green cast, from the bamboo leaves and moss to the bluish-rosy green of the bamboo trunks; even in shadow the moss glows iridescent green. The air itself is saturated with green. Are the millions of microscopic water droplets hanging in the heavy air all reflecting green?

In a Japanese July the fullness of these greens reveals the presence of water in garden and forest, in city rice field. Light and water feed photosynthesis, the process by which green, the color of life, emerges. Water swells leaves, propels new growth with its distinctly lighter color, feeds grey-green fungus and lichens on tree and stone. The undulating, moss-covered ground of Saihoji seems fluid; roots and old stumps emerge from moss like rocks from a retreating wave, like flotsam riding a rolling swell.

In the gardens of Kyoto—in Shugakuin, in Katsura, in Shisendo, and, above all, in the moss garden of Saihoji—the overwhelming presence of the color green and the recession of others permit an appreciation of the range of shades and variations in texture. It is easiest to understand green in these gardens, but I begin to see the significance in the green mountains that form a backdrop to Japanese villages and cities and in the subtle, gentle green of the tatami mat upon which I sat, ate, and slept. The memory remained with me even in parts of the city where I could see no green. It remains with me still.

In Kobe city, at the end of an elegant lunch, I am served a single cup of green tea and, in a glass bowl, three cherries on ice. Perhaps it is the red of the cherries that draws my attention so sharply to the greenness of the tea. The tea seems like a distillation of the Japanese landscape; in drinking it, I drink the landscape.

Dynamic Medium of Process and Meaning

Rock erodes to sand, cemented sand becomes stone, erodes to sand once again. Fire consumes plants and releases seeds, ashes mix with soil to nourish new seedlings. Steel, forged from iron ore and fire, exposed to air and water, turns to rust. Stones cut from quarries, stacked to form walls, fall into ruin, and the rubble is used to build anew. Materials are dynamic, constant but constantly changing, moving, growing, decaying, transforming. Artists and craftsmen often say materials are living, that they have "an active presence, a character, a capacity for change."[14] To see materials as static is an illusion. If the human life span were a day, flowers might seem as enduring as rocks, if we lived a thousand years, rock might seem mobile.

Flowing, molding, pressing, hammering, forging, cementing, growing; dissolving, eroding, grinding, tumbling, cracking, crumbling, scuffing, decaying: materials manifest process. River cobbles and river-run gravel are tumbled smooth and rounded; quarry-cut cobbles and crushed stone have sharp, angular edges. Sedimentary rocks are laid down in layers, deposited by water or wind and carry the imprint of context: ripples, shells, leaves, seeds. Metal, concrete, and plastic flow into a mold and harden, taking the mold's shape. Bud scars on twigs and grain in wood are records of annual growth reflecting irregularities of context. Plants—pruned, pollarded, espaliered, clipped, left freely growing—are clues to social and cultural context. Materials are shaped by processes in context—material, formal, spatial, functional, social, and cultural.

Minerals assume an "angle of repose," the steepest slope they can sustain without reinforcement: grains of sand fall naturally into a gentle slope; clay can hold the sheer drop of a cliff until it shears off; the silty soil of Laguna's hillsides slips, slumps, and slides when wet. Joints and fractures in rock are the lines along which it erodes and breaks into blocks, chunks, or sheets. How long rock retains its shape depends upon its durability, its resistance to surface erosion and internal decay. Some rocks are harder than others; some dissolve. Harder rocks resist erosion to form hills; softer rocks erode to form valleys. Limestone landscapes in water-rich regions form gently rolling karst terrain with many sinkholes over underground channels and caverns. Materials give form potential and yet impose limits to corporality and meaning.

Air is breath, plants live and die, stone endures. Sand—countless tiny loose particles—records processes, the ebb and flow of tides, the passage of people or animals, but these traces are easily erased, thus sand's meaning of immeasurability and impermanence. Stone has mass and strength, and often stands for permanence, timelessness, and immortality. Political monuments are commonly made of stone; the shrines of wood at Ise, an exception, express the paradox of enduring impermanence. The meanings of materials are both inherent and invented, traditional and potential.

Water is paradoxical: yielding yet powerful, transparent yet reflective, a leveler, eroding mountains into plains, cutting valleys, smoothing stones. Seeking level, it fills valleys, forms flat, reflective planes. On the sea's horizon, it traces the horizontal line that orients and anchors. It flows, even as ice; glaciers flow down valleys between mountains of grey rock, break up into icebergs where they meet the sea. Water absorbs, carries, and releases other materials; it is a link among them—earth, air, and living tissue. Translucent, it takes on the color of air, of suspended sediments, of bottom. In Taoism, water expresses *wu-wei*, "the strength of weakness."[15] It cleanses, a symbol of spiritual purification used for ablution, holy water, baptism. Many natural springs in Ireland are seen as sacred and are adorned with flowers, rocks, and pictures of the Virgin Mary.[16]

Fire is comforting in hearth, candles, and campfire, and awesome in lightning, explosion, and forest fire. It consumes and destroys, transforms and renews; indeed, many types and groups of plants require fire to sustain them. Fire burns off woody growth in prairies and releases pine seeds in forests. After a fire has ravaged prairie or forest, green shoots emerge from the blackened earth. No wonder fire is a symbol of transformation and regeneration for many religions and cultures. At Notre Dame in Paris, thousands of candles burn in memory of the dead.

Trees and flowers live, grow, reproduce, and die. People impose meaning, as metaphor, upon flowers and trees. Flowers are laid on graves. And Dylan Thomas said of trees, "The force that through the green fuse drives the flower / Drives my green age; that blasts the roots of trees / Is my destroyer." But not all trees reproduce, a plastic tree, for instance. Only a human can create a plastic tree, for it cannot regenerate or make another tree. Plastic trees and flowers are used decoratively, but they are never *just* decorative, for cultural associations are too strong.[17] Martha Schwartz used plastic plants in her rooftop Splice Garden for the Whitehead Institute for Biomedical Research in Cambridge, Massachusetts. The garden is simultaneously lighthearted and serious, witty and chilling, a garden version of gene-splicing and artificial life. The thin brown trunks of the plastic trees with their imitation bark have protrusions like pruned branches. There are two "spliced" forms, one with a Japanese, one with a French garden motif, the two separated by a sharp line. The ground on either side is aquarium gravel in two shades of green, the Japanese blue-green, the French a dark green; the walls behind are painted two corresponding shades. Circles of raked gravel radiate from round, plastic shrubs on the Japanese side; large blocks in geometric shapes on the French side are covered with Astroturf, some topped with a basket of plastic flowers. In Splice Garden, material and form, together, express and reinforce meaning.

Materials arouse senses, carry meaning, pose limits. Deployed deliberately, to modify process and form and extend their meanings, materials furnish precision and nuance. Used in ways which contradict intended meaning, they may undermine and obscure it. Ignorance of craft, of materials, their properties, and performance in context can lead to unintended irony and to failure: when the stone facing of a monument or a plantation of trees, meant to endure, disintegrates or dies; when a masonry wall, shaken by an earthquake, collapses.

FORM: SHAPE AND STRUCTURE

Unyielding Axes, Disintegrated Grid: Chantilly

JUNE 1992. The gardens of Chantilly, northwest of Paris, are a huge clearing in a forest that once covered thousands of acres. Laid out by André Le Nôtre, the designer of Vaux-le-Vicomte and Versailles, these gardens were the scene of great parties and pageants in the seventeenth and eighteenth centuries; the forests were the site of elaborate hunts. I stand on the terrace above the gardens, looking out over many great basins of water, rectangles and circles reflecting sky—the water parterres. The chateau behind me, fortified by moat and walls, was built in the early sixteenth century on a plateau above the river and looks out over a broad flat floodplain.

I walk down a long flight of steps from the terrace, along a water parterre lined on one side by rows of small trees with straight trunks, their crowns clipped into green globes like the plastic trees in Schwartz's Splice Garden. The path ends at the edge of a canal, reputed to be the largest garden canal in the world (more than a mile long); Le Nôtre worked at Chantilly for twenty years, realigning the Nonette River and digging the canal out of marshes in the 1670s. I walk to the end of the canal to see the basin I know is there, and it seems to take forever; old prints depict visitors of past generations, some walking, some riding on horseback, in carriages, or sailing up the canal. The scale is vast, not a garden one can see comfortably on foot; at walking pace, I find the views monotonous, changing too slowly. I pause at the end of the canal and take a different route back through the trees on a flood terrace above the canal.

Disintegrated grid. Chantilly, France.

I am here not only because Le Nôtre considered Chantilly one of his finest works, but because a student once gave me a photograph of the place, showing the forest on a misty morning with three straight paths leading off into the distance at angles to one another. The image has haunted me since. As I leave the bright gardens, sun reflecting off the canal and basins of the water parterre, I enter the shadowy forest on a straight path that crosses diagonally another straight path, both lines of light. Cutting straight paths through the forest was Le Nôtre's first act. Paths, broad and narrow, crisscross through the woods, going off in different directions, disorienting. The Piste des Lions is one of the broadest and once led straight through the forest for miles right up to the gate of the chateau. Trees along the widest avenues through the forest are sheared up, flat as a wall.

I walk up the Piste des Lions, a path of soft, deeply raked earth at least twenty feet wide, until I realize it is for horses, not people on foot, and move over to the wooded footpath alongside. To my left, through the border of trees, is the broad piste, lit by sunlight, to my right the darker woods. The footpath is narrow, just wide enough for a single person, and meanders, as if made by someone wandering in the woods. There is a main path, and smaller paths that wander off and come back (or not). This is a weird woods. Spooked by a sense of enchantment, I stop to reason why. Birds twitter, a cuckoo, at least six other songs overlaid. Except for a few beeches, the trees are lindens; all fairly young, they fan up together and bow out in clumps, like stump sprouts. Some clumps have one or two fat trunks with dozens of smaller trunks, mostly slender saplings. No rotted trunks are lying around, no stumps are visible among the thickets of trunks and saplings. But there is one clue in the occasional large holes six feet or more across and four feet deep, which seem to occur mostly along the piste, not further in. There is a strange quality to the shape of the trees and the structure of the wood. I begin to draw what I see and realize that the trees were originally planted in rows, each tree a node on a grid, then cut at about the same time—or did they die, gradually, within a decade or more of one another? New shoots had sprouted from the base of each stump, decaying the orthogonal grid. The bizarre overlay of geometries is a relief after the rigid Euclidean geometry of Le Nôtre's plan at Chantilly. A grid of planted trees established the forest's original structure, now altered by stumps sprouting randomly around the base. Paths for horses and riders cut straight through the woods; then people, wandering, made curving paths seemingly at random.

MARCH 1997. I return to the forest of Chantilly in early spring. With a map of the forest in my hand, and no new leaves yet on the trees, I find my way easily through the forest that was so disorienting to me before. The forest is divided into numbered plots, labeled on map and on signs on the trees. Each plot is different, from tall trees with stump sprouts cut, the strongest, biggest stem left to grow, to shrubby thickets. Some are planted on a grid, others seem not to be; in a few plots, there are signs of cutting. One huge tree, its stump six feet across, was cut within the last year, its former crown still visible in the vacuum it left in the forest canopy; trees around it bend away from where its branches once spread. In some sections are holes twenty feet across where trees have come down, in others newly planted allées of beech, trees sixteen to eighteen feet apart, branches trimmed up above head height.

Months later, I read that Chantilly is part of an old royal forest; near Paris, it was a popular place to hunt, managed for hundreds of years as a game preserve for deer, boar, and pheasants.[18] The strange geometry I saw was the consequence of coppicing, of cutting trees, permitting stumps to sprout, then cutting the sprouts at intervals to create a bushy woods with food and cover for beasts of the chase. The tall trees here and there, eight to ten an acre, are "tellers" left as source of seed. All in all, an artificial forest if ever there was such a thing, a forest of the chase. But the birds don't seem to care that the forest has been planted, cut, re-grown, an artifice.

Shape versus Structure

A leaf's shape may be ovoid or lobed, a tree's shape round or vaselike, but the leaf's and the tree's structure is axial and branching. A terrain's shape is flat or rolling, mounded or bowl-shaped, its structure layered or massive. Shape expresses form's surface contour, while structure is the relation of its parts to the whole—a flower and its bud, petals, stamen, incipient fruit; a mountain and its slopes, summit, underlying rock; a town and its streets, buildings, gardens.

Shape is the more obvious and tangible; structure may be concealed. In the Bluegrass region of Kentucky, the bedrock of flat, layered limestone is hidden beneath the paradox of rolling karst terrain—dissolved by water—and revealed in river-cut cliffs and road cuts, echoed in walls of flat, laid stone. One sometimes sees the same structure in limestone paving: flat-bedded sheets, eroded into little hills and hollows—a miniature landscape. Erosion, decay, and destruction uncover or highlight concealed or unrecognized structure: decay of tree exposes growth rings in its core; weathering exposes; fire reveals the infrastructure of streets after homes burn. Structure permits perception of a whole that might otherwise be seen as unrelated fragments, and of parts that would otherwise be intangible.

Shape may change while structure remains constant. The dogwood tree, where bud and flower are one, is another paradox. The hard grey bud opens and its four-part sheath separates, softens, and grows into a four-petaled, white flower; the structure is constant, the shape changes. So, too, the shape of a beach shifts, daily, seasonally, over the years; its structure (the relation of sediments to water level, wave height and length) endures.

Drive a peg into the ground, attach a string, and move the string around the peg—you have inscribed a circle in landscape, a shape of gathering and enclosure, the most efficient shape to bound an area, like Indians' kivas in the American Southwest, the Vikings' circular settlements at Trelleborg, or the amphitheater at Roskilde, both in Denmark. Structure describes how a shape (or any landscape element or feature) evolved, developed, or was made, the word *structure* from the Latin "structura," to build. It defines a shape's proportions (broad or narrow, symmetrical or asymmetrical) and its complexity (simple or compound, regular or irregular). Shape may be explicit or implied, the whole not present; in an arc the circle is implied, the mind completes the shape through knowledge of a circle's structure.

Circle and sphere, square and cube are simple shapes. Shape is a superficial form of similarity, a low order of pattern. The more irregular or complex shapes are, the more significant congruence among them. The shapes of rock crystals and coral reefs are compound, the gradual accretion of similar shapes. Trees and shrubs of different species, pruned into a complex, uniform arc by persistent wind, is a significant similarity. But the sun, ripples in a pond, tree rings, a wheel, a Viking fort, and a kiva have little in common besides a circular appearance: ripples and tree rings expand from a center; tree rings, forts, and kivas enclose interior space; wheels spin. The sun, we imagine, has a spinning interior.

Geometries of Process

In Australia's central desert, spheres and rings of green and grey spinifex stand out against red sand. What is the shape of a spinifex plant—and when? It is round and roughly spherical at first but, as the plant grows outward, its center dies; gradually, the plant forms an expanding ring around its hollow origins. A shape reflects, at a given moment, the limits and potential of its materials, the processes that shape it, and the particulars of its context. Sand dunes shift with wind, a shoreline shifts with water currents. Volcanoes spew molten rock, which hardens into new landforms, and scientists imagine jagged mountains eroding into gently sloping plains. Sheep and deer prune tree canopies into a flat-bottomed shape at the height of their reach; the clipped trees fill out again when browsing ceases. Trees, gardens, and towns are shaped by movement, growth, cultivation, exchange, and decay. Skylines of many American cities changed after 1960, when private developers began to build high-rise towers for downtown offices; the shape of inner-city neighborhoods changed too as houses and businesses, abandoned by owners moving from city to suburb, fell into ruin.

Shapes of mountain ranges, riverbanks, sand dunes, trees, and snow crystals are poised at a moment in time, their beauty lying in a peculiar combination of order and disorder, harmoniously arranged, form reflecting the processes that produced it. Benoit Mandelbrot calls such forms, and their congruence across scales of time and space, "fractal" geometry, "the geometry of nature." Fractal shapes come from complexity and turbulence, they are infinitely long and self-repeating, like Mandelbrot's description of a shoreline, or like traces of tidal rivers in mud, branching ferns, or the edge of a cloud. A sensibility steeped in classical geometry might see such forms as too complex to describe, as simply disordered, or, as Frank Lloyd Wright did earlier, as able to be abstracted into triangles and circles, grids and radiating lines. As fractals, such complex patterns can be described, with relative simplicity, through repetitive processes like bifurcation and development. Snow crystals, in their combination of stability and instability, of symmetry and randomness, of repetition and variety, are fractal forms. Each snowflake or ice crystal embodies both the process of its formation and all the changing weather patterns it has experienced. Water, crystallizing, forms a growing tip with a boundary that becomes unstable and sends off side branches. The structural similarity of snowflakes comes from limits and potential of its material, water; the seemingly infinite variety of shape is caused by variations in context, in the precise combinations of wind, sun, humidity, and temperature to which each is exposed as it forms. Knowing the structure of ice crystals and how their growth is affected by context, it is possible to read those contexts in the shape of each flake. And the same is true of larger landscapes.

Fractal geometry provides a way to describe and appreciate the complex form of villages and older urban districts admired for their variety and quality of wholeness. Such places evolved with a peculiar combination of order and disorder, through purposeful process and repetitive use of built forms, the shape of buildings, streets, and squares varying in response to differing conditions of context—physiographic, economic, cultural, and individual preference. In some new towns, on the other hand, the form of houses, and even such details as exterior paint color and landscaping, are prescribed. And redeveloped urban districts are often a hodgepodge of idiosyncratic buildings and leftover space.

Similar kinds of structure underlie landscapes and their features, both naturally occurring and designed. Axes—of snowflake's branching, river's flowing, city's streets—are lines of movement, whether actual or implied, straight, serpentine, or spiral, singular or branching; they depend on quality of movement, conditions of origin and growth. One major axis, a broad processional route paved with stone, oriented north-south, extended through Beijing, led straight through the Forbidden City connecting the throne room in the palace to the Temple of Heaven. The Champs-Élysées is an axis built by Louis XIV to accommodate the movement of his court back and forth between his Parisian palace, the Louvre, and Versailles, expressing the link between the two. The main street in Aspen Farms and Main Street in Disneyland are axes of movement and meeting. Two axes, at right angles, aligned to the compass, defined the Roman *castrum*—a military camp, and later, a square, fortified town—two roads crossed at the center, puncturing the walls at four gates. This pattern is still preserved in towns like Ljubljana in Slovenia and Cologne in Germany, both originally established as Roman castra.

A city's grid, like a spider's web, is made by overlapping lines of movement, a lattice structure regularly or irregularly shaped. A square grid, quickly surveyed and settled, was common in colonial towns and frontier territories from those of ancient Greece to the Americas: from the ancient Greek city of Priene, to Mexico City, Philadelphia, and the American Midwest. Like the Roman castrum, Philadelphia has two major north-south, east-west streets (Market and Broad) that are central axes within a grid of streets. Benjamin Franklin Parkway, built more than two hundred years after the grid was surveyed and settled, cuts diagonally across it, slicing squares into odd-shaped slivers; such breaks from underlying structure signify something.[19] In this case, the desire to transform an old neighborhood into a new district of cultural institutions and to link two important monuments: City Hall at the intersection of Market and Broad and the site of the new art museum on a hill across town. One can also see cities with a gridded street pattern like Philadelphia's as a modular structure, square-shaped blocks of land bounded by streets. Modular structure, in towns, buildings, tiles, and honeycombs, comes from packing together modules of similar shape.

Most human settlements, like all landscapes, are stratified, spatially and temporally: streets and buildings over underground sewers and basements; multistoried houses with street-level common rooms for entertaining visitors and second-floor private rooms; penthouses on upper floors of skyscrapers. Just as the layered structure of sandstone, shale, and limestone reflects their formation from successive depositing of sand, silt, and clay, so the ground under cities reveals layers of previous settlements. Nested structure, too, is a form of stratification: Imperial Beijing was structured by a series of concentric, rectangular, walled enclosures; the innermost precinct, surrounded by a moat, was the emperor's Forbidden City with the palace at the center; the Forbidden City was enclosed in turn by the walled, administrative imperial city. Nested landscape structure, one part enclosed within another, may also convey a sense of refuge as one moves progressively inward. Courtyard gardens within houses of dense city districts in Kyoto are secular havens, the fenced enclosures of Ise religious refuge; in both, there is a progressive contrast between outer, public realms and inner, private ones, between secular and sacred.

Certain settlement structures are more rigid and inflexible than others, others more open and flexible in accommodating change.[20] Those with circular structure pose particular problems and specific opportunities, for a circle is complete in itself. A circular park is the heart of the University of California-Irvine campus, bounded by a path, lined by buildings; the university has expanded greatly, but the park at its center remains sacrosanct. Had it been another shape, a rectangle, for example, it might have been encroached upon by buildings. In this case, inflexibility was an advantage. Like a circle, stratified structure is less adaptable for it can expand or contract only by accretion or erosion, one layer at a time. Modular structure expands through repetition, axial structure along lines of growth. The grid, on the other hand, is particularly flexible because it accommodates growth along multiple lines of movement.

Marker and Vessel of Experience and Meaning

Elms trees are tall and vase-shaped: long branches sprout high on the trunk, arching up and out like ribs in a Gothic vault. Parallel rows of elms, planted close so their branches meet, create a cathedral-like space beneath the trees. Cherry trees are short and branch close to the ground; an allée of closely planted cherries encloses an intimate space. The Naiku shrine at Ise is raised on a rectangular platform supported by enormous boulders; fences define its inner, most sacred spaces. Space is shaped and differentiated by the form of landscape features: a void enclosed by trees, hills, buildings; an area marked off as distinct or special or forbidden. Open or enclosed, monumental or intimate, such spatial qualities depend on the form and scale of bounding plants, landforms, or walls. In the beginning, according to Genesis, the earth was without form, and thus void. Form orders space: the poet Wallace Stevens describes how a jar placed on a hill reorders the landscape around it; buildings do the same.[21]

Shape, like material, is sensual—visible, tangible, even audible. Anyone who drives on a country road, up and down hills and around curves, *feels* the shape of the land or, sailing a boat, the shape of waves and wind. In landscape, shape is continuous, related, connected to other shapes. The sighted person perceives these as a whole; to the blind person, this continuity is invisible, seemingly fragmented, heard as "various broken sounds spread across a nothingness," until "rain presents the fullness of an entire situation all at once, a sense of perception of the actual relationships of one part of the world to another."[22] Shape has texture: fuzzy, spiky,

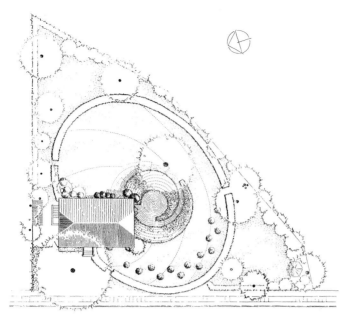

Geometry and function. Sonja Poll's Garden (1970). Denmark. (Plan drawn by Sonja Poll)

or smooth to touch, and it modulates movement: directing and deflecting running water or crowds of people, focusing and reflecting sound—amphitheaters are often bowl-shaped, to gather people and project sound.

Paths that follow cardinal directions, the rising and setting of the sun, or that link important landmarks provide a sense of orientation; mazelike paths engender confusion. Vitus Bering Park in Horsens, Denmark, both confuses and orients. A spiraling path leads to an elliptical lawn near the center, and two diagonal paths slice shortcuts across the park. The curving path is grass, lined by tall, dense rhododendrons all over eye height; straight paths are paved and flat. The effect is disturbing, yet reassuring; to encounter a straight path is to find a way out of the spiral. The whole can be experienced only by exploration, fitting for a park that honors the explorer and cartographer after whom the Bering Strait was named. C. Th. Sørensen designed it in 1954–56, anticipating by several decades later trends in landscape and urban design; which, like Vitus Bering Park, were inspired by the Russian constructivists. Parc de La Villette in Paris, which combines a meandering path with several straight ones, is an example.

Sonja Poll's garden at her house north of Copenhagen, designed by Sørensen (her father), has a complex geometric structure: ellipse, spiral, and circles of hedge, lawn, paths, patio, and flower beds play against the triangle of the property's boundaries and the rectangle of the house. The spiral path leads from the back door down to a small circular patio enclosed by a rounded bank that provides

Spiral path. Sonja Poll's garden. Denmark.

Where are the people in all these places?

a sense of rest and refuge. The oddly shaped leftover space between elliptical hedge and boundary fence is a convenient place for vegetable garden, compost pile, tool-shed, and greenhouse; an awkwardly shaped property turned to advantage.

Geometry, for Frank Lloyd Wright, was "an aesthetic skeleton" that held symbolic meaning: "Certain geometric forms have come to symbolize for us and potently to suggest certain human ideas, moods, and sentiments—as for instance: the circle, infinity; the triangle, structural unity; the spire, aspiration; the spiral, organic progress; the square, integrity."[23] Through "subtle differentiations of these elemental geometric forms," and "a sense of [their] symbol-value," form could be made to *signify*, an idea he exploited for both buildings and gardens.[24]

A circle represents both movement, around a central point, and also stasis, a shape with no beginning and no end, T. S. Eliot's "still point of the turning world."[25] It is a paradox complicated by another paradox: a circle's outline has no hierarchy but its structure, with a center, has. Jens Jensen's "council rings" for parks and gardens in Illinois and Wisconsin were circles of stone with campfires in the center, where people could gather to talk, tell stories, perform. Jensen saw the council ring as a symbol of democracy and of "the brotherhood of all living things."[26] A circle is associated with heaven in many cultures, the annual cycle of seasons, with birth and death, change and becoming. There are more squares than circles in human-built landscapes, and more circles than squares in "natural" landscapes. Is this why squares so often represent reason and order?

In sacred architecture, circle and square, sphere and cube are often combined. The exterior of Woodland Chapel at Forest Cemetery is square and rustic; the interior is square, but within the square ceiling is a circle, and from that circle springs a dome, a half sphere with a central skylight. A circle of simple, Doric columns supports the circular opening in the ceiling under the dome. A soft light washes the dome and strikes the stone floor within the circle—an abstraction of a forest clearing. The body of the dead is placed here in the light under the dome; the mourners sit in shadow.

So, too, the plain buildings of the Shaker Village at Pleasant Hill, Kentucky, give no clue to the flights of ornament within. Who, seeing the austere exterior stone and brick walls, could imagine the arched doorways, vaults, and curving rails of Center House? or the elegant curves of the two spiral stairways in the Trustees' Office—except, perhaps, from a clue in the fantail over the door and the glazing in the third-floor window above the door? This structure is not coincidental; it represents the Shaker belief of a grace-filled inner life nurtured within a plain and austere exterior.

Mont-Saint-Michel's single pilgrimage path is a hierarchical structure, leading from worldly base to hilltop shrine, a spiraling, then a straight, vertical axis, and continues on inside the church, along the main axis from rear to front toward the rising sun. The parts of the whole are ordered along a gradient of importance. Indeed, all axial structure is hierarchical, each part subordinate to a dominant spine. Not surprising, then, that axes are common to religious and political landscapes. In Rome, Paris, and Washington, principal streets link cultural landmarks and political monuments—secular shrines.

The layered structure of Kansas City, Missouri, is hierarchical, the layers both horizontal and vertical: poorer people in inner city, in urban valleys; the wealthier in outer suburbs, on ridges. Anyone attending a convention in Kansas City need never encounter the tumbled down buildings and vacant lots of the valley between hotels and convention center. New hotels are on a bluff, connected to the downtown center by a viaduct that leapfrogs the poor districts, sight unseen, below.

In a coordinated structure like a grid, all parts that have similar importance carry equal weight, though certain orthogonal lines in the grid may be emphasized, for example, streets crossing at the center of a castrum or a city. A grid structure, easy to survey and plot, is sometimes seen as a sign of colonization, but a grid has also been a symbol of democracy. Paul Klee used a grid in paintings to give order to diversity. G. N. Brandt used a similar strategy in his design for Mariebjerg Cemetery, north of Copenhagen, where a grid of high evergreen hedges disguises changes in topography and unifies the whole. The visually separate, rectangular modules framed by the grid are landscape rooms for different styles of burials: wooden crosses marking graves within the dappled shade of a wooded meadow; family tombs set within ferns and ivy under the dense shade of evergreen trees; a serene space carpeted by clipped lawn where ashes are scattered; the graves of children in a place enclosed by lilacs under the spreading branches of an old oak; and many others. The repetitive structure of the grid emphasizes the different landscape styles within each precinct and the particular attitude about death exemplified in each.

Formal composition is fundamental to design, but form without substance, at odds with process, may fail to function, alienate those who use a place, and even put them at risk. Sørensen delighted in formal play; his compositions have complex and sophisticated geometry, but they do not neglect material, process, and performance. Great landscape authors like Sørensen and Brandt fashion forms and employ them to shape and structure space, to evoke feeling, hold meaning, and perform function.

Performance Space: Places of Need and Use

Uluru, Stourhead, Cooper's Place

The heart of Australia is a vast red desert thousands of miles across. To many who live in the cities and towns that hug Australia's coastline, the Center is a threatening chaos, but to Aborigines who dwell there, the Center is highly ordered, a complex mosaic of sand hills, claypans, dry channels, rock holes, and rocky outcrops, each with a precise relationship to water, plants, animals, and myth in a landscape rich in food and charged with meaning.

Bands of Aborigines move deliberately within this domain of food and water sources and sacred places defined by inherited song. Songs of how ancestors sang them into being, and with them the right to use the paths they relate, are passed from one generation to another. The continent of Australia is laced with these ancient paths, visible only to those who know the songs that describe the way, that tell of the relationships among rocks, water, animals, and humans, and that link present time with the forming of the world during the Dreamtime. The songs tell of movement and guide hunters and gatherers of food, legends of origin recalled in everyday rituals of digging for bush potatoes and witchetty grubs, gathering bush banana, hunting wallaby.

The small aboriginal bands have estates of sufficient size to support them with water and food, the fuzzy boundaries of each band's estate overlap adjacent ones; contiguous bands are joined by the songs they share. The locations of paths and sacred places are not fuzzy, however; trespass on a sacred site is forbidden except by those who "keep" the place and those they permit to accompany them.

Rituals celebrate landscape and reenact its formation through dance as well as song. Settings for rituals are created by clearing the ground, constructing a windbreak, and inscribing elaborate symbolic patterns in packed earth: a circle as a water hole, a camp site, or a food-bearing bush; wavy lines as a watercourse; arrows as a path.[27] In the 1970s, aboriginal artists from the central desert began to transfer these compositions to canvas, with methods and compositions strikingly

The climb. Uluru. Australia.

similar to those of traditional ritual art.[28] Typically, the artists work outdoors on canvas spread on the ground, often a group working on a painting together, an affirmation of shared territory and responsibility to the landscape they live in. Many artists begin with a red ground, then add concentric circles—perhaps a rock hole. These paintings and ritual settings are maps of territory as an Aborigine might see it. Walbiri see water underground, witchetty grubs and honey ants crawling in roots; they paint mythic landscapes with water, grubs, roots, terrain, branches, superimposed, fusing past, present, future. In *Witchetty Grub Dreaming at the Site of Mount Wedge*, four small witchetty bushes frame a larger, central bush, all five lying in a claypan surrounded by sand hills.[29] At each bush a woman sits with digging stick, rooting for witchetty grubs. The grubs are shown within the roots of the bush, below ground. Such paintings fuse mythical events with events of daily life, expressing a unity, across time, with natural processes and the landscape they shape.

Uluru rises out of this desert, like an island in the sea, like Australia itself—an immense monolith marking the center of a continent. Water streams off courses eroded into the rock, like rivers of a miniature continent, isolated by desert-sea as surely as Australia itself is surrounded by vast stretches of ocean. There is even a continental shelf of plant life around the base, supported by more abundant water there, the runoff. Of great significance to Aborigines are Uluru's several sacred sites, perhaps the oldest continuously revered place in the world.

Refuge. Uluru. Australia.

The first white explorers who reached it in the late nineteenth century named it Ayre's Rock, but local Aborigines continued their subsistence culture until the 1940s, when cattle stations began to encroach upon their foraging territory, depleting water sources. Today the rock is a symbol of the outback for all Australians and the destination of tourists.

Some tourists to Uluru climb, many watch others climb, then take in the rock at sunset, but most see this landscape from an air-conditioned tour bus, mainly on the move, only its broad outlines visible. Those who step down from the tour bus and walk into the landscape, away from the road and parking lots, enter a different world of green foliage, blue and purple wildflowers, vivid, red-orange ground, with a base rhythm of humming flies punctuated by birdsong. None of this is visible or audible within the moving bus with its closed tinted windows.

Aboriginal rangers have built a path for visitors across the sand plain with its wildflowers and spinifex into a mulga grove and on to the base of Uluru. They lead small groups along the path and tell stories: how to gather spinifex, how to beat and heat it to form glue, how to make fire and find food, how the Liru warrior ancestors—poisonous snakes—came across this plain and threw their spears at the Kuniya ancestors, leaving the pockmarks one sees on the rock today. The tourist path, named Liru, recalls aspects of the dreaming tracks.

The English who colonized Australia were blind to the paths and signs that ordered the Aborigines' landscape. To them it was foreign, a chaotic wilderness. The landscape they introduced, still being built in the desert today, is a pastoral landscape, its roots in eighteenth-century English landscape gardens and their ancient precedents in Roman poetry. From the time that Joseph Addison, in the early 1700s, urged the English landowner to "make a pretty Landskip of his own Possessions," English gentry shaped their estates to express the integration of agriculture, art, property, power, and politics.[30] Their landscape gardens tell stories that can be decoded only by those who can read the signs. Stourhead, in southwestern England, is such a landscape garden. To the modern visitor with no intimate knowledge of classical literature, its landscape is merely picturesque; to an eighteenth-century English gentleman, it represented the power of privilege and empire.

At Stourhead, one descends from the house down wooded slopes to the lake below and enters a calm, carefully ordered world. Follow the path around the lake—now enclosed in woods, now open to a carefully framed, postcard-perfect view—and an allegory unfolds, for one who can read it. Sculptures and buildings embellish the story, and Latin inscriptions yield clues to their meaning: lines from Virgil's *Aeneid* refer to the founding of Rome, others to Alfred, the first English king, or to the builder and owner, the eighteenth-century banker Henry Hoare, a juxtaposing of classical and Gothic styles that parallels the links between ancient Rome and powerful, mercantile England.[31]

Stourhead is literally just that, the head of the river Stour, whose source is numerous springs within the valley. Monuments mark the springs: one is a Gothic cross, moved from its original location near St. Peter's Church in Bristol; another, a sleeping nymph and a river god who points the way to the Pantheon, presiding over a spring that wells up within a grotto. The statue recalls the story from the *Aeneid* in which "the God of the place, old Tiber himself," foretells the founding of Rome. The path leads to a replica of the Pantheon, past a hermit's cave to the Temple of Apollo, across a Palladian bridge to the Temple of Flora. Hoare, unlike many other landowners, who moved entire villages to make way for their landscape gardens, incorporated the village of Stourton into his Arcadian composition. The church spire and the cottages across the way compose a peaceful scene visible from the Pantheon across the lake. Stourhead's self-contained world was a refuge for Hoare and his family from the political turmoil of London and Europe. It stood for the owner, embodying, in his own words, "the fruits of industry and application to business and [showing] what great things can be done by it, the

Storied path. Stourhead. England.

envy of the indolent who have no claim to temples, grottos, bridges, rocks, exotic pines and ice in summer."[32]

This English landscape style spread throughout the British Empire and beyond. Nineteenth- and twentieth-century garden suburbs in England and North America adopted it, and so, more recently, have corporate office parks, asserting the power of property, the status of the owner, and alluding to the continuity of Western culture.

"Only land is power" reads a message scrawled across the wall of an abandoned building in Boston's Roxbury neighborhood. This message would not have been lost on eighteenth-century Englishmen, nor is it lost upon residents of North American inner cities who transform abandoned vacant lots into community gardens, only to be forced to relinquish them for parking lots or if land values rise, for buildings, nor is it lost upon those whose gardens are held more securely in common trust.

Forty people garden at Cooper's Place, a community garden in Roxbury. Each gardener has a plot and all tend a common rose garden with a sitting area open to the entire neighborhood. The sitting garden, reached through two gates under rose-covered arbors, is an anteroom to the allotments beyond, through another arbored gate. Behind the individual plots is a common herb garden and another sitting area for the gardeners, and, alongside, an orchard. Many of the plants the gardeners grow—peanuts, sweet potato, collards, and watermelon—reflect their southern origins. The sustenance provided by their land is spiritual as well as physical and social: as one gardener said, "I love to plant; I love to watch anything grow. I kneel down in that dirt and take up a handful of it. I say this is nature . . . this is God's thing and I enjoy it."[33] One gardener tells of how she goes out into the garden early in the morning, when all is calm and peaceful, to pray. Here, she says, she feels nearest to God.

Twenty years ago the garden was just another vacant lot, composed of four house lots whose property boundaries were invisible with no trace of the four original houses save the stone retaining wall along the sidewalk broken by steps that once led to the four front doors. In 1975, a group of local senior citizens transformed the lot into a community garden. For six years, the gardeners tended their plots, though they were aware that the ultimate destiny of the land they tilled was beyond their control. In 1981 they acquired the land, and two years later they secured funds for improvements from the city. In 1984 my graduate students in landscape architecture developed new designs for the garden, one of which was then built by unemployed youth enrolled in a landscape training program at a local community college.

I had to help six landscape architecture students at the Harvard Graduate School of Design—all white, middle-class, raised in suburbs—to enter the landscape dialogues of forty elderly urban gardeners—African American and Hispanic. Each student was asked to start the semester by staying with one of the gardeners for the weekend. The next week we met with the gardeners to discuss their dreams for the community garden my students were to design for them. My students and I had framed a series of questions to elicit our clients' hopes; one asked the gardeners what their favorite place in Boston was. The response was a surprising consensus: "The Fenway Rose Garden." "We want a rose garden!" Whereupon Beth Arndtsen, the student who had posed the question, visited the Fenway Rose Garden, but it was January and the garden was closed. Undeterred, she scaled the locked fence to study the place; her design for the new community garden adapted its white arbors, its climbing roses, its gravel paths and flat lawn. When each of the students presented a design three weeks later, the forty gardeners chose Arndtsen's. It was built and planted a month later, in March 1984, and it still thrives there.Had the question not been posed, we might never have realized how important a symbol the Fenway Rose Garden was for them. Ironically, the Fenway Rose Garden itself was then in jeopardy; landscape historians were petitioning for its removal from the Fens on the grounds that it was not part of Frederick Law Olmsted's original design for this landmark landscape.

From Linwood Street, in Roxbury, today, the white arches and vivid red and pink roses spilling out over the fence can be seen a block away; closer, the scent of roses fills the air. One enters the garden under a white, rose-covered arbor through an unlocked gate into a formal sitting garden, with a small panel of grass surrounded by a gravel path lined with flower beds. Cooper's Place, named for Ed

Territory reclaimed: Cooper's Place. Boston. (West Philadelphia Landscape Project)

Entrance, sign of welcome: Cooper's Place. Boston.

Cooper, a neighbor, gardener, and activist, is a local landmark. There have been weddings there, and it has stimulated neighborhood change. Before the garden was built, the apartment building next door and two houses across the street were vacant. They are now renovated, repainted, and repopulated. The gardeners had a dream of converting four empty garages at the rear of the garden into a center for canning fruits and vegetables and for environmental education. This seemed hopelessly beyond reach in 1984, but, in 1997, the group broke ground for the center; they had raised $450,000, mostly from foundations, to build it. The gardeners are extraordinary people, but the garden's design, too, was key to its success. The designer gave form to the power of the gardeners' dreams and created a place of beauty and refuge that inspired confidence, hope, and affection.

Despite differences of time, place, and culture, the landscapes of Uluru, Stourhead, and Cooper's Place are fundamentally similar. The phenomenon of territory, embodied in the use of land and the feeling of belonging to it, is common to all three. Australian Aborigines *are* their territory; they belong to their territory, not only the source of sustenance but also the repository of their history, a link to past and future generations. Aboriginal country consists of all those places that hold meaning through inheritance and personal experience. Aborigines separated from their country lose an essential part of their identity. The property of the English gentleman was the source of his power and his vote in Parliament; through the land's embellishment as a pastoral landscape he identified himself and his nation as the inheritor of Rome. His territory was not his own local property alone but England itself and the expanding empire. The land of Cooper's Place was hard-won; held in common it testifies to the achievement of individuals who worked together to achieve common goals. Each gardener shares ownership through use of the land; the plants grown there are a link not only to the past and to the larger community, but also to new hope for the future.

The boundary at Cooper's Place, a chain-link fence four feet high, is a more unambiguous demarcation of territory than exists at Stourhead or Uluru. One can see through the fence at Cooper's Place and talk across it; along with the carefully tended roses it signals that this area belongs to people who care for it. Vandals have left the garden untouched. The unlocked gate to the sitting area says this is private property where others are welcome. The locked gate to the allotments beyond marks them as private, with entrance by invitation only.

At Stourhead, unlike Cooper's Place, boundaries are often concealed. The ditch, or ha-ha, that keeps pasture in view and the sheep out of the garden is invisible from the house. The valley is a world in itself, with property boundaries invisible from within the valley since they lie beyond the enclosing hills or disguised behind dense planting. The inclusion of the village of Stourton within the view from the garden extends the boundaries of the estate beyond the territory it occupies. Thus is the larger world of the village and its inhabitants absorbed into the gentry's domain.

In aboriginal territory, there are no walls, fences, or gates at all. Overlapping boundaries between adjacent estates reflect the belief that many people together hold a country. Traditionally, one attains the right to a particular estate through prolonged association and care. Territory is defined by knowledge, by knowing the stories that plants, animals, and landforms embody. The paths that create territory are not just for traveling from place to place; they also express relationships and responsibilities across multiple, contiguous estates. Dreaming paths, some hundreds of miles long, trace ancestors' movements across the land, connecting significant places and sacred sites within the estates the path crosses. Places linked by a dreaming path are "one country."

Like the aboriginal dreaming paths, the path at Stourhead links a series of landmarks or signs that tell stories connecting the present with the past. The roses and white arbors at Cooper's Place are shared stories of past and present and link it to that other, well-tended public space, the Fenway Rose Garden. The Cooper's Place arbors have come to stand not for the community garden alone, but, beyond that, for a landmark that defines the larger neighborhood. At Stourhead, the Pantheon and the Temple of Apollo provide both a prospect from which to view and reflect upon the landscape and its stories and a refuge from sudden showers. The benches set under the rose arbors at Cooper's Place are likewise both prospect and refuge. Both are a refuge from the world outside just as the central desert of Uluru is now a refuge, for Aborigines, from Western culture.

Territory is established by the limits of the processes which create it. A watershed is a territory through which water flows to a particular stream or river; a tidal zone is the territory created by sea's ebb and flow. The boundaries of both are marked by extent of movement. A habitat is the area within which an animal forages and mates; a nation is the domain in which authority dictates that certain actions proceed in certain ways according to law. Paths, boundaries, and gateways are conditions, not things, spatial patterns defined by processes. Paths are places of movement, boundaries limits to movement, gateways places of passage and exchange. A path is maintained by movement. Once a process ceases, space becomes a shell of past practices.[34]

Places of Need and Use

I once spent a week walking footpaths in the Wye Valley of western England, armed with an ordinance survey. The first day's route was easy to follow: cutting through pastures, on stiles over fences, across wheat fields on narrow tracks through the grain, along the river Wye, then up, among a milling flock of sheep, to a hilltop pasture with views out over the rolling green and gold patchwork to the Black Mountains of Wales. The next day, my hosts sent me further afield, and the way was less easy to find and follow, though the path was clearly marked on the map. I walked along hedgerows through high grass, climbed over stiles blocked by wire fencing, crashed through cornfields, stumbled down a long slope

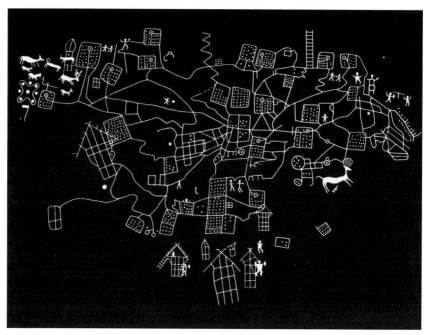

Territory, path, boundary, gateway, prospect, refuge, source, sign. Bedolina petroglyph
(ca. 2500 B.C.)

covered in bracken, chased by a bull. My hosts were members of a local society
dedicated to keeping footpaths open; they kept records of which paths had been
walked, and when. The paths near their home were well maintained by their own
frequent walking; they had made neat paths through nearby wheat fields by tram-
pling a track when the plants were young and the farmer gone to town for the afternoon. Public footpaths on private land are remnants of an earlier landscape
predating the Enclosure Acts. Public access, or right-of-way, is granted by English
common law on the basis of traditional use; that right is relinquished if the path
is not used at least once a year. My route was duly recorded, its right-of-way en-
sured for another year.

Most people tend to follow a path if there is one, as do cows and goats. On
the large, sloping plaza at the foot of La Grande Arche, at La Défense in Paris, a
straight, slanting path begins, ending nowhere special—Sven-Ingvar Andersson's
whimsical stroke. The plaza is grey, of granite pavers, the path is white, of marble.
I stood and watched people and path one late afternoon. Adults crossing the plaza
altered their movement as they reached the white strip: either they changed course
and walked up or down the path, or, as they crossed it, deflected their line of
movement slightly. Two little girls bicycled down the marble strip and back up the
plaza, again and again, for nearly an hour. Two older boys on roller blades came,

set out cones of orange plastic along the path, and skated down, weaving in and out. Cyclists and skaters took turns.

Territory, boundary, path, gateway, meeting place, prospect, refuge, source, and sign are types of spaces basic to human habitats. I call them *performance spaces* to emphasize that they are generated by active processes and are not simply formal and fixed, as commonly seen.[35] My own approach sees space as a setting for performance of activities; it begins with the processes that generate places, rather than with their expression in particular forms, and then asks what settings are necessary to sustain these processes. Each kind of performance space is derived from archetypal needs and activities and the means invented to meet or accommodate them. Some needs and activities are basic to survival—moving, finding sustenance, stimulating senses, reproducing, growing, identifying, and controlling, and making/building. Others are social—belonging, communicating, trading, playing, learning, and conflict. Others, for humans, are spiritual needs—reflection, worship. The places we dwell in, gardens, homes, neighborhoods, towns, or cities, must, at the very least, satisfy these needs. This approach draws from the study of humans and culture and from landscape ecology and animal ethology. I have tested its relevance to landscapes of different cultures: from Uluru to Cooper's Place, from West Philadelphia to Japan, Versailles and Stourhead to Kongenshus in Denmark and Forest Cemetery in Stockholm. Performance spaces are also relevant to inorganic processes and other life forms to the extent that the processes that generate those spaces are shared.

There is a complex interplay between processes and the territories they engender. A simple path may be created by something moving—people, cows, a river—but most paths are not simple. A promenade path is for walking, meeting, talking, playing, displaying; a ritual path or pilgrimage route is for procession and worship. There are paths for every movement, for work, trade, invasion, teaching, learning, pleasure, travel. One place may be the setting for more than one archetypal activity: the channels of a tidal estuary are for moving and exchanging, but so is a trade route. Gateway denotes a threshold, a place of passage: a garden gate that opens and closes, a bridge point of entry into a city, a harbor of access to some hinterland. A sign may be words on a billboard or a post, but Uluru is also a sign, as are the roses at Cooper's Place and the monuments that mark the springs at Stourhead. All convey meaning. Patterns are of diverse scale: a garden, a building, a neighborhood, a city, a region, a nation, yet the functions served are the same; a garden wall, a building wall, a city wall, the wall of China, all are boundaries.

What I call performance spaces have been described by others, though not exactly in the same way; most others focus on a few types rather than many types or on form rather than process. Anthropologists and geographers are more likely to see such spaces as generated by cultural practices, architects more likely to see them as visible forms with process secondary, if there at all. In *The Experience of Landscape*, the geographer Jay Appleton, for example, examines the roots of refuge

Sign. Chaco Canyon. New Mexico.

and prospect in the adaptive behavior of humans and animals.[36] Christian Nor-berg-Shulz, an architectural theorist, refers to domain, path, and node as the archetypal elements of human settlements; Kevin Lynch, another theorist, refers to district, path, node, edge, and landmark.[37] In *Image of the City*, Lynch was con-cerned with identifying, wayfinding, and memory, his goal to define the elements people use to form mental images of a place by which they then find their way. He used these elements to assess and design the "legibility" or "imageability" of a place, to understand how well people could grasp and remember an image of the whole. Both Norberg-Schulz and Lynch compiled lists of elements from observing urban form and people's response to it. Architects and urban designers have used Lynch's list for decades, as if it were comprehensive (he never claimed that it was), though it omits certain important settings, like prospect, refuge, and source.

The architect and planner Christopher Alexander sees specific spaces for be-havior as patterns that combine to create a "pattern language": global patterns on the scale of a region or town ("City Country Fingers," "Ring Roads," "Web of Shopping"); neighborhood patterns ("Green Streets," "Holy Ground"); building and garden patterns ("Entrance Room," "Zen View," "Tree Space"). The 253 pat-terns he describes in *A Pattern Language* are derived from his observations of places that, in his judgment, embody a quality of "wholeness," "the quality with-out a name."[38] Many of these patterns are wonderful and inspiring, others are idiosyncratic, formalistic, and formulaic. His insight that the character of a place

Gateway. Death Valley. California.

comes from patterns of events interlocked with geometric patterns in space is important and seminal, but his frequent focus on form rather than on the processes that shape it leads him to define patterns like "City Country Fingers," in which he stipulates that cities be no more than one mile wide, interspaced with farmland no smaller than one mile wide (so city residents can walk to it). He fails to take account of differences in terrain, soil fertility, drainage patterns, and so on. His dicta are sometimes vague, even mystical. Yet the problems that Alexander's theory poses and the gaps it contains challenge others to address them; his early work, less sweeping in both scope and claims than the later work, had a formative influence on my own thinking. His *A Pattern Language Which Generates Multi-Service Centers* identified all the functions of a community center, breaking them down into constituent parts; he drew formal and spatial relationships that made those activities possible and that evoked feelings.[39] His great contribution is his insight into the relationships among form, function, and feeling and his gathering of hundreds of examples of successful fit among these three.

When John Widrick went back to the drawing board to revise his design for a meeting place at Aspen Farms Community Garden, described earlier, he redefined the problem by focusing on the processes that would ultimately animate the space. He discarded his original proposal, a square area in the center of the garden, and began to consider the constellation of activities surrounding meeting: movement, exchange, gathering. This reformulation enabled him to envision the meeting place as a broad path with places to sit alongside, a main street running right through the garden rather than as a plaza. His success depended on the ability to move fluently between performance and space, between an understanding of general principles and of the particular context of the garden and its gardeners. To concentrate on formal qualities of space and neglect performance is to mistake the shell for the practices which shape and activate it; both are important.

Performance, Space, and Meaning

Many years ago, I heard René Dubos tell a group of landscape architects how "early man was imprinted by the soils, rocks, springs, and rivers among which he developed," "his mind and bodily responses . . . shaped by the information he derived from his senses," how humans, like all living organisms, "retain structural and functional evidences of their distant evolutionary past."[40] I chiefly remember his description of early humans and his discussion of the importance to their survival of refuge (a protected, secure, and comfortable place), of prospect (a vantage point that affords a broad view of prey and predators), and of water. His advice was to make a landscape to which people will be instinctively drawn: create a sense of refuge, provide a prospect and the presence of water.[41] His reflections on prospect and refuge made me take notice of such settings in landscape and made me wonder what other fundamental human, social, and cultural processes exist and what settings they might require.

Nourlangie Rock, an aboriginal dwelling now in Kakadu National Park, was occupied until the 1960s by people who lived as hunter-gatherers. It is a "found" dwelling, not a built one, reached by a hot climb through a dry, tropical woodland. There are only three narrow passages into a shelter created by an overhang and a tilted rock. It is shady, cool, and breezy, for the openings between the two rocks function as wind catchers, affording relief on a hot day. The roof is high, the interior spacious; walls are covered with rock paintings of animals, dangerous spirits, and Lightning Man, a fearsome, mythical figure. Rock paintings in Kakadu date as far back as nine thousand years or more, and as late as the 1960s.[42] As I stood looking, through an opening, out over the countryside, I thought of Dubos. As I did on another occasion in a very different place. The drive up South Mountain near Phoenix to the topmost overlook is several miles from the base; the view is of the valley below and cascades of mountain ranges beyond, one behind the other. Seen from above, the sprawling city seemed miniature and more comprehensible than when driving or walking within it. On a late afternoon, midweek, there were only a few cars, but the enormous parking lot indicated the many to come. By sunset, hundreds were there, couples sitting, arms around each other, families, groups of young men, black, white, Hispanic, Asian. Most just watched, quiet, as the sun went down and the city lights came on.

A prospect is not always pleasant. I sometimes think about the new residents of Åvangsgården—a doctor and a businessman—who tore out the hedges under the trees around the house to gain a view to the fields. The hedges had protected the farmhouse from strong Danish winds and driving rain, and perhaps the farmer, my Danish father, had welcomed a refuge, sacrificing prospect, since the balance between his income and his expense was so precarious. A prospect from West Terrace Park in Kansas City once made me feel elated, then depressed, and, ultimately, ambivalent. In searching for that park, I had passed through a neighborhood of vacant lots and dilapidated houses, onto a bridge over several layers of expressways and viaducts, through a renewal neighborhood to the remnants of the park; framed in the open arches of the refurbished hillside park was a vista of abandoned and decaying factories and warehouses.

Whether uplifting or depressing, the combination of refuge and prospect seems to encourage reflection, and places designed for meditation often combine the two. The verandah of the Ball House by Glenn Murcutt, near Sydney, Australia, is one such example, as are Shonantei, the teahouse at Saihoji, a Buddhist temple garden in Kyoto, and the Hill of Remembrance at Forest Cemetery in Stockholm. Like the Ball House, the teahouse at Saihoji is in a woods, its verandah elevated above the ground and protected on three sides—back, floor, roof. Here, though, the view is down to a lake, rather than out to distant mountains. On top of the Hill of Remembrance, the visitor is surrounded by a low wall of stone within a square of trees open to the sky at the center.

The form of a path may convey a message: straight is the shortest way between two points; a path that goes nowhere prompts a question; meandering invites a stroll. The Japanese stroll garden, with its sharp bends, pulls one's gaze downward; its twisting, turning path conceals then reveals views, giving a sense of flux and mutability. Paths may make allusions, intended or unintended: two paths diverging in a wood may remind one of Robert Frost's poem "The Path Not Taken." At Rousham, in England, the path tells a story; it winds through the garden leading the stroller from one carefully framed scene to another.

Paths, boundaries, gateways, prospects, refuges, and other territories have meaning even when dysfunctional. Two monumental arches on either side of the entrance to Newport Coast Road from Coastal Route 1 to Irvine, California, resemble victory arches, like the Arc de Triomphe in Paris, calling up associations with gates to European cities and triumphant armies. But they are signs, not gates; the six-lane road does not pass under them, nor can anyone walk through them since the other side is blocked by dense planting. They are hollow signs, literally; a rap on the surface brings not the solid sound of stone, but the hollow sound of empty space enclosed by plywood. Gates that permit one to pass by, but not to enter are, as it happens, an apt symbol here, for the road ahead is lined with gated communities, their entrances locked, presided over by guardhouses. The public highway runs past but the private communities are inaccessible to all but the residents and their guests.

So powerful are associations with elements like gateways that use at odds

Hill Garden: Taliesin North. Wisconsin.

with their fundamental meanings may produce unintended responses. Fountain and spring are symbols strongly associated with life, health, and sustenance. Seneca urged ancient Romans to "raise altars to springs at head of rivers," and many urban fountains, from Trevi in Rome to Bethesda in New York, were built to celebrate a city's water supply. Fountains in contemporary hotels and shopping centers, on the other hand, sustain no life; they are nonfunctional, no one drinks from them. They smell of chemicals and mock the meaning of fountain as source. Dubos would probably agree that people are drawn to water, but that not all water sources are useful, comforting, or appealing.

The vocabulary of performance space is so pervasive, within and across cultures, that it is often taken for granted. Children learn it early in their own play and in organized activities. On a visit to a weekend scouting encampment in Denmark, I was struck by how quickly and effectively the ten-year-olds created a series of communities using a few simple materials. Each small group chose a site, pitched tents, built a table and bench for eating, dug a hole for garbage, strung up a boundary fence of twine, and hung a sign that announced the group's name. Territory, boundary, path, gate, source, gathering place, prospect, refuge, and sign: these settings encompass a common heritage that every culture embroiders upon, inventing forms to express its distinctiveness, even as they connect, through shared patterns, to the larger world.

The Nature of Material, Form, Process, and Performance: Frank Lloyd Wright's Taliesins

Frank Lloyd Wright saw "land as architecture" and shaped its outward appearance to express his vision of its inner structure.[43] His writings, drawings, and built work all testify to his lifelong passion for nature and landscape. He wrote dozens of essays on the subject, more than any other architect, living or dead. He was a keen observer of natural form, an experienced architect of landscape; hundreds of drawings display his interest and insight: rhododendron and pine captured in a few pencil strokes, plans covered with detailed notes on planting and grading, sections showing deft modifications to terrain. Like the Japanese landscapes he admired, some of Wright's greatest works are large compositions of buildings and gardens, roads and waterways, fields and groves.[44]

Wright's understanding of nature was grounded in his family's Emersonian philosophy; he was steeped from early childhood in countless quotations, discussions, and sermons drawn from Emerson's writings.[45] His knowledge of landscape came from experience; observing and shaping landscapes were part of everyday life from the time he plowed, planted, hoed, and harvested fields as a boy, to when as a man he terraced hillsides, planted gardens and groves, dammed streams to generate power and make lakes and waterfalls, laid out contours for plowing that traced curving landforms, and selected sites for Sunday picnics.

The key to understanding Wright's approach to landscape lies in those places where he made his home over decades: the Jones Valley of southern Wisconsin and the desert of central Arizona. He was born to the first and chose the second, and the two must be seen together, as he experienced them, the one in contrast to, clarifying, the other. Taliesin North (1911–59) and Taliesin West (1937–59) are structured by similar principles but of different shape, each in dialogue with the other, each with its own landscape.

Buildings were central to Wright, his primary means of integrating varied landscape features in a unified composition. One cannot imagine Wright as the designer of a place like Stourhead, where the main event, the park in the valley, is a separate world from the house. Wright's landscapes are inconceivable without the structures that order the landscape even as they respond to it. The terraces and gardens of Taliesin emanate outward from the dwelling; the reverse is also true, landscape suggested the form of the buildings, the size and placement of windows. It is often impossible to say where building ends and landscape begins, his work part of a larger tradition of architecture that embraces the idea of landscape and building as continuous, where building interiors resemble landscapes.[46] When I am inside Wright's buildings, I find myself looking out to distant views of hills, lakes, trees, and buildings, following the plane of interior floor to exterior terrace, then, tracing the line of walls and roofs as they slide into terrain in a fusion of building and earth. I find myself, as Wright himself did with Japanese architecture, stumped to determine "where the garden leaves off and the garden begins . . . too delighted with the problem to attempt to solve it."[47]

Just as eighteenth-century English landowners embellished their estates—planting groves, damming streams to form lakes, moving villages, building landmarks to guide the gaze—so Wright transformed Jones Valley into a celebration of the landscape of southwestern Wisconsin. The landscape appears sculpted, and indeed it is. A grove of trees rounds off the angular top and ragged slopes of Midway Hill; curving roads and rows of crops accentuate the rolling landforms. Wright would certainly have agreed with Humphrey Repton's assertion that "to improve the scenery of a country, and to display its native beauties with advantage" is an art; Repton's three principles—utility, proportion, and unity—were among Wright's own.[48]

Over the years Wright changed the hill garden above the house radically, transforming it from rough pasture in a grove of trees into an open, rounded mound. By the late 1930s, the profile of the hill garden was a smooth curve covered with soft, closely clipped grass. Originally, the ridge was flatter on top, its form less perfectly round. Over the years, he removed the trees and their stumps, replaced the long grass with clipped lawn, inserted cut stones into the turf—an idealized version of limestone ledges—and rounded and smoothed the landform into a representation, an abstraction of a hilltop. So, too, he rounded off the valley as a whole through a gradual simplification of the given form. Ironically, like much of the rest of the landscape Wright graded and planted, the mounded slope and ledges of the hill garden have often been seen as naturally occurring rather than constructed. Many assume that the ledges and smooth terrain have just always been there. They are mistaken. The hill garden at Taliesin North is a rounded mound, like a breast or pregnant woman's swelling belly, enclosed by angular walls of stone and surmounted by a tower, which originally housed a dovecote.[49] Given Wright's belief in the symbolism of forms and also the association of doves with love and devotion, one can read the circular mound as feminine and the square enclosure as masculine, then interpret it further as a memorial to his murdered lover, Mamah, as representing the fertility of the valley embraced by the lover and architect.[50] The wall surrounding the hill garden sets it off from the surrounding landscape. From at least the 1920s, there was a distinct difference between the two; rough meadow of long grasses grew right up to the wall and was juxtaposed to the clipped grass within the enclosure. Wright often juxtaposed the ideal and the real, abstracted landscape form and given form, the cultivated and the wild. Experience of contrasts heightens each.

Wright was a performer and built each of his homes and gardens as a stage for the many daily, weekly, and seasonal rituals he designed for his family and apprentices. The tea circle, a semicircular niche with a bench halfway up the steps, is a pivotal place that negotiates a graceful transition between the lower courts and the hill garden. It is shady and breezy on a hot summer's day, a delight to the eye,

Prow garden and Taliesin West, 1949. Arizona. (Historical Collection of Herb and Dorothy McLaughlin)

to the body in movement. Taking tea in the tea circle became a daily practice at Taliesin from the 1930s if not before: "The four o'clock tea bell brings the Fellowship together for a welcomed respite from the day's work. Cooling sounds of ice rattling in tall glasses fall on ear as we climb the steps to the circular stone bench of the 'council ring.'"[51]

After 1938, Wright divided his life between Wisconsin and Arizona, journeying twice each year by automobile back and forth, his schedule driven by seasonal heat and cold, the cycle of spring planting and fall harvest. The juxtaposition of the two landscapes clarified each and kept his perceptions fresh. The property he bought for Taliesin West was near Phoenix at the foot of the McDowell Mountains on a gentle, south-facing slope with panoramic views over Paradise Valley to distant mountains. The hills behind have heaps of shattered rock at their base, all covered with desert varnish, black and red from many years' exposure to cycles of moisture and evaporation. The ground is hard, with rocks scattered across the surface as if cast there. Two deep washes structure the site, their steep sides, breadth, and long heaps of loose rocks and gravel clues to the violent force of waters crashing down the stony hillsides after rainstorms. Dozens of small, shallow washes lace the area. Wright sited Taliesin West up against a hill between a large wash to the west and a smaller wash to the east. Here, as he put it, "we decided to build ourselves into the life of the desert."[52]

His Taliesin West is a complex of buildings, courtyards, and gardens aligned, notched, and knit into the landscape: walls, roofs, pergolas, and paths catch sunlight and cast shadows; sight lines point to distant landforms; walls cut into, extend above, reach out to the immediate terrain. Segments of the main path and most of the buildings are aligned along a straight line—the spine of the complex—aligned so that the walls of the buildings receive both morning sun and afternoon light, and so that ends of the main path point to distant landforms. No isolated axis, this spine is embedded within two grids, as a line of one grid and a diagonal in the other. All the disparate parts of the place are held within the lattice structure formed by these two intersecting grids. Buildings, gardens, paths, and patios are set into the slope in some places, elevated on a platform above the desert in others. Lines of movement as one walks through Taliesin West zig and zag along the lines of the two interlocking grids. It is a landscape meant to be walked through.

I never feel a stronger fusion between patterns of landscape and life than I do at Taliesin West. As I walk back and forth between Guest Quarters or Sun Cottage, dining room, archives, library patio, and prow garden, shuttling along Taliesin's paths, I feel woven into the landscape, immediate and distant. Approaching and moving through the complex along the spine, I enter at grade, descend a few steps, turn and turn again, ascend, turn down the main path with a wall and the ground behind it at shoulder height, then turn to walk under a loggia, down a few steps, onto a platform elevated above the desert—the prow garden. As in a Japanese stroll garden, I am turning repeatedly, my eye drawn to the desert and the "borrowed" view of landmarks in the distant landscape.[53] As I walk through the garden, the paths bring a distant mountain into view again and again, at a bend in the path, framed by the loggia, repeatedly hidden and disclosed. Convinced this must be an important landmark for Wright, I asked its name. It is South Mountain, the site of Ocatillo, a temporary camp Wright designed in the 1930s that presaged important discoveries, and a new direction, in his work. At Taliesin North, too, Wright framed views of landmarks with personal significance: the Romeo and Juliet windmill, his first commission; Bryn Mawr, Bryn Canol, and Bryn Bach, local hills given Welsh names by his mother's family.

In Taliesin West, Wright took the materials of the desert and reordered them to construct walls and paths. Desert rocks—huge boulders, sharp-edged stones, rounded "goose-eggs" from the washes—were set in a rosy matrix of concrete made from desert sand to form the walls of platform and structures. The rocks float in this matrix, their positioning startling in its dynamism, unrelated to the positioning one would expect in a wall, prompting one to wonder about the processes of their formation. As Wright said, "Here in Arizona, one is much closer to the cataclysm," and it is just this sense of cataclysm that the walls convey.

The prow garden at Taliesin West is the counterpart of the hill garden at Taliesin North. Desert and garden meet at the wall in Taliesin West and the view is elevated, as in the Wisconsin hilltop garden; though here desert wilderness not fertile fields once surrounded the garden. The plants of the prow garden were those of the desert, massed as single species and reordered in planters and beds of angular shapes. Yucca fills a large bed next to a triangular-shaped pool in the sunken part of the garden. The garden is an oasis open to the desert, jutting out into it. The wall does not enclose the oasis but marks a boundary, inviting comparison between the domesticated and the wild, the human-built garden and what Wright called "this incomparable nature garden . . . a grand garden the likes of which in sheer beauty of space and pattern does not exist . . . in the world."[54]

Wright took care to distinguish between outer and inner form—shape and structure—but the irony is that he himself often fell into the trap of imitating external shape and ignoring inner structure. Jensen chided him for designing flat roofs that echoed the horizontality of the prairie's ground plane but were poorly adapted to the region's heavy snowfall. Hence the leaky roofs for which Wright is famous. Taliesin West was built into the land, the geometry of its plan inspired by the angles of the surrounding terrain, but floods that swept down off the nearby slopes sometimes washed right through the buildings. Whenever Wright responded only to landscape's surface form, rather than to the processes that shaped its underlying structure, he ran into trouble.

"Structure is the very basis of what I call reality," wrote Wright in 1937, the year before construction began on Taliesin West.[55] Years earlier, just after building Taliesin North, he had asserted that structure was "at the very beginning of any real knowledge of design. And at the beginning of structure lies always and everywhere geometry."[56] By structure, he meant the way elements are united into "a larger unity—a vital whole."[57] Though his definition of structure remained fundamentally the same, it evolved between 1912 and 1937, the years in which he first built Taliesin North and Taliesin West. In 1912 he was stressing that structure was "pure form, as arranged or fashioned and grouped to 'build' the Idea" and that geometry (Euclidean) was "the grammar of the form," "its architectural principle."[58] At Taliesin North from 1911 to 1914, he grouped the squares, rectangles, and circles of buildings, terraces, and gardens in a highly sophisticated play of shapes within a single grid. By 1937, when he declared, "Nature could not have static structure first if she would," he was emphasizing the organic, dynamic quality of structure: a product of creative process, unfolding, shaping and shaped by function.[59] At Taliesin West, he established a complex lattice, a structure of spine and grids that has accommodated changing needs and expansion relatively gracefully over the past half-century. The two Taliesins thus represent a profound shift in his strategy of structure, from static eternal geometry to dynamic organic structure.

There is often an unresolved tension in his works and texts between the two.

Wright returned each year to Arizona and Wisconsin full of ideas for change, seizing afresh the task of reshaping buildings and gardens: "It was pandemonium for two weeks—tearing out walls, rebuilding," recalls Bruce Pfeiffer, a member of the Taliesin Fellowship since 1949.[60] The Taliesins, brilliant essays on design to accommodate growth and change, were built and rebuilt, shaped and reshaped, in successive paroxysms of creative destruction. Their very essence was change, their current form the result of adding and subtracting, accretion and erosion, growth and decay. As one of his associates, Cornelia Brierly, observed, "Mr. Wright never cared about things lasting. He was satisfied just to see them take shape."[61]

Over his lifetime, Wright worked out a personal vocabulary and adapted it to many different places. Apart from his native terrain the landscapes that moved Wright most powerfully were those whose underlying structure is expressed clearly in the shape of their landforms and plants, as in deserts.[62] His work *had* to respond when he moved from the gently rounded deciduous trees and layered landforms of Wisconsin's Driftless Area to the spiky desert plants and angular landforms of the arid Southwest. How apt that the Wisconsin hill garden is a rounded mound enclosed by a square of layered limestone walls, the prow garden a triangle elevated by walls of rocks tumbled in mortar like talus at the base of desert mountains. The Taliesins are masterful compositions of landscape elements, influenced by Wright's own experience, ideas, and ideals, and those of his time and culture, further shaped by the context of place. As Wright said, speaking at Taliesin West, "In inhabiting the two places, you learn. You have the open book of nature. On the one page you have efflorescence, richness, ease . . . a form of decay. Perhaps this vegetation that grows all over so abundantly is a form of mold that comes upon the more accurate elements—the stone foundation of things. But when you get out here, you're back to the foundation."[63] In the landscapes of Taliesin North and Taliesin West, the same author speaks but with a different dialect in each.

5
Dynamic Weaving, Fabric of Stories:
Shaping Landscape Context

Context comes from the Latin word "contexere," to weave, an active root that be-lies its static common meaning. Context weaves patterns of events, materials, forms, and spaces. A tree, growing, is context—a weaving together—of leaf, branch, trunk, and root; decaying and transpiring, a tree shapes larger weavings of soil and atmosphere. A river, flowing, is context for water, sand, fish, and fisher-men; flooding and ebbing, it shapes bars, banks, and valley. A gate is context for passage, its form determining how things flow through it: narrow gates constrict; gates of screens block large things and permit smaller ones to pass through. Con-text is a place where processes happen, a setting of dynamic relationships, *not* a collection of static features.

All snowflakes, snowdrifts, leaves, trees, gates, and towns would be identical if active context did not shape them; varying contexts create the seemingly infinite shapes of snowflakes, as of trees, rocks, and people. Abundant water swells living tissue; drought shrivels it. In shade, leaves grow larger than in full sun; crowding and shading by other trees force a tree to grow up not out; persistent wind bends branches and trunk. Pruning shears, and deer teeth too, cut branches to stubs from which twigs grow thickly; breeding for fruit causes more profuse flowering. Earthquakes crack and shift huge blocks, condensation and evaporation "varnish" desert rocks red and black, a sculptor cuts and polishes. Working shapes a body's posture—stooped or straight. No feature of landscape is immune.

Through context, materials acquire meaning. Stone is heavy; moved over long distances—taken out of context—it signifies force, power, or wealth. The pyramids of Egypt, each man-made mountain the tomb of a single man, a pharaoh, are impressive not only for their size, but for the enormous blocks of stone, cut, moved, and stacked by thousands of laborers. So, too, are the "sarsen" or "foreign" stones of Stonehenge and Avebury on the chalky Salisbury Plain, and the Travertine marble from Italy transplanted to modern corporate offices in New York and Los Angeles. Botanical and zoological gardens replete with plants and animals from the far reaches of empires in late nineteenth-century Britain and France and ancient Mesopotamia represent the far-reaching power of those civi-lizations. Not only culture, but individuals provide context and meaning. The Tal-iesins of Wisconsin and Arizona were shaped by, and acquire meaning within, the context of Frank Lloyd Wright's life and work. The meaning and impact of the Vietnam Veterans Memorial or of the Hill of Remembrance at Stockholm's Forest Cemetery depend, in part, upon the visitor's own context.

Six trees. Saihoji. Kyoto, Japan.

Mountain, Sea, River, Forest: Japan's Deep Context

Mountains rise out of the sea and form the islands that are Japan. Eighty percent of Japan is mountainous. Where mountain and sea meet, waves pound against steeply sloping rock. A narrow band of flatland emerges between mountain and sea, broadens out into plains at the mouths of large rivers to form a platform for Japan's largest cities. On this edge between mountain and sea, most Japanese live. For centuries, heavy rains have eroded the rock of steep hillsides, washing sediments down to the sea to form the coastal plain. Volcanoes like Mount Fuji created plains of lava and ash. Mountains are the source of land; no wonder Japanese revere them.

Mountains afford a prospect over the land that, from a distance, provides an illusion of control. But the landscape is in uneasy repose, its surface composure obscuring the violence that has forged it. The mountains of Japan are ranged along lines that trace the collision of continental plates. Earthquakes rock mountains and shake low-lying flatland like jelly. Volcanoes spew fire and ash. Typhoon-driven rain cuts into mountainsides, and tidal waves engulf coastal lowlands.

The mountains of Japan are steep and flatland is precious, hence the extreme density of settlement and the high cost of level land. Cities, towns, villages, farms, and industries compete for space on the scant flatland; nearly every piece is intensively used. Houses, stores, warehouses, and rice fields abut abruptly with no transition. Everything is worked-over. Even heavily forested hillsides are often terraced beneath the trees. The flatlands are managed, rivers restrained and confined, enclosed by levees that limit their floodplain and create more habitable land. Within the levees are vegetable plots, sports fields, and practice courses for driving. Like the prospect from mountain over land, the shaping and the managing of Japan's landscape convey a false sense of control. In densely packed Japanese cities most streets are narrow with little or no sidewalk; the gates or doors of houses and stores open directly onto streets shared by pedestrians, bicycles, and cars. Yet, even in dense urban districts, tiny gardens are wedged between buildings midblock, a luxury of use that is astonishing.

My *ryokan*, a small inn with three guest rooms, is crammed into the interior of a block in a dense maze of narrow streets in old Kyoto. Yet inside, one wall of my room looks into an enclosed garden, filled with shrubs, carefully pruned. Below the threshold is a large, round stone. Water fills a basin hollowed out of the rock, beside the water a bamboo dipper. A narrow gravel path leads between the shrubs to a shrine, and a small tree forms a canopy over the whole. The morning sun on the garden throws a yellow-green light into the room. The tiny garden is a green world. Two clogs wait on a stone beyond the sliding door—an invitation.

From humble urban garden to monastery and imperial estate, Japanese landscape literature compresses and condenses features and ideas, concentrates meaning in miniature, paradox, and detail. Though the courtyard garden at Ryoanji is only twenty-five yards long and ten yards wide, on many levels it stands for Japan. Fifteen rocks in five groups, each group surrounded by an apron of green moss, rise out of a sea of raked gravel, a distillation of Japan's deep landscape structure: the juxtaposition of mountain and sea, stone and water, with the narrow band of settlement between. The garden is at once microcosm and cosmos, like so many Japanese landscapes, a landscape of paradox. The stillness of stone is felt more deeply through juxtaposition to moving, rustling trees beyond the wall. The sand is still, yet raked lines imply motion. The composition seems open, yet at least one rock is always hidden. The garden is both clear and obscure, a difficult simplicity derived from complex ideas, reduced, rather than from an easy, simplistic statement. It is difficult to experience Ryoanji with the receptive and reflective mind it deserves. Unresolved contradictions intrude, jarring the senses.

I enter Ryoanji through a huge parking lot filled with cars and tour buses. Large groups, including masses of uniformed schoolchildren, throng the path between the parking lot and the gate into the park. The mood of the crowd is of an outing or a festival. The path is lined with souvenir shops, ice cream stands, and tea shops along one side, toilets on the other. The crowd fans out in the park beyond the gate, but converges again in the building adjoining the courtyard of stones. Inside the building, I pass a souvenir shop and then, unprepared, walk out onto a veranda overlooking the stone garden. I sit and try to absorb the garden. Though a few other visitors stand or sit alone, most are here in groups; a sign says, "Please be quiet," but a loudspeaker blares intermittently. Teenagers are jostling, joking, and chattering, the surge of their hormones at odds with the repose of the garden. I leave, disappointed.

A final paradox: I experience the garden more intensely in memory than I did in actuality. The image of rocks, moss, gravel, wall, and trees beyond is etched into my mind.

In Kyoto, I learn to look and listen for water. Water is present everywhere—in rain, rice fields, and rivers, in green leaves and gardens, in ponds and stone basins, as throughout mountainous, humid Japan. Streams flow through hillside gardens and rice fields, down into the city, along the streets in shallow, stone-lined canals, and on into the broad floodplain of the Kamo River. At dinner the first night, I am startled by the sound of ducks and moving water beneath the ryokan's window. I had entered the ryokan down a long, narrow path squeezed between two buildings in the dense, old Gion neighborhood, and, from the front, there had been no hint of the canal behind the house.

The next day, I see stone-lined canals threaded throughout the city below street level, alongside or behind the buildings. Many are neglected and without public access; most buildings turn their backs on them. Many canals have unsightly utilities along their banks, one exception, "Time," is a commercial building on a busy central corner designed by the architect Tadao Ando. Its lowest floor opens onto a broad, shallow water channel below street level; steps lead down to the water. The water flows over stones that have been laid on the bottom of the channel, tracing a rhythmic pattern on the surface. The water slows as the building curves inward, broadening the channel, then accelerates as it is constricted farther on. Water sounds muffle the street sounds above. It is a small, waterside refuge. Several blocks away, the dense maze of the city is interrupted by the Kamo River. People are walking, sitting along its banks on a summer evening. The outdoor terraces of restaurants nearby open to the expansive space. Here is an opportunity to achieve at a larger scale what "Time" has accomplished on a small scale, a promise not yet fulfilled. Nineteenth-century prints by Hiroshige show that some canals in Japanese cities were once lovely promenades lined with cherry trees; so could this be.

The City of Kobe built a river park along the course of the Toga, a river which streams down off the mountainside and through the city to Osaka Bay in a broad, stone channel. At low flow, water trickles along the base of the channel, and fountains on either side shoot arcs of water across the channel at the foot of the hill, just below the Shinkansen train station. Children and adults fish and swim in the channel; in flood, water fills the channel. The entire park is within the one-hundred-year floodplain; terraces mark the height of the average annual flood.

Forest envelops the mountains of Japan and once covered the lowlands as well. The forests are structured by light; straight trunks of the tallest trees carry their leafy canopy toward the sun, smaller trees reach long slender branches up through the shade of the canopy. Each part of the forest—from fern to shrub to canopy, from air and water to soil and life—is linked to other parts and to the whole, united by light and water. Forests are finely layered, leaf upon leaf, life upon life. Like the canopy of a tree, the roof of a traditional Japanese house extends well beyond the walls; the drip line on the ground below the eaves is like the drip line at the edge of a tree's canopy. Beneath a tree one is sheltered, but still outside; in a traditional Japanese house inside and outside merge in a similar way. In Japanese gardens, I looked through branches to sky and water, through water to reflections of trees, rocks, clouds, and sky. In garden, as in forest, each detail has its place within the whole, all linked by deliberate impulse, by idea. Parts of the whole may be distant or even absent: at Shugakuin, the mountains across the valley are part of the garden; at Ryoanji, water is present in its absence. In the Japanese garden, as in the forest, are many details, many layers.

Even a Japanese tea whisk is linked to landscape. The whisk is made from a single four-inch segment of unadorned bamboo, each filament straight and light, like a single trunk of bamboo; together they form a grove. Above a short, uncarved handle, its stem splits into 172 filaments that alternately lean in and fan out, curling at their tip, held separate by black thread woven between them at the point where they lean in or fan out from the handle. The eighty-six filaments that push in toward the center meet below their tip, forming a conical mass, then curl outward. The eighty-six long, slender filaments that arc out curl inward at their tip. Similar, but not identical, each filament stands out as a separate unit, yet together they shape the outer form of the whisk. The whisk is linked to landscape, too, through the greenness of the tea the whisk blends from teapowder and water. And it recalls the garden, the traditional setting for the tea ceremony. Such dialogues are the context of individual, group, and landscape over time.

Elemental Landscapes

Tree

An old tree stands in grass at a wood's edge, its trunk and branches thick, its bark deeply ridged. Older branches are low and spreading; younger branches, on the shady side, shoot straight up: half a wolf tree. The tree encompasses a moment and a lifetime. Each twig shoots forth new growth, extends its reach toward light. Buds swell and burst, from one bud a new leaf unfurls, first white, then green, from another a flower. Each flower in short-lived glory, petals separating, wilting, falling, leaves a budding fruit, a house of seed that will yield new life. The leaves, now full, face to sun, fill out the shape of the tree briefly, then shrivel and fall, expose the frame of trunk, branches, and twigs. Its fruit drops to earth and rots—a rich bed for seed within. Sprouting seed sends shoot to sun, root to soil; branching twig each year adds height and branches at growing tips. Each brief cycle adds to the tree's history: a small scar on a twig is a leaf stem that used to be; a large scar on its trunk marks a lost branch. Ridge upon ridge of each twig, rings within rings of trunk, mark the years; the length between each ridge, the width of each ring, tell the chapter of a growing season: years of abundant water, air, and nutrients;

years of drought, pollution, starvation. The tree itself, some day, will slough its bark, drop leaf and limb, die and decompose. Or cut, it may regenerate, send up saplings from the base of its stump.

A tree connects earth and sky by the sunlight it transforms into leaves and wood, the nutrients it draws from earth, the water and air it transpires, the energy it stores as potential fire and warmth, food in sap and fruit, refuge for the animals and other organisms it harbors. A tree canopy establishes a shadier domain, cooler and moister than the surrounds, the edge of its domain the outer reach of the leaves—the drip line. A tree modifies habitat to sustain itself and nurture its seedlings: decaying leaves alter soil chemistry and create a spongy humus that holds moisture, a soft medium for root growth. Some trees, like black walnut, release chemicals toxic to other plants or, like Norway maple, suck up so much water and nutrients that other plants cannot survive. Not only a context, not only a participant in, but a shaper of context, a tree modifies and orders environments to suit its needs and ensure survival.

A former field, open to sun, encouraged the old tree's spreading; the grove, grown up since on one side, gave it the partial, wolf-tree form. The grass beneath is clipped, so seedlings sprout but do not grow to trees. The old tree grows on a farm no longer, but is now surrounded by a grid of garden rooms in a cemetery north of Copenhagen—Mariebjerg, one of G. N. Brandt's masterworks. The tree, an oak, stands in a large, square, grassy room, enclosed by a frame of lilacs, blooming. The lilacs, open at the bottom, are a transparent screen of slender woody stems. A yew hedge forms an opaque, green frame around the whole. The space between the two hedges, lilac and yew, is an ambulatory around the little clearing with its graves. I enter the garden through an opening in the hedges, cross the grassy threshold between them, step into the clearing where small gravestones are set flat, flush in grass, within a large grid, only partly filled. Tiny white daisies grow in grass, and myrtle's clear blue-violet flowers beneath the pinks and purples of the lilacs. Sweet scent of lilacs, fresh smell of grass, birdsongs of many layers fill the clearing: a raucous, repetitious note, a long, melodic song with many variations, a dove's whooo / whooo / whooo. Birds in the hedges twitter and flit like children in the leaves. The old, broad-spread oak spreads branches over the graves, as if to protect them. The lilacs lean into the clearing, reaching for sun.

Planting the framework of hedges to encompass the old oak, *just so*—off center, at the edge of the clearing, the edge of the wood—was a master stroke, so was choosing this place for the burial of children. The small garden is just as poignant in late autumn, without leaves, with vivid contrast between big trunk and branches of the oak and twisted, slender lilac branches reaching into the clearing toward the tree. Beyond the oak tree's canopy, moss fills the space between the stone squares. "Sleep well, little Jan," say the words on one.

My association of lilac hedges with playing under rosebushes as a child is personal; so are the memories they prompt of children laughing in the leaves, unseen behind hedges in Eliot's poem, of Whitman's reference to lilacs by the dooryard blooming in his elegy on Lincoln's death.[1] But I am not the only child who has played beneath bushes. Verbal literature draws so heavily from landscape literature that it is difficult *not* to make such connections. Great landscape literature stirs personal memories, carries common meanings, and derives power from both.

The transformation of humans into trees, trees with human qualities, gods in trees are common stories: Philomen and Baucis, Daphne and Apollo, threatening forests in Grimm, *sakaki* ("plant-god") trees in Shinto temple precincts. Gerda Gollwitzer has collected illustrations of trees in art and literature from many regions of the world over three thousand years.[2] Words describe, prints and paintings depict Daphne growing into a tree, her hair and fingers sprouting branches, toes rooting, as Apollo, chasing, reaches out to grab her. The many parallels between trees (or plants and animals) and humans led scientists in the early twentieth century to describe forests as communities, to see in them human values, such as harmony, cooperation, invasion, dominance. Since the 1950s the view of plants as individuals with overlapping territories, favored by many American ecologists, is seen by some as a response to a shifting emphasis in the larger culture from community to individual.[3]

On a prairie, in a desert, a tree is a sign of water; a forest is a reservoir. A tree is a pump, powered by sunlight: sun evaporates water from leaves, sucking water and nutrients from soil via paths in roots, trunk, branches, and twigs. Where water is ample, forest is the norm, and a single, freestanding tree an anomaly, for trees tend to live in groups, branches and roots interlocking, big trees shading smaller ones. Forest alters habitat far more effectively than any single tree; it creates conditions for plants whose requirements (light levels, soil chemistry) and rhythms (time of leafing and flowering) are compatible with the trees' own. Trees are enormously successful organisms; on land, if they have light and water (ice or snow won't do) their domain is limited only by the activities of animals (grazing) and humans (burning, cutting). Out on the prairie, a green line of cottonwoods, visible from many miles away, announces a river; even with leaves off, these large, coarse trunks and many fine branches and twigs form distinctive silhouettes against the sky.

River

Water moves in a swirling helix, pushing a river into a series of sweeping curves that meander across the land. Its force swings against one bank, eroding and erasing, scooping a deep pool, sweeps across the other bank more slowly, releasing sediments from suspension, forming riffles, laying down new ground. A river moves across valley floor over time, cutting and dumping, cutting and dumping, shifting its course, cutting off channel fragments to form crescent lakes or "oxbows." Islands move slowly downstream as flowing water hits one end and,

River meander. Dinan, France.

deflected, erodes the shore, carrying sand and silt down river, released to sink in the eddies at the island's tip, a point bar.[4]

A river has form through time. It laps against, flows across land, its shore an elusive line, moving up and down and across the landscape. Swelling, it rises up and rages, cutting earth, dumping mud, then, dwindling, shrinks back within its banks, leaving terraces on the plain to mark the bounds of periodic flood. No rain, and yet the river flows, in drought, drawing underground water from rains of thousands of years ago; trees, still green and living, tell the presence of water underground. Lining the Todd River in Alice Springs, Australia, on a low, broad, meandering band of grey sand are big, spreading eucalyptus trees, the only sign of water for much of the year.

Rivers gather water from sky and land, from within earth and rock, carrying, concentrating, sorting grains of sand, silt, and gravel, the debris of the discarded and the dead. Places of concentration and exchange, fertile, rich in food and water, rivers connect destinations, charting paths into remote territory, their mouths gateways between sea and hinterland. Animals and people gather along them; all principal cities in the world were once on rivers: at mouth, confluence, or limit of navigable waters. Some are synonymous with civilizations: the fertile crescent formed by the Tigris and Euphrates, the Nile, the Tiber, the Yangtze. Rivers are boundaries, and can be barriers; bridges and ferries permit crossing and mark passage, real and mythical, like the passage from life to death over the river Charon.

Riverbank. Dinan, France.

In Dinan, France, a monumental arc of poplars marks the sweeping meander of the river Rance, the arc representing the *idea* of that sweep, smoothing out
the irregularities of the riverbank. Through the abstraction and echo of the horizontal form in the vertical dimension, a line inscribed by humans on the landscape, the experience of the river is intensified. Individual trees set in a tight,
evenly spaced row along the banks of the river assert their own quirky growth,
more apparent in contrast to the regularity of their placement. Dinan's core is a
fortified medieval town set on a hill, the river valley, once its trade route, now a
park—a green chasm between the old city and its modern suburbs. The riverway
is a precinct apart from the old and the new; its form is more sinuous, its tempo
more leisurely, yet it is a landscape on the move: flowing, swinging, cutting into
rock along the outer arc, laying down a broad terrace along the inner curve. The
flat plain, its edge marked by the poplar arc, advances, accreting sediments carved
from hillsides upriver. The rough green wall of woods rising beyond the poplars
cloaks the steep slopes, cut by water flowing.

Water springs from rock and seeps from soil into pools, pools spill into
streams, and streams converge to form larger streams and rivers deep and broad.
A river flows from sources to sea. Gravity pulls a river down, from high ground to
low: water tugs at rocks and roots, rushing streams strip stony slopes, swift currents run through rocky rapids, waterfalls plunge over cliffs. It slows on flatlands,
spreads, and swings in broad, sweeping curves. Near its mouth, wide channels di-

verge within the estuary into wandering meanders—curves within curves within curves—engraved on shifting mudflats. The river dumps its load of silt among marshy grasses and watery earth, then spews out to sea the sediment it has ferried so far, staining seawater brown, tan, or red earthy tones, creating a broad sloping undersea shelf marked by shifting sea color—from light to deeper blue.

What is a river, then? Mountain spring, seep, rill, rapids, meanders, marsh, mudflats, mouth, shoals. Its bounds are the banks within which its waters ordinarily flow, the flatlands onto which its water floods, the upland ridges from which the water runs, the extent of the underground reservoir from which the river draws. A coastal river links land and sea; winds drive waves, tides tug the sea upriver.

Runners of rapids, stalkers of fish, and river watchers know what rivers signify. Mark Twain said knowledge prevented his experiencing the Mississippi poetically, but, for Norman Maclean, river knowledge is the source of poetry. He tells of "becoming the river" in watching it flow by and knowing how it was made: "As the heat mirages on the river in front of me danced with and through each other, I could feel patterns from my own life joining with them. . . . And I sensed that ahead I would meet something that would never erode so there would be a sharp turn, deep circles, a deposit, and quietness."[5]

Cloud

Out on the plains, as on the ocean, where the sky vault is vast, clouds approach, visible from great distance, pass overhead, transform: a cloud moves slowly across the sun, edge lit, sun disappears behind then reappears as the cloud moves on; shadows move across the land; a shaft of light breaks through, shines now on hill now on meadow. High clouds and low clouds: one flows quickly east, the other drifts slowly west—dizzying.

In clouds, as in rivers, water, air, and dust combine; sky, river, sea, mountain, and valley are contexts for cloud. Cloud color, shape, and structure reveal temperatures, speeds, directions of flowing air, and proportions of water and dust: heaped clouds and layered clouds; tall and short; high, feathery filaments—frozen ice particles; amorphous grey, white, black. Clouds describe the surface over which air flows—the quality of terrain: they hover over islands, roll like waves over mountain ridges, flow down valleys and lie in gentle dips and hollows. Morning mist rises over rivers, fog over seas. Sea of air, sea of water are one sea.

The artist James Turrell works with light and sky to design "sky spaces"—apertures in ceilings and walls, the bowl of a volcano crater—to frame a view of the sky, offering an experience of the sky alone. An artist cannot shape the sky, but Turrell shapes perception to "set up a situation to which I take you and let you see. It becomes your experience. . . . It's not taking from nature as much as placing you in contact with it."[6] Turrell's sky spaces recreate the experience of lying in an open meadow where the sky fills the view. One is absorbed as clouds scud past, lending depth, color shifting gradually, at dusk when blue becomes darker and deeper extending into violet, then pierced by the first star, all in a slow but steady succession toward black of night and emerging starlight. Turrell installed a series of works in the home of an Italian patron, where, through one small window framing a view of the sky, he was led to reflect on the physical laws that govern the universe, that connect his body and world to other worlds.[7] In city and forest, where buildings and trees crowd the horizon, such an experience of sky is rare except from a rooftop or in a meadow, or through a skylight. Turrell transformed the skylight into art that prompts contemplation of time, change, and the rhythmic dialogue between humans and nature.

Boundary between cloud and sky may seem distinct from a distance, but becomes wispy as one approaches; within the cloud all is edge, all wisp. The edge of a cloud is infinitely long—archetypal, fractal form. Walk up a mountainside into cloud, downhill into valley fog, sail into sea fog, and the boundary blurs into a zone, not an edge. Within a cloud, the world seems ethereal, elusive, without substance. No wonder the Hopi believe the clouds are the domain of the dead. A cloud cannot be touched, but it can be felt, cool and moist. In the Bible, clouds portend and conceal, they are the unseen hand of God, or God's apparition: "And the LORD said unto Moses, Lo, I come unto thee in a thick cloud."[8]

Mountain

Moses said he spoke with God on the mountain and saw the Promised Land beyond the river Jordan. Mountains, in many cultures, are where gods and humans meet, the axis mundi where earth rises to meet sky, where the human is dwarfed into insignificance, where otherworldly light seems to glow, haloes around backlit peaks, ridges silhouetted from behind by brilliant light.[9] At Roden Crater, an extinct volcano near Flagstaff, Arizona, Turrell is shaping a series of earthbound spaces to engage skylight from sun, moon, and stars. One among hundreds in a field of volcanoes, the red and black cone rises up out of the Painted Desert. Turrell chose it for the shape of its interior bowl, a curvilinear horizon framing the sky, inducing a sense of celestial vaulting, of the sky as dome. He is reshaping the bowl to intensify perception of sky's color and vaulting, is building chambers and tunnels within the mountain to reveal specific celestial phenomena and varied aspects of light in space. Roden Crater is both sacred space and astronomical observatory.[10]

Mountains emerge out of ancient, ongoing violence and inexorable, eternal erosion. The volcano field near Flagstaff is the scene of ancient explosions that threw up magma—or molten minerals—from inside the earth, leaving cones of red, purple, and brownish-black. Around Sunset Crater, the last to erupt, lava fields of spiky, blasted, black cinders are still barren more than nine hundred years later. The seismic shudders and jolts of California are still thrusting up mountains; the San Fernando earthquake of 1971 lifted the San Gabriel Mountains of Los Angeles six feet.[11] Uluru emerged as the rock around it in the center of Australia eroded away. The rounded, tree-cloaked slopes of the Smoky Mountains in

North Carolina and Tennessee are the remains of higher peaks whose eroded sediments form the Eastern Coastal Plain and Atlantic Shelf.

Mountains are context: colder at peak and on north flank, warmer at base, on south and west, more moist to north and east, dry to south and west. To go up a mountain, or from south slope to north, is to seem to travel hundreds, even thousands, of miles. In temperate climates, the tallest peaks may have arctic conditions at their summit where summer comes late and fall early, and plants of the tundra grow in alpine meadows. Drive down the Blue Ridge Parkway through North Carolina to the Smoky Mountains in late May, in and out of spring, as the road rises and falls, as it follows northern, then southern, slope, runs along a ridge, dips into a valley. The mountains' lowest slopes are deep green, the color lightens with height to pale lime just below the black-green coniferous forest. Deep green fingers follow mountain valleys up and fade into lime, a sign the valleys are warmer. In the lowlands, trees are fully leafed in their dark summer color; as one rises, their color becomes brighter, then paler, finally, there are only tightly furled buds and bare branches. White flowers of dogwood and pale-pink azaleas of mid-mountain spring furl back into winter. Topping a ridge, plunging down the mountainside, is to fall into summer.

The long road up from Denver over the Rockies through Kenosha Pass, gateway into South Park, is squeezed between mountain walls of overwhelming mass and scale; the driver feels gravity in rockslides along the road, in their angle of repose. Solid, crumbling, at rest, in motion, enduring, and changing. Plants on hot, dry southern and western slopes are sparse, with rocky soil exposed as reds, greys, browns. Dark green spruce stand, needles stiff, on moister, cooler northern slopes, and yellow aspens flicker; then, on a rise, at ten thousand feet, South Park stretches out, its vast meadow below rimmed by distant mountain peaks, jagged, snow-covered above timberline. Landforms and plants within the valley-park look soft, but feel hard and prickly. Soil is thin, plants sparse; rocky fragments and plants are sharp, even the grasses feel like pins. Aspens' yellow lines and patches trace disturbance: fire, landslides, mining. As people stop to see the view their voices carry, mingle with aspens' rustle, insects' clatter-buzz, wind across ears a noise like blowing in a seashell, sound of trucks in low gear coming up hill, whoosh of cars coasting downhill into the park, air horn of a truck bearing down on a car, its weight carrying it downhill.

The Rocky Mountains split the continent; the peaks along the western boundary of South Park are part of the Great Continental Divide. Like all mountains, they shed and store water, rain falling on their back slopes drains west to the Colorado River and the Pacific Ocean, its waters to be drunk in Utah, Arizona, Los Angeles; rain on the front slopes flows to the Mississippi via the Platte. The Rockies' thawing snowpack feeds streams and rivers of the drylands on either side. So, too, the Sierra Nevada in Spain divide Granada from the Mediterranean coast, a relationship of mountains, earth, and rivers that the gardens of the Alhambra pre-

Mountain, river, stage. Lovejoy Fountain. Portland, Oregon. (Maude Dorr, Courtesy Office of Lawrence Halprin)

sent in miniature; they are abstractions of a mountain stream. Water gushes from fountains in walls, spouts in thin streams from fountains in floors, flows softly from the basin in the Patio de la Reja, streams down from the hillside gardens to city and river below. Distant snow-covered peaks are the fountains' source.

Studies of water movement around rocks, of rocky slopes, with their planes, fracture lines, ledges, and talus, fill many pages of Lawrence Halprin's notebooks. In drawings, he records his observations of mountain streams in the Sierra Nevadas, and traces his transfer of understanding to the design for Lovejoy and Ira's Fountains in Portland, Oregon. At Ira's Fountain across from the Portland Auditorium, the progression from springs, to tributaries, to downstream water-falls is telescoped into the space of a city block. The sheer volume and force of the falls and the mystery injected by the many water sources, some half-hidden, com-bined with the steep drop to the base of the fountain and the dense screen of pines contribute to an experience of water that echoes its importance as a source of elec-tric power in this region of mountains and rushing rivers.

At the base of the fountain, waterfalls roar: water funneled down a shoot and over the edge falls free; water streams down the face of tall, slanted slabs; a thin stream, caught by a notch in lip's edge, arcs out—a line of light. Above the falls, water spouts from several sources, disappears, reemerges, clashes, mingles, flows over the edge. Water color and movement change: reddish brown over cobbles, dark green in deep places, white to light green in foaming waves and spray. Here

People as context: basketball moves. East Oakland, California. (Lewis Watts)

and there, running over rough conglomerate, water catches on protruding stones, tracing many white foamy lines, each stone a point of origin. The ground at the upper level slopes from side to side, top to bottom, tilts, and seems to shift. The expansion joints in the concrete are irregular, like joints in rock. Water's sound is lighter here, higher pitched.

Human

"Don't forget, the biggest attraction isn't here yet," said Walt Disney, the day before Disneyland opened in 1955. "What's that?" "People. You fill this place with people, and you'll really have a show."[12] No matter what one may think of Disney's theme parks, he had a point.

At Ira's Fountain, the landscape is truly theater, a stage, scene of action, not a static scene. Even without people, the fountain has drama in patterns of water and surface, light and ripples play off surfaces. Water movement invites action, the flat slabs at the base ask to be occupied. The plaza accommodates many players and watchers within its nooks and crannies. Within two hours one Saturday morning in early May, a limousine pulls up and a couple in wedding dress emerge to pose beneath the fountain for a photographer who balances his tripod on a sloping slab, a daring mountain biker rides up and down the steps and across the slabs below the falls, three women in wet suits pose in a kayak under the falls for a host of photographers, a man in a red-and-black-checked flannel shirt, jeans, and boots lies on his back, his bare belly rising to the sun, two children drop leaves in a stream, then chase to watch them flow under, over, around, and through. In Lawrence Halprin's works, people—walking, talking, sitting, dancing, playing— are part of the landscape; his designs require people to complete them. People animate his places, their movements an improvised dance within a choreographed framework. As Halprin said of the Portland fountain, "Though the environment itself is visually exciting it was conceived as a place for involvement. . . . The score for people's activities remains open and nonfixed. The composition was unfulfilled until it was occupied."[13]

People-watching is a popular pastime in virtually all cultures. Much of the attraction of tourism is the pleasure of watching the novelty and also the recognition of other people, for all cultures share common landscape genres—thoroughfares, homes, sacred landscapes—that also reveal each culture's distinctiveness. As actors on a stage (or gone from it, leaving it empty), people provide context. Where human settlement is dense, one might never see a landscape without a human figure, and there is scarcely any place on earth without mark of human occupation. The Scottish Highlands are a ghostly, emptied landscape in glen after glen, but stone walls and sheep pens on hillsides and a path are signs of habitation. Many are drawn to wilderness like this where they may walk for days and meet no other human; many are repulsed by other wildernesses recently abandoned in inner cities.

Statues of human figures populate some landscapes: mythical, heroic, and evocative characters like Hercules at Vaux, the "British Worthies" at Stowe, generals on horseback, the Little Mermaid on a rock in Copenhagen Harbor. Partially buried human forms evoke a sense of the horrific, like the open, toothy mouth of the giant at Bomarzzo, in Italy, through which one enters a cavelike room. A statue of three soldiers, looking like lost boys, stands near an entrance to the Vietnam Veterans Memorial in Washington, D.C. When the memorial was first proposed without human figures some people objected; the soldiers' statue by Hart was added a few years later. Hart believed that without the human figure Maya Lin's design was elitist and that his was populist, "for the figure is a necessary element if public art is . . . to be truly public."[14]

But is the unpeopled wall really unpeopled? And does it not touch fears? "It is what people do in the space and the things they leave there that moves me as a foreigner without any connection to the culture or war," said one of my students after visiting the Vietnam Veterans Memorial. The statue of the soldiers makes a statement; the wall invites reflection and initiates a dialogue. The intimacy of the personal objects at the base of the wall recalls mementos left at the feet of statues of saints in pilgrimage churches. The narrow path keeps people in close file, alongside the wall of engraved names, a ritual of respectful remembrance. The Lincoln and Washington monuments, visible at either end of the path's axis, are imposing and superhuman; the wall is more human in scale, more personal: the people honored here are connected to Lincoln and Washington by line of sight, and much more.

The human body is the basis for landscape's measurement, both relative in scale (micro, human, superhuman) and precise (foot, yard, mile). A day's journey on foot or horseback once measured land area. The Japanese land measurement was once the *tsubo*, the area of rice field required to feed a family for a year. Body's form embodies stories about the evolution of the species and the life history and habits of the individual, about place and culture. The human body and mind are both natural phenomena and cultural artifacts. Adornment tells stories of societies; people decorate their bodies with paint, precious metals, feathers, shells, bones, and fancy dress to advertise their social identity and status, attract mates, celebrate rites of passage and religious ritual. The feet of Chinese women were once bound to make them tiny. Current fashion in the West favors the skinny, yet the diets many savor are rich in fat. Human bodies are bound within the natural world, exchange with air, water, animals, plants in every breath, swallow, and bite.

Human evolution, Loren Eiseley said, is an "immense journey" from sea shallows to space beyond earth. Bodies and minds bear the marks of the contexts that shaped and shape them: sea and savanna, city and cyberspace. Of the body's many substances the primary is water: "The river is within us, the sea is all about us."[15] Eiseley describes human bodies as "little detached ponds," "sacks of sea water."[16] And the "most enormous extension of vision of which life is capable: the projection of itself into other lives. This is the lonely, magnificent power of humanity. It is, far more than any spatial adventure, the supreme epitome of the reaching out."[17]

Bird

"To you they are birds, to me they are voices in the forest," a Kaluli man told anthropologist Steven Feld.[18] In the Papua New Guinea rain forest, where the Kaluli make their home, are more than 150 different birds. Birds are ancestors named by their sounds. Kaluli sing with birds, insects, and running water; for them composing a melody is like "having a waterfall in your head," songs come from birds, and have trunks and branches.[19] Kaluli do not sing in unison, but, like birds, in response to one another. In ceremonies, dancers turn into birds. Kaluli aesthetics evolved within rain forest ecology; the concept of "lift-up-over-sounding" is important in Kaluli song, like layered birdsong, song echoes the layered forest. As Feld reminds us, many composers of music, from composers of the blues to Olivier Messiaen, have drawn similar inspiration from birds.[20] Stories of transformation — from human to bird to human — are common also among North American Indians, as are associations of specific birds with human qualities: eagles with power, hawks with aggression, ravens with trickery. Birds share many processes with humans: they speak, mate, nest, have territory, navigate, hunt, flock.

My closest experience of birds as voices in the forest occurred one early spring morning on a field trip taken to look for migrating birds; a class of twenty ten-year-olds and a half-dozen adults walked through Carpenter's Woods in Philadelphia, a place well known to birdwatchers. After some time, we found a place in the woods to sit and hold an informal Quaker meeting, since the children had missed the weekly meeting for worship back at school. For half an hour, I listened to layered birdsong shape an audible space that matched the layers of the forest, from sources in trees high above and down beneath bushes. Their songs were many and diverse: cheeps and chirps, tweets and twitters, buzzes and melodic phrases. Children, adults spoke, intermittently, between long pauses, as they were moved to, in varied voices, like the birds.

Rachel Carson opened *Silent Spring* with a chilling description of a spring when no birds sang: "There was a strange stillness. It was a spring without voices."[21] The passage from parking lot to the central plaza at the Salk Institute in La Jolla, designed by Louis Kahn, is a built analogue of Carson's fable. I approached as a pilgrim, prepared for epiphany by color photographs of the place, and found disappointment. I entered buildings and plaza through a stand of trees where birds were singing, across a carpet of grass and wildflowers between grove and gate, and stepped into a stark, glaring plaza of white stone.[22] Directly ahead, water ran into a long channel incised in the white stone, pointing to sea and horizon. Water was almost invisible and inaudible, unlike the Alhambra, where it had been omnipresent. I stayed several hours, and during that time, a few researchers in white lab coats hurried across the plaza from one building to another; two talked for a while, huddled under the building's overhang at plaza's edge. My only company on the plaza was an architecture student, photographing and taking notes. How devoid of life the plaza was, I realized most fully when I walked back through the gate into the grove full of birdsong. The oasis, the refuge, is not within the walls; it is outside, among the trees.

Unlike the Islamic precedents it draws from as models, Kahn's design is not an oasis at all, but, at the heart of the institute, a silent abstraction, with its gesture to the horizon, the ocean. The sterile white plaza resembles an ideal of a laboratory; yet when I peeked in the windows of the working laboratories inside, I saw a fertile clutter. Ideas arise out of obscurity and jumble, and only afterward seem crystal clear. The plaza may represent the product of scientific research; it does not reflect the process of discovery. Nobel laureates tell stories of how the context of a community, conversations, and even chance remarks were key in developing their ideas. But here was a rigid core devoid of life, sound, and movement in an institute devoted to medical research—to life. Later, I learned that Halprin was to have designed the plaza, but that he and Kahn had disagreed fundamentally over what its nature should be. Halprin felt it should have places to sit, meet, and meditate, be full of water's sound, birds' song and flutter. That would have made less of a visual impact perhaps, been less photogenic, but more delightful and fruitful, more in tune with the meaning and function of the place.

Where Mountains Meet Plains: Denver

Great, upright, red rocks, thrust from the earth, rising hundreds of feet, strike the boundary between mountain and plain along the Front Range of the Rockies. The red slabs are the ruined remnants of ancient mountain peaks, of rock layers that once arched high over the Rockies. My eye follows the angle of their thrust and completes that arc, transported millions of years into the past to an understanding of the powerful processes of mountain-building and erosion. Nestled up against these foothills, Denver rests on sediments many hundreds of feet deep, their fine grains eroded from slopes of ancient mountains once high above the Rockies. Beyond the foothills are suburbs, and beyond the suburbs, further east on the Plains, city, farm fields, and rangeland.

I find more magic in the fractured, tilted zone at the mountains' base than in the younger peaks of these mountains. Rocks rise high out of the ground, huge and dramatic; elsewhere, only a small surface is exposed, emerging from the grass. I walk over these submerged giants, imagine them extending downward to their foundation, waiting for erosion to wear away soil and plants, to expose them. The rock is soft, brittle, broken, the surface of the large strata smooth and rounded. Grasses grow in depressions of the rock faces, lichens, bright yellow-green and grey-green, climb the tilted flanks of red, rose, pink, and mauve rock; black streaks where water travels. Green cedars, rooted in the rock-strewn ground, are tough, their foliage coarse. Sun shines on smooth rocks, casts smooth, dark shadows; junipers cast many tiny, jagged shadows. Dialogues in color and form. In the open, on the foothills' flank, I look up to see thin, transparent clouds, ethereal against red rocks and blue sky, hovering overhead—mountain wave clouds flowing gently eastward. The wind, gusty and fierce coming off the mountains, almost blows me over the edge. It calms for a few seconds or minutes, then more gusts kick up red dust-devils. Whirlwinds whack my face with grit.

A path of red sand, ground from rocks, runs between two cedars, a gate, a sense of passage from one domain to another. I think how different this rocky terrain is from the domain across the road below with its soft rounded hills eroded by sharp gullies, windblown silt of the Plains. Three deer cross the slope ahead; I pick my way off the path to follow their track. The sound of water trickles down the swale, across the path.

Red Rocks Amphitheater is set up among these foothills west of Denver, facing east, its flat stage dwarfed by the red slabs that frame it and the panoramic view across the city and the Great Plains. The dialogues of material, form, and territory are those of the surrounding foothills. Concrete steps mixed with red sand give a

Identity of place: mountains, plains, Denver. Red Rocks Park.

rosy tint; in some places, red sandstone slabs. The cedars of the slopes are planted in rows in large stepped terraces; they line the steps down each side of the theater. The path from the lower parking lot leads around huge, tilted rocks, under ledges, down to the base of the amphitheater—a beautiful passage. Design in such a setting should be just this recessive, not calling attention to itself; it takes a self-confident designer to be so understated. The amphitheater was built in 1941; more recent additions are less successful; the new canopy is an eyesore, so are new steps of grey, untinted concrete. Gravel has been added to the parking lot, also grey; it is not of the place, not red. Traces of the earlier, red gravel are visible beneath the grey. All are jarring, misguided "improvements." The original designer, Burnham Hoyt, was more sure, more deferential.

Sitting, looking out over Denver and the Plains, I feel the hill at my back and the huge sweep of rocks to each side of the amphitheater, a sense of refuge. The sun is hot on my arm; its light catches the top of the foothills' parallel ridges. Beyond the hogback, a sharp, vertical ridge, the soft, eroded hills are clad with brown-green; beyond are the houses on the plain and the trees of the settlements where once was only grass. From the amphitheater is a view of the city and a prospect for reflecting upon the deep structure of the region and the place of humans within it.

A few days later, I sit on one mile of sediments in the Central Plains Experiment Station in Munn, Colorado, about eighty miles northeast of Red Rocks

Contextual shaping: Red Rocks Amphitheater.

Amphitheater listening to stories of the place told by a University of Wyoming professor of range management clad in a shiny, blue nylon shirt, jeans, cowboy boots, and a tooled belt. During the worst storms of the Dust Bowl years, he is saying, soil from Colorado blew all the way to the Atlantic Ocean, and folks in eastern cities choked on it; it brought home to them what was going on in the Midwest. The semiarid climate of the High Plains supports a short-grass prairie; without irrigation, no trees grow except in floodplains and depressions. Eleven inches of rain per year—almost desert; cactus grow here: small, rounded barrel cactus and tiny prickly pear.

The grassland looks soft, but crunches underfoot; there is a crust on the soil. The prickly cacti are low, unobtrusive, an unwary walker may get a spine through the boot. Out here on the experimental range are no trees, even in the swales: "It is next to impossible," another professor is saying, "to generate runoff in this landscape, it is absorbed so rapidly into the soil." I discover how quickly air and wind parch skin, mouth, and nose. We are a group of fifty landscape ecologists and landscape architects out on the High Plains for an entire afternoon, and no one has thought to bring drinks.

The next day, I drive east out onto the Plains again, off the main road into the grassland, grazed and ungrazed. I drive for miles without seeing a single tree. My eyes adjust to the compressed spectrum of color and detail, to the subtle shifts in color across broad patches of landscape, a mosaic of pale greys, yellows, and browns of many fine-grained details—silver-grey dead leaves, pale green lichen, golden composites, straw-colored grasses, brown earth, fence posts weathered brown. The terrain is hilly, sometimes quite steep. Occasional gullies cut across the landscape, their edges sharp, steeply cut like a long rip torn in the land. The soil is soft silt, windblown—loess—piled up in places into rounded dunes. Coming down into a gully beside an eroded hill, I am shocked to see several trees, dark, bold, and coarse.

Roads reveal the landscape: bending around rock and curving with the slope of the foothills, straight and right-angled on the Plains, where the gridded system is important for wayfinding. At regular and reassuring intervals I know I will find another coordinate—even if the road is closed to passage, it means there are some people around somewhere, though it is hard to know what is public road and what is not. At one intersection (all gravel roads), a sign says, RD something. The road is on the map, but a cattle grate and a notice attached to a fence post say, PRIVATE PROPERTY—NO TRESPASSING. Off the main roads, I am turned back by such signs again and again.

Today, the weather is sunny with high clouds, cool and windy, the wind blowing off the mountains, sagebrush rolling wild, plastered against the mountain side of fences. The plains are about the sky—sun, clouds, wind. Wind blows across my ears and whisks clouds across the sky, their shadows racing across the landscape. What is golden one minute becomes charcoal grey or dull brown the next. There is only the sound of wind, and that is constant; wind pushes at me, slams the car door.

The Plains are open: the landscape is big, the sky vault vast, the scale of a single person (or even a group) dwarfed. Nothing is vertical except what people have introduced: a windmill, cruciform telephone/electric poles, a series of fence posts. I can see for miles across the rolling plains with no point of orientation. Up in the foothills the height, openness, and prospect were reassuring; I knew where I was, could see where I had come from and where I was going. There were refuges—behind rocks or junipers, in the protected overhang of a huge tilted stone. There were clear choices for routes: up, down, along the slope, down into a valley. Down on the Plains, I have no reason to chose one direction over another, except to avoid the low sun of late afternoon. Out here I feel compelled to head toward a ridge for a prospect.

Each farmhouse is planted round with trees, the huge older trees diminishing the houses, often bungalows no more than one floor high; trees are planted as close as ten feet from the house, straight vertical trunks in sharp contrast to the broad horizontal sweep, marking each a special place. The farmhouses stand against the sky, isolated, except for these trees. I understand why the settlers planted trees so close together and near the house, a detail one can latch onto. I drive back toward the city and see trees again; they tame the landscape, give to the openness a locus.

Denver and other cities along the Front Range Corridor—Fort Collins, Boulder, Colorado Springs—straddle the zone between Rocky Mountains and

Deep context: sky, wind, open, dry. High Plains. Colorado.

Great Plains. Denver, a city of trees, is an oasis of irrigated green within the arid landscape, a refuge from this wide open land. It is buffered from the extremes of mountains and Plains by the presence of both: from mountains' steep, rocky ravines by Plain's soft slopes; from Plain's drought by snowpack and mountain streams. To James Michener the South Platte River that flows through Denver is "a sad, bewildered nothing of a river. . . . It's a sand bottom, a wandering afterthought, a useless irritation, a frustration, and when you've said all that, it suddenly rises up, spreads out to a mile wide, engulfs your crops and lays waste your farms."[23] A wide river of shallow, braided channels, it is clogged with sediments carried down from the mountains. It flows through willow thickets and cottonwood stands across the high dry plains to the Missouri and on down to the Mississippi and Gulf of Mexico. Long dry periods are punctuated by cloudbursts that swell streams and rivers and, especially when augmented by springtime snow melt from the mountains, swiftly convert dry creek and river beds to wide, raging torrents. These rhythms are part of the deep context of this place; they become part of each life that dwells here.

Rhythms of high peak flows separated by long periods of extremely low flow are a challenge for the designers of storm sewer systems. Denver's sewers were once open gulches; many were converted to underground pipes, but the enormous size required to accommodate peak storm flow made conversion often im-

Response to deep context: house in grove. High Plains. Colorado.

practical. Over the past twenty-five years, therefore, Denver has built a new storm drainage system of parks and parkways. The channels through which the stormwater flows are the paths through which people walk, ride, or kayak, the form congruent with the deep context of the region. The channels and the water flowing make this context and its rhythms legible within the city even as they link outlying farmland, suburbs, and downtown. It is a storm sewer/open space system that is not only functional and sustainable, but also beautiful and meaningful. Skyline Plaza, part of a downtown redevelopment project, steps down into a sunken garden that pools water after heavy rains; it prevents flooding downstream by letting the water seep gradually into the sewer. Harvard Gulch, a storm drainage channel and linear park, has replaced the narrow, dirt gulch that once flooded adjacent houses. The original plan called for an underground storm sewer; instead, the water now flows through a park whose sinuous landforms echo the movement of water, even when it is only a small trickle. Where the level of the channel drops, a weir breaks the water's erosive force. At high water the weir is exciting, but even at low flow, its sculptural form recalls the power of water at high flow. Where the South Platte River moves through downtown, at the confluence with Cherry Creek, there is a park and a plaza where people come to watch the kayak races and sit by the river. The plaza has another purpose, designed to absorb and deflect floodwaters, its broad terraces alternately submerged or exposed. At high water, lower terraces are ghosts whose form, under water, makes a trace on the surface.

The Enduring and the Ephemeral

Weather is the ephemeral expression of wind, rain, heat, and cold from minute to minute, day to day, season to season. Climate is the pattern of long-term variations; deserts, prairies, and forests express its enduring patterns. At continental and global scales, seasonal patterns of rain and drought, heat and cold, produce corresponding associations of plants: deserts, prairies, dry woodlands, temperate forests, coniferous forests, and tundra. Prairie grasslands, like the American Plains, grow in regions with moderate rainfall—more rain than in desert regions, less than in forested ones, all temperate grasslands have similar characteristics, so do deserts and forests.

Some contexts are more enduring than others. Still, *enduring* and *ephemeral* are relative terms: to human eyes, mountains seem unchanging—an illusion fostered by the perspective of human perception and life span; the sediments washed off eroding mountains onto the Great Plains are a mile deep east of Denver.

Cultural contexts may also be enduring: Thomas Jefferson is part of the landscape context of Charlottesville, Virginia, and of the American Midwest. The influence of Roman language, law, and literature on landscape extends way beyond the Mediterranean region and the territory Romans once occupied. The pastoral landscape, celebrated at least as early as in Roman literature, has been working itself out over millennia, further strengthened by the biblical tradition of pastoralism: "He maketh me to lie down in green pastures; he leadeth me beside the still waters."[24] It becomes deep, not permanent, not universally cross-cultural, but enduring, persistent, over time and place in Western cultures despite great differences of climate and terrain. Rolling lawns with groves of trees—in estates and suburban tracts, office parks and cemeteries—are evidence of the pastoral landscape's deep cultural context.

Even hunter-gatherers, through fire, change species composition and the pattern of plant communities. How closely the form of the visible, surficial, human-made landscape relates to the enduring context of geology and climate depends mostly on the extent and intensity of human activity and its congruence with deeper context. To many, farmland is a natural landscape, but all agricultural methods impose a cultural order.[25] To many, even most, cities are unnatural, but a more enduring natural environment is there, camouflaged by the surface of buildings, roads, sewers, and parks.

The grid, which in the nineteenth century was laid across the landscape of the American Midwest and West, an idea at first, then a real grid of fences and roads, a framework to domesticate the western wilderness is superficial, not deep, context. From the humid East to the drier West, the grid holds within it many settlement forms, all visible on a clear day if one travels by air, for example, from

Two contexts: beach ridges across the midwestern grid. North Dakota. (Alex S. MacLean/Land-slides)

Chicago to Denver: on the Nebraska prairie, wheat fields conceal older fields and small streams that erosion will deepen into gullies; in Colorado, pivot irrigation displays a pattern that seems bold and distinct. But, as with patches and corridors of forest, meadow, and fields of a single crop, both wheat fields and pivot irrigation reflect a particular culture more than deep context, the landscape surface a cultural artifact, many of its features ephemeral.

The hedgerow and small field landscape many English love was originally a response of ancient farmers to deep context. Size and shape of prehistoric fields varied, with larger, rectangular fields on gentle slopes and small, irregularly shaped fields on steeper, rougher terrain.[26] But changes to field boundaries over the centuries responded to shifts in ownership patterns, market demands, rural occupations. The landscape of today was created through a succession of enclosures to create pasture for sheep, some as early as the fourteenth century, some from the enclosure acts of the eighteenth and nineteenth centuries.[27] A shift from sheep to food crops and the introduction of large agricultural machinery are now transforming this landscape once again, from the patchwork of small enclosed pasture to large open areas. Still, surface structure is often ephemeral, disappearing after successive changes, while traces of an earlier cultural landscape and of a deeper structure remain. A stile over a fence and a path through a field mark footpaths that predate the enclosure acts and to which the public still retains the right of passage. Left unplowed, unmowed, or ungrazed, the landscape will be reclaimed by forest, but, on the downs of southern England, farming practices over millennia have so altered the soil's structure that it will no longer support forest. Deep context is enduring, its rate of change prolonged, but even deep context can be altered over time.

Sea is the deep context of the Netherlands, literally lowlands. Dialogues between seawater and land, flood tides and dikes, boats, travel, and trade have structured culture and settlements over hundreds of years. The polder landscape of canals and fields reclaimed from sea—from long and thin to broad and vast—were such dialogues, their forms shaped by changes in technology and new sources of power, from hands to windmill to bulldozer. Polders are part of the enduring context of the Netherlands, sustained through many years of labor, but now many are being flooded and returned to sea, reminders that agriculture may be deep, but not eternal. The context behind this profound change is not just the nation, but the European Community. And the sea itself. Some polderlands, like the Danish heath, are seen as marginal agricultural land in the context of Europe as a whole.

The deep context of a city is invisible to most, buried under layers of human constructions; and yet it exerts a powerful influence upon the urban landscape. Skyscrapers in Manhattan, built where bedrock is within reach of foundations, hide the rock, but the skyline reveals it. Boston's Lower Beacon Hill was tidal estuary until filled in the nineteenth century, with houses built on foundations of submerged wooden pilings, sound as long as they were under water. Modern residents forgot what Bostonians once knew: if groundwater drops below the pilings' tops, they rot and no longer support the buildings. When surface structure obscures or opposes deep context, only energy, materials, and information can sustain it.

Landscapes like the Alhambra in Granada mark fleeting human triumphs, but they also celebrate what endures: the mountains, rivers, and the warm, dry climate of Andalusia; the thousand-year presence of the Moors, their gardens, irrigation systems, and knowledge. The great gardens of Le Nôtre extol the deep context of the Île-de-France, physiographic and political, still a region of concentrated power to which resources of the country flow. Eighteenth-century English landscape gardens, like Stourhead, reveal, in contrast, not simply the rolling physiography and lush climate, but the power of gentry compared to royalty. Mariebjerg and Nærum present enduring aspects of Danish nature and culture, and Ryoanji represents deep contexts of Japan.

In the history of a place the deep contexts are constants that successive human generations must readdress. Traditions, values, and policies may change, but deep context remains key to the history and future of a place—why it was settled, its initial location, its transportation routes, its economic development, and the health and safety of its residents.

Anomalies: Things Out of Context

Landscape features may coexist, juxtaposed, and yet be unrelated, anomalies of material or form out of context, shaped by a different context from the one that predominates. Glacial erratics—anomalous boulders—were shaped by local conditions elsewhere, thousands of years ago, when glaciers flowed across the land, scraped chunks of rock, and carried them many miles to be left behind when the ice retreated. Stone walls and old building foundations engulfed by woods in New England are clues to changes in human use of land, just as hedgerows in England are artifacts of agricultural landscapes that no longer serve the original purposes. Like the wolf tree in a woodland of younger trees, so a mansion surrounded by tiny urban row houses may tell a story of abandonment and recolonization. Anomalies reveal variations in context otherwise hidden, disguised, unrecognized, or forgotten. On prairies, in deserts, trees in swales signal water underneath. Wooded thickets on vacant lots in American cities, on abandoned farm fields, and bombed ruins in Berlin are reminders that the larger context there is forest, and absence of forest an anomaly of culture.

A channel's width, depth, and shape describe the amount of water that normally flows and the height of regular and occasional floods. The signs are there even when no water flows: wadis, wide shallow dry boulder-strewn strips, are desert streambeds; seldom, but repeatedly, water rages down their broad reach. A wadi, its bed dry, is still a river, as anyone knows who has ever seen it full or dug into its gravelly channel to find water. In Phoenix, the huge, dry floodplain of the Salt River is not a wadi; its waters are diverted upstream by the Granite Reef Dam into the Northern and Southern Canals and dispersed into hundreds of miles of smaller irrigation canals and ditches.

"Sometimes I went south to visit our German neighbors and to admire their catalpa grove," says the narrator of Willa Cather's *My Ántonia*, "or to see the big elm tree that grew up out of a deep crack in the earth and had a hawk's nest in its branches. Trees were so rare in that country, and they had to make such a hard fight to grow, that we used to feel anxious about them, and visit them as if they were persons. It must have been the scarcity of detail in that tawny landscape that made detail seem so precious."[28] An anomaly is often a landmark; it may become sacred, like Australia's Uluru. Different cultures occupying the same landscape at different times often embrace the same significant landscape features: high points and churches in England, sacred springs and Christian shrines in Ireland, aboriginal sites (Uluru) and Australian tourist destinations (Ayre's Rock). Anomalies sharpen the perception of a larger context that might otherwise be taken for granted: a clearing in the forest, a grove on the prairie. Sometimes, even, anomalies or rarities are valued more highly than the common landscape. National parks in the United States and Great Britain often preserve the most extraordinary landscapes, remote from human settlement, anomalies of natural phenomena.

The geographer George Seddon calls this the crown jewel approach, in contrast to Denmark's, of preserving the most typical—whole everyday landscapes where many people live.[29] But then, Denmark is a relatively homogenous landscape; it has no Grand Canyon or Peak District. Surely it is important to preserve both rare and common landscapes.

An anomaly confounds expectation, a puzzle that prompts a story to explain it: a dry wadi or oasis in the desert, an island in the sea, a mountain on a plain, seashells on a mountaintop, poppies in a field of rape. How to explain anomalous patterns is at the heart of both myth and science. Erwin Panofsky, reflecting on the connections between Roman temples and medieval market crosses in English gardens, on the one hand, and Palladian temple front and romantic "Silver Lady" on the Rolls-Royce radiator, on the other, concludes that these apparently incongruous juxtapositions are clues to the character of English culture, the opposing forces of rationality and intuition, classicism and romanticism.[30]

As I walked through the woods in the Quabbin reservation of central Massachusetts some years ago, I stumbled across old stone walls and foundations half-buried in leaves and undergrowth and large trees growing out of old cellar holes. A paved road ran through the woods for several miles, then headed for the lake, disappearing beneath its waters. The road once led to seven towns in the flooded valley now occupied by Quabbin Reservoir, towns drowned to provide water for the city of Boston. If you did not know the story, you would be tempted, as I was, to find out. Or to speculate.

Identity: The Power of Place

A place is particular, a tapestry of woven contexts: enduring and ephemeral, local and global, related and unrelated, now and then, past and future. Landscape context is a fabric whose strands are narratives of landscape elements and features, both the persistent and the fleeting. Many stories have been shaped over tens of thousands of years, others over several human lifetimes, still others are just now emerging. There are deep stories, dialogues that have become interwoven, embedded, in place over time. Every place has ongoing stories, recognized, concealed, and lost. Some take longer to tell than others, some are short; some have an ending, others are open, still unfolding. All that has happened in a place, all the lives lived there contribute to a sense of place; identity is defined by the common and by the rare alike. An idiosyncratic anomaly like Watts Towers in Los Angeles, a fantasy built from discarded crockery and scraps of metal, can help define identity of a place.

When Dolores Hayden first moved to Los Angeles and set out to trace the history of her new urban landscape, she discovered many untold stories, and founded the Power of Place project to bring them to light. The result was a landmark project that tapped "the power of ordinary urban landscapes, to nurture citizens' public memory, to encompass shared time in the form of shared territory through walking tours, public art, and publications."[31] Hayden concentrated on

Los Angeles downtown, the site of the original Spanish pueblo founded next to a large Native American village, Yang-Na, and documented the successive activities that structured the landscape there: vineyards, citrus groves, flower fields, oil fields, manufacturing, and real estate development. Most traces of earlier activities have been erased, but remnants remain in street names, isolated citrus trees, a winery, a produce market, a flower market, an oil company. Hayden challenges designers and artists to envision new public spaces that would reveal these former urban landscapes and those who lived and worked in them, men, women, and children, Native Americans, Hispanic, Anglo, African, Chinese, and Japanese Americans. Many place stories here in Los Angeles (and everywhere) are concealed, forgotten, or uncelebrated, especially those of women, poor people, ethnic and racial minorities. Hayden's purpose is not to introduce competing stories into the public realm, but to celebrate the diversity of identities that have contributed to the American landscape, and to forge a new and fuller sense of place.

In the Mill Creek neighborhood in West Philadelphia, a place where my students and I have been working since 1987, as in most older American landscapes, is a rich fabric of stories. Its principal thoroughfare, Lancaster Avenue, was the nation's first turnpike, and before that an Indian trail that followed a ridgeline. From the Busti Mansion, built by one of the first large landowners, there is still a prospect over the valley below. The Pennsylvania Institute, a hospital on the opposite hill, was a nineteenth-century landmark of treatment for the mentally ill. Most houses standing today were built after 1876. A small African-American community already lived there then, served by an African Methodist Episcopal Church and a "home for colored orphans." At the turn of the century, European immigrants predominated, including Italians and Jews from Russia. A large Caucasian population remained until the 1970s; today the population is almost entirely African American. The story line of the Mill Creek itself, once visible from the windows of mansion, hospital, and orphans' home, is now buried in a sewer but is still powerfully present in its consequences.

There are painful stories in Mill Creek, stories just as important to remember as stories of mills, mansions, and immigration. A 1934 study of Philadelphia's housing, which became the basis for red-lining, documented building age and condition, race, income, and education of residents. Mill Creek's older houses (some in poor condition, some with flooded basements), its population of different races and ethnic origins (some with relatively low incomes), led to the lowest rating, red, for the entire neighborhood. Over the next fifty years, homeowners and businessmen there found it difficult, often impossible, to get mortgages, bank loans for improvement or expansion, and fire and theft insurance. Mill Creek is shaped by all the processes at work in inner-city America. New homes and businesses in suburban areas, subsidized by federal highway, mortgage, and infrastructure programs, fueled new construction beyond the city line in the headwaters of Mill Creek, funneling more runoff and sewage into the sewers, increasing floods, bursting pipes downstream in West Philadelphia. Segments of Mill Creek sewers have collapsed repeatedly since 1930, destroying homes and even lives, yet federal grants subsidize new suburban sewers, not the maintenance of old inner-city ones, including this one, which carries runoff from suburban development. The place was laid waste by the violence of neglect that Robert Kennedy called "slower, but just as deadly, destructive as the shot or bomb in the night . . . the violence of institutions; indifference and inaction and slow decay."[32]

"You mean there really *was* a *creek!?*" an eighth-grade student said as she examined a photograph from 1880 showing stream, mill, men dwarfed by the huge sewer they were building, new row homes in the distance. A map of 1915 indicated the spot where the photograph had been taken, and a 1961 newspaper photograph showed a deep, gaping hole, porches hanging, falling; a broken sewer, parts of houses, a truck down at the bottom. At the start of the school year, a teacher in Mill Creek's Sulzberger Middle School told me that her students called their neighborhood The Bottom. So they already know it's in a floodplain? "No, they mean it's at *the bottom*." Both meanings of the word can be read in the area around the Sulzberger School: standing water after rain; slumping streets and sidewalks; tumbled-down buildings, some boarded up, some occupied; vacant house lots, rubble-strewn; whole square blocks of abandoned land, men standing around street corners on a workday afternoon, jobless.

Front and back doors of the middle school open on different worlds. The six front doors, in the solid, three-story, brick facade on high ground, face a small neighborhood of well-kept homes. Aspen Farms, the community garden designed by my students in 1988, is just a block away. The school's back door, a full story lower, is in the bottomland, so are the playfields and, across the street, the Mill Creek Housing Project, many units unoccupied, walls covered with graffiti, grass overgrown. The contrast between care and devastation is striking: drive down one street between well-kept homes; turn the corner onto fallen-in houses. The scene repeats as you turn, turn again: care, waste, care, waste. The islands of care are mainly on higher ground, where houses have well-used porches, many carpeted with plastic lawn, furnished with chairs and potted plants, where open lots are gardens or off-street parking. The sea of waste in between the islands is mostly in the bottomlands: houses with cracked foundations, buckled porch posts, tipped roofs, boarded-up buildings; vacant lots filled with rubble and trash, thickets of sumac and ailanthus trees.

In the 1997–98 school year, 130 sixth, seventh, and eighth graders at Sulzberger Middle School, together with my students at the University of Pennsylvania, learned to read the neighborhood's landscape, to trace its past to understand its present and envision its future. The tools they used were their own eyes and imagination, the place itself, and primary documents like maps, photographs, tax records, census tables, steam-railroad timetables. The students wrote and drew their visions for the future and a group of seventh graders even wrote and sang a rap: "Pipes BREAKING / Street, it be a-SHAKING / Houses, it be TAKING / Underground / Where rats run round . . . / . . . What are we going to do with the vacant land, ya'll? / We can build a boxing ring / So we can all / brawl / And play basketball. . . ." The ideas they proposed were published in a booklet, "Power of Place: Visions for Our Mill Creek Neighborhood"; some may actually be built.[33]

Reading the Mill Creek landscape is a skill anyone can learn. Even without maps of the topography or the sewer, one can follow the buried stream's course by connecting the low spots, keeping slopes to either side, walking from vacant lot/meadow to slumping playground to community garden to new homes built on "open" land. The children tracked the creek, proud of their special knowledge of things happening underground, unseen by most adults.

The Mill Creek Housing Project was designed by Louis Kahn, one of America's most famous architects, and built in 1954. The dark, tiny doorways of the project's row houses have no porches, no places to pause between sidewalk and house; neither prospect nor refuge, the doorways are used only for passage and concealment. Yet even the most modest older homes in the neighborhood—row houses with no porch or garden—offer a stoop, a place to sit and watch the street.

The City Planning Commission's Plan for West Philadelphia, published in 1994, made no mention of either the historic landscape or the buried river; a new project, Nehemiah Homes, was built in the bottomland downstream from the Mill Creek Housing Project, as an isolated enclave for first-time homeowners. Small groups of new houses within the established blocks of long-time homeowners, experienced in community building, would have appeared less heroic, certainly less visible, but would have been much more likely to survive.

In summer 1997, a group of Sulzberger Middle School students, teachers, community gardeners from Aspen Farms, and my research assistants from the University of Pennsylvania worked together to gather stories about the Mill Creek and its namesake neighborhood, and to find ways to tell those stories of the urban landscape in the school's curriculum. The students and teachers wore T-shirt advertisements of light blue; on the back, in black letters, they say, "ASK ME ABOUT THE MILL CREEK." And people did.

SUSTAINING THE FABRIC OF PLACE: JAPAN

For thousands of years the Japanese have integrated the traditional and the new. Shinto customs and shrines exist side by side with Buddhist temples, often combined; papers inscribed with wishes and tied to trees, a Shinto custom, are a common sight in Buddhist temple precincts. Buddhism came to Japan long after Shinto was established as the indigenous religion, but it prompted many changes in Shinto practices. In Shitennoji, a large Buddhist temple complex in Osaka, where there are many Shinto shrines, one, simple and beautiful, is dedicated to a god of the earth, its central feature a large stone, covered with soft, green moss.

Beneath the moss is a carved relief of Buddha.

At times, the contrast of old and new in Japan is extreme: in Tokyo, a man sweeps the street with a broom made from a branch and twigs; on an adjacent lot a construction worker in hard hat pushes earth with a bulldozer. Tea whisks and *tatami*—straw mats three feet by six feet and several inches thick—like much traditional Japanese design, are admired greatly, but they are now relics, no longer part of the flow of daily life for which they were fashioned. How to embrace the new while preserving and renewing the best of the traditional is a dilemma for Japan today. Some Japanese architects have successfully integrated tradition and innovation. With wedding receptions and honeymoons now big business and with weddings in Christian chapels a popular trend among young Japanese, many Japanese hotels have built wedding chapels. Tadao Ando's design for the chapel at the Rokko Oriental Hotel in Kobe fuses Shinto and Christian, traditional and modern, Japanese and Western. His Rokko chapel complex has a fan-shaped reception terrace, a corridor with an anteroom, and a small chapel. Built of concrete, glass, stone, and steel, not the old wood, tile, paper, and tatami, it seems very Western in style, recalling modern Finnish churches. And yet, fundamentally, it is Japanese, as I found out when I visited.

I step across the gap between the curved edge of the reception terrace and the straight edge of the corridor and enter a world apart. The long corridor—with walls and vaulted ceiling of blue-green, frosted glass and a floor of black stone—stretches into the distance to an open end that frames a distant view of green—trees, shrubs, and grass—like the view of the garden from the teahouse at Katsura. Translucent walls meet black stone floor flush, filling the corridor with a diffuse, disembodied light. I feel suspended in light, the green view at the end my only connection to the material world. A long way down the corridor, the door to a chapel opens abruptly to the right. I turn sharply into the small, dark anteroom to face a concrete wall that curves into a vertical strip of clear glass—the landscape beyond abstracted to a thin line of illuminated green. Another sharp right turn, and I stand at the chapel's threshold, the chapel walls are of warm, dove-grey concrete. The left wall of floor-to-ceiling glass faces the green hillside against which the chapel nestles. The floor of elegant black slate draws my eyes downward, and the green view beyond the glass wall pulls my gaze outward, a tension between interior floor and outdoor landscape reminiscent of the correspondence between tatami floor and garden at Shisendo, at the ryokan.

As I leave the chapel, I face the translucent, blue-green wall of the corridor, wall glowing with light reflected from the landscape beyond, visible only as blurred outlines with an intensification of green near the ground and blue toward the sky. Like a shoji screen or the white silk screen at Ise.

Modern architecture like Ando's is singular; a comparable integration of new and traditional has seldom been achieved in the larger landscape of contemporary Japan. Rather, far-reaching changes in valued landscapes—foundations of myth, art, and religion that connect modern Japan with its origins—are breaking the continuity of culture, in an engulfing wave of change that has not been resolved with the past. Only an understanding of the deep context of the Japanese landscape and a careful discarding and adapting can resolve this dilemma: how to find open recreational space in the city amid competing claims for the same, scarce land? How to accommodate automobiles without destroying city and countryside? How to weigh the relative importance of new housing and of rice fields?

A long workday, a six-day work week, and short annual vacations make urban open space essential to quality of life in Japan, but how, in the context of scarce open land, can space be found for playgrounds and ballfields, for places to stroll and sit, and for the increasingly popular but land-consuming sport of golf? Activities that extend over large areas in North American cities are compressed here. Gas stations are compact, with little pavement, no visible pumps. There are no vacant lots, for open space is precious. Every bit of land is used, even rooftops. Groups of workers perform daily calisthenics atop office buildings. Parks and sports fields compete with houses, businesses, industry, hospitals, schools, highways, and parking for the same scarce space. Many Japanese live in apartment buildings and have not even a tiny garden. But in and around Japanese cities are green open areas; the largest are temple grounds, rivers and riverbanks, and forested hillsides. Sacred sites have long been associated with water and hills, but so, too, have places for entertainment. In the Tokugawa era from the seventeenth to nineteenth centuries, along riverbanks and at bridges, in temple grounds and outside temple gates the rules governing behavior were more lenient than in ordinary urban areas. These sites attracted entertainments of many kinds and became a sort of free space "exempt from both conventional social norms and clear-cut property relationships. They were a kind of 'sacred' place where freedom and protection were assured."[34]

I step out of the Tennoji subway station in Osaka into a steady rain and wander around a dense district of old houses and narrow streets, packed with dozens of temples. The temple grounds are shady, green oases, enclosed by high stone walls. From the street the only hints of these gardens are the treetops poking above the high walls and occasional views through the gates. I pause at each gate and step beneath its wide, wooden canopy to peek into the garden within, glad for shelter. Despite the rain, one temple precinct is filled with children running and playing; preparations are under way for a festival later in the day. I return several hours later to find the festival in full swing, the grounds packed with people and booths of food and games that spill out through the gate onto the adjoining streets.

Small neighborhood temples, serving a local population, are an informal play space for children. Larger temples, with many priests or monks, have more formal, landscaped grounds, dignified and subdued—a place to stroll, not play. The fact that temples do not pay taxes on the land they occupy is a major concern of city government in cities like Kyoto, where temples are numerous, but so long as they permit public access, temple grounds are an important civic resource, a place for recreation and reflection, embodying and perpetuating cultural tradition, in dense urban districts a refuge. In Kyoto, the forests and gardens of hillside temples, monasteries, and imperial villas preserve forested hillsides and maintain the flow of cool air off the hills into the city on hot summer nights, but in other cities, development of hillsides for housing and resorts is eliminating space for recreation, destroying the traditional relationship between mountain and settlement, and blocking hill-to-valley breezes.

Automobile ownership in Japan is growing, and so is traffic congestion. In large Japanese cities, dense settlement, narrow roads, and irregular street patterns make the subway the most efficient mode of transportation. Efficient subways, thronged with people late into the night, busy, interior arcades, and the active street life of Japanese cities fill many Americans with nostalgia for the lost vitality of American central cities. But in smaller, less densely settled cities, as in the Mie prefecture, where bus and rail lines are less convenient than the car, parking on streets has become a major problem. The widening of streets and creation of space for parking is causing large-scale demolition of older buildings in such cities. Competition for space is not new, but what is new in Japan is not only the growing number of automobiles, but the importation of settlement patterns that require enormous amounts of space. So, for example, new urban districts in Tokyo and Osaka have become virtually indistinguishable from similar developments in Dallas and Houston. Where tradition and innovation once enriched one another in mutual readjustment in Japan, a growing gulf is now separating the old and the new. Rapid economic growth and the importation of Western styles of architecture and urban development, fueled by education of Asian designers and planners in the West and the increasingly international scope of professional practice in design and planning, all have contributed to the swift changes and to the lack of integration. The dilemma is one many cultures face: how to reconcile tradition and change.

One of the most startling sights to a Western visitor is the occasional rice field in Japanese cities—seemingly isolated anomalies, unrelated to anything around them. Like the tatami mat in a room, the green carpet of the rice field extends from boundary to boundary of the property, often with only a few inches between it and adjacent apartment houses, stores, or warehouses. An eye grown used to the greys and browns of streets and buildings and garish signs suddenly sees the rice field, an intense, living, growing green. How could it survive in the densely built city of extremely high land values? Rice must be important.[35]

The emperor grows rice within the grounds of the Imperial Palace. Rice is the offering brought to the shrines at Ise. Rice has structured the landscape of country and city. Rice and fish are the staples of Japanese diet, the one from the earth, the other from the sea. Historically, coastal fishing village and inland farm village formed a unit, and it was the demands of rice cultivation—flat terraces connected by water channels—that structured inland villages. Many Japanese cities are built on the rice fields of former villages, and contemporary urban form often reflects that earlier structure of field and village. City blocks may reflect the shape and size of the rice fields they replaced. Rice fields are a reminder of the origins of the Japanese measurement system, the basis of dimensions for room and house. The *tan*, a standard measure of land, was originally the area needed to produce rice to feed a family of four or five people for one year. Before the seventh century, the size of one tan depended upon the land's productivity; after the seventh century, the tan became a standard size, three hundred *tsubo*; one tsubo is the size of two tatami.[36] Traditional Japanese rooms are modular, composed of varying numbers of tatami, woven from a reed that covers the rice-stalk padding inside. The bowl of rice, tatami mat, room, house, and the block on which they are situated, all are related; all parts of a whole felt, but not seen in a single glance. The rice fields of city, country, and palace, the rice-straw ropes that bound and mark sacred places, the rice of thanksgiving offered at Ise, these are all part of that whole.

How, for example, to weigh the importance of new houses compared to the importance of a small rice field? The rice field yields rice for a single family or at most a few families, an apartment building would house many. On a deep level, the city's green rice fields yield more than food. They permit city dwellers, especially children, to appreciate the relationships among sun, earth, water, and plants; to see the connection between nature and food. These rice fields permit one to *feel* history, to understand, not just to know abstractly, the landscape history that structures the city blocks and streets of Japan. Such prompts help transcend the overwhelming concreteness of the present, serve as an aid to imagining the reality of other times, both past and future.

Foreign rice is less expensive than homegrown rice, but rice is more than food. In Japan, mountain, sea, and forest form the warp; rice is an important thread in the weft. Pull that one thread—rice—and a portion of the pattern that is Japanese culture unravels. No wonder urban, as well as rural, rice fields have government subsidy. Culture is a fabric, the deep context of the natural landscape, the warp against which the weft of human intervention and elaboration weaves a pattern.

Landscape context is complex and dynamic, woven of many strands, in multiple dimensions. In landscape, speaking in context demands more than using local materials and imitating forms common to the regional landscape. To speak in context is to distinguish deep and lasting contexts from those that are superficial and fleeting; it is to respond to the rhythms and histories of each and to project those contexts into the future. To guide such contextual expression is the function of the grammar of landscape.

6

Rules of Context:
Landscape Grammar

A leaf on a tree is similar to a noun in a sentence. Nouns are not green, and leaves are not words, but the relationships among leaf, its growing or wilting, its context in twig, branch, and tree are like the relationships of noun to verb to sentence. This insight is Gregory Bateson's: "Both grammar and biological structure are products of communicational and organizational process."[1] In other words, "Anatomy *must* contain an analogue of grammar because all anatomy is a trans-form of message material, which must be contextually shaped."[2] But Bateson limited this analogy to the "creatura," living things; he failed to see that entire landscapes and their features—rivers, clouds, and mountains, not only trees, birds, and people —might not only be analogous to, but even *embody*, grammar and language.

Through grammar, meanings are shared; grammar is an aid to reading and telling landscape more fluently, deeply, expressively, and gracefully. The language is living, so grammar—derived from speech and the literature of landscape—is timeless, yet not rigid, but evolving and various. There are formulas, rules—arti-facts of inherited usage—but also free expression, the renewal of language through the invention of new patterns.

Readers do not use grammar the same way tellers do. Readers decode mean-ing, move from perception of an element to an appreciation of its function, to un-derstanding. Tellers have a message to relate and search for ways to express its significance by the choice and ordering of landscape's elements.

Elements like water or path unite to form features, like river or fountain, and features, in turn, combine to create larger landscapes, grammatically ordered to convey "wider and more varied patterns of meaning than in and of themselves."[3] Such rules govern the creation of leaf, tree, and forest, gate and garden, street and town. Trees and birds participate in grammar; they do not choose to obey its rules, and cannot break them. People follow the rules some of the time, but sometimes break them and sometimes invent new grammars. Multiple, overlapping gram-mars coexisting is what makes human landscapes so interesting and complex.

PRINCIPLES OF GRAMMAR

Landscape grammar has no right or wrong, despite its rules, except perhaps when function is impaired or when choice leads to a sickness or dying. Grammatical principles are descriptive, not prescriptive; they reflect usage, aid the reading and making of landscapes, but do not demand they be made in a single, specific way, though some ways may be more adaptive than others. Codifying landscape grammar is a daunting task because contexts are multiple and change continually. Consequences must be assessed. Certain landscape statements carry a price: a town in the path of a river's flood, or a house on a landslide-prone slope. Landscapes that do not agree with the enduring context of a place may be riskier or more costly to build and maintain. With no single appropriate answer to a decision to stress or underplay a particular tense in landscape, a mistake in tense is made only if chosen materials, forms, or processes deny, undermine, or fail to convey an intended meaning.

Combining Grid, Water, Path, Meeting: Ancient Priene

In Priene, a colonial city in Asia Minor built in the fourth century B.C., elements combine to create a larger landscape of function and meaning. Priene was constructed on a hillside above a river's floodplain, where it was well defended from both natural hazards and human enemies. It was originally a seaport settlement; the hill spur on which it stood jutted out into the sea that separated the city from Miletus, its neighbor across the water to the south. The site today is more than seven miles inland.

Priene's layout followed the then-current method of Greek town planning, a grid plan coordinated with the sloping terrain. Streets, houses, and public spaces were subordinate to the overall grid, with the acropolis on a hilltop high above the town, the whole surrounded by a wall. Priene, carefully sited on sloping ground, demonstrated the flexibility of the grid. The main streets ran, more or less level, along the line of the slopes, and the secondary streets—narrow alleys—stepped up and down the slopes; the grid was aligned so that one street ran down the center of the one long valley that cut into the hillside. The houses were sited, as Hippocrates and Aristotle recommended, on the south-facing hillside to capture sun; they stepped down the slope so sun could reach houses across the street.[4] Most public buildings and temples were built where slopes leveled out. Curving seats of the outdoor theater, facing out, open to the sky, were set into the hillside below the acropolis, and the long *stadion*, a racecourse, rested on more level ground below the town.[5]

The structure of the hills around Priene is layered rock—marble and schist; water trickles through cracks in marble, underground, and flows out as hillside springs. The ancient water supply was both natural springs (exposed within the town by the terraced terrain and marked by fountains at several intersections) and an aqueduct that tapped mountain springs behind the town. The water system, like the grid plan, was typical of towns built in Greece itself after the fourth century B.C. Engineer and scholar Doris Crouch thinks Greeks chose sites for their colonial towns that resembled the geological context of their native country, confident of their ability to adapt their familiar town planning and water management practices there.

The lines of Priene's grid followed patterns of events—water's flowing, above

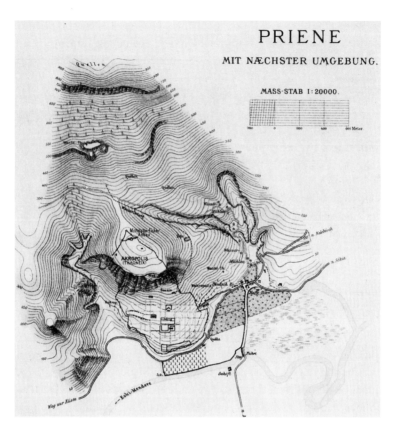

Coordinating town and terrain: Priene. Mid-fourth century B.C. Turkey.
(Wiegand and Schrader, 1904)

and below ground, and people moving. Both lines of the grid and the movement served function and meaning. Lines became paths for water and people, boundaries for buildings; points of intersection with springs became sources of fountains and spaces for public gathering. Just as a word's meaning is mere potential until shaped by specific relationships with other words in context of phrase, clause, or sentence, so the meaning of an element of landscape is merely immanent until shaped by relationships with other elements in context. Flowing, water, grid, path, boundary, and source (and the streets, drains, and fountains they comprise) pose potential relationships, suggesting combinations, permitting fusion, or promoting integration. Paths as lines of movement are potential links between disparate entities—people, animals, water. Grids and axes, both structured by points and lines, have potential to coincide or intersect, as in Priene's (or Philadelphia's) street grid with embedded principal axes.

Water and air in Priene, as elsewhere, share the same components, in different proportions, as rivers, seas, skies, and clouds. Clouds, intermediate in water composition between sea and sky, link the two; when fog forms, sea and sky are indistinguishable, seemingly fused, disorienting to anyone out on the water. When two or more elements are fused the many become one, but the parts retain their identity. Like Priene, the Vietnam Veterans Memorial in Washington, D.C., can be divided into phrases: the wall itself is like a noun phrase, moving along the path a verb phrase. Wall and movement are modified: the wall by the material, stone, as by an adjective; moving, by path's descending and rising, as by an adverb. Like any landscape text, the memorial is composed of many such phrases, both subordinate and coordinate (the stones are subordinate to the wall, but coordinate to each other and to the mortar). Like all landscapes it is a complex composition; qualities of embeddedness are shared by all landscapes and all other languages—verbal, graphic, mathematical, or musical.

A landscape has many contexts, interacting (contingent, coordinated, subordinated) or independent, with highly related (congruent, echoing, convergent), or loosely related, or even unrelated, patterns (discontinuous layers). These multiple contexts may be fused (node on a web or network, when a tree's wood and fruit are also part of a system of lumber and food production and distribution, when plants grow in a certain soil or when a road follows a ridgeline); parallel (when a road runs alongside a river); nested, overlaid, overlapping (edge as zone; forest edge, porch, and portico); intersecting, interwoven, interlocking, continuous, interrupted (nonconforming rock layers, 1960s urban renewal that tore down whole blocks).

Grammar of verbal language combines morphemes into words, words into phrases, phrases into clauses, and clauses into sentence, but too close a comparison between verbal and landscape grammar must be resisted. Yet, like landscape, verbal language is continuous, neither linear nor segmented. The segmenting of verbal discourse is a process of combining, of sentences into paragraphs or stanzas, into chapters, poems, and books, ordinarily the province of composition. Composition is also the process of the composing of landscape, of selecting and combining landscape elements in significant ways, according to rules of grammar and traditions of rhetoric and style. Style is a way of doing things, a characteristic system of expression an individual or group employs.[6]

Scale and Tense: Micro, Macro, Past, Future

Elements—water and stone, circle and grid, path and prospect, moving and growing—have no scale, but landscape contexts do. The scale of the Great Plains, unbounded by mountains and forests, is vast; up close, landscape features like trees and buildings give the Plains a more human scale. The Smoky Mountains, though tall, are cloaked in dense forest; small clearings in the hollows have an intimate scale. An overview, like the prospect over the Plains at Red Rocks Amphitheater in Colorado, conveys a sense of connection across space and time, a possibility of seeing past routes and future direction, how parts fit into a whole.

"The world at arm's length—roughly one meter in scale—is the world of most artifacts and of the most familiar living forms."[7] Thus begins *Powers of Ten: About the Relative Size of Things in the Universe*, a remarkable journey in photographs and text across the known world: zooming from beyond our galaxy down in scale to a proton, in forty-two progressive views, each representing a power of ten. A collaboration by the designers Charles and Ray Eames, the physicist Philip Morrison, and the educator Phylis Morrison, it is an essay on scale, the relative size of things in the universe. Of the distance traveled, imaginatively, only about a dozen of the scales—from the moon to the surface of our skin—have been directly experienced by humans, the others have been seen through telescopes, the transmissions of robot ships, through microscopes and traces left in experiments.

An area one meter square is at the heart of human experience, the scale of human companionship, conversation, touch, the size of a desktop, of a small gate and its threshold, a narrow sidewalk, a bench for one person or two, close together. The next smaller scale, exponentially—10^{-1}, or ten centimeters—is intimate, that of a hand close-up, the latch of a gate, an individual flower or leaf, the detail of tree bark, grain of marble, a frog, a small spiderweb. One step smaller—one centimeter—is the scale of a fingernail, a spider and a fly, the joining of materials as in metal latch to wooden gate or mortared joint between bricks.

Increasing dimensions to a space ten meters across, one arrives at a domestic scale: the size of a single house or small garden, the domain of a family in some parts of the world; one can hear a human voice clearly from ten meters away, though one cannot touch and can barely distinguish facial features. This is also the scale of a tree's territory—the height and breadth of its canopy, its drip line, and extent of its roots underground. The only animals larger than ten meters are whales.

An area one hundred meters square, just over two acres, is of civic or palatial scale: of a city block with buildings, yards, streets, and sidewalks, encompassing many homes or businesses, of a large plaza, a stadium, the base of a skyscraper. The Fenway Rose Garden in Boston, the lawn around it, and the basketball court nearby all fit within such a space, so does the Taj Mahal with its four minarets. In the countryside, two acres is the size of a small pasture or a garden that will support a family with food. The giant sequoia, the largest known individual organisms, reach one hundred meters in height.

In the view from one thousand meters (one kilometer) in the air, a height sustained by an airplane approaching a landing, individual people are not distinguishable, but cars, boats, gardens, buildings, a segment of highway are. One thousand meters (one kilometer) square, approximately two hundred acres, is the area of a neighborhood with many blocks, its network of streets and hundreds, even thousands of homes. It is the size of the Fens with all its paths and ponds, Rose Garden, sports fields, and parkway. Small farms, each with house, garden, barn, pasture, and fields, like Åvangsgården in Denmark, are two hundred acres, as are large gardens like Stourhead. The horizontal span of the George Washington Bridge in New York City is a thousand meters.

In a landscape ten kilometers across (about six miles), the layout of downtown and inner city is discernable, their neighborhoods, streets, highways, and blocks. Rivers and parks are visible at this scale, and one can still make out the largest individual buildings. Ten kilometers is a cruising altitude familiar to airplane passengers; Mount Everest reaches this height above sea level.

Looking down at a landscape one hundred kilometers across, the scale of the entire metropolitan region of Chicago or Philadelphia or a portion of Los Angeles, one can see the structure of principal streets and highways, river and park systems; no buildings are visible. This is the scale of a moderate-sized watershed, of Philadelphia's Schuylkill River or Boston's Charles; one can see the surficial traces of fault lines across the Los Angeles region. It is a vantage few people have seen except on maps or in photographs taken at high altitudes.

At one thousand kilometers across, larger patterns of rivers, lakes, clouds, mountains, and plains appear, but the mark of humans is more difficult to discern. This is the scale of the Great Plains, the Rocky Mountains, a large hurricane, or the watershed of a great river like the Missouri or the Ohio. Forests have been cut, rivers dammed, rock quarried, cities built, but from this perspective, little has changed in thousands of years. At ten thousand kilometers across, the earth itself fills the area, swirling clouds reveal air's movement; at one hundred thousand kilometers, the familiar picture of spaceship earth, seen from space, a sphere of blue sheathed in an atmosphere of swirling white.

Space is not segmented into scales, but continuous. A seed is part of fruit, fruit part of tree, tree part of forest. Path, garden, neighborhood, town, region, nation are nested contexts, each enclosed within a larger whole and context for features at smaller scales. This successive, sometimes hierarchical, relationship of parts and wholes in landscape gives its language a nested structure. Rules of grammar—modification, agreement, correspondence, subordination, and coordination—apply across scales, as well as within.

To be comprehended, patterns must be brought within human range by enlarging the micro and miniaturizing the macro. Designers' drawings and planners' maps represent landscapes enlarged or reduced; the scale they choose depends on the actions they intend. Urban designers typically work from the scale of building, street, and plaza to neighborhood, architects within the scale of a building, from doorknob to threshold to chair to exterior walls, with all its features and furnishings—scales at which environment can be seen, touched, smelled, heard. Planners work at the scale of an entire neighborhood, region, or even nation, ordinarily not concerned with sensual experience. Landscape architects work at scales from garden to metropolitan region, and thus bridge design and planning, a distinctive and important role. When professionals focus on a narrow range of scales (from gate handle to garden, for example) without addressing larger contexts of scale (neighborhood and region), they may introduce elements that do not agree with those contexts and may, therefore, be unsustainable. Similarly,

Correspondence across scales: cracking ice. Massachusetts. (Alex S. MacLean/Landslides)

when planners focus on scales of neighborhood or region and neglect domestic and local scales, their proposals may not agree with those smaller contexts and produce failures or unanticipated consequences.

A strength of Christopher Alexander's "pattern language" is that it reflects landscape's nested quality; his patterns are arranged from the metropolitan scale of "Distribution of Towns" to the intimate scale of "Half-inch Trim," though most of the patterns fall between the dimensions of one meter to one hundred meters: personal, domestic, civic, and neighborhood scales reflecting the architect's and urban designer's scope of concern. Alexander does not specify how to combine them, though he does advise the reader to pay attention to patterns at more than one scale.

A similar device to the Eames' and Morrisons' "Powers of Ten" could be constructed to illustrate scales of time: from the length of a deep breath, to the time spanning the lives of people known to a single person, to the time of the earliest surviving landscapes shaped by humans, to the age of fossils. Tense in landscape is relative; it is rare to find an entire landscape in a single tense. At Vizcaya, the former estate of John Deere in Florida, worn stairs of stone embedded with fossilized animals and vegetables resonate with the smell of rotting plants in the surrounding tidal swamp. Like the rounded river cobbles in the Patio de la Reja's fountain in the Alhambra, made smooth by years of running water, the worn steps, fossils, and smells at Vizcaya summon a sense of ongoing time and collapse the past and present. As do shoots sprouting from a cut stump. The tumbled-down houses and abandoned land in Philadelphia's Mill Creek, occupied by so many unemployed, convey a sense of past that has no part in the future.

Hadrian's Villa in Tivoli, east of Rome, is a rambling ruin that once housed thousands of people. Like the skeleton of a dead tree sticking out of one of the vaults, action here appears over, apart from the ongoing process of decay. But there are signs of repair, explanatory plaques, railings to protect visitors from falling, all introducing a sense of the present, some, depending on materials and form, calling attention to the contrast between the past life of the place and its present.

Loss of past can be self-inflicted. Dallas performed a lobotomy on itself when it destroyed all vestiges of its past downtown, replacing older buildings and squares with new commercial office buildings and a cultural district. Reconstructed colonial and pioneer villages are similarly disquieting. Both kinds of places seem in limbo, detached. East Berlin, in physical suspension for many years, is undergoing a shocking transformation, eradication of the recent past, replacement by the new. Not so in West Berlin after the war, where new construction was integrated into remains of old buildings damaged by bombs, as in the Kaiser Wilhelm Memorial Church. The East German government owned all the railroads, and because they used no more than a few lines, in many railyards and along rights-of-way tracks and land are now overgrown. Around East Berlin are many railroad bridges, now lush ruins. The Ruins, the eye-catcher visible from the courtyard behind Sanssouci, in Potsdam, is perched picturesquely high up on the hillside; it conceals a reservoir that feeds the fountains of the park, a built version of a late eighteenth-century German painting of a Roman aqueduct in ruin. "We have too many ruins now," said a German friend.

In Orange County, California's South Coast Plaza, Isamu Noguchi's sculpture *Lima Bean* is the only sign that the land now covered by mirrored-glass banks, office towers, parking garages, and lawns was, until recently, beanfields. A present tense, without obvious antecedents, pervades the freshly clipped, cleanly edged green grass, brightly colored flowers, polished metal fountains, and trendy signs and lamps. No spent flowers, dead leaves, or old buildings hint at past lives. Nor is there anticipation of the future, for southern California's mild climate produces no single time of blooming, no pronounced seasonality, just an ever-agreeable present.

In Philadelphia, spring moves by at fast forward; one day is cold and blustery, branches bare, then air is warm and breezy. One late afternoon in mid-April, the sun fills the air with brightly lit dots of color—greens, browns—leaves brightly backlit. Three days later, trees are almost fully leafed out. The air is full of falling bud cases and petals; insects zing around, light catches their wings. Every day sees major changes. I feel the future rushing toward me in landscapes like these.

Modifying, Agreeing, and Corresponding

At Parc de Sceaux, outside Paris, the ground is graded plane—flat and tilted— and trees are clipped into cubes and cones. Long parallel rows of sycamores,

Growth and form modified and subordinated: clipped allées. Sceaux. France.

lindens, and hornbeams are planted close, their leaves sheared into a solid green mass that frames the mansion and forms an entry to the park. Beyond the house, thirty-six cones of evergreen yew dot a tilted plane. Their sides show a lighter green, new bright green growth against deep-green, older growth and brown, where the yew has been cut back sharply. Clipping modifies the yew's growth, makes it bud more densely, become more opaque, and introduces a tension between outer form and internal, branching structure. This part of the garden is bounded on two sides by a long, clipped, rectangular wall of yew. Beyond the green wall, woodland trees grow freely.

Imagine how shocking it must have been when plants were first pruned into cones and cubes. Why would anyone modify plants' growing, so extremely, without a strong intent? To demonstrate mastery? Reveal an underlying ideal? Contrast reason and irrationality? Now it has become a formula: topiary. Some people find topiary repulsive, to others it is fashionable or fun. Sven-Ingvar Andersson takes it as serious fun, as he said in an essay of 1967 soon after he had planted Marnas, his "henyard" garden of hedges and topiary birds in southern Sweden. First he planted the birds as "eggs," young hawthorn trees cut "into tight balls, so that the birds will not grow bare-legged," then later, little by little, he shaped them into hens twelve feet high.[8] He described how he expected his garden to grow over the next forty years, said he knew a lot could go awry between then

Agreement: wind, tree, house. Sea Ranch. California.

and now, but, despite the uncertainties, he was not worried about the outcome:

> My confidence stems not so much from a sense of my own ability to manage the affair, but from two facts: the simple pattern of the planting and the material, hawthorn. If I always proceed with a respect for the placement of the hawthorns and their existence as living organisms, they will always form a clear pattern that can adapt to whatever serendipitous circumstances are introduced by myself and by time. The hawthorns, on the other hand, permit enormous variation, from the meter-high closely clipped to the freely growing twenty-foot tree. But not beyond those limits which lie in being a hawthorn, which means that every single cell, whether it sits in the roots or in the skin of the fruit has a predetermined number of chromosomes with a particular set of genes, which can vary a little bit and give each plant its unique individuality, yet still ensure similarities in form and mode of meeting external conditions.[9]

Is it right or wrong to clip trees, flatten and tilt slopes, lay a grid of streets on hilly ground? Neither right nor wrong, necessarily; it all depends on meaning and consequences. Limits are imposed not by a moral criterion, but by the materials, forms, processes, and behavior, depending on their nature.

At Sea Ranch, a residential development on the northern California coast, someone planted a tree against the exposed, windward corner of a house near cliff's edge, overlooking the Pacific Ocean. Dwarfed, pruned by wind, its branches splay back, embracing both sides of the home, as if protecting. The tree's form agrees with wind's force and direction and building's shape. To read protection in this requires an imaginative leap between outstretched branches and arms. The tree had no message for people, its dialogue was with wind and house.

The wide path up the Hill of Remembrance in Stockholm's Forest Cemetery is steep at first—climbing eased by low stone steps, deep, stone-dust treads, landings every dozen steps; then the slope tapers, steps pass between trees through an open gateway atop the hill, ending just inside low walls.[10] At the beginning of the ascent, steps are set into the hillside, so the slopes enfold the climber; at the end, frames of trees and wall enclose. Form and material shape the experience of path and refuge; all modify processes of movement and grieving, in agreement with the meaning its author intended: "To give form to a sorrow that cannot be told," an experience of difficulty, comforted.[11]

Shapes of valley floor and terraced slopes reveal where floods have been and where they will return. Shape of river's banks and the structure of its branching agree with patterns of rain falling and the qualities of material over which it flows: branched in uniform rock, trellised (parallel branches and sharp turns) in fractured terrain, braided rivulets over unconsolidated sediments, interrupted over limestone (a stream may disappear into underground channels dissolved in the rock). Channels straight and long are rivers modified to agree with human purpose, confined by design to direct water for human use.

Frank Lloyd Wright once laid out a grid of gardens on the Wisconsin hillside below Taliesin North; it faced the road, presented a vivid pattern, and people drove by just to look at them.[12] Unlike the grid of streets and drains at Priene, however, form and function did not agree; this was a poor location for such a layout and for gardens, the slope too steep, the soil too erodible. Wright soon replaced the gridded gardens with grass and trees. When first built, the prow garden at Taliesin West, composed of desert plants, agreed with the climate of Phoenix; now it is filled with grass and tropical flowers, which are at odds with the climate, and must be irrigated.

The Wisconsin River near Taliesin is dwarfed by the vast valley through which it flows. Where valley and river do not agree, the valley has been shaped by a different river or process, in this case, thousands of years ago by a glacial lake with far more water than the present river's flow. The Salt River, or Rio Salado, is an enormous grey, dry channel of gravel that divides Phoenix from Tempe. The river is empty, its waters distributed by hundreds of miles of canals into thousands of gardens and swimming pools. Forms of river and valley ordinarily agree; forms of valleys in the same rock and region correspond: agreement, in relationships between a landscape element or feature and the processes that shape it; correspondence, to analogies across entire landscapes, at micro and regional scales. The gridded streets of Denver correspond to the larger grid of the American Midwest; the process of surveying and settling links their disparate scales and locations. Water flowing through unconsolidated sediments produces the correspondence between patterns of sand in a gutter, along sandy banks of a river, in broad, braided channels of the South Platte River, hundreds of miles long.

In Phoenix, in September, it is more than one hundred degrees at midday and extremely dry. Animals' rustle, birds' song are still until after sunset. High, thick walls protect lush, garden oases. In the desert beyond the walls, plants are widely spaced to gather water, many emerge only after rainfall. Ocotillo is tall with long, tough, thorny stems that flare out from the base, as in a vase, leafing out after rain, blooming scarlet in spring. A fence of ocotillo stems looks dead brown until rain falls, and then, after a few days, it turns green—a living fence, memory of rain, barometer of the past. The rocks of Taliesin West, varnished bright orange-red and black, mark many years' exposure to daily cycles of heating and cooling, evaporation and condensation. To lack of water and strength of sun all desert plants and animals, rocks and rivers respond, giving the landscape a pervasive and powerful order. Not sameness, or even similarity, of material and form, but correspondence—tough skin, compact form, spaced for water, dormant between rains, nocturnal activity—gives a sense of coherence to deserts and to all landscapes.

Understanding landscape grammar provokes question, answer, and appropriate response. Failure to understand leads to misreading and inappropriate action. In the mid-1980s, when architects and urban planners failed to read the vacant blocks in Boston's Dudley Street neighborhood, the result, in part, of the blocks' location in an old floodplain, they proposed to build new houses in the bottom of the abandoned valley. My students and I proposed alternative designs in agreement with the landscape structure: houses on higher ground and parks and playgrounds over the buried stream and within its former floodplain. New houses and town commons sponsored since by the Dudley Street Neighborhood Initiative have followed this strategy.[13]

Order: Coordinating and Subordinating

W. G. Hoskins compared the English landscape to a symphony that "is possible to enjoy as an architectural mass of sound," but whose impact is greatest when: "we are able to isolate the themes as they enter, to see how one by one they are intricately woven together and by what magic new harmonies are produced, perceive the manifold subtle variations on a single theme, however disguised it may be."[14] Enduring landscape context is akin to symphonic theme and restatement, responses to that context by populations over time are like Haydn's many variations. But not all landscapes are harmonious. English footpaths with no relationship to either old sheep pastures or more recent wheat fields, that correspond, instead, to an even older pattern of common fields, are a Shostakovich landscape, full of clashing orders and discords, not the lush harmonies of Brahms.

Disorder, wrote Rudolf Arnheim, "is not the absence of all order but rather the clash of uncoordinated orders."[15] Arnheim defined order as "the degree and kind of lawfulness governing the relations among the parts of an entity" and com-

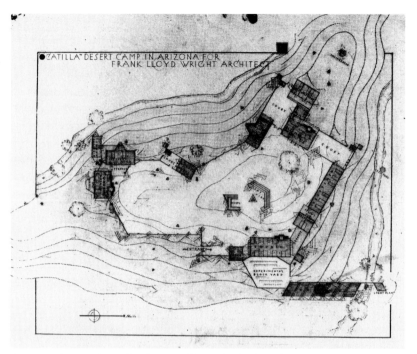

Correspondence and coordination: Ocatilla. Frank Lloyd Wright. (© 1998 The Frank Lloyd Wright Foundation)

plexity as the multiplicity of the relationships among those parts.[16] The greatest works of landscape literature, like great compositions of music or art, combine high order with high complexity, a difficult union, but: "complexity without order produces confusion; order without complexity produces boredom." The easiest way to achieve a sense of order is by repeated use of homogeneous landscape materials or forms—green lawn at Stourhead and Forest Cemetery. Hierarchy orders landscape by subordinating some features to others—the central axis at Versailles, nested domains at Ise. Coordination achieves order by granting elements similar importance—the grid of garden rooms at Mariebjerg, ellipses at Nærum. Chaotic order, not random, but seemingly accidental, is the most difficult of all; Halprin and his associates designed the surfaces over which water flows in Ira's Fountain in Portland to create specific patterns of turbulent flow.

Frank Lloyd Wright experimented with all four kinds of order—homogeneous, hierarchical, coordinated, and chaotic—to compose landscapes of high order and high complexity. In Taliesin North he used homogeneous material—local limestone and sandstone—for buildings and walls. His compositions, up until the 1920s, were coordinated by a single orthogonal grid, sometimes leading to problems on steeply sloping or irregularly shaped terrain, as in the gridded gardens at Taliesin North. Working in complex topography on large landscape compositions in the 1920s, he gradually adopted structural strategies more appropriate to irregular terrain. At the Johnson Compound in Death Valley, an unbuilt project of 1924, he provided hierarchy with several axes aligned in response to terrain and views. When he drew a new site plan in 1925 for vineyard, gardens, and farm buildings at Taliesin North, he coordinated them within a new grid oriented roughly perpendicular to the line of the slope, at a forty-five-degree angle to the grid of the earlier plan. At Ocatilla, a temporary desert camp where he lived for a few months, Wright overlaid two grids, each aligned with the terrain, sowing the seeds of design that would come to fruition in his Taliesin West. He often juxtaposed architectural form derived from Euclidean geometry to the complex, seemingly random, order of plants' growth: at Taliesin North in the cantilevered terrace over wild slopes below and hilltop garden enclosed by wall with freely growing grass beyond; at Taliesin West in the prow garden raised above the desert.

At Priene, in Asia Minor, points where water springs from the hillside are nodes around which fountains and important public spaces for meeting—temple, agora—are coordinated. Intersections in the lattice of Wright's Taliesin West are potential nodes, some activated by crossing paths, sculptural objects, entrances to buildings.

Following and Breaking the Rules

Local Dialects, Invented and Imported Grammars

Grammar is a living pattern reflecting both timeless rules and the contingencies of time and place. The deep context of a place is the foundation with which new expressions agree, correspond, are coordinated, subordinated, or not. Attending to the grammar of enduring context entails a response not only to the physical context of landforms, plants, and plant communities, but also to temporal context, to rhythmic daily and seasonal changes of light, temperatures, and water characteristic of a place, and to enduring aspects of cultural context. Design that reveals and agrees with deep context is likely to be more functional, more economical, more sustainable over time than design that disregards it.

Local landscape dialects emerge out of dialogue with enduring contexts of place; traditional vernacular landscapes are a consequence of collective learning, trial and error, finding what works and repeating it, refining through experience. They tend to correspond more closely to local conditions than do landscapes of cultures of highly developed technology. English hedgerows of hawthorn and beech; New England walls of glacial boulders dug from fields; layered limestone walls in Kentucky blue-grass country and the Driftless area of Wisconsin; split-rail fences in Virginia/North Carolina; barbed wire and wooden post fences in the Midwest: all are boundary types particular to the cultural and material context of place (property ownership, land use; local stone and plants). Vernacular landscapes may also include features that do not work in a place, such as those imported by immigrants. But the Hispano-Islamic gardens at the Alhambra in Granada are classical works in congenial dialogue with the natural and vernacular landscapes of Andalusia, with their mountains and rivers, their steep, terraced hillsides, fountains, cascades, pavements of river cobbles in flowing and geometrical patterns.

Glenn Murcutt studies a site for a building by observing its processes—wind blowing, sun shining, fire burning, animals moving, plants growing, water flowing. Then he designs in agreement with these processes, including the ways of his clients' lives. Form and materials of his buildings correspond to vernacular structures, not because he imitates, but in response to similar features of enduring context. Design attuned to enduring context can go beyond conventional understanding of regionalism's focus on indigenous materials and forms of vernacular settlements and buildings. In fact, as in Murcutt's buildings, imported materials and distinctly contemporary forms introduce a present tense and, thereby, heighten an awareness of layers of time.

Parc Sceaux and other seventeenth-century French gardens near Paris, like Vaux-le-Vicomte, Versailles, and Chantilly, were bold inventions. With their broad, flat terraces and sheets of water in basins and canals, these gardens were keyed to the floodplain landscape of the Île-de-France and the powers of their royal and aristocratic patrons. But the geometry and visual effects of Le Nôtre's designs relied also upon strict accuracy of measurement in design and construction. In the eighteenth century, the title "geometer" referred to all mathematicians, computation ability was a sign of intelligence, and many of the well educated were proud of their arithmetical computation.[17] The gardens also display an understanding of military engineering.[18] These gardens were ordered by a grammar invented not only as an expression of the deep structure of the landscape of the Île-de-France—the floodplains and canals—but the intellectual and political context of the time as well.

In composing landscapes, humans participate in, and elaborate on, dialects of place, perhaps even choosing to depart from and replace the rules with a grammar of a different place and time, or one simply invented, idiosyncratic. The landscape of every place engenders expectation. When form deviates from that norm there is a reason, conscious or unconscious, intended or unintended. Designers who know grammar may break the rules deliberately for the sake of meaning, for the sake of powerful new expression or new relationships. But designers who flout the rules without reason or in ignorance produce, at best, gibberish, a jumble of forms and materials, of meanings that add up to no meaning, like many landscapes today; at worst, potential catastrophe.

The International Style of architecture and planning, so influential in the twentieth century, is responsible for the proliferation of high-rise towers amid a broad, bland landscape of grass and concrete, appropriate to no place. In Jeddah, air-conditioned towers block sea breezes from penetrating the city; in New York City, it produced a no-man's-land of wind-swept plazas. In Mexico City, concrete buildings and pavement replaced three stones that had been quarried for buildings and pavement in the Valley of Mexico from pre-Columbian times. The black, the grey, and the red stone were formed concurrently in volcanic eruptions: the black stone is basalt, lava spewn from volcano mouth; red stone *tezontle* is rock that was molten but remained within the volcano. The lightweight red stone traditionally was used more in walls, the grey stone in details—ornament, frames, thresholds, the heavy black stone in pavement. Recently, Mexican architects and landscape architects, like Mario Schjetnan, have introduced stone from the Valley of Mexico once again in buildings and pavement.[19] Lack of correspondence between the pervasive concrete of International Style buildings and plazas and the indigenous volcanic stone used traditionally forfeit a story linking the built landscape to the vulcanism that shaped (and still shapes) the Valley of Mexico. Failure of agreement between the enduring context of vulcanism and landscapes and buildings designed in the International Style, ill-adapted to earthquakes, have had deadly consequences: pilotis, free plan (post-and-beam construction with non-bearing or curtain walls), separate stair shafts sheared off during earthquakes; roof gardens add weight at the top where it is most dangerous. The old pyramid form is very earthquake-resistant, so is the patio form that gives a rigidity and stability to the structure.[20]

The interior gardens and thick-walled buildings built by Spanish missionaries in Mexico and southwestern America, on the other hand, were oases in a hot, dry climate, learned from the Moorish culture of southern Spain, brought there, in turn, from northern Africa and the Middle East. But the green trees and lawns of the English landscape garden exported to India, Australia, and Africa as a sign of home, comforting to imperial bureaucrats and an assertion of British dominance over local cultures, were not so adaptable; to export is not necessarily to adapt. When built forms are repeated across the world without an understanding of the processes that originally generated them and in ignorance of the story lines of the place to which they are exported, their narrative can become boring, alienating, unsustainable, even disastrous.

Grammar Observed and Ignored: Chestnut Hill and Mill Creek

A big rock juts out of the Schuylkill River in Philadelphia just upstream from the East Falls Bridge. When the river is in flood, only the barest tip of the rock pokes above the water; once or twice a year, even the tip disappears, marked only by lines on water's surface. At low flow, the rock's stony ridges emerge, a warning to boaters of deeper rock below the surface. The rock is part of the fall zone, a series of waterfalls and rapids that mark the place where the soft sediments and gentle slopes of coastal plains meet the Piedmont's rocky hills—the end of navigable waters from the sea. From the vantage of a satellite one thousand kilometers above the earth, the Coastal Plain is clearly visible, as are the Appalachian Mountains and their foothills, the Piedmont. The rock in the Schuylkill is a part of this larger complex that structures the entire eastern seaboard of the United States from New Jersey to Georgia, as well as the Philadelphia metropolitan region.

William Penn sited the new town of Philadelphia in 1682 on a strip of relatively level, forested land between the Delaware and Schuylkill rivers just north of their confluence. Like the fourth-century builders of Priene, Penn aligned the lines of the grid—the city's future streets—with the landscape's structure: parallel to the two rivers and perpendicular, connecting them. The low, gently rolling plain and small creeks were no great obstacles, and the city grew within this frame of streets and squares. Penn's vision of Philadelphia as a "greene countrie towne" was influenced by current ideas in town planning. After the Fire of London in 1666, for example, John Evelyn and others put forward proposals for widening and straightening the streets, and for introducing a new grid of streets with squares filled with gardens and trees. Penn's plan for Philadelphia expressed those ideas.

Philadelphia's principal source of water from the early nineteenth century was the Schuylkill River. The fall zone was flooded by a dam built in 1821 to power the waterworks to pump river water to a reservoir atop Fairmount, from which it flowed by gravity through pipes to the city below. Philadelphia's Fairmount Park, one of the world's largest urban parks, was created along the banks of the Schuylkill and its tributary, Wissahickon Creek, to protect the water supply. Today one can walk eleven miles from City Hall, at the center of downtown, to the city's limits, without leaving park: up the sloping plain of the Franklin Parkway to Fairmount, now capped by the Philadelphia Museum of Art, on the broad walks along the banks of the Schuylkill, up a narrow trail in the steep, rocky, wooded Wissahickon Valley to northwest Philadelphia and Chestnut Hill, a "railroad suburb" built in the late nineteenth and early twentieth centuries. The path from downtown to Chestnut Hill tells a story of Coastal Plain and Piedmont, of flat plain, then rolling terrain, of houses and sidewalks of brick, then of stone, of cosmopolitan London plane trees, then native eastern hemlocks and beeches.

As the city expanded to north and west, and as the streets of the grid were extended, they hit the steeper slopes, deeper valleys, and broader streams of the Piedmont. In Chestnut Hill, the grid deforms and disintegrates as it approaches the slopes along the Wissahickon and its tributaries. Here, the park boundaries coincide with the valley's upper slopes; woods extend up tributary creeks into neighborhoods where houses, walls, and terraces are built of the native stone—Wissahickon schist—patterned after English Cotswold cottages and French villas, the gardens landscaped with plants native to the region's forest. Though styles of houses and gardens were imported, the designers responded to the grammar of deep context. Thus the grid is subordinate, deferring to the landscape's structure; stone and plants of gardens correspond to the materials of the region, the plants are in agreement with its climate and soil. The community's main street and spine,

Grammar observed: Wissahickon. Fairmount Park, Philadelphia.

Germantown Avenue, predates the extension of the city's grid and cuts across it, lined with older houses, part of the enduring cultural context. Before it became a park, the Wissahickon Valley was an industrial landscape, with more than thirty mills and numerous houses and inns. Most of the buildings have been removed, and, since the turn of the century, a forest of oak, beech, and hemlock has grown up protecting the city's water supply and the neighborhood's property values.

In a different neighborhood, another tributary to the Schuylkill, Mill Creek, became not park, but sewer. When the urban grid pressed westward from city center into the rolling hills and valleys of West Philadelphia in the 1880s, row houses packed the grid, in some sections with little or no yard at either front or back, and no parks to relieve the dense fabric. Anomalies, large properties—a mental hospital, a mansion, a large playground, a huge vacant block—either predated the city's expansion or resulted from development that ignored the grammar of deep context. Buried in a sewer, its floodplain filled in and built on, Mill Creek still drains and still carries all the stormwater as well as the wastes from half of West Philadelphia, but the size of the pipe, about twenty feet in diameter, is too small to agree with the huge quantity of sewage and stormwater it needs to convey. In consequence the wastewater cracks, then undermines the sewer, and, once or twice a year, sometimes more often, the sewer overflows, and brown water spouts from inlets and manhole covers.

For more than sixty years, in Mill Creek, the ground has fallen in, here and

Grammar ignored: burying Mill Creek (1880s). (Philadelphia Water Department)

there, along the line of the sewered stream. A playground was built by the city on the site where, in 1961, several blocks of housing had collapsed and been demolished. Now, sagging streets and sidewalks and cracked walls reveal ongoing shifting and foretell future cave-ins. For many years, the creek has ripped open the grid, undermined buildings and streets, slashed meandering diagonals of shifting foundations, tumbled buildings, and vacant land across the urban landscape. Young woodlands of ailanthus, sumac, and ash have grown up on older lots, urban meadows on lots recently vacated.

Most community gardens in this part of West Philadelphia lie within the old floodplain of Mill Creek. Gardeners at Aspen Farms know there is a buried stream in their neighborhood; they see its effects in and around their garden. Houses across from the garden have sunk several feet, and the plots in the back corner, where the garden slopes toward the old streambed, need water less frequently, since the soil there is often moist. The Spruce Hill Garden was built where a house collapsed over a tributary to the Mill Creek. A crack now spans the entire height of a house across the street from the garden; the building has sunk down over that same old streambed. Just one block away, 43rd Street, a low point, floods every time it rains.

After a heavy rain, the Schuylkill flows milky brown, the water surface glazed, oily, and lumpy, like a thick soup of sediment and sewage. Normally, rain falls,

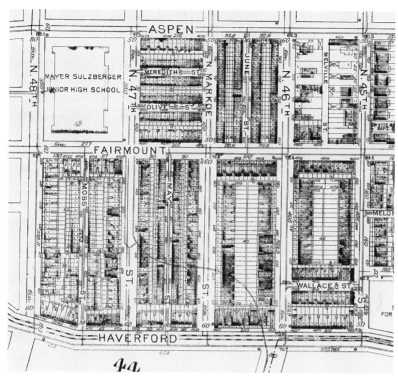

Grammar ignored: houses built over sewer. (G. W. Bromley, 1927)

Consequences of ignorance: vacant lots in Mill Creek. (West Philadelphia Landscape Project)

flows quickly across the paved floodplain to the sewer, then on to a treatment plant for cleansing before discharge into the Schuylkill. After large rainstorms, there is too much sewage and some flows directly into the river—a combined sewer overflow. The mixture of sanitary sewage, stormwater runoff, and river water flows downstream past parks and docks into the Delaware River and its estuary. Mill Creek overflows past the place where Philadelphia draws its own water, but cities downstream, like Wilmington, Delaware, take in its discharge. The consequences of ignoring landscape grammar in the Mill Creek neighborhood and other communities extend far beyond their own boundaries.

Grammars of place embody collective wisdom accumulated over generations of life in a particular landscape; their rules are guides it is foolish to ignore. But grammar is a flexible system, not a straitjacket of dictums. It does not dictate how the language of landscape should be used or what meanings ought to be expressed. The methods by which authors combine individual elements to compose landscapes, the rhetoric they employ, and the ideological agendas they promote are the subject of pragmatics, poetics, and polemics of the language of landscape.

Three

USING THE LANGUAGE OF LANDSCAPE:
PRAGMATICS, POETICS, AND POLEMICS

For thus it was designed:
Controlled disorder at the heart
Of everything, the paradox, the old
Oxymoronic itch to set the formal strictures
Within a natural context, where the tension lectures
Us on our mortal state, and by controlled
Disorder, labors to keep art
From being too refined.

—Anthony Hecht, "The Gardens of
the Villa d'Este," *The Hard Hours*

The henyard at Marnas.

7
Shaping: Pragmatics
of Landscape Expression

CREATING A FRAME FOR STABILITY AND SERENDIPITY: MARNAS

Driving down a country road in Sönder Sandby, past fields of wheat and farm-steads tucked behind hedges of the broad, rolling cropfields and pastures of Skåne in southwestern Sweden, I see it would be easy to miss the tiny, old, half-timbered house. It is partly hidden by tall green hedges against the road. Four willow trees form a narrow gateway between house and hedge; slow and turn sharply to enter, pull past the hedge and enter a garden fantasy with clipped balls of privet, tall top-iary birds, and spherical purple flowers on long green stems. A coiled green hose and a basket of cut flowers lie on the path, catching the late afternoon sun, signs someone must be nearby. High, living walls of hawthorn bound and screen other garden rooms: sounds of shovel digging lead to where the gardener is, in floppy straw hat, wooden shoes, and overalls, planting yellow yarrow brought over from Lutyen's Deanery in England.

Marnas, named for Marna, an earlier tenant, is Sven-Ingvar Andersson's weekend home. The house is much as it was a hundred years ago, with no indoor plumbing and a stove to heat its three small rooms. The garden is a laboratory and workshop, where, for thirty years, Andersson has tested new ideas and pursued ancient practices: growing pears in bottles for brandy, clipping hedges, making soil from wastes. Tasks depicted in the Breughel print that hung opposite Andersson's desk at the Royal Academy of Fine Arts in Copenhagen are carried out here.[1] For him, traditional gardening is a link "through history to human ex-istence and evolution."[2] Marnas is a personal playground, too, with past projects and ongoing experiments: a woman of boards, a sculpture of branches, an over-grown wall of brick that was once a barbecue pit. The garden's grid of hawthorn hedges encloses eleven rooms, large and small: secret gardens, leafy passages, a garden room of strawberries and vegetables, another of compost, another of fire for burning woody refuse, one vacant, "an empty pot for useful things."[3] Six top-iary hens, twelve feet tall, clipped from hawthorn, sit in a "henyard"—a flowering parterre—the largest room, near the old house. Birds twitter; a hedgehog pokes out from under a hedge, waddles down the allée, ducks under another hedge.

When, in 1967, the editors of *Arkitekten* asked Andersson to write an essay on complexity, he sent in "A Letter from My Henyard." It was a reflection on the gar-den at Marnas, a philosophy of landscape and life, a manifesto, gentle, but pointed, light and deep, playful and critical, spontaneous and composed, a reminder that, in landscape, ideas are tangible and values have consequences.

Andersson foresaw the time when he no longer would have the strength "to hold clippers or clamber up ladders" and when it would be difficult to find folk to hire. He planned the garden's future form as a hawthorn grove, the grove it is now beginning to be, growing from gridded hedges. Though the trees were planted when he wrote, there were still no hens in the "henyard," since the hedges were only a foot high and the "hens" still "eggs"—clipped balls of hawthorn: "I have a definite idea of how my henyard will end, but that which lies between *now* and *then* is an open plan. . . . A lot can happen before the henyard becomes a hawthorn grove." The fixed framework of the hedges was in place, but many decisions were still to be made: how high should the hedges be ("It's hard to clip them if they are over four and a half feet, but I would like to enclose the henyard a bit better")? Should the tops be clipped horizontally or follow the terrain, or be cut at several different heights ("A plane at just the right level will make a completely enclosed space in the lower part of the garden, and a view out over distant hills and ridges from the higher hedge room")? What about the spaces between the rooms, should they be voids between the parts of the garden that "mean something" or rooms in themselves—leafy passages "filled with fine shade-loving plants or birdcages or moss-covered stones"? "From the rectangles one could peek in at these wonders through openings in the hedges." How consistent should the various parts of the garden be? There were many possibilities:

> positive and negative space structure, different room heights, open and closed spaces, spaces that gather themselves around something which happens on the ground plane or that open to the clouds; passages that follow the district's in-between spaces and passages that wind through the garden seemingly independent of the primary structure? Shall I perhaps make my playground into an illustration of "Complexity and Contradiction in Architecture" or shall I let form follow function in the hope that less is more? There are many "Intentions in Architecture" to choose from, and to the ecological requirements of the hawthorns I can add my own social needs.[4]

Or, he asked, should he simply yield to "the free play of forces and accept chaos as the aesthetic of our time"? Humans, "like hawthorns, are very adaptable, but still bound to their genetic structure" in whose "genetically fixed pattern there is a need for stability, on the one hand, and for freedom, growth, and individual development," on the other. "The task, then, is to find the balance." Plan only details that express the essential framework, let the others emerge—that was the answer he built into his garden. Leave room for impulse and serendipity. "The only ideal city planned in detail that still functions well is the botanical garden at Padua. . . . But then it is plants that are concerned there," not people.

Most people do not consider making a garden as speaking, and do not begin to garden by reflecting on what they want to say, and yet, nonetheless, they are

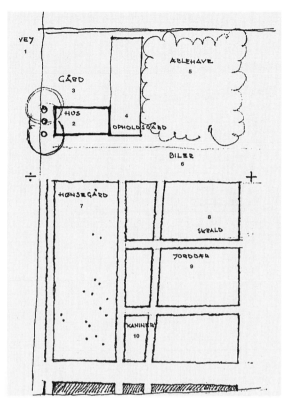

An open plan: Marnas (1967).
(Sven-Ingvar Andersson)

Legend: (1) road, (2) house,
(3) courtyard, (4) patio,
(5) apple orchard, (6) cars,
(7) henyard, (8) bonfire,
(9) strawberries,
(10) rabbits' place.

speaking, even praying, through their gardens. Though human capacity for language may be innate, we learn the language of landscape primarily through living in, building, caring for a place. How and why people choose to express themselves as they do, how to know what is appropriate, is the subject of pragmatics.

People need a place to shape their environment, writes Andersson. The need for self-expression is at the root of community gardens as it is of his own hawthorn hens. What rationale could justify the aesthetic double standard that asserts the architect's right to experiment, he asks, yet confines the user "behind a nice facade" and windows with "neutral curtains," and denies them the right to exuberant expression "that could be the true folklore of industrial society?"[5] Andersson's garden at Marnas embodies themes and strategy similar to those G. N. Brandt explored in Denmark at Mariebjerg Cemetery and C. Th. Sørensen at Nærum Garden Colony. All three demonstrate an interplay of order and complexity; in all three a fundamental structure establishes order, but time, circumstance, and the gardener's improvising add complexity.

Marnas celebrates transience within constancy, it is an open experiment steeped in tradition, changing as plants grow and as the gardener ages. In Andersson's essays, I read of his earlier garden with the leftover privet shrubs "that decided they

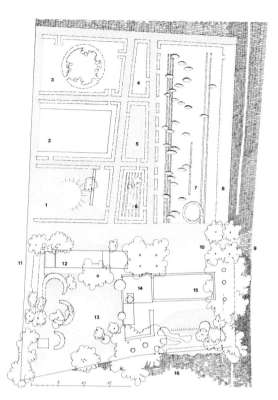

Elaborated framework: Marnas.
(1976) (Sven-Ingvar Andersson)

Legend: (1) bonfires and sitting,
(2) kitchen garden, (3) compost,
(4) Beata's garden, (5) sun garden,
(6) flower garden, (7) henyard,
(8) tunnel arbor, (9) country
road, (10) parking, (11) field,
(12) outhouse and guest house,
(13) old orchard with privet
hedges, (14) patio, (15) house,
(16) meadow.

wanted to become birds;" I discover his topiary garden, and learn how Marnas was
designed to "hold the dream" of the gardener as an old man sitting under a
hawthorn grove.[6] I read the plans from 1967 and 1976, and view a succession of photographs, recognizing the grid of hedges that enclose the many garden rooms. The
birds clipped from hawthorn, now more than twelve feet tall, occupied their
"henyard" from the beginning, but some of the early rooms are barely recognizable
in the one I know now. His daughter's sunny little garden is now a shady room filled
with lilies of the valley; his grandson's special place is not beneath the trees as
Andersson imagined but under a structure of branches and old boards built to
shelter tender plants. The "orchard" has become a guesthouse with a privy and a
closed gazebo, its walls the old windows of the architecture school retrieved from
the trashpile. One fruit tree survives; I sit under it, looking out, as Thomas Jefferson did from his gazebo at Monticello, toward the blue distance of a "sea" view.

Andersson had written in his 1967 essay, imagining his later years:

> If I am so fortunate to live to a patriarchal age and feeble senility, and if my henyard
> hasn't been torn down for a rocket launching pad or some other useful thing, some-
> time near the turn of the century, I will sit in a grove of hawthorns with a rug round
> my legs. Perhaps there is a little clearing which lets the sun reach the ground in a few

places, but mainly all that I have shaped has disintegrated now I no longer have the strength to hold clippers or clamber up ladders. My son-in-law has no interest for this sort of thing and folk cannot be hired for garden work. Nonetheless, I am satisfied. The hawthorns are grateful for the freedom to develop a lovely, healthy growth. In early summer all the branches are decked with masses of yellow-white flowers, like whipped cream, which later fall to the ground like a silent snowfall, leaving the crooked stems standing black against the white ground. In fall, the branches are weighed down by dark red fruits and by all the birds that thrive in the sheltered world of the thorn grove and enjoy its edible fall dress. If I am truly fortunate my great grandchild will dig holes under the trees.[7]

Between then and now was an open plan, one whose structure so far has been flexible enough to hold the dream.

Authors' Sources

To make even a small garden, like Andersson's small garden—let alone a neighborhood or city—requires hundreds of decisions: which flowers, which vegetables, which fruits, shrubs, trees to plant, how to arrange them; whether to fence the garden and how, with what kind of entrance gate—material, hinge, handle, latch—with paths straight or curving; how to cultivate, mow, prune or permit plants to grow without shaping. The task is complex. Each choice limits further choice, raises questions, and presents other opportunities; each decision is significant, conveys meaning. How daunting then to set a frame for an entire neighborhood or city, one people will live in for dozens, even hundreds, of years. Where and how does one begin a landscape? There is no single "right" way, as Andersson made clear.

Composed landscapes are made from the landscape phrases of an author's experience not constructed laboriously from landscape elements, just as Northrop Frye and T. S. Eliot said poems come from poems, are made of poems, not words.[8] Sven-Ingvar Andersson's garden comes from his experience of birds, his family's farm, the hedges of Brandt at Mariebjerg and Sørensen at Horsens and Nærum, the clipped shrubs and raked gravel of Shisendo. So, also, Lawrence Halprin's Portland fountain comes from rocky streams in the Sierra Nevada Mountains, Murcutt's buildings from the Barcelona Pavilion and Farnsworth House of Mies van der Rohe, and from the eucalyptus trees, sun, wind, and water of Sydney harbor.

Every person belongs to a set of themes that connects each to lineages of experiences, values, beliefs, practices, and theories. Andersson's work is linked to that of Sørensen and Brandt, but also to that of Steen Eiler Rasmussen, Sven Hermelin, Frederik Magnus Piper, Pieter Breughel, Kazimir Malevich, Geoffrey Jellicoe, Kevin Lynch, medieval monks, anonymous farmers and gardeners.[9] Life themes shared across generations and cultures lead to landscapes and also forge friendships among teachers, students, and colleagues—living, dead, unborn.

Sørensen regarded Le Nôtre (1613–1700) and Ligorio (1500–83) as colleagues; he kept their portraits, like those of family, in his bedroom, and emulated the precision of their geometry, but more freely, with ellipses and spirals.[10] In the Philadelphia offices of Andropogon (named after a grass), a landscape architecture firm specializing in landscape restoration, hang photographs of Ian McHarg and the ecologist Jack McCormick. Among my own pantheon are Frederick Law Olmsted, Frank Lloyd Wright, C. Th. Sørensen, Paul Klee, T. S. Eliot, John Dewey, Patrick Geddes, Lewis Mumford, Ian McHarg, Lawrence Halprin, Kevin Lynch.

Reproduction and Adaptation

Many gardens imitate others: a mother's or a grandfather's, an English cottage garden, a Japanese rock garden, a wildflower meadow. They echo memories and lineages, a fondly remembered person or place, love of things English (or Italian or Japanese), desire for authority, reverence for the wild. It is easier to copy or adapt an existing pattern than to invent a new one, but one learns from copying; to make a self-reproducing landscape, for example, is to understand the processes that shape, structure, and sustain it. When Olmsted designed the Fens in Boston no one had ever built a marsh before, and the project yielded new knowledge and new techniques.[11] He had to figure out what to plant, how, and when; though he consulted with experts and engaged a contractor who assured him that he was up to the task the first attempt was an utter failure. Olmsted had based his design upon a general understanding of natural processes of water movement—tides, currents, and flooding—and plant growth and succession, gained from prior experience, but he had no existing built models to guide him. Nevertheless, he undertook this risky experiment on a public project very much in the spotlight. In collaboration with the city's engineer, he worked out a plan for the basin to receive rising floodwaters and for the tidal gate to enhance water circulation and regulate water exchange between the Fens and the river. He engaged Charles Sprague Sargent, director of the Arnold Arboretum, to advise him on plant selection and on methods for establishing the marsh. In the first phase, in 1883, more than a hundred thousand plants, grasses, flowers, shrubs, and vines were planted in a space of two and a half acres.[12] Many species, both native and exotic, were included so that if some died, the odds were that others would survive. Some plants were intended to play the role of "nurses" to shelter more tender plants from sun and wind until the more vulnerable could take hold. But, for some reason, almost all the plants died before the end of the first year and had to be replaced. Furious and mortified, Olmsted wrote the contractor, "The mere loss of so many plants is the smallest part of the disaster. The whole plan is a wreck."[13] The Fens were replanted; within ten years the new marsh looked as if it had been there forever.

Olmsted, understanding the significance of the Fens and Riverway, urged his partners to follow it carefully, day by day: "The aims are novel, the conditions are novel. You cannot trust to usage." As he said in 1893, the Boston projects would be "points to date from in the history of American landscape architecture, as much as Central Park. They will be the openings of new chapters of the art."[14] New chapters, yes, and yet, projects like Olmsted's Fens (1880s) and Aldo Leopold's Sand County farm in Wisconsin (1930s) were relatively rare until the 1970s, when such landscape architects as Darrel Morrison and Andropogon Associates began to specialize in landscape restoration, experimenting with seed collection and in planting and management methods like burning and seasonal or annual mowing. Landscape restoration is now a field in itself, though is more often practiced as a science than an art.

Architects, typically, focus on adapting their buildings only to the formal geometry of landscape, if they consider even that. In his book *Design Thinking*, Peter Rowe describes an architect who approached the design of a new health facility and hotel by adapting the layout of a "classical villa" as the point of departure, because of a "correspondence between the villa type and the problem at hand"; the architect did not engage landscape explicitly except to address the view toward a lake.[15] Rowe also describes the various working methods of other architects in designing building complexes and urban districts; few mention landscape at all. Architects like Glenn Murcutt are exceptional.

Landscape authors collect phrases to use. They gather small details, like the way two materials are joined, or how grasses grow in shallow water, how sun shines through backlit maple leaves, how a path is set into a hillside, how an edge of rough stones keeps walkers on an unfenced path. And they compile larger features from work that has preceded them: how the grid at Mariebjerg, Priene, or Philadelphia, and the ellipses at Nærum provide predictability yet flexibility. Laurie Olin's notebooks are full of such observations: drawings of details among sketches for projects under way.[16] Christopher Alexander's pattern language is a collection of such phrases, meant to be selected by a designer and adapted to a given situation. Reproducing and adapting are designers' strategies as they are of life itself. Adapting a phrase or "precedent" is like recombination (taking genes from two parents). The choices of model and what to adapt to are key. A designer may use an Italian hillside villa as a model for a project on a sloping site, or a mountain stream as a model for a fountain. A designer is foolish to adapt a plan to the form of a hillside or incorporate a nearby tree without taking account of the processes that shape them, unwise to adapt to weather since it will change tomorrow. A wise designer adapts to the enduring patterns of landscape.

Composing a landscape is so complex a task, it is no wonder many designers imitate precedent. Not a bad way to learn, unless the application becomes dogmatic and rigid. Or unless patterns are copied without returning to the original for inspiration, thus losing meaning. To use a form or phrase without knowing its roots is to miss the sense of the original discovery. The vocabulary of forms—streets, gardens, parks, and buildings—often deferred to as precedents, is not merely a reflection of enduring human needs; each represents a response to the particular cultural values and practices of its time. Some forms may still have the capacity to express contemporary purposes and values, but many do not. Geoffrey Jellicoe adapted historic motifs inventively, altering and juxtaposing them in surprising ways that made them seem fresh. "To copy a historic form of the past is to raise a corpse from the dead and pretend it is alive," says Jellicoe. "Only the spirit can be alive to activate the present."[17] There is need not only for continuity of tradition, for enduring precedents that still seem appropriate, but also for invention. Both are necessary if landscapes are to express contemporary cosmology, speak in an age when photographs of atomic particles and of galaxies are commonplace, when time and space are relative, not fixed.

Abstraction and Invention

Frank Lloyd Wright expressed his reverence for nature not by imitation, but by abstracting landscape features, as in the perfectly rounded form of the knoll in the hill garden and the steps/ledges cut to appear as layered bedrock but with edges straighter than those in an unbuilt landscape. Wright saw himself as bringing out the ideal, the inner nature, not imitating outward appearance; it was a process he equated with civilization, one that "the true artist *imposes* on natural forms."[18] For him, abstraction also meant a progressive geometrization of outward form; he saw natural features as underlain by "an essential geometry." At Taliesin West, he abstracted the formal structure of the landscape, the angles of mountain peaks and talus at the base of nearby hills; he applied that triangular geometry to the form of house and garden and to the structure of the whole. "Abstraction is stark form," he said in 1937, "in abstraction it is the structure or pattern of the thing that comes clear, stripped of all realistic effects, divested of any realism whatsoever."[19] Hill garden and prow garden at Taliesin North and West are each abstractions, the re-presentation of their landscapes.

Brandt, the author of Mariebjerg Cemetery, built his own garden as an abstraction of three archetypal landscapes—farm, garden, and wilderness—each, a small garden room. Nearest his house is an orchard garden with clipped grass lawn, a frame of apple trees and surrounding hedge, a small rustic teahouse built of branches, and green apples on the ground in summer—a serene combination of formality and informality. Next to the orchard is a water garden, after that a tiny woodland. At its best, abstraction teaches, presents a larger and more complex landscape idea in a compressed form.

Like Wright and Brandt, Halprin prefers abstraction to imitation, but he engages landscape processes more fully, distinguishing between "copying nature's pictures" and "using her tools of composition."[20] Ira's Fountain in Portland is not a mere visual copy of a river but an equivalent experience; it reproduces the ways water moves in a rocky, mountainous landscape, condensing a mountain stream into a single city block. The many variations in material and form of the surfaces over and through which water flows there produce a great variety of waves,

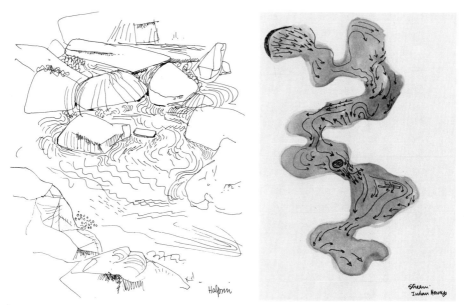

Author's sources: studying water movement. (Lawrence Halprin, Courtesy Office of Lawrence Halprin)

ripples, eddies, and sounds. Others have imitated the form of this fountain, but not the process by which it was conceived or which it represents, and without his attention to details of water flow; in consequence, their designs are far less engaging, often boring. In designing with process, in contrast, Halprin draws from arts like dance and music that share the dynamic qualities of landscape, particularly modern dance that entails improvised movement within a choreographed framework. Another fountain in this mode is the "beach" at Parc André Citroën in Paris, a large, inclined plane of stone, like the slope of a beach, with more than one hundred water jets, whose spouting varies, like waves breaking then running up the beach in the shifting zone between water and land, inviting play. An abstraction of a beach, provoking a similar response to water from players and observers.

Among landscape designers there has been much preoccupation about invention and the avant-garde in the late twentieth century, leading some authors to produce landscapes that are new and inventive for their own sake. The results have been mixed, among them some alienating or irrelevant public spaces and some successful experiments. In seeking the radically new, authors have introduced unconventional materials, imagery, and composition, but few have worked in fresh ways with landscape processes themselves.[21] Schwartz's Splice Garden uses conventional materials in shocking ways and materials like plastic not ordinarily associated with gardens. SITE employs common imagery in surprising, even surreal, ways, like the cars submerged in asphalt at the Ghost Parking Lot. The result of authors' borrowing of formal strategies, like montage and collage, from art has sometimes been a confusing collision of forms and materials. The better of these, however, such as the plan for Bernard Tschumi's Parc de La Villette in Paris, is more puzzling on paper—structured by seemingly unrelated axes, curves, and grid—than it is in fact. Much larger and more elaborate than Sørensen's Vitus Bering Park in Denmark, built thirty years earlier, the plan for Parc de La Villette, which resembles it, has follies—small, bright-red buildings—each a slightly different form, laid out on a grid. The follies stand out against green lawn, their bright color and varied character making them easy to spot as landmarks; the grid is oriented to the canal and the main promenade.

Murcutt uses metaphor to envision buildings that are like contraptions to engage landscape phenomena like sun, wind, rain, fire, plant growth, and animal movement. The Ball-Eastaway House is on a wooded site in the semiarid sandstone belt surrounding Sydney, and the house of corrugated iron seems, at first, a foreign object inserted into this ancient landscape, an alien spaceship on a large, rocky outcrop. But, gradually, the house tunes one in to this tough, scruffy landscape, prone to bushfires fed by the oil of eucalypt leaves. The iron walls form a thin, but tough, fire-resistant skin for the house. Sprinklers set into the iron punctuate the line of the house just under the roof, ready to spray the walls and roof in case of bushfire. The sprinklers are both fire extinguishers and sculptural ornaments. Murcutt saw the dry floodplains of rivers in the Sydney region, where rain falls seldom but comes in torrents when it does, as an analogy for the gutters of the building and designed them wide like the broad floodplains. The downspouts are large columns, their generous diameter in agreement with both the volume of water they must drain and the size of the eucalypt leaves that are swept along with the water, their round shape describing the spiraling movement of water. Downspouts end several feet above the ground, depositing the eucalypt leaves in a nest-like pile that softens the impact of water hitting the ground, preventing erosion. Water from one downspout falls onto a rock ledge that slopes away from the house, leaving a black streak like the marks left on Uluru and other rocks by waterfalls. Gutters and downspouts are neither imitations nor abstractions of natural form, but analogues, expressing and accommodating the movement of water.

Metaphor is a powerful aid to imagining new forms, but some metaphors and their translation into form are irrelevant, clichéd, incomplete, or inappropriate. The library at the University of California–San Diego has an awkward tree-like form, a too-literal imitation of an obvious metaphor: tree of knowledge. Jørn Utzon's church at Bagsværd, north of Copenhagen, expresses a metaphoric link between earth and sky; the corridors are roofed with glass vaults through which sky is visible. The rolling white ceiling resembles clouds, and you sense the sky, and look up to clouds. And yet the metaphor would have been more powerful had he used rainwater to reflect light and express actual connection, as in Murcutt's house at Bingie, between earth and sky. The drainpipes and gutters at Bagsværd are visible, but closed, the water not used, a missed opportunity.

There is a tradition of garden laboratories among Scandinavian landscape architects like Per Friberg, Sven-Ingvar Andersson, and Henrik Pøhlsgaard; successful experiments find their way into clients' landscapes, the failures remain unreplicated. Friberg's garden, in southern Sweden, is like an inventor's laboratory full of ongoing experiments; some have been in process for thirty years. Half-built projects and sculptures lie around; parts of the garden are like different episodes in an open-ended story. A few years ago, he began to experiment with the front lawn, laying out large square patches of lawn in a grid defined by mowed strips. He treats each patch differently, leaving grass at different heights, mowing at different times, sowing some with wildflower seeds. The American landscape architects Michael Van Valkenburgh and John Lyle also have made garden laboratories; so has the Scottish designer Ian Hamilton Finlay. Van Valkenburgh has strung mirrors in his garden, photographing them at different times of day; he sprayed a chain-link fence with water one winter to create an ice wall, trying diverse techniques and quantities of spray, then later used the idea in a commission. In design thinking, inventive solutions often emerge through a process of trial and error, of trying out alternatives, building and refining them. Frank Lloyd Wright certainly proceeded this way, building ideas at the Taliesins, then leaving some and tearing out others, but when he experimented with clients' buildings the results were sometimes less happy.

House in Palm Grove, Palm Grove in House

Driving up the Pacific coast north of Sydney, Australia, the architect Richard Le Plastrier described how he came to design the house he is taking me to. A man wanted to build a house in a palm grove. When Le Plastrier went to the place he found a tall man gardening in the palm grove; the man wanted to build a house so he could live in his palm garden, but was stumped how to do it and reluctant to start. Le Plastrier designed a house in a garden and a garden in a house.

In the cove, the sun glints on palms growing on the hillside in the center of a little valley. The house looks more like a walled garden with palms inside and outside than a house. Around its periphery are walls of deep red, rammed earth; the path to the door turns sharply around and under large cabbage palms, through a gate into a narrow vestibule with glass and slat roof, then into a small open, roofed area, and then to the door into the house.

The whole is garden, sailboat, and Japanese house combined. The house is open, the conventional separation of house and garden broken down; the interior walls of sail canvas can be rolled up or down. The tight galley, bath, and storage space are ranged along one wall, the bedroom is next to a pool with a large window that looks out over dark water in which goldfish swim. Sailcloth moves in the wind, catching silhouettes of palm fronds in sunlight; other sailcoth walls are furled, as along a boom. The woodwork is especially beautiful, like the most finely crafted sailboat, and fitted, without nails or screws. A Japanese house: sliding screens, rooms like platforms, open, with few doors. Along the inner side, facing the garden, the walls dissolve into columns matching the columns of the palm trees, whose segmented trunks are echoed in the segmented wood columns and vaults of the roof over the living room. The parallel is intentional, the perfect home for a devoted gardener. The references to boats and Japan are not incidental. Le Plastrier was once the Australian national champion for single sail-craft racing, and studied, worked, and lived in Japan after working for Utzon on the Sydney Opera House.

For Le Plastrier, landscape comes first, the building must grow from it: "Landscape is everything, the broad structure, as well as the details." He often begins a job by spending a week or so living on the site and drawing. He builds the houses himself, with the help of contractors, and continues to refine the design throughout the process of building. The vault of the palm house was not resolved until the building was in process; Le Plastrier walked every day among the palms, searching for a solution. Yet landscape is not truly everything, for each building also grows from the patterns of the client's life. He spends time with the people for whom he designs so that he can understand better how they live. Like Murcutt, who does the same, many of his closest friends are former clients.

THINKING, BUILDING, CARING

Designers who express themselves in the vernacular landscape of everyday speech tend to shape landscapes directly with their own hands and tools. Formal speech, reserved for special situations, is employed primarily by professional designers, usually in the service of a client who expects artful expression. Professionals tend to speak more indirectly than those who are not professionals, using drawings, plans, and specifications to tell others how to carry out the design. Landscape architects structure future form not only by direct shaping of material, form, and space, but also, indirectly, through anticipating how process will continue to mold landscape, and by devising a plan for management of change over time. The great challenge of landscape expression is the complexity of the medium and the fact of its abiding change. The smaller the scale, the greater the role of direct shaping through working drawings and on-site adjustments; the larger the scale, the greater the role of indirect shaping through guidelines and policies. The most indirect shaping (often with no intention of landscape expression) is through policies that create a context that shapes landscapes, in turn.

Shaping Directly: Trial and Error

I stroll through the big garden-to-be, south of San Francisco, along paths between curving white lines of plastic pipe, flexible as a garden hose. Some large boulders have already been installed, partly buried, next to the future fountain; the rest of the garden is still bare dirt. Workmen have staked the flexible pipe following Halprin's plans and now stand by, ready to move them on command. As I walk on the paths and look down the lines they trace around, up, and down gentle hills and valleys, Halprin signals adjustments. "You can't do this in public work," he explains to me. "When contractors have bid on a project they won't stand for this, and it damages the way you design. The design becomes a paper design, more geometric, less is changed in the field. And it's not easy to work with curves, since horizontal and vertical curves need to be adjusted carefully in place. Contours on surveys are never exact enough."[22]

I am reminded of one of the most successful gardens of curves ever made, the Donnell Garden, north of San Francisco in Sonoma. Halprin worked on this garden as a young associate of Thomas Church in the late 1940s, one of the last projects he undertook with Church before opening his own office. He worked on site using a garden hose to lay out paths and edges of beds. Perhaps "Capability" Brown worked at Bowood in England this way in the eighteenth century, on site, to achieve the cinematic curving landforms. The landscape architect A. E. Bye tells how he designed a long, curving entry road to an estate by driving a truck across the fields where he felt it should go, then staking the tracks he had made in the long grass. Many of the gardens Bye has designed have large, undulating lawns, their subtle curves emphasized in low light and melting snow. They were shaped directly on site by bulldozers directed by Bye or his staff. He rarely makes construction drawings, preferring instead to start construction with an idea, then work it out in dialogues with site, builders, and clients: "So often the unexpected occurs in garden construction. While moving soil on the Hering property [in Connecticut] we suddenly exposed limestone rock formations of astonishing complexity and drama . . . we stopped there."[23] Such direct shaping by an author is uncommon among designers today, and students seldom learn it.

The architecture studio Kinya Muriyama taught at the University of Pennsylvania one year was an exception. He asked his students each to design and build a portable teahouse, full scale, then to form small groups and site their houses together. The culmination of the studio was to set the tiny houses in a landscape, drink tea in them, and reflect. The students were startled when they took their houses outside for the first time and found that the ground sloped and undulated; it was not flat like the desktop, paper, and floor they had designed and built their structures upon. One group, drawn to a lovely grove of pines on a small rise in the middle of an open field, struggled to place their houses without destroying what had attracted them to the grove in the first place, yet many architects view a landscape or "site" as a passive foundation waiting to receive significance through a building.

Learning through doing was an important part of Wright's Taliesin Fellowship, and still is, after his death. At Taliesin West, apprentices select a site in the desert, put up a tent, and build a foundation platform or more elaborate dwelling. Some such buildings have been continuously adapted and inhabited over the years. Apprentices learn through living on that site, selecting it, constructing their

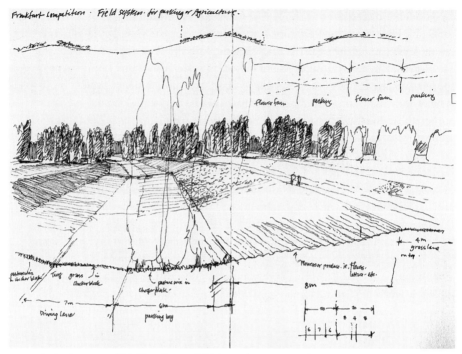

Author's sources: Thinking about a field for parking or agriculture. (Laurie Olin)

own shelter with materials at hand (gravel, sand, rock from desert, and wood, metal, glass scrounged from the workshop) and discovering the consequences: one shelter recently built down in a wash will flood to about three feet in a big storm. Wright himself built things over and over, or the apprentices did, until they got it right; there are no drawings or other records of many changes made at the Taliesins during Wright's lifetime.

Unlike Bye and Le Plastrier, who work on residential projects for individuals or families, most landscape authors today do not build the landscapes they design unless, like Wright, it is their own; instead, they work out ideas through drawings and models and direct others' labor through drawings and text. This is especially true when projects are public or of great scope: parks, plazas, entire new communities. In large firms, designers may not even make their own construction, or "working," drawings, and landscapes may be translated by intermediaries from drawings to reality with little or no dialogue between designer and laborer.

The Map Is Not the Place: Virtual Landscapes

While Murcutt does not construct buildings himself, several builders work with him repeatedly; he prepares all the drawings himself, from initial sketches to working drawings, and, in the drawing, works his way toward the making. Then he refines the design, making small adjustments while construction is under way. Françoise Fromonot calls Murcutt a craftsman because he is a sole practitioner whose drawing is an instrument of making.[24]

Drawing is a way of knowing and thinking, not just a diversion or even a medium of artistic expression; it is as natural for some people as speaking and writing is for others.[25] Making notes in the form of maps and sketches leads the author to see significant details and relationships. Even those who shape landscape directly use drawing to advance thinking and communicate ideas; Le Plastrier starts to design a building by drawing the landscape on site. Professional landscape authors commonly draw on sheets of transparent tracing paper to simulate, think about, develop, test, and refine their designs, laying one sheet over another, drawing over and over the sheets, copying some things from the sheet below, discarding others, a process of recapitulation, trial and error, a condensation of the vernacular method without the expense of actual building. The process calls for recursive passes until a "mutation" (creative breakthrough) occurs (and is recognized). As in the role of accident and serendipity in evolution, further trial and error in context, at enlarged and reduced scales, determines survival of a design. Designers inhabited such virtual landscapes long before computers were invented and they now inhabit digital drawings and maps.

Drawings and maps also permit one to construct views not presently visible to the eye or to present selective information. Topographic maps and section drawings, used together, are aids to the understanding and the modifying of landscape. Contour lines, representing points of equivalent elevation, enable one to envision landform and test modifications. It was by plotting the vacant lots on a contour map of the Dudley Street neighborhood in Boston, that I was first able to understand the correlation between low spots and vacancy. Identifying similar low-lying areas in other neighborhoods, before actually visiting them in person, permitted me to predict where concentrations of vacancies would occur. Through a section drawing, a "cut" through a landscape along a line drawn on a topographic map, one can see the slope of the ground plane and the relationships of soil, rock, and artifacts underground to things above ground.

Building and studying a physical model is an aid to developing, testing, and refining landscape designs in three-dimensional space, and also in time, particularly effective in visualizing complex processes like water and air flow through a landscape of complex shape, like a town. Take a model of the entire downtown of Dayton, Ohio, with all of its buildings and streets, then cover the surface with plastic pellets, and put the model in a wind tunnel, as my students and I once did, and watch bare areas—windy spots—and piles of pellets—places with poor ventilation—emerge, often in unexpected places but with an underlying pattern whose cause can be deciphered through experiment. Add new buildings and trees to streets and parking lots in the model, test it again in the wind tunnel, and solutions to many seemingly intractable wind problems can be found. Without model and

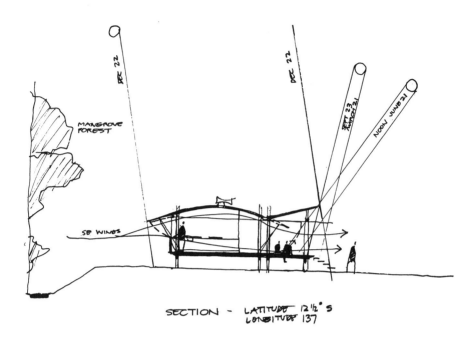

SECTION – LATITUDE 12½° S
LONGITUDE 137

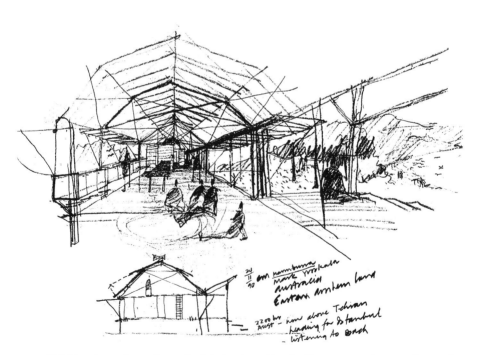

Thinking about a house for an aboriginal artist and her family. Eastern Arnhem Land. Australia.
(Glenn Murcutt)

wind tunnel these problems would be felt in place, but the cause would be invisible, and the pattern impossible to appreciate, especially for an entire downtown.

And yet the drawing, map, or model is not the place. The same year I discovered, by plotting on a contour map, the connection between buried stream and vacant blocks in the Dudley Street neighborhood, architects for a local community development corporation were already designing several hundred new houses to be built on that same vacant land. The maps they were using contained no topographic information! When I first pointed out to them that the stream is a contributing cause of the original deterioration and abandonment, they found the idea difficult to believe. Unable to read contour maps, they had not been able to see the pattern in the first place, then found it difficult to incorporate that understanding into their work. Later, after reviewing my students' drawings and revisiting the site, they conceded the point and changed their plans. The information that is included on, or omitted from, maps and drawings limits what is expressed. One problem with the kind of drawing architects use to conceive buildings' mass and relationships, a "figure-ground" diagram, in which buildings are shaded black and their context left as white, is its implication that landscape context is blank. Similarly, functional diagrams or "space planning" drawings can lead to neglect of meaning, feeling, and art.

Drawing and model building are no substitute for fieldwork. I once was asked by planners at the Boston Redevelopment Authority to review their plan for Roxbury, about to be unveiled in a press conference. The planning process had been criticized in the community and controversy was anticipated. When I walked into the room that held their huge model of the neighborhood and scanned it, I saw new houses erected on the site of the garden of Cooper's Place, already a local landmark and the site of at least one wedding! Fortunately, the Boston Natural Areas Fund had already acquired the property from the city (the property map the planners had used was out of date), so the garden was not in jeopardy. But the error revealed problems with the planning process itself, which had relied too heavily upon secondhand information, too little on local knowledge.

Shaping Context Itself

As design through time, landscapes may entail a succession of designs, sometimes requiring alteration or even deliberate destruction of early phases through growth, succession, or thinning. This is particularly true of the restored "native" landscapes—wildflower meadows, marshes, and woodlands—that Andropogon Associates design, each requiring unconventional methods of maintenance—burning, for example, or selective thinning. In such landscapes, many vigorous plants may look like weeds and be destroyed unwittingly. Well-meaning clients may undermine the landscapes they originally chose by failing to care for them appropriately. In 1984, after ten years in the business of design, Andropogon had completed few landscapes they were still proud of. As a consequence of their experiences, the Andropogon partners changed the way they practiced and decided to insist, as a condition of their contract, on consulting not with the property's owners alone but also with the workers who shape it directly, those who mow, fertilize, prune, and rake it. Whenever possible, they go on advising and training staff, fine-tuning the landscape design for years after its construction. Landscapes are not finished when they have been constructed. It may take years to implement a design, for it to evolve; the way a landscape is managed can change it fundamentally over time. Shaping the context in which landscape is shaped is an act of design.

A landscape author can work alone at small-scale design, say for a garden, but cities and regions are, necessarily, collective cultural projects, accretions of millions of decisions, actions, and events, coordinated and uncoordinated, planned and unanticipated. All too often, such larger landscapes grow by regulation that restricts without enabling, or by default, rather than by expression of a common vision. Here lies the heart of the long-time tension between designers and planners. Planners of large landscapes typically rely upon regulation as a tool of shaping, while designers chafe against regulations since rules limit scope to invent. The best designers and planners discover new solutions by redefining the problem. Charles Eames was once asked if design admitted constraints; his answer: "Design depends largely upon constraints." Had he ever been forced to compromise? "I have never been forced to accept compromise but I have willingly accepted constraints."[26]

Sanibel, a city and barrier island of fabled beaches off the Gulf Coast of Florida, is a seashell-hunter's and bird-watcher's paradise. Half of the island is national wildlife refuge; by 1974, the other half was rapidly being engulfed by newly built resorts. Residents and environmentalists, on one side, and developers, on the other, were poised to do battle. Wallace McHarg Roberts and Todd, the firm I worked for at the time, was hired to prepare a comprehensive land use plan for Sanibel that would, among other things, have to hold up in court. I began by preparing maps of the island, "virtual" images of the place drawn from published sources, aerial photographs, and others' field surveys showing topography, geological development, water regime, flood zones, plant associations, wildlife habitat, historic settlement, land use, zoning. Then I entered into a dialogue with the place itself. A clear pattern emerged from the place on my first visit, reinforced by the maps.

Residents of Sanibel thought that the city's problem was the outside developers who were building a swath of condominiums along the gulf beach. The problem turned out to be far more complex. Hurricane floodtides for the ten-year storm, that is, a storm with a statistical probability of recurring once every ten years, were ten feet above sea level, but no storm that severe had occurred in thirty years, long before most people had moved there. No hurricane had hit the island since the causeway from the mainland was built in the 1960s. In the 1920s storm tides twenty-five feet high had swept over the island, yet no place on the island was above ten feet in elevation; the two beach ridges were only five feet above sea level, except for a few isolated higher spots. The few old-timers who had survived the last one told me it hadn't been too bad, but when I mapped the historic buildings that remained in Sanibel on the topography map, I saw that they all stood on the highest points on the island (between five and ten feet above sea level) and, even so, were up on stilts! The houses most residents lived in had been built at grade on lower elevations, and were sure to be inundated in the next, overdue ten-year storm.

A single main street ran the length of Sanibel Island along a ridge, with mangrove swamp and muddy bay beach on one side, freshwater wetland and gulf beach on the other. The mangrove swamp was principally a wildlife refuge for alligators, pelicans, herons, roseate spoonbills, and dozens of other bird species. The interior wetland was a freshwater reservoir, filled by rainfall; it supplied the island's drinking water, and the lagoons and sloughs that were home to alligators and other wildlife. The gulf beach ridge was a low dune between the Gulf of Mexico's saltwater and the freshwater wetland; the gulf beach of white sand was perfectly oriented to the currents so that new seashells washed up with each high tide. It was a nesting ground for enormous sea turtles that hauled themselves up the beach, laid their eggs, and returned to the sea. At one end of the island was a low-lying place of shifting sands, a guzzle breached by hurricanes. These eight physiographic and ecological zones structured the island, its human history and land use, its nonhuman populations, as well. Each zone supported the island's human and nonhuman populations in important ways: protection against flood, prevention of saltwater intrusion into the freshwater lens, sustenance of marine and other wildlife.[27]

The new zoning we proposed to the city was based upon the landscape's value for the health, safety, and welfare of Sanibel's residents. Regulations governing new development stipulated performance requirements that must be met in order to sustain that value: storm protection, for example. This type of zoning is much harder to administer than the conventional kind, which stipulates precisely what type and density of use are allowed and which are prohibited. Performance zoning, however, is more flexible; it permits a skilled designer to overcome problems with an inventive solution.

WEAVING A FABRIC

I have a shawl woven mostly of silk, with some wool and cotton, whose fabric reminds me of landscape. It has the colors, shapes, and complex structure of Wright's Taliesin West, the fixed framework and fanciful serendipity of Andersson's Marnas. Like landscape, my shawl was a collective project. One weaver, Randall Darwall, chose the materials, dyed the yarns, strung the warp, and set the vocabulary; another weaver, Fayette Watkis, wove the weft, composing and improvising within the prepared context.[28] The exact same warp yielded several other shawls that looked like very different cloth; although the underlying context was the same, the improvisations in the weft produced new patterns. The finished fabric of my shawl shimmers, not alone from the silk threaded through, but from the play of hues; threads transforming color, brown at one end, slipping through green, to purple at the other end, many stories or one story line with many phases; the shawl ends in a palette of knotted twists. Once you have seen such a fabric others seem routine and regimented. Darwall is like a landscape author who sets the frame within which the future landscape will develop, to be shaped by many others.

Sea Ranch, a condominium community on the north California coast built in the 1960s and 1970s, is like a Darwall shawl. Lawrence Halprin identified the warp; his plan for Sea Ranch was a score, a framework delineated in accord with the seacoast landscape of sun, wind, fog, beach, eroding cliffs, wind-pruned trees, open meadows, and drainage ways. The score provided a roadway, areas for clustered housing, and a set of rules for building. Order and experiment were both part of the plan, as the individual actors, human and not—designers, builders, owners, plants, winds, cliffs—improvised within these constraints. The designers who wove the weft (Joseph Esherick, Charles Moore, Donlyn Lyndon, among others) responded to the rules, each in their own way; the result was extraordinary.

In landscapes, particularly ones where there are many authors, the key is to establish a framework that provides overall structure—a structure not arbitrary but congruent with the deep context of a place, to define a vocabulary of forms that expresses the natural and cultural processes of the place, and then to encourage a symphony of responses to the conditions of the place and the needs of the specific people there. The result should be a dynamic fabric, complex but coherent, that will evolve to meet changing needs and desires, connecting past and present.[29]

Framework, Themes, Improvisation: West Philadelphia

Rows of brick houses with stoops line Westminster Street west of Lancaster Avenue in West Philadelphia; none have gardens, there are no street trees, and on a sunny summer day, the light is glaring, the street hot. In 1987 the narrow lot on the corner of Westminster and May streets had been vacant for many years, full of trash, junkies' needles, and an abandoned car. Ten years later, in 1997, a canopy of big green leaves spans the narrow lot, sheltering a garden room beneath, a dark, shady oasis. From a distance, the canopy looks like a tree, but from the gate at the sidewalk one can see that the leaves are growing on vines, supported by, entwined on, a wooden structure. Four posts are the corners of the room, four beams connect them, holding up the ceiling of green. Westminster Community Garden does not look designed, but it was, deliberately, by a landscape architect, not as a finished design though, rather as a framework, a warp, for eight gardeners to weave their weft upon. The neighbors who care for it had never gardened before, they simply wanted to get rid of the vacant lot eyesore across the street. They asked for an outdoor room to sit in, with flowers and vegetables, a barbecue pit, a tool-

Bottom-up: rebuilding community. (West Philadelphia Landscape Project)

shed. Ruth Loewe, one of my research assistants, designed an enclosed outdoor room, a garden with a curved path flanked by flower beds leading to a large, square wooden frame—an arbor—like the frame of a house. Beyond are the "backyard" vegetable plots. Within days of its construction in 1988, the framework was embellished. One neighbor brought treasures culled from flea markets: a ceramic dragon, a pedestal birdbath, a concrete bench with a lion's claw base, an old metal porch chair, a grill, a shade umbrella. Neighbors installed two sections of wrought-iron fence to create a gateway at the entrance, angled out like outstretched arms, and put up an old mailbox next to the white gate. They nailed a horseshoe and hung an American flag over the arbor's entrance, and installed a big, black iron kettle at the back, a reminder, to one, of her childhood in the South. One of the designer's greatest contributions in an inner-city neighborhood like Mill Creek is the translation of others' dreams into a form they can build upon and adapt, making it their own. The importance of the garden goes beyond an agreeable place to sit or to grow flowers or vegetables in; as one person said, "It's doing something for the neighborhood. Even the drunks want to help us do another one." Westminster was one of the first gardens built as part of the West Philadelphia Landscape Project.[30]

The designs for the Westminster garden and Aspen Farms are emblematic of the West Philadelphia Landscape Project as a whole; they embody its goals: to build an urban landscape that is a symbol of pride and hope, that reveals natural

Top-down: restoring water quality. Schuylkill River. Philadelphia. (Alex S. MacLean/Landslides)

processes and local resources, improves environmental quality, stimulates other initiatives, and builds skills and knowledge within the community that will lead to economic opportunity. Community gardens are apt models, tangible examples of transforming nuisance into beauty. They provide the opportunity for people to create their own place, to develop and display skills, knowledge, and accomplishments. Gardens create local heroes, leaders who become a source of advice and counsel for others with similar dreams. Adept at reading landscape, community gardeners teach others such literacy.

From 1987 to 1991, while Loewe, Widrick, and other research assistants worked with neighborhood residents and staff of Philadelphia Green to design and build gardens, I searched for, designed, and tested ways to approach rebuilding the larger urban landscape that would combine a comprehensive overview with a grass-roots perspective.[31] Conventional, top-down planning had not worked well in the past. Although public investments had been made, the results were not sustained: new houses, playgrounds, and streets were poorly maintained and often vandalized; none altered the underlying social conditions of unemployment, poverty, and abandonment. The neighborhood's many success stories were largely the result of private initiatives by groups and individuals within the community: vacant lots transformed into gardens, improvements to homes and residential blocks. Still, the bottom-up approach was likely to miss broader issues, such as the relationship of the Mill Creek sewer to regional water quality.

I started by defining a framework that was in agreement with the deep context of Mill Creek, the watershed and the community, then identified a vocabulary of landscape improvements appropriate to the context, and cited models of success that already existed in the neighborhood.[32] I called the product a framework for action, not a plan, for it is an open-ended guide that identifies opportunities for change; it does not prescribe a particular method or outcome or scheduled period of time. Like Aspen Farms' main street and the structure of Westminster, it is meant to be filled in through the actions of a host of individuals and groups: schools, churches, businesses, and public agencies. The framework of floodplain, traffic corridors, and grid of streets is inscribed by water flowing in valley bottoms and sewers, by people driving and walking along streets and sidewalks, building and settling blocks of homes. Water, flowing from north to south, cut the valley, undermined buildings, and created open land. People, moving east-west between city and country, made the primary paths, drawing commerce; settling and building, people plotted the city's grid, filled the blocks with homes, churches, schools, businesses.

At the heart of this proposal is the Mill Creek floodplain, to be designated as a special district in which low-lying land, once vacant, would be used to hold rainwater, which would then seep gradually into the sewer, preventing combined sewer overflows in the Schuylkill River. Not all the property in the new district need be public property; some could be owned by community groups or by businesses that tolerate, and even benefit from, periodic local flooding: a garden center and nursery or a miniature golf course. Revealing the presence of the buried creek is an important part of the proposal because many who live here do not even know the creek exists despite its persistent influence on their lives. The floodplain district would structure an urban landscape in agreement with the neighborhood's enduring context, analogous to such greenways and plazas as Harvard Gulch and Skyline Plaza in Denver and Olmsted's Fens and Riverway in Boston.

Within the framework of floodplain, traffic corridors, and city grid is the potential for improvisation. Originally built with block after block of rows of identical houses, with few variations, there are now gaps—large and small, connected or not—that were created after one or more houses were abandoned and destroyed. These vacant lots are a resource for reshaping small neighborhoods to meet the needs and suit the taste of the people who live there: gardens, orchards, outdoor workshops, sitting areas, play lots, and parking spots between houses on blocks where once there was no outdoor space at all except street, sidewalk, and porches. Reinvestment is likely to proceed house by house, block by block, variations on a theme. To aid this process, my research assistants and I defined a vocabulary of block types and vacant land types and produced dozens of sketches of possibilities intended to inspire people to imagine and invent.[33] These ideas were refined and tested in Aspen Farms, Westminster, and dozens of other community landscape projects designed and built between 1987 and 1991. What was learned in the process of talking with people and evaluating built products informed the planning, which, in turn, influenced the design of other projects.

Since 1990, my students and I have developed this framework further and worked within it. We created a digital database that fits the top-down/bottom-up approach, linking the scale of the city to that of the street corner, making available to the general public information and tools that were once accessible only to large public agencies and institutions.[34] One can look at a map of West Philadelphia on the computer screen, then zoom in on a smaller area, down to the scale of a few blocks or a single property, finding increasingly detailed information about land use, vacant land, buildings, sewer, floodplain, topography, and population. The database runs on a personal computer and was designed for use by both governmental and grass-roots organizations; an atlas of selected maps is also available on the Internet.[35] Among other uses, the database is providing course material for a new curriculum for a local middle school.

To be sustainable, community development in an inner-city neighborhood like West Philadelphia must address the issue of education, leadership, and employment prospects for youth. In 1995, my students and I, with gardeners from Aspen Farms, began to work with teachers and students at the Sulzberger Middle School to develop a new curriculum in which the neighborhood is an extension of the classroom. Children from sixth to eighth grades, working with students from the University of Pennsylvania, study their community's natural and social history and design and build outdoor classrooms on vacant lots. In summer 1997, one group of twelve- to fourteen-year-olds constructed a model of the Mill Creek watershed, built a pond and butterfly garden at Aspen Farms, created their own website, where they published descriptions of their landscape projects.[36] In fall 1997, a class of sixth graders studied neighborhood trees as part of their science studies, and planted and tended a nursery for street trees. In 1997–98, an eighth-grade class worked on a proposal for a miniature golf course in which water hazards store stormwater after rains and the eighteen holes tell Mill Creek's history. Students chose and wrote the stories, designed the golf course, and developed a business plan as part of their social studies, language, science, and math curriculum. At the end of the year, they will present their proposal to community leaders and staff of the West Philadelphia Empowerment Zone.

Landscape projects alone cannot solve problems like poverty, unemployment, and the physical deterioration of housing and public infrastructure, but even small, incremental improvements to the urban landscape significantly improve how neighborhoods look and function and the quality of urban life. Successful landscape projects serve as catalysts for other community development projects and as important adjuncts to social programs such as education, job training, and employment. Such projects have given Sulzberger and Penn students the opportunity to apply knowledge they are learning in the classroom and to effect tangible change in the neighborhood. And they give Penn students like

Loewe and Widrick the opportunity to learn by testing theory in action and to appreciate the complexity of the idea and reality of community. As Hayward Ford, president of Aspen Farms, told Widrick, "It isn't all a bed of roses. There are fifty different people, with fifty different ways of seeing things and fifty different ways of doing things. And everybody, of course, is always right."[37]

The West Philadelphia Landscape Project is atypical in many respects. It is a research project, the staff are faculty and students at the University of Pennsylvania, and there is no client in the conventional sense. This has advantages and disadvantages. Though the planning work has no official standing, neither is it bound by political expedience. We work with partners who wish to collaborate— community gardeners, teachers and students, public officials—and we make available the results to anyone who is interested. But we have no authority to implement our plans. Staff of the Philadelphia City Planning Commission and of the Philadelphia Redevelopment Authority attended presentations of our work and received copies of our reports, but no mention of the Mill Creek appeared in the city's *Plan for West Philadelphia* in 1994![38] The Philadelphia Water Department, on the other hand, made the Mill Creek Watershed an area for special study, and we hope to work together on demonstration projects that prevent flooding, improve water quality, and enhance environmental education and community development.

My work establishes a landscape structure, as Andersson's garden at Marnas does, that lends stability and welcomes change. Like Murcutt's Ball House and the house at Bingie, it is an actual and metaphorical expression of natural processes and the patterns of people's lives. Like Le Plastrier's house in a palm grove, it seeks to dissolve boundaries between human artifacts and nonhuman phenomena; the act of construction becomes part of the creative process. It has a score like Halprin's that inspires the creative contribution of others. Yet mine is a different sort of practice from any of these. I choose my clients, and they do not pay me. I influence how people think and act, but I have little control over the precise shape that their built products take—their houses, their gardens, their neighborhoods. The products I am most proud of are the people I have taught to read and speak the language of landscape and the frameworks I have composed to inspire and order their creative contributions.

8

A Rose Is Rarely Just a Rose:
Poetics of Landscape

Landscape materials, phenomena, and forms are emphatic, paradoxical, analogical: wind is an exaggerated breeze, water is yielding yet erosive, roses bloom and wither, so do humans. A rose is rarely just a rose; it is encrusted with meaning accreted through centuries of poetry, painting, gardens, and rituals of everyday life. And still roses are mined for fresh meanings by reformulation, surprising and provocative juxtapositions and combinations.

In Western cultures, where words have primacy over images and other symbols, figures of speech and rhetorical devices such as emphasis, metaphor, paradox, irony, address have been codified elaborately, even excessively, in literature but are rarely applied to landscape.[1] The failure to recognize the potential figurative power of landscape in its own right, not simply as a backdrop or a frame for a building, is common. Yet all but a few figures and tropes, some of which turn specifically on wordplay (onomatopoeia), are present in landscape literature.

Thomas Jefferson employed the figurative qualities of landscape masterfully; later architects have modified and weakened his remarkable vision. His design for the University of Virginia at Charlottesville used two parallel rows of pavilions and colonnades to define a central lawn and frame a view to the Blue Mountains. One end was left open, the other closed by a large building, the library, facing the mountains. Thus Jefferson linked two sources of knowledge: books and nature. When, in the 1890s, the university's board of visitors elected to close the open end of the space with a new building by the architect Stanford White, the view to the mountains was blotted out, and the Lawn became an enclosed space, internally oriented, losing the reference to nature Jefferson had intended and provided.[2] Some architects have lobbied to remove the trees from the Lawn so that the buildings can be seen more clearly, but it is the trees that intensify the experience of the buildings.[3] The contrast of the trees' branching, fractal form to the crisply Euclidean geometry of the architecture initiates a dialogue: in early morning, in late afternoon, low light casts shadows of branches against the smooth round white columns—a dialogue between organic and inorganic, romantic and classical, metaphor and source.

Figures of Speech and Rhetoric

Landscapes designed by Martha Schwartz are laden with overlapping figures and rhetorical devices, provocative and disturbing in their effect. The courtyard of the

Metaphor and source. University of Virginia.

Rio Shopping Center in Atlanta employs various figures of speech: hundreds of gilded frogs, larger than life, sit, equally spaced, facing a forty-foot-high geodesic globe and a central fountain that would otherwise be insignificant. Here there is anachorism (a form of anomaly), interrogation (a form of address), and, for emphasis, placement, exaggeration, and parallelism. The effect is surreal. Why frogs? Why facing the fountain? Schwartz calls the choice of frogs serendipitous; they were one of the least expensive garden ornaments available in Atlanta.[4] But a frog is not just a frog; it is a potent symbol, a sign of fertility in certain cultures, linked to water in most. It has a dark meaning, to some Christians, of avarice, a grasping at worldly pleasures.[5] Was this an ironic message in a place devoted to shopping? Some years after construction of the Rio Shopping Center, the *New York Times* published a story entitled "Silence of the Frogs."[6] It reported that, all over the world, frogs are disappearing, for reasons unknown, though some speculate that loss of habitat, environmental poisons, and the thinning ozone layer are causes. When I think about the Rio courtyard, I am haunted by the silence of the frogs. Landscape as language, richly figurative, attracts meaning beyond that originally intended and foreseen.

Emphasis

Placing emphasis on one thing requires downplaying the importance of something else, and this raises questions. Why emphasize one thing over another? And to

Placement, framing, parallelism, address: Katsura. Kyoto, Japan.

what end? Emphasis without meaning is boring; repetition without variation may become monotonous. Overuse of emphasis creates confusion: when one building and landscape after another strives to be bigger, brighter, more ornate, or more distorted than the ones that preceded or that surround it, the result is cacophony.

Placement. To set something first or last, as a manor house at the end of a long avenue of trees, establishes a hierarchy. Planting a grove of trees atop a hill makes the hill seem higher. Siting a monument or building on a mountaintop or hilltop stresses the structure's importance (the statue of Christ, the Corcovado, at Rio de Janeiro, Greek temples, Christian churches on older sacred sites); so does putting a fountain at the center of a garden or a piazza at the center of a town. Placing the Statue of Liberty at the entrance to New York Harbor at a time when most immigrants arrived there by ship gave it far more significance than if it had been erected in the middle of Central Park. The position of Louis XIV's bedroom and the statue of Apollo along the same central axis at Versailles implies a commonality between the two. So does the placement of Philadelphia's City Hall and Art Museum at either end of a broad tree-lined parkway, the significant connection between civics and culture.

Framing. Framing brackets; it separates from context, focuses attention by screening undesired or irrelevant views, by directing the gaze. Gates, walls, hedges, and groves of trees may frame objects, scenes, or distant prospects by enclosing with distinctive color, texture, sound, or scent. Low, protruding roofs of Japanese teahouses direct the gaze downward, evoking humility; windows in buildings and arcades at the Alhambra frame expansive views to distant hills and sky, conveying a sense of power. Richard Long and James Turrell play upon and within, and twist this tradition of framing: in "England 1967," Long placed a freestanding frame of dark wood in rolling parkland; in his "skyspaces" and at Roden Crater, Turrell frames the sky, isolating shifting light and clouds to focus contemplation.[7]

CONTRAST. An oasis in the desert, an island in the sea, a grove on the prairie, a clearing in the forest—all contrast with context. The more homogeneous and extensive the context, the more powerful the potential contrast: hot and cool, wet and dry, light and dark, colored and monotone, open and enclosed, large and small, loud and soft, rough and smooth, pungent and sweet. Freestanding elements on a plain become landmarks, even icons: the windmills and hedgerows of Holland, grain elevators on the High Plains, stone pillars at Stonehenge on Salisbury Plain, Uluru in Australia's Red Center. Bright, reflective surfaces in landscapes with dark, overcast, or misty climates are mirrors, signs, beacons. Well-watered urban landscapes in the arid American Southwest lose impact when too prevalent, when the line between irrigated and dry is haphazard. In an oasis, less can be more.

EXAGGERATION. Mountain is an exaggeration of hill, wind of breeze. The wind's force is increased when funneled through a small opening—the Venturi effect. Plants bred to exaggerate a desired form, color, scent heighten effect, so do "weeping" beeches in arboreta and neon-bright azaleas in suburban yards. Which attributes are selected for exaggeration is significant. Steps or paving stones far wider than human gait make one feel smaller; if the contrast is of superhuman or extrahuman scale a person may feel insignificant. A person feels more comfortable, important, or powerful when a landscape feature is a smaller than normal scale: the bridge over the pond in Boston's Public Garden; Denmark's Legoland, a combination of miniaturization and exaggeration with diminutive buildings, landscapes, and towns constructed from little Lego blocks. Exaggeration can also deceive: steepening a slope creates a sensation of height, forced perspective an illusion of distance, magnifying size in contrast to surroundings, a surreal effect. "Homage to the Magnolia," a walk in the garden at Sutton Place, an estate near Guildford, England, is a surreal landscape inspired by the painter Magritte.[8] There, five "monster Roman vases" frame and "herald" the view to a magnolia tree "too small and tender . . . to terminate such a lengthy vista." In the words of the walk's designer Geoffrey Jellicoe, "The purpose is to disorganise the mind by a deliberate incongruity in the juxtaposition of disparate objects, preparing it for the tranquility of the Nicholson wall," an abstract sculpture in a garden room beyond the walk (see *Allegory* below).[9] Toward the end of his career, Jellicoe was fascinated with the unconscious and explored landscape design "the unreasoned fantasia of the subconscious, released in all their fun, oddity, and awesomeness."[10]

Exaggeration in religious and political landscapes diminishes the individual and heightens a god, ruler, hero, country or state. The vast scale of the gardens at Versailles—the time it takes to walk from one end to another, the broad avenues, the long staircases, the canal that stretches into the distance—underscores the power of their builder, Louis XIV. The Mall in Washington, D.C., with long, flat sheets of water and stretches of lawn, has a breadth, length, and openness that make gauging distance difficult; it takes much longer to walk from place to place than one anticipates. At the Lincoln Memorial, one feels dwarfed by the many steps, the superhuman statue, and the high pedestal. Gigantic representations of human features emerging from ground or water herald the heroic or monstrous: the huge head and arm of Titan emerging from the middle of a pool in a fountain at Versailles; a gateway at the entrance of Oral Roberts University in Oklahoma formed by a cast of the founder's hands, clasped in prayer. The attribute chosen for exaggeration is significant. In Baghdad, two enormous swords cross over an avenue to form a Victory Arch more than 130 feet high, the entry to a military parade ground; the hands that hold the swords, modeled on a cast of Saddam Hussein's forearms with a sword in each fist, seem to explode out of the earth.[11]

The roots of landscape hyperbole may lie in phenomena like the awesome height of the Alps and dangerous force of storms. Frequent use diminishes its effect. In the seventeenth century, the jet of water on the Titan fountain at Versailles was unusual and dramatic, but higher jets of water now surge up, hundreds of feet, from lakes all over the world, so commonplace they fail to impress. A desert town, Fountain Hills, Arizona, boasts "the world's tallest fountain."

DISTORTION. A twisted or misshapen condition has been more fashionable in some eras than others, chic in sixteenth-century Mannerism and in twentieth-century postmodernism, with twisted axes common in buildings and streets. Distortion seems more disturbing in living things than in buildings, plazas, or streets, perhaps because of the association with genetic birth defects or mutations caused by radiation or toxic chemicals. In southern Sweden, there is a forest of naturally deformed beech trees (*Fagus sylvatica tortuosa*), their trunks and branches twisted and misshapen like the forest trees of Disneyland's Snow White ride. Some of the beeches, with their sharply bent branches, resemble Japanese calligraphy; others have curved, drooping branches that spring from the trunk at odd angles. Huge stones mark the boundary, frame the place in monumental scale. On a summer evening the low light, filtered through leaves, is reddish-brown. This is a profoundly disturbing place. Sven-Ingvar Andersson, who took me there, reports that the trees' deformed condition is genetically determined. Because it is so rare, the forest is protected by law. Once, he says, few other trees grew here, and there was little to distract from the trees and their bizarre forms. Now, ironically, with the forest protected by law, other trees have appeared, eliminating the uniformity of species that made the variety of distorted forms even more apparent. Andersson first visited this place at the age of twenty, and it depressed him greatly for he could not imagine being able to design a place as powerful as this; but why not plant a grove of them?[12]

ALLITERATION, ECHOISM, ASSONANCE. Arching fountains at Generalife in the Alhambra that repeat both sound and shape are alliterative. The wind in the poplars at Åbenrå in Denmark echoes and alludes to the sound of rushing water; this is echoism, as is the sound of the artificial sea at North Point Preserve in San Diego's Sea World, ironic since the real sea is just beyond, though invisible and inaudible. Repeating shapes of trees or landforms, as in roofs that echo treetops in Murcutt's Ball House or mountains at Taliesin West and Denver's Harlequin Plaza, is also echoism. Rattling leaves of bamboo and dry leaves of beech hedges is assonance, "a resemblance or correspondence of sound or shape," providing a kind of rhyme between sounds or shapes that echo, but do not allude to each other.

On a walk through Parc de La Villette in Paris a few years ago, I heard birds in song, but saw only one bird. As I moved forward, the sounds grew louder, and, at a turn in the path, I saw a row of speakers, spaced evenly, set among the plants in a garden border, and sat down to listen, entranced, to the wonderful music, a mix of instrumental music and sounds of the world, composed in what seemed a random blend and sequence. The music incorporated surrounding sounds as if they were an intentional part of the whole—birdsong, rustling leaves, the rushing traffic of the *boulevard périphérique*, the sound of feet walking on the bridge overhead, faraway voices and clapping.[13] I continued to hear the music as I moved on (or did I?), more aware of the tone, rhythm, and orchestration of sounds around me, no longer certain whether I was hearing music or just perceiving ambient sounds in a new way. I was tuned into the sounds of the city and heard an order, the underlying base tones of traffic, then repetitive and random sounds in combination, a passing train, construction hammers. That was the first time I had experienced what R. Murray Schafer calls a "soundscape," the characteristic sound, frequency, and rhythms of a place, alliteration, echoism, assonance. Since that day, I am more aware how sound shapes context, and sounds became less ephemeral, more easily recalled.

RHYTHM. Rhythm is a succession of accented beats or pulses, a pattern of sounds, sights, or sensations, a periodic recurrence or regular alternation with interval, meter, cadence: parallelism, epanaphora, epanalepsis. Rhythms emerge out of a contextual background; they go with or against, in counterpoint. In landscape, the rhythm of movement is most visible when documented on film or video, then viewed at a faster speed than normal. In Disneyland, the stroll is the rhythm, in basketball the dribble, the run, and the jump.

PARALLELISM. Parallelism repeats a formula or structural pattern to create order, establish a rhythm, emphasize a feature that departs from the pattern (an anomaly). Trees in an allée or avenue direct attention to a monument at the end, as the trees along the Franklin Parkway in Philadelphia direct attention to City Hall and the Art Museum at either end; when the trees were replaced recently, there was a controversy over whether species should be varied, for the sake of ecological diversity, or whether all the trees should be the same species, for the sake of visual effect, a conflict between the pragmatic and the rhetorical. In the end, a mixture of species was planted. Alexander Pope satirized gardens in which such repetition is taken to an extreme: "Grove nods at Grove, each Alley has a Brother, / And half the Platform just reflects the Other."[14] The pattern need not be, literally, parallel: at Nærum Garden Colony, the many freestanding elliptical hedges of hawthorn and beech reveal the rolling topography, rescuing the scheme from monotony. The repetition of bright red follies at Parc de La Villette, all about the same size and set on a grid, heightens the differences among the follies. The uniformity of parallel colonnades linking the pavilions that flank the Lawn at the University of Virginia highlights the variations among the pavilions. In the square-shaped Villa Rotondo in Vicenza, the repetitive symmetry of identical facades emphasizes each of the varied landscapes that confronts each loggia: formal garden on one side, then woodland; orchard and vineyard; distant fields and floodplain. Though the plan of the building is frequently reproduced, its landscape context is rarely shown. Yet Andrea Palladio, the villa's designer, cites its landscape context as the reason for this unusual four-part symmetry. The building is a foil for the landscape:

> The site is as pleasant and as delightful as can be found; because it is upon a small hill, of very easy access, and is watered on one side by the Bacchiglione, a navigable river; and on the other it is encompassed with most pleasant risings, which look like a very great theater, and are all cultivated, and abound with most excellent fruits, and most exquisite vines: and therefore, as it enjoys from every part most beautiful views, some of which are limited, some more extended, and others that terminate with the horizon; there are loggias made in all the four fronts.[15]

EPANAPHORA AND EPANALEPSIS. Disney's gates to each land in the Magic Kingdom repeat to signal a beginning; equidistant road markers announce the beginning of a new segment. Bands of stone headers at intervals across a brick sidewalk that mark the beginning of each segment of pavement provide variety that sets up a visual and audible rhythm. Progressive passage through a ritual landscape is often signaled by a series of walls, gates, shrines, or signs. At Ise, a succession of gates into nested enclosures marks the entry to increasingly more sacred domains; pilgrims may not proceed beyond to the innermost. A million pilgrims a year journey to Juazeiro, Brazil, home of a Roman Catholic "holy man" who died in 1934, climbing two miles up a steep hill on the Rua do Hortoa to a huge statue of Padre Cicero. Concrete statues along the route mark each Station of the Cross and prompt a prayer or action; pilgrims tie ribbons and drape flowers around the statues of Christ, slap or spit at the figures of Judas and Herod's soldiers.[16] All of these

Placement, framing, parallelism, address, metonymy: Sceaux. France.

landscapes are epanaphora, repeating an element to mark the beginning of a series of segments or motifs.

In epanalepsis an element or combination of elements is stressed through repetition, such as notes in birdsong, words in a refrain, or the diverse fountains at the Alhambra and Generalife, each similar in sight and sound—the low bubbler, the arc, the wall gusher. Many of the low bubblers are in small courtyards and under porticos in shade, where their soft sound is amplified, their shifting shape expanding in ripples. Arcs in larger, open courts are transformed by sun into curving lines of light, their splashing sound bright; gushers spout from terrace walls and rush into basins. The visitor moves through the gardens to these water refrains, variations on a theme.

Climax and Anticlimax

CLIMAX. In climax, the "highest or most intense point in an experience or series of events," intensity and significance increase step by step. When a canoist runs a river, toward a waterfall, water flows faster, the rushing roar grows louder, then comes the climactic drop into crashing water. So, too, a view or monument at the top of an ascending path (the church at Mont-Saint-Michel, the grove on the Hill of Remembrance in Forest Cemetery). Ecologists once saw a succession in plants' growing mounting to a "climax" in a sequence of stages: from a cut forest a meadow grows, then woody seedlings of shrubs and trees emerge, sun-loving trees grow into shady woodland, which die off, in turn, as forest trees grow higher. The perception of climax as the ideal of progression was in part a human idea projected onto landscape.

ANTICLIMAX. In anticlimax, there is a failure to live up to expectations: when the end of a journey disappoints, when no water is discovered in a desert waterhole, when no view and nothing else of significance appears at the end of a long, ascending path. The eye-catching ruins atop a distant hill, seen from Sanssoucci (the palace that lends its name to a grand estate in Potsdam outside Berlin), draw the eye; up close, after a long ascent, the climber finds no ruins at all, simply columns placed artfully akilter, to hide the reservoir that feeds the fountains of the park. Jellicoe prevented such a letdown in his design for the long walk at Sutton Place, whose terminus in an insignificant magnolia is not anticlimactic but provocatively surreal. After nineteenth-century tourists to Niagara Falls complained that "the Falls fail to astonish," Frederick Law Olmsted was hired, in 1886, to prepare a plan to redress the disappointment. He changed the rhythm and varied the sequence of visitors' experience.[17]

Anomaly

Landscape that is incongruous is anomalous; taking something out of time or place provokes notice and promotes discovery. To take something out of context on purpose can be crucial to invention and humor.

ANACHRONISM. In anachronism, the antique is placed out of time, in a modern setting, or vice versa. Replicas of gas lamps, benches, railings, and fences from the nineteenth and early twentieth centuries, common in American parks of the late twentieth century prompt questions. Why reproduce the old? Why not simply adapt it? Or invent anew, as in Paris and Barcelona, where lamps, benches, and fences in new parks are frankly contemporary, as the celebrated Paris Métro entrances once were? Battery Park City, a new residential and commercial neighborhood at the tip of Lower Manhattan, combines sleek modern buildings with a landscape that reflects nineteenth- and early twentieth-century style, but is surrounded by the city's crumbling infrastructure: potholes, decaying parks, aging subways. Perhaps the ubiquitous reproductions in the United States are expressions of nostalgia for a period when more substantial investments were made in the urban public realm.

The use of modern materials like plastic, steel, and concrete or of frankly contemporary styles to reconstruct or interpret historic landscapes is also anachronistic. Andersson advocates such an approach when the purpose is renovation or renewal, but not when it is reconstruction (which must, by definition, employ historically accurate materials and construction techniques). Renovation, he sees as guided by an understanding of the original conception and the elements that contributed to its artistic quality, not a copy, but an artful translation. Free renewal, as defined by Andersson, preserves not the form itself, nor even the spirit, but rather the original's artistic quality, an approach he supports when documentation or funding are inadequate to make reconstruction possible and when too little of the original is left to support renovation. Better a new form with a strong artistic concept than an imitation devoid of the aesthetic qualities that made the original memorable.[18] His design for Urienborg, Tycho Brahe's observatory and garden on the island of Ven, between Sweden and Denmark, is a fusion of all three, reconstruction, renovation, and free renewal.[19]

PROCHRONISM. World's fairs and expositions typically display a representation of something in the future as if it exists already. Disney's EPCOT (Experimental Prototype Community of Tomorrow), intended to "entertain, inform, and inspire," was envisioned as a showcase for American industry and research.[20] In "Future World," each exhibit is sponsored by a big corporation: "Wonders of Life" by Metropolitan Life Insurance, "The Living Seas" by United Technologies, "Universe of Energy" by Exxon, "Horizons" by General Electric, "Journey into Imagination" by Kodak, "CommuniCore" by UNISYS, "World of Motion" by General Motors. All demonstrate the conviction that environmental and social problems can be resolved by technology. In Kraft Foods' "The Land," a film titled *Symbiosis* praises "working in harmony with nature and listening to the land," implying that pollution has been overcome. The film ends with a lone farmer, hands in back pockets, staring across a field of grain, as if the family farmer is still alive and well, but then the camera pulls up to show development nearby. Since the category "farmer" has now been dropped from the U.S. census, this scene is deeply ironic. The landscape and buildings at EPCOT recall those of the 1939 New York World's Fair. This is yesterday's tomorrow, an anachronism whose landscape, with its swirling bands of brilliant blooms, is meant to reassure the visitor that the future will be a happy place.

ANACHORISM. An anachorism is a foreign element, something out of place rather than out of time. Exotic plants transported in the late nineteenth century from the outposts of the British Empire to the Royal Botanical Garden at Kew are anachorisms, so are the pastoral parks and gardens with green lawns and groves exported from Britain to Australia, India, Africa, and, today, to the American Southwest.

ANASTROPHE. Anastrophe is an inversion of the normal or expected order for emphasis, or humor, or priority. Thus, casts of human legs, upside down, stick up out of the pavement in SITE's plaza outside the railroad station in Yokohama, Japan. The sponsor, the Isuzu Corporation, wanted the plaza to feature their cars and allude to their work in high technology for outer space. Inspired by photographs of astronauts floating upside down in space capsules, SITE designed an inverted plaza with upside-down cars and legs cast from citizens of Yokohama. A field of Texas bluebonnets, the state flower, hangs upside down from the ceiling of Austin's airport, waving in the breezes of the ventilation system. "The Hanging Texas Blue-

Metaphor and simile: Harlequin Plaza. Colorado.

bonnet Field" is part of a larger commission of hedgerows, windbreaks, and allées designed by Martha Schwartz to lead travelers from the airport's parking lots and roads to the entry.

Metaphor

Metaphor involves a transfer of meaning from one thing or phenomenon to another, an "imaginative, often unexpected, comparison between basically dissimilar things."[21] Seen broadly, "all figures of speech that achieve their affect through association, comparison, and resemblance"; seen more narrowly, "a figure of speech that concisely compares two things by saying that one is the other."[22] Is the distinction between simile and metaphor relevant in landscape? What would landscape examples be of *simile*, a direct comparison, and *metaphor*, a condensed simile? Is it a matter of how literal the comparison? Is the gravel at Ryoanji, raked in wavy lines to look like water, a simile? Is Astroturf a simile for grass? Are ruins as memento mori, a reminder of human mortality, or Patio de la Reja, as the hydrologic cycle, metaphors? And is a metaphor the same as representation? Ryoanji and Harlequin Plaza, in an office park outside Denver, represent landscape, are they similes or metaphors? Mirror-clad pyramids at Harlequin Plaza echo the form of Rocky Mountain peaks, the checkerboard paving echoes the midwestern grid. What transfer of meaning is here, a "fanciful or unrealistic comparison"? Harlequin Plaza was once highly controversial, regarded by many as a polemical landscape that asserted the authority of art, flaunted concerns for function, and failed to respond appropriately to its context. But the designer George Hargreaves took elements of the office park's "anyplace" character and used them inventively, calling attention to the distant mountains and highlighting the unsettling character of the new development. The plaza is a metaphor that can be read on several levels.

Tree of life, tree of knowledge, tree as man or woman—are all metaphor or are they simile? At the heart of the campus at Århus University in Denmark, oaks, long-lived trees of strong wood and native to Denmark, are a symbol of the nation. Here are multiple metaphorical dimensions. The landscape architect C. Th. Sørensen proposed planting acorns instead of larger trees at the university, symbolic, in economic terms, of construction beginning just after the Depression and during the German Occupation. Sørensen said, "When my newborn daughter Sonja is eighteen, she will walk under the oak trees"; and she did.[23] The oak tree has become the symbol of the university; a large ceramic relief of an oak, *The Tree of Knowledge*, hangs at the main entrance, the only explicit reference to the landscape's metaphorical meaning.

SYNECDOCHE. A part that stands for the whole, a synecdoche, is often a landmark, a clue that points to an entire landscape, city, or nation: Half Dome for Yosemite, Eiffel Tower for Paris, Empire State Building for New York, the Mall in Washington, D.C., for the nation. The fountains built by American cities at the end of the nineteenth century, like Bethesda Fountain in New York's Central Park, symbolized and celebrated new public water systems. The name Bethesda alludes to the pool in Jerusalem where an infirm person "was made whole of whatsoever disease he had," making explicit an implicit link between water and health.[24] Today's windmill fields and powerlines, parts of the networks of power on which modern culture depends so heavily, render that network visible.

METONYMY. When an attribute of a person or thing stands for the thing itself, it is a metonymy. As a child, I thought the Iron Curtain was an actual metal drape drawn across the landscape of Europe, casting a long, dark shadow. For many people the Berlin Wall came to represent just such an idea. Buckingham Palace and Westminster stand for the British monarchy and parliament, much as the White House stands for the presidency and Lafayette Park and the Ellipse are now known as President's Park, or as the Hill represents Congress. A New England village green stands for the town; Disneyland's fairy castle for Fantasyland, Main Street for the midwestern small town. Landscapes have often been seen as representing the people who occupy them. In the early twentieth century, the Prairie Style of landscape and architectural design celebrated "the prairie spirit" where prairie plants and landscape stood for "native beauty," and the "independence and progressiveness of the pioneer" who settled the prairie.[25]

Houses and gardens built to represent their owners are employed by art and literature, as well. In Jane Austen's *Pride and Prejudice*, Elizabeth Bennet dates her love for Mr. Darcy from her first view of his estate: "Pemberley House was a large, handsome stone building, standing well on rising ground, and backed by a ridge of high woody hills; and in front, a stream of some natural importance was swelled into greater, but without any artificial appearance. Its banks were neither formal nor falsely adorned. She had never seen a place for which nature had done more, or where natural beauty had been so little counteracted by an awkward taste."[26] "A man's home is his castle" was a sixteenth-century English reference to Roman law.[27] Such nineteenth-century landscape designers and authors as J. C. Loudon in England and Andrew Jackson Downing in the United States advised how a middle-class villa garden could be landscaped in the style of an eighteenth-century English estate.[28] There is a direct link between the design of such English estates, with house and garden standing for owner and rustic cottage for rural ideal, and the design of American suburban grounds as pastoral miniestates. Is the separation of the workplace and the home that is dictated by modern zoning an extension of the idea of Everyman's home as his/her "castle"?

PERSONIFICATION. Personification, identifying the nonhuman with the human (a tree is like a man, but not the reverse), abounds in popular culture: the Old Man of the Mountain in a rocky cliff, the willows that weep in cemeteries, the ravages of fires, floods, and earthquakes as Mother Nature's revenge. In gardens, allusions to classical literature are personified in sculpture: at Vaux-le-Vicomte, two statues overlook the central canal, the god of the Anqueil, the local river, and the god of the Tiber. Are we, thereby, invited to compare Vaux with the great Italian gardens or France under Louis XIV with the Roman Empire? It was the god of the Tiber who foretold the founding of Rome and reassured Aeneas of his future victory. At Stourhead, the statue of the god of the Tiber is an explicit reference to this passage from the *Aeneid*.[29]

EUPHEMISM. A landscape euphemism dresses up nasty things or things people prefer not to confront, the dress or screen standing for the thing screened, for example, garbage bins and service areas around large office buildings behind a green screen of shrubs or trees. A planted island in an intersection in River Oaks, a wealthy Houston suburb, a "designer" pump station that pumps sewage to a treatment plant rather than dumping it into Houston's Buffalo Bayou, a pudgy putto holding a basin on his head, drapery concealing his groin. Resort landscapes are euphemisms designed for play, with no signs of work save by those who wait on those who play. What a society chooses to screen in euphemism is a clue to its values and its anxieties.

CONCEIT. Schwartz's Splice Garden, on the roof of the Whitehead Institute in Cambridge, Massachusetts, relating the act of gene-splicing to the juxtaposition of French and Japanese garden styles, is a conceit: the relating of two quite dissimilar things—the plants representing living things, the inorganic plastic material standing for artificiality. The Splice Garden can be read as an allegory, as well, for the plastic cannot reproduce itself; after ten years it is faded and brittle, essentially dead.

ALLEGORY. An allegory is an extended metaphor, a story that can be read on more than one level, whose purpose is to enlighten and instruct. Mazes have been built as allegorical objects of amusement and means of religious experience. The maze at the Shaker settlement in New Harmony, Indiana, was described in 1822 as "a most elegant flower garden with various hedgerows disposed in such a manner as to puzzle people to get into the little temple, emblematical of Harmony, in the middle. The Labyrinth represents the difficulty of arriving at Harmony."[30] Parallels have been drawn between the maze and life's hazards: "The world's a lab'rinth, whose enfractious ways are all compos'd of rubs and crooked meanders."[31]

The landscape of Sutton Place, designed by Jellicoe, is an elaborate allegory of "Creation (the lake landscape), Life (the gardens), and Aspiration (the Nicholson Wall) . . . and like all allegories, is intended to lift the spirit for a brief period out of the present."[32] The lake, in a shape suggestive of a fish, was conceived as the beginning of the allegory, with three hills representing father, mother, and child. Around the house are a kitchen garden, a swimming pool garden, a wild garden, a surrealist garden, a paradise garden. To reach the paradise garden from the house, one must cross a moat with lily pads on stepping-stones, for, says Jellicoe, "the allegory is that you must have a hazardous journey if you are to reach" paradise.[33] The secret garden, "the heart of the allegory," was inspired by *Midsummer Night*, a painting in the client's collection by Atkinson Grimshaw (1876), of a fairy and woodland. The Nicholson Wall, thirty-two feet long, sixteen feet high, is a carved abstract relief sculpture of white marble by Ben Nicholson that stands at the end of a dark reflecting pool in a garden room framed by hedges.

CLICHÉ. As twisted axes and fragmented spaces became fashionable in postmodern landscapes and buildings they lost their original bite and became clichés. As symbols of rebellion against modernism and as commentary on the fragmentation and chaos of contemporary life, they were metaphors whose power was eroded through overuse. A concrete path rolled up at the end like a carpet is a pun; seen more than once, it is a cliché, the standard fate of obvious puns, which lose impact and become annoying with repetition. However, when Peter Walker and Martha Schwartz used Astroturf to clad sloping planes of plywood, alluding to Le Nôtre's inclined planes of clipped grass, and in the context of other, similar allusions, in their roof garden in Boston, they reclaimed the lost meaning through reformulation and novel use.

Paradox and Irony

Paradox and irony, the one contradictory yet true, the other an incongruity between what is and what seems to be—expected and actual, expressed and intended—are closely related and often combined. Both are dualisms, but irony contrasts surface meaning and underlying reality. Denver's Rocky Mountain

Arsenal is both: a toxic dump, contaminated by nerve gas and abandoned, yet a wildlife refuge rich with a diversity of plants and animals.[34]

Denmark in June: blue sky, no clouds, clear air, bright sun, white light, cool breeze, cool air, hot skin; Konza Prairie, Kansas, in October: how soft the hills look to lie in, light yellow grass stems softly curving; close up, sharp limestone chips on the ground, grass stiff and prickly. Both are paradox. So is water, both solid and gas, visible and invisible; so, too, are built landscapes, like parks or planted prairies, that are commonly seen to be naturally occurring, while natural meadows on vacant urban lots, unplanted and untended, are perceived as artificial. Both, in fact, are natural and both are constructed. The false idea of natural as excluding the human causes this error. Every landscape is inherently paradoxical, a fusion of the managed and the wild.

Japan is a landscape of paradox. Violence and repose, discord and harmony, excess and economy, complex and simple, hidden and revealed, large and small, extraordinary and everyday, enduring and ephemeral, traditional and new. Juxtaposed, each contrast prompts contradiction and confusion; fused, they have rare depth and resonance, the simultaneous presence of contradictory qualities that enhance the experience of each. Japanese gardens are especially renowned for this phenomenon, but it is present, too, in villages and shrines of traditional character. Today, the fusion is disappearing, while juxtaposition remains, the consequence of a growing sense of unresolved contradiction and cultural confusion.

ANTITHESIS AND OXYMORON. Antithesis opposes antithetical elements by placing them in a balanced, parallel structure; oxymoron fuses contradictory elements in a single expression. It is easier for opposed elements to make each more striking and more significant, the juxtaposition of clipped and uninhibited growing like the three parallel rows of lindens framing an interior ring of freely growing horse chestnuts in the Place des Vosges in Paris, or the branches of elms at the center of Kongens Nytorv in Copenhagen encircled by rigid, stubby twigs of clipped elms. A view of a city skyline seen against a leafy foreground is also antithesis: Boston from Mount Auburn Cemetery; Philadelphia from Belmont Plateau in Fairmount Park; Houston from Buffalo Bayou.

Stone seems the antithesis of decay, but fossiliferous limestone, composed of plant and animal remains, is an oxymoron. Vizcaya, an estate near Miami, Florida, is surrounded by dense, subtropical forest. Its house, terraces, steps, railings, and paths are built of limestone that teems with fossils, animal and vegetable, including large corals, resembling slices of brain. The garden air is full of the dank smell of rotted organic matter. Schwartz's Splice Garden employs both antithesis and oxymoron: Japanese and French garden motifs are juxtaposed; all the plants are plastic. A plastic flower is an oxymoron, a condensed paradox that owes its effectiveness to synthesis, not juxtaposition, of contrasts; so is a roof garden, for gardens embody a sense of groundedness and a garden absorbs water while the pur-

Paradox, oxymoron, conceit: Splice Garden. Cambridge, Massachusetts. (Alan Ward)

pose of a roof is to shed it. Richard Long's circles of rocks and branches seem to deny the circle's structure; circular in shape and chaotic in structure, they are oxymorons. The disintegrated grid of the woods at Chantilly owes its magical quality to the fusion of planted grid, chaotic regeneration, and random dispersal of seed.

The curving line of poplar trees along the river Rance in Dinan in northwestern France is both antithesis in the contrast of arc and meander and oxymoron in the paradox of chaotic growth of trees planted in a precise arc. These are among the oldest devices in garden design, as Anthony Hecht reminds us in "The Gardens of the Villa d'Este."[35] Even an unbuilt landscape, like inert rock formed by flowing minerals, can be so read. Alexander Pope criticized gardens for lacking such contrast: "No pleasing Intricacies intervene, / No artful Wilderness to perplex the Scene."[36] If ever strictly true or not, it is no longer so, for with few armies of gardeners to clip, pluck, plant, and mow, even Versailles now has its wild, vegetative ruins.

Community gardens in the Mill Creek floodplain are both paradoxical and ironic: they stem from lack of use and also from preservation, from closed opportunities for investment and from new reconstruction. The successional meadows on vacant lots—both nuisance and resource—are also paradox. To be appreciated as a resource, the paradox must be seen: the meadow must show signs of use, of care, for example, through a carefully designed and maintained edge or fence, a frame of care that helps viewers perceive beauty.

ANTIPHRASIS. In antiphrasis, a material or form is used in a manner contrary to the expected, the expression contrasting sharply with what is meant. Schwartz employed this form of irony in her proposal for a New York City roof garden.[37] It looks like any other garden until its 897 daffodils bloom in spring, their bold yellow spelling IGNORANCE before they fade, leaving green, then brown leaves. In summer, purple Greek anemones spell EVIL, in early fall, Peruvian lilies emerge as orange MONEY, followed by BLISS in blazing red amaryllis. Flowers are used incongruously to challenge their common association with purity, beauty, and love.

LITOTES. A litotes is an affirmation of something through understatement, through the negative of its opposite (e.g., she is no fool). The opposite of hyperbole, it is an ironic understatement of the negative of its opposite: "Less is more," said Mies van der Rohe; "less is a bore," declared Robert Venturi. His firm's design for Franklin Court, on the site of Benjamin Franklin's house and print shop in Philadelphia's Independence Park, is not a mere replica; a white steel frame outlines the house that was once there, another the print shop. Franklin Court is a litotes, the understatement in the "ghost" structure, the white steel frame that outlines the house that was once there, the irony in incongruity within a historic district, the mocking of more literal historic reconstruction.

MEIOSIS. Meiosis is an understatement that belittles by using materials or forms "that make something seem less significant than it really is or ought to be." Schwartz's experiments with materials normally not associated with gardens, not only plastic flowers and Astroturf, but Plexiglass, wire glass, colored aquarium gravel, chicken wire, fish netting, and bagels, have been read by some as meiosis, as attempts to belittle, to undermine the meanings of gardens. The cover of *Landscape Architecture* magazine for January 1980, which featured a photograph of Schwartz's Bagel Garden, provoked an immediate, and virulent, reaction; letters to the editor filled pages of the magazine for many months with protests. Some landscape architects suspected she was poking fun at *them*, not at the garden itself. The Bagel Garden had low boxwood hedges in two squares, one inside the other, with purple flowers in the center, and ninety-six weatherproofed bagels sitting on a square strip of purple gravel. Schwartz said she was taken aback by the reaction: "Why are you all taking this so seriously? I was just having fun." The Bagel Garden (and much of her other work) employs rhetorical devices familiar to twentieth-century art—collage, Dada, Pop Art—long since no surprise to the art world, but an outrage to some lovers of gardens.

DRAMATIC IRONY. In dramatic irony's double vision of the future observers see what's coming, actors are blind to it. Overviews of a maze where viewers watch others wandering and can anticipate the dead end the wanderers will reach or their successful emergence, these are a form of dramatic irony. So are tricks in gardens where water shoots out unexpectedly, drenching the passerby, while others watch knowingly.

Irony: gateway to Newport Coast. Orange County, California.

Irony can also be in the eye of the beholder, unremarkable to some, ironical to others. To me southern California is steeped in irony and paradox: a paradise with perfect climate, iridescent sky, ocean beaches, snow-capped mountains, freedom of movement across a region laced with freeways, but an apparently idyllic landscape subject to violent ruptures of earthquake, wildfire, mudslide, riot. The outsider there sees the future as predictable and inevitable, homes destroyed on unstable hillsides or fault lines; the insider ignores the danger or assumes it won't happen to them. The population of Orange County has generally opposed governmental interference and control, yet neighborhood codes in Irvine limit what color owners can paint their houses. The triumphal arches on either side of a public roadway to gated communities are an irony, so is Fort Pendleton, a de facto nature preserve where soldiers learn means of destruction.

Address

At Disneyland, a visitor is addressed by a statue of Disney, himself, hand in hand with Mickey Mouse: "I think most of all what I want Disneyland to be is a happy place . . . where parents and children can have fun, together." Address announces, appeals, or prays to someone or something not present or unable to answer: a place, an idea, a supernatural being, a dead person. Laying flowers on a grave addresses the dead, while the dead address the living through gravestones.

APOSTROPHE. Sharp turns in paths of Japanese and Chinese gardens, an interruption for effect, focus attention on a view, increase awareness of the process of

Address. Mariebjerg Cemetery. Denmark.

walking, are apostrophes, whose original meaning from the Greek is "turning away." At the Vale of the White Horse in southwestern England the horse's outline, scraped into the chalky bedrock, faces the sky above not the valley below (most photographs of this monument are taken from the air, a view unattainable by those who first traced its outline thousands of years ago). Shrines with lit candles and offerings in churches and at roadside shrines address Mary. At Ise, coin box and rope are a shrine to the winds: throw coin into box, pull gong, bow twice, clap twice, bow, and back away. Trees within Japanese temple precincts covered with twisted paper and wooden plaques tied to branches are pleas for help in passing university exams or for the health of a child.

Aposiopesis. In aposiopesis a statement or address is broken off, to be completed in the imagination: an eroded cliff whose former outline can be visualized; a path or line with continuation implied; a path to the edge of a cliff or to a prospect whose continuation is the view, an incomplete circle to be completed by viewer. House and churches were moved and graves disinterred before the Quabbin Valley in central Massachusetts was flooded in 1928 to create the Quabbin reservoir; the roads remain, leading hikers through the woods of the Quabbin Reservation past old stone walls overgrown to the lake's edge, where one continues in imagination on a road leading under water, past former farms and homes, to old towns. The frame outlining the former silhouette of Benjamin Franklin's house at Franklin Court in Philadelphia, not a reconstruction, is an aposiopesis, in this case, less is more, and in no way a bore. Andersson's design for Urienborg, Tycho Brahe's garden on an island between Sweden and Denmark, is also aposiopesis. The original formal garden had a four-part symmetry, and Andersson chose to reconstruct one quarter only. It is deliberately incomplete, suggestive rather than exhaustive. An invitation to imagine.

EXCLAMATION AND INTERROGATION. On New Year's Eve of 1903, when Isabella Stewart Gardner welcomed her first guests to Fenway Court, a version of a Venetian palazzo (built with architectural details transported from Italy to Boston), they were enchanted by the garden within the house. There is no sign of it from the entrance or through the dark, narrow vestibule; the visitor emerges into a covered courtyard garden, three storys high, filled with light and the brilliant color and scent of flowers year round. This is exclamation, a strong statement standing out from its context. When designers say a building or garden makes a statement, they usually mean it embodies an exclamation. Interrogation resembles it, something unexpected but one prompting a question (!?), an anomaly, a path that ends in a wall, an unexpected juxtaposition like the golden frogs at the Rio Shopping Center or the huge vases in Sutton Place.

EXPRESSIVE CONTEXT: EUPHONY, CACOPHONY, MOOD, MYSTERY

If personification attributes feelings, thoughts, intentions to the nonhuman world, expressive context attributes the ability to evoke or amplify human feeling to landscape features and phenomena. Life-threatening events, such as wildfire, flood, hurricanes, and tornadoes seem to elicit similar feelings from people of different times and cultures. Sunlight and darkness, heat and cold, evoke common responses that vary from culture to culture and within a culture. But do landscapes embody gloom, mystery, confusion, calm? Or do they merely receive projected humans feelings? Authors and artists use landscape to signify or reinforce mood: many stories, written and painted, portray a dark pine forest, a sunny meadow, or a "looming" mountain to establish an atmosphere of gloom, cheer, fear. Poussin, Claude, and many other painters depict Aeneas meeting Dido in the cave as a thunderstorm pours rain and hail; "booming sea" and "howling" treetops are a stormy setting for the turning point in Yukio Mishima's *Sound of the Waves*.

A sense of melancholy or pathos, influenced by English poet-philosophers and their landscape gardens, fashionable in early nineteenth-century United States, was cultivated in that century in new "rural" cemeteries like Mount Auburn near Boston. Mount Auburn's designers sought to evoke sadness and promote reflection through "winding paths leading from sunny lawns through areas of cool dark woods, . . . dark and reflective water bodies, flowing streams, material evidence of the ravages of nature such as blasted tree trunks or of deciduous plants displaying nature's cycle of symbolic seasons, and vistas of great distance, height, or depths."[38] Many nineteenth-century cemeteries seem maudlin today.

In euphony landscape patterns are perceived as harmonious, in cacophony as discordant. At Paley Park, a narrow park on East 53rd Street in New York, a waterfall masks the cacophonous traffic noise on the street. The Villa d'Este in Tivoli and the Villa Lante in Bagnaia, both in Italy, employ water for euphonious effect. Jellicoe describes how, inspired by the Villas d'Este and Lante, he designed four cascades for the garden at Shute House in England meant to create a harmonic water chord as the water moves downstream through successive cascades striking trebles, altos, tenors, and bass.[39]

How one arrives at or enters a place, the transition between outside and inside, the nature of boundaries and gates, is critical to mood. So is sequence: the order of experience, the rhythm of movement, anticipation and the element of surprise.

Magic Kingdoms: Disney's Worlds

Walt Disney told designers what he wanted visitors to feel: "I want them, when they leave, to have smiles on their faces. Just remember that; it's all I ask of you as a designer."[40]

Arrival at Disney World outside Orlando, Florida, is designed to put "guests" in a carefree mood, to create the sense of entering a world apart. Off the highway at the Disney World Exit, one drives for miles through Disney-owned territory, manicured parkland with signs in brilliant red, green, purple, and yellow that are unlike real highway signs. Park the car, then ride a tram to the ticket booth, buy tickets, and board a steamboat bound for the Magic Kingdom. There, a journey begins, across water, to an apparent island. Landmarks stimulate anticipation; the spires of Cinderella's Castle suggest a royal domain, synecdoche for the Magic Kingdom. At the dock one walks up a red path, under a sign that says, "Here you leave today and enter the world of yesterday, tomorrow, and fantasy," through a short, dark tunnel to the Town Square, full of bright shades and sounds, and roaming actors in costume. Munchkin land. It is as though, like Dorothy in *The Wizard of Oz*, having gone to sleep in real black and white, one wakes up to Technicolor and fantasy! In both Disneyland in Anaheim, California, and Disney World in Florida, red, yellow, and orange flowers, red paths, nostalgic music in major key create an upbeat setting; diminutive buildings suggest that one is a giant, ruler of the kingdom. California and Florida as their sites are no accidental choice; both are warm, sunny vacationlands.

Main Street, in both places, is a straight axis with a Victorian train station at one end and Cinderella's castle at the other, framing views to both. Seen from Town Square, the castle is a lure, an eye-catcher in garden terms, or "wienie," as Disney called it. Cars, buildings, lampposts, even trees are smaller than normal. One feels larger than life. On Main Street the buildings decrease in scale with height: the ground floor is 90 percent of normal height, the second floor 80 percent, and the third floor 60 percent.[41] Anachronisms are deliberate, so are the prochronisms of Tomorrowland, presenting the future as the present. Victorian materials and motifs like the exaggerated ornament on Main Street stores and the soundtrack of old tunes like "School Days" evoke nostalgia. Tomorrowland, with its sleek chrome rockets, its moving sidewalks (the "WED-way People Mover"), and a landscape swirling patterns of colored flowers reminiscent of Roberto Burle Marx's gardens of the 1940s in Brazil, is a dated fantasy, neither then nor tomorrow.[42] A bronze plaque at the entrance to Disneyland underscores the intention: "To all who come to this happy place: welcome. Disneyland is your land. Here, age relives fond memories of the past . . . and here youth may savor the challenge and promise of the future."[43]

Just as Disney's cartoons use exaggeration and distortion to evoke response in the audience, so the Magic Kingdom's landscape functions as expressive context. In Mickey Mouse's Birthdayland (Disney World), enlarged lawnmower, garden hose, windowboxes, shutters, picket fence, clothesline, watering can, rake, paths are neither awesome nor threatening, but comforting, familiar icons of American suburbia of the 1950s. In comparison to the miniature scale of house and yard, these huge objects make one feel simultaneously small and big, a child again yet an adult. Mickey and Minnie's car is parked in front of a garage with a huge lock. Why a lock? What's inside? The simulated landscape of the rides (trees with twisted trunks and branches in Snow White) titillate fearful delight in young children, the only kind of intended paradox in the park. The rides are allusions to cartoons and movies; as Disney said, "We're trying to tell a story in those rides."[44] Artists drew storyboards of the rides, and Disney "described the entire Snow White ride as if it were a movie cartoon, visualizing all the park's attractions for the designers just as he had brought cartoons to life for his animators."[45]

"If you can keep a place clean," said Disney, "people will respect it; if you let it get dirty, they'll make it worse."[46] A staff of six hundred copes with Disneyland's dirt; during the day, white-clad sweepers eliminate spills and litter; every night after closing, crews hose down the entire park, pluck faded blooms, replace trampled plants.[47] "Just make [the park] beautiful and you'll appeal to the best side of people. They all have it; all you have to do is bring it out."[48] Perhaps Disney was right, at least about Americans; as funds for maintenance of urban parks shrank in the 1980s and parks became littered, vandalism seemed to increase. Boston's Public Garden—fenced, well maintained, with swan boats and miniature bridge, and formal flower beds changing by season—seemed to inspire decorum and discourage mischief, while Boston Common—tattered and littered, its frog pond often dry—seemed to attract litter and graffiti.[49]

Still, obsessive cleanliness accompanied by much euphemism can seem cloying and oppressive, like the white painters' cart and the white cleaners' carts at Disney World with their tools, paint, soap, and disinfectants and, no doubt also, deodorizers for tidying up after the (real) horses that defecate and urinate on Main Street. Those who maintain and clean the park are themselves dressed up in sparkling white costumes. Other maintenance is hidden or tucked away on the perimeters, unacknowledged. There is an underground city that supports the domains above, reached through doorways with signs that say, "Members of the Cast Only." On the perimeter of Walt Disney World in Florida, a sign says, "You are now leaving WDW." But you aren't really. The warehouses and fire station that service Walt Disney World, all color-coded, are just outside next to the road, though there is no sign of any connection to WDW.

Disney regretted that he had not controlled the land surrounding the original Disneyland in California; the hotels, restaurants, and bars that grew up around his theme park created a "honky-tonk" context at odds with the park's family atmosphere. He also realized that there was more profit to be made in food and lodging than in the park itself. The purchase of 27,500 acres in Florida, more than 150 times the size of his California Disneyland, provided greater scope to shape the visitors' context and extend it through hotels and campgrounds, each with its own fantasy theme.

For James Rouse, developer of Columbia, Maryland, Baltimore's Harborplace, and Boston's Quincy Market, as for many other developers, Disneyland is a model. In 1963, he told the graduating class at Harvard's Graduate School of Design,

> I hold a view that may be shocking to an audience as sophisticated as this, and that is, that the greatest piece of design in the United States today is Disneyland. If you think about Disneyland and think of its performance in relation to its purpose—its meaning to people more than its meaning to the process of development—you will find it the outstanding piece of urban design in the United States. It took an area of activity —the amusement park—and lifted it to a standard so high in its performance, in its respect for people, in its functioning for people, that it really became a brand-new thing. It fulfills the functions that it set out to accomplish unself-consciously, usefully, and profitably. I find more to learn in the standards that have been achieved in the development of Disneyland than in any other single piece of development in the country.[50]

Disney's Magic Kingdoms are expressive landscapes with the power to move people. Designers and developers of new residential communities and shopping centers have learned much from Disney, and many parts of southern California, and of America, now resemble this world: themed communities and shopping malls with vivid flowers, turn-of-the-century lamps and benches, outdoor soundtracks of upbeat music. Bounded domains with guarded gates, kingdoms unto themselves managed by central authorities, invite prospective residents to live out their fantasies and leave crime and the poor outside. There is danger in longing to inhabit fantasyland, to forget real life, the mistakes of the past and the problems of the present, the genuine promises and risks of the future.

In fall 1993, I took part in a one-day workshop to advise the National Park Service on the future "Site Character" of the White House landscape, newly dubbed President's Park. Traffic and trees, monuments and barriers, sights and sounds were all discussed in the context of the presidency, the state of the nation, and Walt Disney. Advisors were asked to prepare statements beforehand about goals for the "desired future" of President's Park twenty years from now, and these were compiled in a document circulated o all participants. Disney's influence was pervasive. "The appearance of the White House grounds at President's Park are at least at the standard maintained by Disney at its theme parks," was one participant's stated goal. Another was, "There are no visually intrusive landscape elements, permanent or temporary. . . . Eliminate, wherever possible, above-ground utilities, mismatched sidewalks (no asphalt), the homeless, cars parked around the Ellipse."[51]

Reportedly, Walt Disney's body lies frozen in a cryogenic institute in Irvine, California, as Snow White's did in the enchanted forest, waiting. If he awoke tomorrow and stepped outside, he might think he was in Disney World.

It is easy to praise Disneyland and Disney World, and easy to condemn them, but no matter whether one is an admirer or a critic, both are models of rhetorical expression. To know landscape poetics is to understand how such settings are fashioned and how they achieve their effects. To use figurative language well is to create landscape literature that is imaginative, affecting, and eloquent.

9

Polemical Landscapes

BERLIN, JULY 1993. I had driven through Potsdamer and Leipziger Platz without even knowing it. There was no "place" there, no sense of deliberately shaped space, just huge tracts of vacant, uneven ground covered with weedy plants. The walls of abandoned old buildings were scarred with unpatched bullet holes. The street I was looking for, Stresemannstrasse, was on the map but did not seem to be where the map said it should be. I parked next to the old German War Ministry and walked down Wilhelmstrasse, rounded a corner, my first glimpse of the Berlin Wall—still standing. A truck was dumping new cobbles on Niederkirchnerstrasse for workers to lay. Until recently this had been part of the no-man's-land between East and West. Thick slabs of smooth granite were stacked for a new sidewalk—a very expensive material. On the side of the street opposite the Wall, a fresh bouquet of red flowers was attached to the facing wall. Later I learned that this street had been Prinz-Albrecht-Strasse; No. 8 was headquarters of the SS and Gestapo, once the most dreaded address in Berlin. The flowers faced the former entry and basement cells where prisoners were brought and held.

This block was the center of institutionalized Nazi terror from 1933 to 1945: the headquarters of the Gestapo, the SS, and the Reich Security Main Office. Warrants leading to incarceration in concentration camps were issued here, all Gestapo activities were masterminded in its offices, genocide was planned and organized here. The buildings were still standing after the war, but in 1949, 1953, 1956, and 1962, they were blown up, one by one, until only two remained. Prinz-Albrecht-Strasse itself has disappeared; its new name, Niederkirchnerstrasse, was adopted in 1951 in honor of a Communist resistance fighter, a seamstress, executed by the SS.[1]

I stepped through a hole in the Wall into a big vacant lot and looked down into a deep trench running the length of the Wall—the cells where prisoners were kept. Two tall mounds—building rubble—rose in the center of the block, overgrown with meadow plants, their yellow flowers bright in the grey misty afternoon. On the other side of the mound was a small museum, The Topography of Terrors, with an exhibit of the history of this block of land, of the Gestapo and the Holocaust. Nearby, under a canopy, was a space filled with sand: the basement where prisoners were tortured. The museum opened in the 1970s, and, in 1982, the West German House of Representatives voted to erect a memorial on the site. A

Destroying the past: Berlin Wall near Prinz-Albrecht-Strasse 8 (1993).

competition was held in 1984, but the winning scheme was, in the end, not built. So what will be? The museum had a temporary quality, as ephemeral as the Wall itself had become; there have been proposals to build a heliport here or a new expressway. Part of the block where a famous palace by the architect Karl Friedrich Schinkel once stood is now a place where people without a driver's license can come to practice their driving; the building rubble is graded into hills and curving roadways.

I stumbled on the Topography of Terrors while looking for the site of the old Anhalter and Potsdam railroad station, the largest passenger station in Europe before it was destroyed by bombs in the Second World War. On the site, left undeveloped for more than fifty years, a woodland had grown up on the rubble, its flora diverse, including many rare and endangered species that had earlier disappeared from the city. I had read an article about the site years ago and cited it in my book *The Granite Garden*, but I had never seen it. I continued to search for the place; it was not on my map. I finally found the site, down the street from the Topography of Terrors, now with only a fragment of the old facade of the station still standing: in front were neat gardens, behind were soccer fields, where once passenger trains pulled in under a great arched shed. I walked way back, hundreds of yards behind the fragment of facade, into a wood of poplar, birch, and locust growing out of parallel ditches, their canopies creating leafy tunnels. I scraped the leaves and moss with my toe and exposed asphalt beneath, then looked down into the ditches and saw I was walking on one of the old railroad platforms. The trees were growing up out of the old tracks, not ditches at all, the yellow brick of the platform walls still visible in spots. These were the freight platforms, backed up to the Landwehr Canal where goods were transferred between barges and trains. Under some trees at the edge of a clearing a group of young people was hanging out, a fire burning. The fringe area was a "wilderness" preserved by West Berliners.

Later, I walked around what used to be walled-off no-man's-land between the Brandenburg Gate and the canal on the south; after the construction of the Wall, this area was mined, and vegetation kept low and open. Parts of it were inhabited now: an area with junked trucks and an old airplane, a place where dismantled sections of the Wall, all spray-painted, were stacked and standing. A hand-drawn sign said, "Bring your passport and get it stamped with the old German Democratic Republic border stamp." A new apartment building with landscaped parking lot and play areas, a new landscape, extended out into no-man's-land and stopped. Even with maps and postcards of the area before and after the Wall was built, it was hard to discover where the Wall once stood.

BERLIN, AUGUST 1966. We crossed on foot into East Berlin at Checkpoint Charlie, left the American sector, walked past the guard post, around barriers across the road, under gunpoint. An East German border guard motioned us toward a white prefabricated trailer, my Danish friend spoke briefly, in German, to the guard who then followed us into the trailer and took our passports. Inside were a few seats and a closed door leading to another room. We waited for what seemed an eternity. My friend (now a diplomat), pretending he couldn't speak German well, had deliberately insulted the East German soldier, and there we sat with no passports. Finally we were allowed to leave, and we wandered all afternoon through grim streets with buildings still riddled with gunshot holes from the war, with horse-drawn wagons, and uniformed men with machine guns standing about. At the end of the day, we crossed back into West Berlin on the U-Bahn, in a train that traveled slowly, creeping through closed-up, dimly lit, abandoned stations patrolled by dogs and soldiers armed with machine guns.

BERLIN, JULY 1993. Standing on Zimmerstrasse at Checkpoint Charlie, I tried to reorient myself and remember how I had felt in 1966. Nothing seemed the same except some signs and a guard tower, but the tower had been moved from the middle of the street to inside a fence along the side and was now a thriving tourist attraction selling T-shirts and other paraphernalia. New office buildings and stores were visible along Friedrichstrasse, just beyond Checkpoint Charlie, in the old eastern sector, and in the distance was a Benneton store, just like one in an American shopping mall. What a landscape of memory this is: old Potsdamer and Leipziger Platz, Gestapo offices, the Wall, Checkpoint Charlie. But it is largely hidden memory. There is potential here for powerful memorials, but instead the past is being erased, the Wall precinct built over. The old no-man's-land along Zimmerstrasse is filling up with newly built apartments.

From the Brandenburg Gate I walked along Unter den Linden to the mu-

Recreating the past: The Schloss (1993). Berlin.

seum island in Mitte. Traces of the Wall were already removed from the Brandenburg, a reconstruction of the prewar landscape installed. The rain was misting steadily. Many postwar buildings lined the street, some prewar, once pocked, now patched, the larger holes with blocks of lighter stone and the smaller pits with what looks like plaster, like a ravaged face covered with makeup. The statue of Frederick the Great on horseback was back in place where it stood before the war; it was put back in the late years of the German Democratic Republic, as that regime came to terms with earlier German history. In 1951, the municipality of East Berlin blew up the Schloss, the residential palace designed by Schinkel. I was surprised, therefore, to see what looked like the yellow-orange facade of the Schloss in the distance. But its yellow walls billowed and flapped, the building an elaborate full-scale replica on painted canvas, facing the river Spree and Unter den Linden. There was a carnival outside, with roller coaster and booths. Young couples dressed in period costumes were handing out flyers in German and English, announcing some businessmen's plan to reconstruct the Schloss on Marx-Engels Platz across from the Dom (the burial cathedral of the Hohenzollern family built in the 1890s). This would obliterate the plaza and mean demolishing a postwar building, now closed because of asbestos contamination. Many East Berliners were saying then that they did not want the 1950s building torn down.

The boundaries between East and West that dictated the fates of Berlin neighborhoods for half a century are being eradicated rapidly. Everywhere the names of streets and squares are being changed. Even the pedestrian stoplights with the tiny "worker" image have been replaced by the banal, nondescript figures standard in West Berlin. Any tourist with a map made before 1990 is in trouble. On one building, a plaque (dedicated June 1993, just one month before I came) commemorates a workers' uprising in 1953, the plaque made deliberately to look old. It is dangerous to erase the past. It prevents dealing with memories and forfeits the possibility of transformation.

POLEMICAL DIALOGUES

Competing ideologies govern the ways landscapes are shaped. Ideologies based on loyalty to a primary authority set the terms of dialogues: the authority of nature, an appeal to the natural; the authority of the past, an appeal to tradition; the authority of art, an appeal to invention; the authority of expedience and efficient function, an appeal to economics and the practical, the authority of power, an assertion of strength, force, or wealth. Design follows from ideology: imitation of nature, rejection of the exotic; reliance upon precedent, rejection of contemporary invention; search for new expression at the expense of tradition; translation of functional diagrams into form at the expense of grace and meaning. All too often each of these is pursued in isolation, with the landscape an arena of polemical monologues. The authority of the past is ranged against the functional present, landscape as art against landscape as expedience, nature as resource against nature as sacred. Tradition is opposed to innovation, function to meaning, ecology to art. Is nature sacred *or* profane? *Can* tradition and innovation be reconciled? Should landscape be shaped as *art* or as *sustaining habitat*? The answer to each of these questions is the same, yes and yes and yes. For these apparent dichotomies are neither incompatible nor antithetical. What is the use of beautiful gardens if the larger landscape is degraded and the planet is dying? Of what benefit to humans is the health of the planet if the everyday world is barren?

Among the vital questions, posed and repeated, are these: Is nature a sacred entity and are humans one with all living creatures, or is nature a wilderness refuge requiring protection from the ravages of humankind? Or is nature just a reservoir of resources intended for human use? Is nature a web of processes that link garden, city, and globe? Is there a history common to all in a society or is there no shared past? Whose history should be remembered and celebrated in public places? Is art separate from the everyday, or rooted in the normal processes of living? Is art the province of the expert, or can, and does, everyone participate? Should places assert or exert power over people or empower them? The opposing answers to such questions lead to opposing natures, histories, arts, powers.

Tensions and contradictions in landscape architecture also stem from the intellectual biases and unresolved conflicts among the disciplines it draws from: agriculture (gardening, horticulture, forestry), engineering, architecture and fine arts, science (ecology), each based upon disparate ideas about the relationships of human to the nonhuman. Agriculture, engineering, and architecture rest upon the concept that nature can be improved upon, ecologists rely on the role of observing, rather than acting upon, nature. To gardeners (and by extension to farmers, horticulturalists, and foresters), humans are stewards charged with managing plants, animals, and their habitats for human ends, for sustenance and pleasure, and nature is both material and process, something to be reckoned with. To most engineers, nature consists of forces to be controlled or overcome. To artists and architects, nature is generally not an active agent but something to perceive, a source of inspiration and of symbolic forms to be drawn upon, a scene to be represented, a site to occupy and transform. To many ecologists, all of the above are interlopers in nature, human disturbers deflecting nature from its ideal, self-regulating state. Fortunately, there are exceptions. Engineers like Ken Wright of Denver have devised drainage and floodways that deflect or adjust to flowing water. Architects like Glenn Murcutt and Richard Le Plastrier regard landscape processes as active agents and design their buildings to respond to wind, water, light, and heat. Artists like Robert Smithson, James Turrell, Alan Sonfist, Newton and Helen Harrison, and Doug Hollis have engaged processes of erosion, water flow, light, wind, sound, and plant growth in their works.

Further accentuating these differences among disciplines is their recognition of, and homage to, different types of authorities in their understanding of the world and in justifying their actions. Most derive authority to some degree from tradition, from systems of rules, and from charismatic leadership, but give each differing weight. Historians of science have shown that science, too, is tradition-bound (until the next paradigm shift), its course swayed by powerful personalities and political and socioeconomic forces, not reason alone; nevertheless, science claims to recognize only rational proofs as a legitimate authority. Architecture, for its part, has long acknowledged the traditional authority of certain exemplary buildings (the Pantheon, the Villa Savoye) and of certain styles (for example, classicism and the vernacular), and most architects seek legitimacy through reference to a stylistic tradition or an original model. Artists, today, claim greater license to flaunt authority than do architects or scientists, and society responds by granting them greater freedom; artists are seldom held as accountable for their works as architects or engineers are.

Landscape architects draw from each of these and from other disciplines, often without examining and reconciling the contradictory beliefs and traditions. This habit of borrowing and applying theory and methods without resolution often places disparate ways of knowing and working in hostile juxtaposition.[2] In programs of landscape architecture, it is not unusual to find students with backgrounds in horticulture, art, architecture, engineering, and ecology all in the same class, with the department's faculty including members of several of these disciplines. Mating these fields in a single faculty is, at best, a rich marriage of ideas, at worst, a shotgun wedding, and few schools or individuals have succeeded in combining these diverse sources critically and inventively. As a result, too few built landscapes fuse the potential contributions of art, science, gardening, engineering. In 1957, Sylvia Crowe described landscape architecture as a bridge between science and art, a profession whose greatest task is to "heal" the "breach between science and humanism, and between aesthetics and technology."[3] Forty years later, landscape architecture is still struggling to integrate its diverse roots.

The Authority of Nature

Reinhold Tuexen, head of the Central Office for Vegetation Mapping of the German Reich, declared, in 1939, that it was necessary to "cleanse the German landscape of unharmonious foreign substance." Subsequently, a team of botanists declared "a war of extermination" against the small forest plant *Impatiens parviflora*, saying, "As with the fight against Bolshevism, our entire occidental culture is at stake, so with the fight against this Mongolian invader, an essential element of this culture, namely, the beauty of our home forest [is at stake]."[4] Under National Socialism, earlier ideas of the natural garden were taken up and their political implications expanded; one designer described, in 1936, an obligation to design "blood-and-soil-connected gardens."[5] These ideas became part of official policy as "Rules for the Design of the Landscape" developed by Heinrich Himmler's staff in 1942 for the so-called Incorporated Eastern Territories of Germany (taken from Poland in 1939): "It is not sufficient to settle our people in those areas and to eliminate foreign people. Instead the area must be given a structure which corresponds to our type of being."[6]

Such exploitation ought to have dispelled forever the illusion of innocence surrounding "nature," one of the most powerfully loaded, ideological words in the English and the German languages. Those who cite nature and the natural to justify their designs or to evoke a sense of goodness rarely examine precisely what such words mean to them. Most are ignorant of the ideological minefields they tread.

"Attack of the Killer Weeds," announced the cover of the Philadelphia *Inquirer*'s Sunday magazine in 1996, alluding to the lead article, "Aliens Among Us."[7] The conflict over the use of native versus "exotic" plants, debated over nearly one hundred years among landscape architects and environmentalists, and among ecological restorationists and horticulturists, has grown increasingly strident. Once confined to the pages of professional journals, it has now spilled over into the popular press. Is it a coincidence that there is a growing movement to support "native" plants and eradicate exotic "invaders," like the Norway maple, just at the time of mounting anger at illegal immigrants and at multinational corporations that move U.S. factories and jobs away to countries with low pay scales? Polemical rhetoric plays on fear of the alien, provokes opposition as well as support, and ironically obscures the real problems some species pose.[8]

Landscape authors who call their work natural or ecological cite the authority of nature to justify their selection of some materials or plants and the exclusion of others, and to support their decisions to arrange material in certain patterns, and to tend the result in certain ways. To call a landscape natural implies the existence of other, unnatural, landscapes that are, presumably, wrong. Yet quite different sorts of landscape designs have been cited by others as natural, much as God is claimed by opposing nations. In fact some designs invoke nature as if it were divine authority. To Frank Lloyd Wright, nature was the manifestation of God: "Nature should be spelled with a capital 'N,' not because Nature is God but because all that we can learn of God we will learn from the body of God, which we call Nature."[9] But for Wright, nature included humans, and the aim of his designs was "truly no less than the creation of man as a perfect 'flower of Nature.'"[10] For many people today, nature is devoid of humans and human constructions.

So, too, the authority of science is cited to augment or substitute for the authority of nature or God. To most landscape architects ecological science is a vital source of principles for landscape design; indeed, the adoption of ideas from ecology contributed to a renewal of that discipline in the 1960s. But, for some, ecology is the primary authority for determining the natural, and, therefore, the only correct way to design landscapes. To these, ecology's most extreme practitioners, ecological design is deterministic; the laws they cite are couched in terms that recall religious dogma. In recent years, debates over what constitutes a "truly ecological practice of landscape architecture" have escalated with certain groups accusing others of "nonecological" behavior.[11] Bitter quarrels have ensued over the proper materials, styles, and methods of ecological landscape design, some advocating the exclusive use of native, and rejection of naturalized, plants, some urging eradication of exotic invaders and condemning planting of foreign species. Some labor to conceal the artifice of their works; others celebrate the human capacity to transform the landscape. Some honor the role of reason in design and promote science as the sole source of truth about nature; others trust personal intuition or even revelation and reject science as a reliable way of knowing.

Such conflicts about competing sources of authority and conflicting ideas of nature engender confusion about certain issues: whether humans are outside or inside nature, whether human influence is, inevitably, destructive or, potentially, beneficial, whether one can know an objective nature apart from human values. Does authority come from principles, tradition, and precedent, from the way things have always been done or were done in some idealized past or by exemplary earlier models, or does authority rest in a rational system of rules or laws, which can be tested, proved, or explained? Some trust the claims of a charismatic leader.[12] Such differences in basic assumptions are so fundamental that resolving these conflicts seems impossible. And yet, clarifying some differences and dispelling confusion is not impossible. Not impossible, that is, if those engaged in the debate define their terms. If someone invokes the authority of nature, implying the right to speak for nature, who has conferred that privilege and why? And what is nature anyway? And how determine its authority? Or balance conflicting claims made in nature's name?

Nature is an abstraction, a set of ideas for which many cultures have no one name, "a singular name for the real multiplicity of things and living processes."[13] A. O. Lovejoy found sixty-six meanings of the words *nature* and *natural* in literature and philosophy from the time of the ancient Greeks to the eighteenth century.[14] The abstract quality of the word also tends to deny the role of the nonhuman as exerting an active force upon the world, on the one hand, while inviting personification (Nature's revenge) of nature, on the other.

The competing claims conceal real paradox. Nature is, in fact, both given and constructed. *Nature*, Raymond Williams called "perhaps the most complex word in the language," "the inherent force which directs either the world or human beings or both" and "the material world itself, taken as including or not including human beings."[15] From the Latin *natura*, which comes from *nasci*, to be born, nature is linked to other words from the same root, *nascent, innate, native, nation*; in English, as in French and Latin, nature originally described the essential or given character of something and only later did it become an independent noun.

As human cultures describe themselves as reflections of nature, so their ideas of nature mirror that culture, their concept of normal or abnormal, right or wrong. The idea of the Fall, of humanity expelled from paradise, assumes that a state of grace within nature is no longer available to human beings. Nor has science been immune; ecologists who describe the "harmony" of nature and the succession of plant "communities" from pioneers to stable climax forest assume an implicit model for human society.[16] Ecology, anthropology, and garden design are laced with Edenic narratives, nostalgic stories of an original state in which humans and nonhumans lived in peace, perfection, and innocence, followed by a state of expulsion, of humans anyway, from nature. In some such scenarios, the most "primitive," least "civilized" "native" peoples are seen as more worthy and as morally superior to the more "civilized" in their relation to nature.[17]

Even in a particular time and place, no agreement exists on the natural way of doing things. Wright and Jens Jensen, fellow residents of Chicago and Wisconsin, friends throughout most of their lives, agreed that nature was *the* authority for design and sought to articulate the moral messages or "sermons" they read in hills and valleys, rivers and trees. And yet the two "argued incessantly about the nature of nature," about what form a natural garden should take.[18] Wright had contempt for "some sentimental feeling about animals and grass and trees and out-of-doors generally," but revered nature as an internal ideal, the very "'nature' of God."[19] It was the task of the architect to bring the outer, often imperfect, form into closer conformity with an inner ideal, its nature, its essence. Wright derived his principles for design from what he saw as the underlying structure of flowers, trees, and terrain; his landscape designs were often abstract versions of actual regional landscapes of prairie or desert.

Jensen's obsession, on the other hand, was to protect and promote the native features of regional landscapes. He saw a correspondence between a region's climate, physiography, and flora and its human inhabitants; landscape, he believed, fostered, then symbolized, a relationship between people and place. His published works do not suggest that he believed humans could improve upon the native landscape: "Nature talks more finely and more deeply when left alone."[20] He revered the primitive, and found his "main source of inspiration . . . in the unadulterated, untouched work of the great Master."[21] Jensen sought to imitate the outward appearance of the local landscape, its meadows, woodlands, and riverbanks: "Through generations of evolution our native landscape becomes a part of us, and out of this we may form fitting compositions for our people."[22] Many of his ideas, such as a correlation between nature and nation and his advocacy of native plants were common in Europe and North America.[23] Contemporary ecological theories drew parallels between plant and animal communities and human communities.[24] German landscape architects under National Socialism carried the relationship between native plants and folk to ideological extremes, using native plants and natural gardens to represent the Nazi political agenda, and there is some evidence that Jensen was sympathetic to at least some of these ideas.[25]

Whatever nature means to landscape architects, they tend to care about it, for the beliefs and values it represents tend to lie at the heart of their decision to enter the profession. For the past seven years, I have asked my graduate students, "What is nature?" Among their responses are clashing perspectives: nature was given as a trust to humans by God; nature is trees and rocks, everything except humans and the things humans make; nature is a place where one cannot see the hand of humans, a place to be alone; nature consists of creative and life-sustaining processes which connect everything in the physical and biological worlds, including humans; nature is a cultural construct with no meaning or existence outside human society; nature is something that cannot be known; Nature is God. The experiential and spiritual aspects of nature are cited frequently, and nature as material resource is seldom mentioned.[26]

Ian McHarg's *Design with Nature*, published in 1969, stimulated fundamental changes in the teaching and practice of landscape architecture. McHarg advocated systematic application of a set of rules derived from ecological science and demonstrated its value in professional projects.[27] His charismatic personality and polemical power captured the attention of the profession and the public; he was instrumental in the acceptance of ideas others had also explored. Today, more than thirty years later, many of these innovations, once seen as radical, are common practice. However, his claim that science is the only defensible authority for landscape design has provoked equally dogmatic reactions from those who seek to promote landscape architecture as an art form and who have set that approach in opposition to "the ecological movement and its detrimental consequences for design."[28]

Is ecology a science (a way of describing the world)? Is it a cause (a mandate for moral action)? An aesthetic (a norm for beauty)? It is important to distinguish the insights of ecology, the science, from ecology as a source of prescriptive principles and aesthetic values. The perception of the world as a complex network of relations, with humans as but one part of that web, has been a significant contribution of ecology, but there has been a tendency to jump from such insights to prescription and proscription, to cite ecology as an authority much as nature was cited in the past as the source of laws for landscape design and as providing a single norm. To Laurie Olin this approach is "a new deterministic and doctrinaire view of what is 'natural' and 'beautiful'" reflecting a "chilling, close-minded stance of moral certitude."[29]

The Authority of the Past

Appeal to the past for authority is as problematic as appeal to nature. Because the history of twentieth-century landscape architecture has been told largely as a history of forms rather than of ideas and expression, especially in the history of naturalistic or ecological design, implicit motives and values implicit in design have generally remained unexamined. Gardens built to imitate nature may appear similar yet express different, even divergent, values and concepts. Although the Fens and Riverway in Boston and Columbus Park in Chicago were built to resemble scenery native to their region, and although both are frequently cited as precedents for landscape restoration today, the motivations that underlay them were different in important ways not usually understood.[30]

The Fens and Riverway, designed by Frederick Law Olmsted and built in the 1880s to 1890s, were revolutionary in function and form, their so-called wild appearance in contrast to prevailing formal and pastoral styles.[31] Built on the site of polluted tidal flats and floodplains, they were designed to purify water and protect adjacent land from flooding. They incorporated an interceptor sewer, a parkway, and Boston's first streetcar line, and together formed a landscape *system* to accommodate the flow of water, removal of wastes, and movement of people. Olmsted conceived them as a new type of integrated, multifunctional, urban open space, one he took care to distinguish from a park. This skeleton of woods and wetland, road, sewer, and public transit structured the growing city and its suburbs. The Fens and Riverway were a fusion of art, agriculture, engineering, and science.

Jensen, designing Columbus Park (1916) in Chicago thirty years later to symbolize a prairie landscape, created a large meadow, excavated a meandering lagoon, and planted groves of trees to represent the Illinois landscape: prairie, prairie river, and forest edge.[32] All the plants used in the park were native to Illinois; they belonged, as Jensen put it.[33] In outward appearance, the prairie river looked much like the Fens, as photographs within about a decade of construction testify. Like Olmsted, Jensen intended his project to expose city residents to the beneficial influence of rural scenery, particularly those unable to travel to faroff places or unwelcome in "neighboring fields, woods, pond-sides, river-banks, valleys, or hills."[34] Yet Jensen's aims and his goals were quite different from Olmsted's. His agenda at Columbus Park, as elsewhere, was to bring people, especially "the growing minds" of youth, into contact with their "home environment," for "We are molded into a people by the thing we live with day after day."[35] Every region ought to display the beauty of its local landscape: "This encourages each race, each country, each state, and each county to bring out the best within its borders."[36] In *Siftings*, Jensen elaborated on environmental influences, attributing certain characteristics among populations of European countries and American regions to the influence of their landscapes. He claimed to see each regional landscape as beautiful in its own way, but he repeatedly exposed a prejudice for the superiority of northern regions and their peoples: "Environmental influences of the hot south have almost destroyed the strong and hardy characteristics of . . . northern people."[37] He drew parallels between people and plants and advocated that only species native to a place be used: "To me no plant is more refined than that which belongs. There is no comparison between native plants and those imported from foreign shores which are, and shall always remain so, novelties."[38]

Olmsted, too, believed that environment influenced human behavior, convinced that contemplation of "natural scenery" had beneficial physical, mental, and moral effects, and that lack of such opportunity could lead to depression and mental illness.[39] But in constructing such scenery, he advocated the use of hardy, exotic plants along with native species, arguing with Charles Sprague Sargent, who opposed using nonnative plants in the Riverway.[40] The upshot was that only native species were planted on the Brookline side of the Riverway (where Sargent had the authority of approval), but a mixture of native and nonnative species was planted on the Boston side (where Olmsted did). The primary purpose of the Riverway was "to abate existing nuisances, avoid threatened dangers and provide for the permanent, wholesome and seemly disposition of the drainage of Muddy River Valley."[41] Jensen's work posed no such goals.

The natural garden movement of the early part of the twentieth century, which Jensen supported, and today's ecological design movement seem to have much in common. Both stress native plants and plant communities as material and model for garden design. And yet, deep differences in the ideas of nature have guided the two movements. In the United States, natural garden design in the early part of the century was part of a larger context of regionalism expressed in art, literature, and politics, a populist movement promoting local roots over the increasing power of the federal government, the growth of national corporations, and the influence of foreign styles.[42] Jensen, in his focus on regional landscapes and native plants, never discussed the value of plants, animals, or biological and physical processes apart from human purpose; his anthropocentric perspective is a contrast to late twentieth-century environmentalism, in which animals, plants, and ecosystems have been accorded value, even legal rights, not for their worth to humans alone, but for themselves.[43]

Among landscape architects the most bitter recent debates have been waged over the authority of nature versus that of art; the authority of past landscapes has been cited mainly in defense of one or the other position, each side constructing its own pantheon of past authorities: "Capability" Brown, Olmsted, and Jensen, for example, versus Le Nôtre, Daniel Burnham, and Thomas Church. The classical tradition of architecture has occupied a similar position among Western architects to that of nature among landscape architects. Much as different landscape architects are inspired by and appeal to nature for authority, so architects appeal to the authority of a classical style in buildings and landscapes, including particular exemplary models. Architects have returned to classical buildings and spaces repeatedly for inspiration and authority, from Palladio to Jefferson to Gunnar Asplund to Albert Speer to Robert Venturi. A classical style has been employed at different times and places for quite different purposes, all appealing to the past for authority, and serving primarily to identify the client with Greece and Rome. But as inheritor of what aspects of those cultures? Art? Philosophy? Democracy? Empire?

I was unprepared for the heated polemical debates among jurists on the Minnesota State Capitol Competition in 1986 over whether or not the new landscape should be in a classical style. "You are an ideologue," accused a fellow juror, a European architect, on the last day of the panel's deliberations for the Minnesota State Capitol Competition, following my support of a scheme he abhorred. By this time I had become inured to such attacks. At the first meeting of the jury, as we prepared to introduce ourselves, he had requested that we each identify our ideological positions so each would know where the others stood before the debate began. Expecting him to lay out a political position of some sort, I was surprised when he and another juror (also a European architect) professed their ideology as classicism.

The entries we had come to judge were proposals for the grounds of the Minnesota State Capitol Building, which had been built in the 1890s in neoclassical style. There were eleven members on the jury: two landscape architects, three architects, a city planner, and several politicians and local businessmen. This was a two-stage review: the first meeting was for two days, its object to select five finalists who would then develop their designs further; the second meeting would be several months later, to select the one to be built. There were more than three hundred entries, each consisting of two panels of drawings illustrating the design, all displayed on easels set up in the National Guard armory. We spent the first day reviewing all entries before assembling to compare notes toward the end of the afternoon and proceeding to narrow the field by eliminating many contestants from further consideration. The subsequent debates were among the least substantive and rational I have ever experienced on a competition jury, which normally affords the most challenging, stimulating, and heated of professional discussions. The two classicists supported those proposals that were in accord with their canon and dismissed those to which they were opposed, including any design in a modernist or contemporary style. The one proposal the classicists favored most was not a bad design, but several others they rejected out of hand were also worthy of consideration; their principal strategy seemed to be to eliminate competing schemes from consideration through appeals to the authority of the past, and further to flatter, ridicule, or intimidate other jurors to win support or cow the opposition, as needed. In the end, the Minnesota Capitol got a classical landscape.

Landscapes of memory are often polemical. Most reconstructions of past landscapes—Sturbridge Village in Massachusetts, Williamsburg in Virginia, and Disney's Main Street—take their authority from the past, but present a sanitized, sentimentalized version of past and present. So do places from which the past has been selectively stripped, like Philadelphia's Independence National Park, a zone of suspended time in a busy city. The core of that park is six large city blocks from which all traces of activity that occurred between 1800 and the 1970s are expunged, all of those buildings—factories, warehouses, stores, tenements—demolished. The remaining buildings, built before 1800 (or reconstructions), are scattered like headstones in a cemetery surrounded by a pastoral landscape of lawn and trees in one section of the park, and isolated within a monumental mall in the other. "Independence," as the National Park Service calls it, is the product of decades of bitter battles over what is significant about the past and how it should be represented. In the late nineteenth and early twentieth centuries, the focus was on Independence Hall and the Liberty Bell as national icons: first, on the reconstruction of the building itself, then, on creation of a proper setting for it. Proposals offered between 1915 and 1930 ranged from modest plazas across the street to a formal vista several blocks long to frame the building, with the Liberty Bell on a sort of altar in the center of a "Great Marble Court" surrounded by neoclassical buildings. From the 1930s on, the idea of a unified historic district grew, seen by some as a tool for revitalizing the surrounding area. Throughout the controversies two things remained constant: the regard for Independence and Carpenters' halls as national shrines. All the plans put forward for Independence included both buildings as foci. The landscape of Independence reflects changing ideas over the course of a century, of history, the nature of the authority it confers, and the role of historic preservation.

The Authority of Function and Expedience

Designers of the modernist architecture and urban design that dominated the landscape of American cities redeveloped from the 1950s through the 1970s invoked the authority of function to overhaul what they saw as "obsolete" neighborhoods and city centers. Entire blocks of older buildings were torn down, in some cases entire neighborhoods; streets were obliterated, and new high-rise buildings went up, surrounded by large, open, windswept plazas. Every city I have ever visited, with the exception of Copenhagen, has many such barren places. Copenhagen avoided similar mistakes by deliberately excluding massive redevelopment from the city's center, and by deciding not to build expressways on the site of the lakes that ring the city along the old fortifications; for years the city looked old-fashioned, with its low skyline punctuated by church steeples and spires of public buildings; now it is recognized as being particularly livable.

Ironically, single-purpose public works, like highways and housing, when pursued in single-minded concern for narrowly defined functional efficiency, often produce dysfunctional conditions. New expressways built between suburbs and central cities from the 1950s on destroyed many old neighborhoods and funneled traffic onto downtown streets, leading to more congestion and demolition downtown to provide more parking. Whole neighborhoods were deemed outmoded and unfit for modern living: "an obsolete neighborhood . . . and a new plan," declared one report. In this case, the authority of function was invoked to condemn lower-income housing in Boston's West End, a neighborhood described as "a defect to the city in terms of cost of services versus tax revenue," to make way for more "efficient apartments," open lawn, and parking lots in Charles River Park, a new upper-income development.[44] Houses were "machines for living," and from the 1940s through the 1960s, old houses in urban neighborhoods were torn down and replaced with new public housing in high-rise towers surrounded by parking lots and lawn. By the 1970s, many of these were deemed unlivable and hence demolished; the most infamous case, the award-winning Pruitt-Igo Public Housing Project in St. Louis, consisting of high-rise towers designed by the architect Minoru Yamasaki, was deliberately blown up in 1976.

It is difficult to convey the emotional impact of such wholesale destruction wrought by urban renewal to someone who did not experience it firsthand. I visited West Philadelphia in June 1969 to look for an apartment, and when I returned to begin graduate school at the University of Pennsylvania in September, entire blocks of homes between campus and my apartment were gone, and cranes were in place, building new towers. During the next year dozens of additional blocks were erased, the empty tracts bounded by temporary white rail fences, the ubiquitous sign of the Philadelphia Redevelopment Authority. In those years, white, wooden rails and open land seemed to be everywhere around the city. Many vacant blocks were not to be built on for twenty years; some are empty today. A friend told me of the trauma of losing her neighborhood, still strongly felt after thirty years. She had grown up in West Philadelphia on a block of rowhouses where she knew everyone; all of her friends lived within a few blocks of each other. At fourteen, after a trip to Boston in summer of 1968, she was shocked when her mother met her at the train station and took her home to North Philadelphia, an entirely different part of the city. Her home and entire community had been wrecked and cleared, people scattered; all that remained of the many blocks was one huge open lot, no streets, not even a brick left. "My mother must have known before I left for Boston, but never told me. I never saw my friends again. I still don't understand why it happened." The lot remained open for many years, until a small shopping mall was built. Such events happened in cities all over the United States in the 1950s and 1960s; the sociologist Herbert Gans estimates that at least a million families were displaced and low-cost dwellings demolished between 1950 and 1980 (not including households removed by urban expressway construction).[45] Many forced to move felt grief for their lost homes even when their physical living conditions were improved.[46] So much was destroyed so fast, so many historic buildings and districts, so many social networks and place memories; the reaction was not long in coming.

In 1961, Jane Jacobs opened *The Death and Life of Great American Cities* with a salvo: "This book is an attack on current city planning and rebuilding."[47] Her book documents examples of functionalism run amok in urban landscapes, and recounts tales of protest, including her own street's campaign to prevent city engineers from lopping ten feet off the sidewalks in order to widen the road and improve traffic flow. In many cities, protests against clearances halted highway construction, but a residue of distrust for planners and city officials still remains in inner-city neighborhoods. Highways and high-rise towers are still read, in some places, as polemical landscapes, as symbols of urban renewal. So are grass and parks: lands cleared were frequently sowed with grass seed; parks were sometimes built as compensation for properties taken for highways, many on the sites of former homes.[48]

Suburban landscapes, too, exhibit the pursuit of function and expedience at the expense of livability: short cul-de-sacs are barren expanses of asphalt, their dimensions dictated by the space it takes for a fire engine to turn rather than by the demands of sociability or play. Designers and residents in many places have successfully protested such regulations (fire engines are told to back up). Local commercial and corporate landscapes increasingly are versions of the chain-store phenomenon, with attendant uniformity of product. Laurie Olin describes how designs for new office parks, rooted in the identity of their region's landscapes, have been foiled by fast-track, large-scale construction firms that work for the same client corporations all over the country and, citing the authority of expedience, are unwilling or unable to adopt local materials and motifs.[49]

The Authority of Art

Richard Serra's *Tilted Arc* was a curving, tilted wall of steel plate, 120 feet long and 12 feet high; it spanned Jacob Javits Plaza at the base of a federal office building in Manhattan. Designed specifically for the site and built with public funds as part of a public arts program in 1981, it was removed just eight years later, following hearings, convened in 1985, provoked by opponents of the work who claimed that workers in the office building despised it as menacing and ugly. In the hearings, the artist and his supporters invoked the authority of art: since it was site-specific to remove it would be to destroy it as a work of art, to render it a mere heap of rusted steel; to do so would be an act of vandalism. The opposition maintained that this space was the only outdoor place in which workers could sit and eat lunch, that the occupation of the space by the sculpture precluded other uses. The attack on *Tilted Arc* in the name of function was ironic since the sculpture was it-self a critique of the plaza built in 1967. Like many such spaces, Jacob Javits Plaza was large, paved, and open, elevated above the surrounding sidewalks, cut off by planters and walls, the only sunny spot occupied by an empty fountain (turned off to prevent water, whipped by winds, from spraying passersby). The old plaza as-serted the power of bureaucracy, the new one that of a cultural elite. Users were well served by neither.

On one level the celebrated controversy pitted the authority of art against that of function, but it was also a clash of political power and ideas over the role of public art and who should control it.[50] Serra and his supporters advocated the autonomy of art, that public art should not be bound by practical and political considerations external to the work itself. In interviews, Serra has described how he strives to create "anti-environments" and how, with *Tilted Arc*, he intended "to dislocate or alter the decorative function of the plaza" so that once it was installed the space would be "understood primarily as a function of the sculpture."[51] Those who opposed *Tilted Arc* on political grounds did so for different reasons: some ob-jected that it failed to symbolize patriotic values or justify civic authority; others protested the use of public funds for art.[52] In the 1980s, such criticisms were not limited to *Tilted Arc*. Critics used many of the same arguments to denounce the design for the Vietnam Veterans Memorial, proposed in 1981, the same year *Tilted Arc* was installed, mistaking similarities in style—abstract, nonfigurative, simpli-fied form—for kindred meanings.[53] Ultimately, the public embraced one and re-jected the other.

Tilted Arc was a watershed for many public artists; as Martha Schwartz com-ments, "The use of the plaza was subverted for the artist's vision, and whether that subversion is appropriate for public art turned out to be a very valuable discus-sion. I changed my mind during that sequence of events about what public art should be. The best public art is art that can speak on many levels, and if you choose not to be engaged with it, you don't have to be."[54] Schwartz, the landscape architect/artist chosen to redesign Javits Plaza, intended her work to be "the an-tithesis of *Tilted Arc*—less self-important and self-referential." Rather than high-lighting the alienating aspects of the open plaza at the base of the office tower, she remade the place entirely to redress the dreary conditions to which Serra had so strongly responded.[55]

Schwartz, herself, designs polemical landscapes and cites avant-garde artists as her inspiration and authority (not Serra); she and others who have promoted landscape as art describe their opposition to function or nature as sole authority.[56] Compared to *Tilted Arc*, her work has elicited tame public reaction. The profes-sional response is another story. Her Bagel Garden provoked outrage when it was featured on the cover of *Landscape Architecture* in 1980; it was accused of being elitist, called an insult. Many objections to it were similar to those raised later against *Tilted Arc* and the Vietnam Veterans Memorial, even though the Bagel Garden was her own garden not a public place. Much of Schwartz's work has been for private clients, as has that of Peter Walker, one of the most influential advocates of landscape as art. His corporate clients have given him scope to realize vast landscapes inspired by Vaux, Versailles, and Chantilly, such as the office estates in Texas for IBM at Solano and Clearlake. The clients reap the prestige such art confers; like Louis XIV, IBM has territorial ambitions, and the landscapes attest to its power.

The Authority of Power

Powerful patrons have long employed the authority of nature, of the past, of function and expedience, and of art in landscapes to demonstrate and legitimize their claims. They have also used landscape to display their dominance and wealth: through the construction of lavish gardens, parks, palaces, and temples to which they control entry; through the erection of monuments of superhuman scale that make an ordinary person seem insignificant and powerless, or powerful only as a member of a group; through the foreclosure of private property or enclosure of common ground for private purposes. English gentry who enclosed lands once open and used communally and then prohibited entry were invoking the authority of power; the hedges, landscape gardens, and sheep pastures they made were symbols of that authority. It was the same when Napoleon III and his prefect Baron Haussmann had entire sections of Paris demolished for new boulevards and buildings to be built in their place.

Mussolini's First World War Memorial and Cemetery at Redipuglia was designed to display the authority of power, as were the Mall in Washington, D.C., the palace and gardens of Versailles, and the Escorial in Spain. In all such places, composition points to the source of power, axial symmetry is usually the principal clue. At Redipuglia, a link is made between the glory of Italy, its military power, and God, as defined by the axis between carved words at the entrance, the tomb of the general at the base of the terraces, and the cross at the top. At Versailles, the king's bedroom was at the center and the chapel to one side; in the Escorial, palace of the Spanish kings, "the royal apartments were arranged around the chancel," conveying the message that "power, to be legitimate, requires piety and orthodoxy."[57] On the Mall in Washington, the Capitol, not the White House, is at the head of the primary axis, an indication that the primary power is vested in the collective, elected representatives of the nation's citizens. At Versailles Louis XIV entertained guests and impressed them with French military prowess; the gardens were displays of engineering incorporating the vocabulary of siege warfare: patterns of terracing like battlement walls, sequences of elevations and ditches, canals resembling moats. Louis XIV, who centralized and professionalized the French army, deployed soldiers as laborers to construct the gardens of Versailles.[58]

In the 1980s, Boston's inner neighborhoods were riddled with vacant land, abandoned buildings, closed fire stations and libraries. The state of these neighbor-

Cultivating paradox: Bird Sanctuary. Bloedel Reserve. Bainbridge Island, Washington.

hoods was invisible from downtown, but downtown prosperity, symbolized by gleaming new towers, could readily be seen from the neighborhoods, providing a stark and disturbing juxtaposition. The new towers, in times of high unemployment and declining local social services, were a daily reminder to residents of inner-city neighborhoods that they had not shared in Boston's economic growth. But the boom was a mixed blessing even downtown. Most new buildings that transformed Boston's skyline in the 1970s and 1980s were private projects constructed in a vacuum of public vision. Rather than contributing to the public realm, they often degraded it, creating dark, windy canyons and barren plazas, icy and windswept in winter, sun-baked in summer. Some buildings, ostensibly public, were and are still really private enclaves guarded by private police. The sumptuous materials lavished on their interiors contrasted vividly with the potholed, trash-filled streets and narrow, broken sidewalks outside.

The political scientist Harold Lasswell, late in his life, warned of the consequences of what he calls "the architecture of opulence—of sleek and commanding office buildings, apartment houses, and other structures"—to contribute to "long-run political destabilization" in that such architecture operates on a worldwide scale to reassure the rich, the strong, and the self-confident and to provoke and radicalize the poor and the weak.[59] He alludes to examples in the past in which powerful ruling elites were lulled by the landscapes of power they inhabited into supposing that the system supporting their privileges was equally robust;

they were, in consequence, unaware of how fragile their base of power. "The disaffected multitudes of our day," Lasswell writes, "are no novelty in the history of civilized systems of public order, save that they are stimulated by instant communication to act in concert on a widening scale."[60]

Landscape polemics at first may win attention for a neglected issue of significance, but, persisting, they harden into dogma, polarizing and leading to loss and fragmentation. Modernist dogma, which claimed to worship function and rejected history, ridiculed tradition, ignored memory, and banned ornament, provoked the historicist polemics of the classicists at the Minnesota State Capitol Competition. The single-minded pursuit of function and expedience that produced the urban clearances of the 1950s and 1960s sparked urban riots, in turn. Environmentalist dogma, which claimed nature as the sole determinant and authority for landscape design, incited others to proclaim the authority of art instead. Polemics spawn polemics. Polemical landscapes produce a counterreaction, if not immediately, then in subsequent generations. The purpose of polemics is not simply to persuade, but to mobilize the converted and set them apart. Today's struggles to redefine nature, history, and art, the efforts of others to follow the course of expedience alone and to invest as little as possible—all are reflected in landscape. There is contest without consensus.

Transcending Polemics

Nature, Art, Past, Function: Bloedel

In a forest, on an island, in a sound, near a city are a series of gardens within a garden devoted to environmental education. The Bird Sanctuary, Anteroom, Garden of Reflection, and Garden of Planes at Bloedel Reserve near Seattle tell stories about identity and difference, freedom and control, tradition and invention, use, abuse, and renewal.

A path leads through meadow, down through woods to a dredged pond edged by trees—the Bird Sanctuary, set between forest and meadow. Small islands make the pond appear larger and more mysterious. By the shore, the water is deep, brownish-black; further out, wind-driven ripples, swan/duck-swimming ripples collide, fracturing its surface into kaleidoscopic greens. Red alders line the shore in clumps of twos, threes, fours, and fives—like sprouts sprung up from the same old stump. As soil slides into the pond, trees lean in, then struggle to stay erect, reaching up to light, their leaves flickering. The trees mark a refuge at the edge of an open meadow that slopes up to sky. The way islands lie, poplars clump, meadow slopes looks deliberate; a feeling mind was at work in their creation. The Bird Sanctuary is an "artful wilderness to perplex the scene," dug, planted, inhabited.[61]

A path in the sanctuary leads from pond through forest to the Anteroom, a wooded moss garden, where it winds around enormous tree stumps. Clumps of alders grow out of the stumps, their many overlapping roots grasping woody car-

Cultivating paradox: Anteroom. Bloedel Reserve. Bainbridge Island, Washington.

casses and fallen branches. Ground, stumps, lower trunks are covered by thick moss: bright green, deep green, upright, creeping, shaggy green growing down from bark. Layers of soft, fuzzy growth, some of long fuzzy tendrils, other mosses branched like tiny leaves or twigs, form a thick cushion. The place has a graveyard air; branches lie like bones buried beneath moss.

The garden is both memento mori and memorial to the forest that was logged so long ago. It juxtaposes decay and rebirth; it celebrates both artful construction and organic regeneration, the power of life to renew a forest once cut for timber. And the paradox grows the more one knows. Bloedel Reserve is funded by a family fortune derived from the timber industry, the site first logged to fund a Territorial University for Washington, with the sale of timber paying for some of the original buildings on the new campus. When the property was sold, the proceeds were used to finance the university's first academic programs.

From the Anteroom's moss garden, the path leads in to the Reflection Garden, a clearing in the forest bounded by a rectangular frame of clipped yew hedges, a mythic space of water set in grass within yew within forest. The top of the hedge, sheared flat, catches a line of light. The long rectangular pool reflects the dark forest and reveals the groundwater beneath the spongy turf. A tree with three trunks holds the eye, an icon at one end. Like the trees beyond the wall at Ryoanji, in Kyoto, the trees of the forest beyond the hedge press into the space.

Cultivating paradox: Reflection Garden. Bloedel Reserve. Bainbridge Island, Washington.

Like pools in French gardens, for example, the one in Courances, dark water brims against green grass. The hedge, clipped on one side, grows freely on the other—an oxymoron. Many individual yews make one, clipped, mass; thousands of branches and twigs intermingle and merge to form walls both massive and opaque, yet delicate and transparent. Viewed obliquely, the plane of yews is dense green; seen head on, it is but a screen, the colors and shapes of plants beyond clearly visible through branches and twigs. The gardens' designer, Richard Haag, calls this a Zen space, and it is paradoxical indeed, a container of emptiness.

Beyond, the Garden of Planes, like the Anteroom and the Garden of Reflection, was once a fusion of Japanese tradition and contemporary Western art. In contrast to the "Don't worry, be happy" story of World Showcase at Disney's EPCOT, where the tensions between identity and diversity have been denied recognition, the Garden of Planes, in its original version, was perplexing, too difficult for visitors to understand. Several years ago the union of identities was erased, and the garden recast into a trite version of a Japanese garden. There is now no perplexity, no difficult questions posed, no responses prompted—except in the contrast between the clichéd banality of this garden and the other three.

The first three gardens at Bloedel are stories about the use, abuse, and renewal of landscape. They do not return the site to some imagined, ideal condition before humans cut the forest, but create a garden in which the evidence of human use—the tree stumps, for example—is incorporated into the whole. These three gardens draw their power from ideas of nature, from past garden traditions, from art, transcending polemics, making the case for an artful, humanist environmentalism, an antidote to the self-hate that underlies so much environmentalism, its misanthropy. They present paradox, thereby provoking reflection.

Cultivating Paradox

Now is a time for telling new tales, for retelling old dilemmas: how to live in the world *and* preserve it; how to sustain tradition *and* foster invention; how to promote freedom *and* cultivate order; how to forge identity *and* value difference; how to appreciate the parts *and* grasp the whole. Paradox, the fusion of seeming contradictions, has never been more critical. Apparent oppositions need to be seen not as unsolvable dilemmas but as part of a larger whole; they need to be fused in undisguised dynamic tension without loss of distinctions, avoiding the tendency to reduce the discomfort that tension engenders. This is a function of art. For humans invent new stories and recover old ones to cope with threats to survival, and relate them in new landscapes. Stories compel, capture imagination, change attitudes and actions, bring about dramatic shifts within a single generation. Landscape stories explain the world, define a place in it, justify actions, guide behavior, reinforce through experience. Art amplifies the power of these stories, making them memorable.

USING / KEEPING. Across Puget Sound from Bainbridge Island and Bloedel Reserve in Seattle, Gasworks Park artfully reclaims a derelict industrial site for a public park. Olmsted advocated removing all artificial constructions in projects such as Niagara, but the landscape architect Richard Haag proposed retaining many of the ghost structures of the old gas plant, some tall and rusting, like reminders or warnings, some painted red, blue, and yellow—sculptural landmarks and play structures, all surrounded by grass. Bloedel and Gasworks are two chapters in the same story, both exploited for energy and materials—vegetable and mineral—then reclaimed, both optimistic, affirming stories about landscape's use, abuse, and renewal. Neither tries to disguise the artifice; the use of antithesis in both is effective. The sites are gardens in which the remnants of human use—the rusting towers at Gasworks, the tree stumps at Bloedel—are incorporated into the whole, the one juxtaposed to green lawn and children's play, the other to plants' growth. Without continued reminding, people readily forget that constructed landscapes can appear wholly the product of nonhuman process. Antithesis reminds that people used the land, then helped build "natural" landscapes; oxymoron prompts the realization that humans participate in many of the world's processes, both destructive and creative.

SUSTAINING / INVENTING. There is always a tension between the attachment to the familiar and traditional and the impulse to start fresh, invent, and revolt; in different times and places, one or the other may be emphasized. Urban renewal of American cities in the 1950s and 1960s broke with the past, ignored ongoing story lines—the context of place—and often failed to reproduce landscapes as habitable and lasting as the ones they replaced. Which traditional landscapes are chosen for preservation or destruction is significant: in Independence National Historical Park in Philadelphia only the structures built before 1800 were preserved, the rest destroyed; in what was East Berlin, much of the landscape built after 1945 and before 1989 is being eliminated. Tradition without invention is stultifying; invention without tradition is alienating. One looks to the past and sacrifices the future, the other breaks with the past and focuses on the future; both neglect and impoverish the present. Haag's Bloedel, G. N. Brandt's Mariebjerg Cemetery, and C. Th. Sørensen's Nærum Garden Colony—oxymorons all—both reinterpret tradition and invent. Bloedel fuses traditional garden motifs (formal pool, bounded outdoor room, moss garden) with the plants and history of the temperate rain forest of the Pacific Northwest. Brandt and Sørensen take the elements of the Danish landscape (grove, meadow, and hedge) and use them freely in strikingly inventive ways. Bloedel, Mariebjerg, and Nærum are landscape expressions that permit the visitor to feel simultaneously the rootedness of tradition and the stimulus of invention.

FREEING / CONTROLLING. Public housing projects like Mill Creek forbid those who live in them to alter them, but then so do the covenant-enforced regulations in affluent Irvine, California, that prescribe color of house (bland earth tones) and curtains (white).[62] Designers must learn how (and when) to relinquish control (whether to enable others to express themselves or to permit nature's processes to take their course) while still maintaining order. *Tree Nursery*, a painting by Paul Klee, shows one answer to this dilemma; it is a framework of horizontal lines within which much variety is accommodated without an overall chaotic effect. Klee was struck by what he called the "patchwork rhythm" of gardens in a landscape. The organization of community gardens like Aspen Farms in Philadelphia depends upon a similar gridded framework of plots, each garden plot a whole in itself, an improvisation on similar themes by different individuals, yet all part of a larger whole unified by materials, structure, and processes. In Granada, Spain, allotment gardens lie within the Alhambra/Generalife, a national landmark, held within a highly organized framework of walls and terraces, enlivening not detracting, complementing the formal gardens and courtyards, where vegetables and nut and fruit trees are planted among flowers and vines. In the Moorish garden no arbitrary boundaries separate the ornamental from the productive, the pleasurable from the pragmatic, the sacred from the secular.

FOSTERING IDENTITY / TREASURING DIVERSITY. Splice Garden presents two garden traditions, Japanese and French, in uneasy juxtaposition—a paradox; the Bloedel Garden of Reflection merges them in a single landscape—an oxymoron—that recalls, simultaneously, Ryoanji and Courances. Schwartz's garden holds no promise of reconciliation between the two identities; Haag presents the possibility of a new identity born out of diverse origins. For me, Schwartz's is a cautionary tale, Haag's an optimistic story. But fusing several identities into a new one is not the only way, nor is it, often, even preferable. It is easiest to appreciate diversity when that diversity does not impinge on one's own identity. Sørensen's design for Nærum Garden Colony and Brandt's design for Mariebjerg Cemetery are landscapes that foster identity and encourage the valuing of diversity. At Nærum, Sørensen resolved the most common source of conflict among gardeners in such communities: how high the common hedge should be clipped. In the normal layout, a grid, each garden shares a fence or hedge with three other gardens, one to either side and one at the back. By proposing freestanding elliptical gardens bounded by hedges, Sørensen permitted each gardener to make a choice, yet gave the overall community its own, striking identity. Brandt accomplished a similar purpose by providing a landscape frame (allées of trees, hedges bounding burial "rooms") that establishes a strong identity for the whole while allowing for the expression of different identities within each room.

At the scale of an entire downtown, Hayden's Power of Place project in Los Angeles interprets the urban landscape as an expression of the histories of many different peoples; it seeks to forge a new identity out of a recognition of diversity rather than celebrate a single history that leaves out many others. The dark side of identity is that it is often defined not by what people have in common, but against those others who are uncommon, those seen as different and, by implication, inferior or unimportant. Perceiving difference seems to be easier than sensing similarity. The human habit of constructing dualisms runs deep: us and them, city and wilderness, nature and culture. But, similarity and difference need to be held simultaneously: the us in the them and the them in the us; the role of natural processes in cities and of human imagination in wilderness; the symbiosis of nature and culture. We need to shift from a focus on the Other to a reverence for all life, to a delight in diversity.

The language of landscape highlights similarities while both acknowledging difference and permitting the assertion of individual and culture within a framework of commonality. Landscapes themselves harbor both genetic and cultural diversity, and collectively, human habitats comprise a record of diverse adaptations to similar conditions. That diversity of response is a resource to be treasured. Some day we may have to sift through the human repertoire for answers to difficult questions.

DIVIDING/UNITING. Children bused miles away to visit nature when all around them are the products of natural processes: water flowing, earth subsiding, wildflowers and sumacs growing in vacant lots, making soil from rubble and detritus. Such an absurdity comes from dividing the world into pieces, nature/not nature, and so on, habits that prevent a grasp of the whole. Children are being taught to value places outside their neighborhood, faraway places they might someday see. Or never.

To see similarities among disparate things is at the heart of creativity. Oxymorons enable us to achieve a difficult unity while experiencing the separateness of the parts. To deny oppositions, therefore, is not to avoid distinctions; to distinguish one need not oppose. Prospects are important to seeing and making things whole, perhaps a reason why sages and prophets climb hilltops to gain perspective. Now satellites have given us a view of Earth from space, from which to conceive the whole in new ways.

"Why are you here?" a neighborhood child challenged me one day. "It's not your neighborhood." "It depends on what you call a neighborhood," I replied. "It can be the block you live on or the place you work or the city you live in, or even your country. I don't live in Mill Creek, but my office is less than a five-minute drive away; I want my city to be the best place it can be, I want my country to offer all its children the same chance to learn and work." Later I heard her explain to her classmates, "She thinks the whole world is her neighborhood. She wants us to be the best we can be."

REAL / IDEAL. Utopias can be dark. Plants hanging from wires in Disney World's EPCOT, or native landscapes that are racially pure, are reminders that one person's ideal may be another's nightmare. Mill Creek Public Housing, and other such projects of the 1960s, now decaying, abandoned, or demolished, remind us that one person's paradise may be another's inferno, that one group's search for personal paradise may condemn others, that the paradise sought by one generation may create a hell for the next. Italo Calvino warned that we live in an inferno of our own creation, "that we form by being together," and that to escape, we must "seek and learn to recognize who and what in the midst of the inferno are not inferno, then make them endure, give them space."[63] William James said those who would change the world must hold the ideal and the real as dynamically contiguous. Community gardens in Mill Creek's old floodplain, rivers restored in Denver, give tangible hope that we may yet achieve a more collective paradise. The park along the river Rance in Dinan, the patio in the Alhambra, serve as landscapes of meaning and value for other places and times. Make them endure, give them space.

The pond at Aspen Farms. (Martin Knox, West Philadelphia Landscape Project)

Epilogue:
Reimagining Mill Creek

Designers are storytellers. Design is a way of imagining and telling new stories and reviving old ones, a process of spinning out visions of landscapes that pose alternatives from which to choose, describing the shape of a possible future. The products of design—gardens, homes, road and water systems, neighborhoods, and cities—are settings for living that convey meaning, express a society's values. We extend these meanings further through processes of construction and cultivation, use and neglect, as we dwell in what began as dreams.

Dream One. Mill Creek Parks

After rains, Mill Creek comes alive above ground, water pooling, forming shallow ponds, flowing through channels into riverine plazas, lingering for a few hours or days, then gradually disappearing, seeping into the sewer below. When the water is invisible, the creek's presence underground can still be seen. In early spring, carpets of blue scilla bloom in grass and under groves throughout the Mill Creek parks. Rows of red maples mark the course of the underground sewer; are rooted in the damp soil of the old floodplain. In spring, their buds swell dark red, leaf out green; in fall, leaves flame red, drop, blow across bricks, onto porches. Artists have designed water fountains there now, spray pools, even manhole covers.

Mill Creek parks meander through West Philadelphia, their diverse character reflecting their sponsors and contexts. Where blocks of rowhouses afford little or no outdoor space except street and sidewalk, there are ball courts, playgrounds, and play fields, sitting gardens, and community gardens, all intensively used. Mill Creek Mini-Golf and the West Philadelphia Garden Center, in the commercial district between Market and Walnut streets, are also among the parks. The parks are not continuous; they are most numerous north of Walnut Street, where there were once many vacant properties. South of Walnut, the parks are fewer.

People of Mill Creek call their neighborhood the Bottoms, using the term differently from their meaning years ago when it was known pejoratively as "The Bottom." Now they read it as fertile bottomlands, a place that regenerates continuously within the context of the creek and its history. They inscribe their own stories, improvising within the frame of creek and streets.

Every schoolchild knows the story and can read the landscape of Mill Creek: where it once flowed on the land, where its shore was the site of a large Indian settlement, where it powered mills to grind wheat and corn, then to weave cotton and wool, where it was buried in a sewer and built upon, where the force of the creek's waters broke through the sewer to flood basements, crumble foundations, and cave in streets. Where the land above the sewer became open once again, a gash of vacant land, trashed and abandoned. There Mill Creek parks were built, and rain now runs off rooftops, streets, and sidewalks into ponds in the parks, ponds that contain the water and slow its passage to the sewer, the treatment plant, and the river. Every schoolchild knows the connection between parks and river and water to drink.

Schools are at the heart of the community's reconstruction. Students' studies focus on the stream, the sewer, the community. They learn science, social studies, history, mathematics, art, and literature in the context of the neighborhood's past, present, and future. They learn the arts of citizenship: how to know a place, how to envision and build its future, how to care for it. Knowing, imagining, building, and caring, they teach their elders and younger children.

Schools have living laboratories—meadows, wooded groves, and ponds, once vacant lots—children care for and study them all as part of their science classes. In the hall is a display of photographs taken every year for the past fifteen showing the once-vacant lots and the growth of meadow and forest occurring over time. Students keep records of plant species growing there, and mount an exhibit every year of their discoveries. A big pond was dug on one vacant property, planted as a wetland, and stocked with frogs, salamanders, and other animals. Seen in the larger context, these outdoor classrooms are islands in the urban fabric, links for migrating birds in fall and spring between the wetlands along the Schuylkill River, the woods and meadows of Clark Park, Cathedral Cemetery, and Fairmount Park.

Mill Creek parks are now models of community development, environmental education, and water management, the first sewered, urban floodplain to be mapped in the United States, the first use of inner-city vacant land for stormwater detention to prevent combined sewer overflows, the pilot for many other projects in Philadelphia that saved millions of dollars. Teams of public officials, engineers, planners, and designers from other cities come to study the parks and the Mill Creek Center at a middle school in the bottomlands. Tours of the park start at the school, where sixth to eighth grade guides demonstrate a model of the watershed in the form of a fountain. The fountain was a collaboration between teachers, children, and artists, and many features were ideas first suggested by a child. It is like no watershed ever seen before: slanted copper panels stained blue-green by water represent roofs; it has basins (water barrels); sloping stone (streets and sidewalks); runnels (gutters); transparent columns of sand, of rock (soil); beds of water plants (wetlands); funnels and pipes (downspouts and sewers); a pool (river). The water enters the fountain in two ways, by rainfall or pipe. When rains come, the three-story school building spouts water off its roof into pools and pipes, running smaller fountains. When it rains really hard, children and teachers grab their raincoats and run outside to watch. And the water can also be turned on, filling the fountain from a pipe.

The play of water in the fountain is never the same. The fountain's pumps, check dams, spigots, and nozzles are controlled at will; some can be pushed, slid, or turned by a single child, others by the combined strength of two or more people. Water is concentrated or dispersed, patterns of flow are varied, as pumps lift the water, as check dams are shifted or slid into place, as spigots are opened or closed, as nozzles are turned to produce a fine mist or a line. Sometimes the play of water is a riot of random patterns, sometimes orchestrated through the coordinated efforts of the players. Water leaves the fountain along runnels that feed a series of pools in a large, sunken section of the school grounds. Usually only the lowest pools are filled, but after a storm the entire lower basin fills with runoff from the roof and school grounds. The magnitude of a rainstorm can always be gauged by how high the water reaches in the stepped basin. Only once in the last ten years has the water reached the top step.

Dream Two. Mill Creek Art Folk Park and Mini-Golf

After many years of planning and waiting, new buildings are being constructed now in the Walnut-Market Corridor, the commercial district and principal commuting route between downtown Philadelphia and the suburbs. Its renewal promises jobs and educational opportunities for West Philadelphia. During all those years, a temporary landscape grew and matured into a striking setting that drew private investment; new buildings were designed to fit within that landscape. The Market-Walnut Corridor intersects the Mill Creek floodplain between 42nd and 47th streets, where the original course of the stream was relatively flat and meandering, with small branches and ponds; by the 1990s, there were many vacant properties here. The new businesses that came are those that can tolerate waterlogged soil and periodic flooding: outdoor markets and parking lots, for example, where rainwater is ponded deliberately. The Art Folk Park was the first new enterprise built here, followed by several large commercial enterprises, the Mill Creek Garden Center and Nursery and the Mill Creek Miniature Golf Course; the popularity of each, in turn, boosted support for other investments.

The Mill Creek Art Folk Park, a large, open meadow visible from passing cars and buses, where artists construct and display their works, has attracted much attention and many visitors. The works change continually; with no formal selection process, most of the artists are little known, except locally, though occasionally a well-known artist creates a piece. Many of the works are quite whimsical, others more serious. There are works by sculptors, painters, muralists, dumpster divas, cartoonists, doll-makers, garden artists; on weekends the park draws photographers, fabric artists, hair-braiders, storytellers, griots, mimes, dancers, musicians, makers of musical instruments, poets. The place has brought together a magnificent local resource, previously unrecognized, once many individuals working alone, scattered throughout the community. The park itself was the outgrowth of an arts program to create new landmarks along the course of the creek, to reveal and celebrate it. The first work built at the Mill Creek Art Folk Park is the only commissioned work there: a fence, whose design was chosen in a widely publicized competition that also served to announce the art park. The fence was to mark and enclose the place, but also to permit those driving by to see the art works within, to allow people to move freely in and out, to be durable and inexpensive to construct. Hundreds of proposals submitted by artists from all over the country were judged by a jury of artists, community leaders, and members of the Art Commission and the Redevelopment Authority's Fine Arts Committee. After the jury's decision, a selection of the best ideas was displayed at the Institute for Contemporary Art. Many of these have since been built elsewhere.

The Mill Creek Garden Center and Nursery occupies several large properties, the principal retail center designed like a garden; here flowers, vegetables, and garden supplies are displayed and sold. Small trees and shrubs are for sale in lots nearby. The garden center and nursery is the largest in the city; its unusual and beautiful design draws customers from around the city and the western suburbs. It is prominently located along a major commuting corridor, and many stop by on the way home. It is a nonprofit organization whose programs are supported by proceeds from retail sales; the nursery and sales staff are youth from West Philadelphia working in an educational and job-training program. Many students work weekends and summers while still in high school, then continue in a full-time two-year program in horticulture and landscape management affiliated with a local community college.

Golfers at the Mill Creek Miniature Golf Course have five sets of holes to choose from—"Piedmont Forest," "Mills and Mansions," "Streetcar Suburb," "Cave-In!" and "Visions." All were programed and designed as part of the Mill Creek Watershed curriculum at the local middle school. In "Piedmont Forest," golfers tee off from a low point into a steep valley cut into the hillside, then gradually make their way up to the top, past springs, enclosed by oak and hickory trees, mountain laurel, ferns, mayapple, and past slopes of exposed grey rock flecked with shiny flakes of mica—Wissahickon Schist. "Mills and Mansions," a round of nine holes, tells the story of the colonial settlement of Mill Creek, with replicas of the cotton mill on Haverford Avenue, the drovers' inn along Lancaster, a slaughterhouse, and the Busti mansion. It leads into "Streetcar Suburb," another nine-hole round that tracks the development of the neighborhood from the Civil War to 1930, each successive hole another decade. The favorite part of this course is the reconstructed segment of Lancaster Avenue with all the stores shown in miniature, and the streetcar terminal. In "Cave-In," each hole represents an actual cave-in event from the 1930s to the 1990s, depicted in a posted newspaper account. Golfers tee off through scale-models of blocks of homes, trying to avoid water hazards and cave-in to reach the green and sink the ball safely into each hole. "Cave-In," in the lowest part of the site, incorporates several stormwater detention ponds; after rainstorms water comes splashing down the hillside into ponds and water hazards. There are unexpected squirts of waters and jets of air—golfers beware. "Visions" vies with "Cave-In" as the most popular course at Mill Creek Miniature Golf; it is an experimental course, a showcase of ideas for the future of the neighborhood where the "landscape" of each hole presents a separate proposal.

Many changes to Mill Creek in recent years were inspired by "Visions," the new plaza next to the old Arena Stage site, for example. Anyone can submit to a selection panel an idea for a new hole in the golf course. The propositions are submitted in miniature models; they range from the pragmatic to the fanciful, inciting crowds to voice their approval or dissent. Other proposals, such as showing Sulzberger Middle School in 2400 A.D. as a ruin, are fantasies. Some engender serious debate over days and weeks, provoking additional submissions in response. Plans for the vacant lot at 48th and Market were extremely controversial and prompted many alternative visions over the course of several years. The golf course began with an idea from one person, a member of the community. University and middle school students developed the idea, produced designs and a business plan, then presented their work to local leaders who decided to make it real. It is typical of the way things work.

Dream Three. The Urban Forest

From the air the neighborhood looks like an urban forest, on the ground, streets are shady, green corridors. A massive reforestation has occurred, block by block; even the narrowest streets are planted with trees. Streets that used to bake all day in the hot summer sun are now shaded; the trees have made streets and homes more comfortable on summer afternoons and evenings. The street is still a stage, but the action is cooler. Students grow the new trees right in the neighborhood in street-tree nurseries on former vacant lots: sixth graders plant small trees in the fall, tend them over the next two years, choose the street where they will be planted, teach residents about tree care, and transplant the trees to streets when they are ready to graduate from eighth grade. The trees are densely planted, and the weaker trees are thinned out to make room for the more vigorous. Each fall, the park commission brings truckloads of leaves collected from city streets for students to spread as a thick mulch, preventing the growth of weeds, keeping the soil moist and soft. Trees from the school's nursery survive much better than ordinary nursery stock.

West Philadelphia's Mill Creek has been the focus of a twenty-year study on the effects of trees on urban microclimate, a collaboration between students, teachers, and university faculty. Before new trees were planted, measurements of temperatures on treeless blocks throughout the community were taken as part of school and university school classes, then continued annually thereafter. Researchers have published papers demonstrating the marked difference in microclimate and human comfort on these streets within ten to twenty years after the trees were planted. Treeless neighborhoods were once ten degrees Fahrenheit hotter on summer evenings than suburban neighborhoods only a few miles away; now evening and nighttime temperatures in Mill Creek are ten degrees cooler than before, as cool as in the suburbs. This urban forestry project brought international attention to Mill Creek, and the dramatic aesthetic transformation has prompted many other cities to imitate it even before the results of the microclimate study became known.

Dream Four. The Grove

A grove of trees enfolds a school, branches reaching, buds unleafing. Leaves, soaking up light, drying, dropping, rotting, make roots' fertile bed. Year by year the grove has grown, ten more trees for every class. Each child, learning, prunes twigs back spurring growth, records changes, tells stories of straight-trunked tulip, multi-stemmed maple, dappled brawny plane, sturdy stocky oaks—red, white, and black—long-limbed yellowwood, delicate dogwood, billowy shadblow, eccentric gingko: many trees, one grove.

Behind the trees, walls of brick, baked yellow clay, rise high. A school sits on a limestone base, built in 1923, say numbers cut in its cornerstone. Windows broad and tall look out: trunks like columns frame the sixth grade's first-floor view, in September a green world closely canopied, then winter's open tracery and spring's pubescent bud, soft stem, downy underleaf. Seventh graders look down from the second floor into dogwood's creamy flowers, tulip tree's green-orange tulips and through branches where birds nest, flitter, flutter, sweep, chitter, stutter, cheep: many motions, one dance; many voices, one sound. From the top floor, eighth graders look out beyond the grove to houses and gardens, to rows of maples, strings of gingko, each line a sign, leading back to the school where they learned to make their mark.

Smell of sun heralds the new year on dry leaves, on apples, on pears along the warm south wall. Fragrant rain signals the coming of the end, as scents unfold, rhythms quicken. By the doors of the school, six yellowwood stand, their blooms blowing across the walk, white confetti in early June. Through this arbored gateway, students pass. They have learned to read what sloping valleys and flowing water tell, what bud scars say. They speak the language that holds life in place. Knowing, they shape the landscape to hold their dreams.

Notes

Full citations are given for all sources not listed in the bibliography. Travel journals, which I have been keeping since 1988, are not cited specifically because they have been used extensively throughout the book; see Sources for details on places and dates. All descriptions in the text in present tense are directly from the journals.

INTRODUCTION

1 See, for example, Spirn, *West Philadelphia Landscape Plan*.
2 See, for example, my essays: "Architecture and Landscape"; "Introduction," in Andersson and Høyer, *Sørensen*; "Texts, Landscapes, and Life," in Høyer, *Andersson*.
3 Unless otherwise noted, all photographs in this book are my own. See also *Telling Landscape*, a book of my photographs, also in preparation.
4 See, for example, my essays "Constructing Nature: The Legacy of Frederick Law Olmsted," in Cronon, *Uncommon Ground*, and "Frank Lloyd Wright: Architect of Landscape," in De Long, *Frank Lloyd Wright*.

1 THE LANGUAGE OF LANDSCAPE

1 See, for example, the tablet of Enannatum I, governor of Lagash, which records the delivery of cedar trees to roof a temple, Mesopotamia, ca. 2900 B.C., and other examples in Gyorgy Kepes, ed. *Sign, Image, Symbol* (New York: George Braziller, 1966). For a review of the literature on evolution of human cognition, see Donald, *Origins of Mind*.
2 Roland Barthes, *Elements of Semiology* (New York: Farrar, Straus and Giroux, 1968), 16.
3 Lakoff and Johnson, *Metaphors We Live By*. Each developed these ideas further in subsequent books: Lakoff, *Women, Fire, and Dangerous Things;* Johnson, *Body in the Mind*.
4 Stilgoe, *Shallow-Water Dictionary* and *Alongshore*. While I admire Stilgoe's work on the language of the estuary, I reject his definition of landscape as including only land, not water, and countryside, not city.
5 Brown (1716–83), Olmsted (1822–1903), Wright (1867–1959), Halprin (b. 1916), Schwartz (b. 1950).
6 Heidegger, "Building Dwelling Thinking," 145–47. Some of these implications have been explored by others, including the geographer Relph, *Place and Placelessness*, and the architectural theorist Christian Norberg-Schulz, *Concept of Dwelling*.
7 Verner Dahlerup, *Ordbog over det Danske Sprog* (Copenhagen: Nordisk, 1931), Jacob Grimm and Wilhelm Grimm, *Deutsches Worterbuch* (Verlag von S. Hirzel, 1885), Arther R. Borden, Jr., *A Comprehensive Old English Dictionary* (University Press of America, 1982). For a review of the histories of the words *landscape, nature, land,* and *country* in English, German, and Scandinavian languages, see Olwig, "Nature of Landscape." See also Jackson, "The Word Itself" in *Vernacular Landscape*, 3– 8. I am grateful to Andre Wink for the translation and interpretation of J. Heinsios, *Woordenboek der Nederlandsche Taale* (Martinus Nijhoff, A. W. Sijthoff, 1916).
8 Webster's *New Universal Unabridged Dictionary* (New York: Simon and Schuster, 1983) and *Oxford English Dictionary* (Oxford: Oxford University Press, 1989).

9   Anthony Hecht, "Gardens of the Villa d'Este," in *Hard Hours* (New York: Atheneum, 1967), 95.

10 Maclean, *River Runs*, 61.

11 Lakoff and Johnson, *Metaphors*. See also Ralph Waldo Emerson, "Nature," in *Essays and Lectures* (New York: Library of America, 1983), 7–49.

12 Stilgoe, *Shallow-Water Dictionary*, 23, 28.

13 Many cultures have no single name or notion for *nature*. The singular quality of the English word masks a real multiplicity and implies falsely that there is a single definition. See Raymond Williams, "Ideas of Nature," in *Materialism and Culture*, 67–85.

14 Jackson, in "The Word Itself," limits the definition of *landscape* to deliberately created, "man-made systems"; Stilgoe, in *Common Landscape*, narrows the definition further, to human-made, nonurban land.

15 Berger and Mohr, *Another Way of Telling*.

16 Bateson, *Sacred Unity*, 310–11, 253–57.

17 Leopold, *Sand County Almanac*, 129–33.

2 READING AND TELLING THE MEANINGS OF LANDSCAPE

1   The passages quoted are from Twain, *Mississippi*, 280–83. Samuel Clemens spent 1857–61 on the Mississippi, first as a cub pilot under the tutelage of Horace Bixby, then as a licensed steamboat pilot. His pseudonym, Mark Twain, refers to water two fathoms deep.

2   It is ironic, given its history, that this Danish province is commonly referred to in English by its German name, Schleswig, rather than by its Danish name, Slesvig.

3   Helge Seidelin Jacobsen, *An Outline History of Denmark* (Copenhagen, Høst & Son, 1993), 101, 105.

4   For a social and cultural history of the Danish heath and its transformation, see Olwig, *Nature's Ideological Landscape*. The Danish edition of the book has additional material on European Union policies on marginal lands as they will affect farmlands previously reclaimed from the heath: *Hedens Natur* (Copenhagen: Teknisk Forlag, 1986). Olwig related these themes to the American landscape in "Reinventing Common Nature," in *Uncommon Ground*, edited by Cronon.

5   Hans Christian Andersen, "Jylland mellem tvende have," *Folkehøjskolens Sangbog* (Odense, DK: Foreningens Forlag, 1964), 712–13. See Introduction for a description of the circumstances surrounding my stay in Denmark.

6   Olwig, *Nature's Ideological Landscape*, 67.

7   Johannes Iverson, *The Development of Denmark's Nature Since the Last Glacial* (Copenhagen: C. A. Reitzels, 1973). Iverson summarizes research on the relationships among geology, soil, plants, and human occupation of landscape in Denmark.

8   From Cicero, *De natura deorum*, quoted and translated by John Dixon Hunt, "The Idea of the Garden and the Three Natures," *Zum Naturbegriff de Gegenwart* (Stuttgart, 1993), 312.

9   Hunt, "Idea of the Garden," 325.

10 John McCrae, "In Flanders Fields," in *The Oxford Book of War Poetry*, edited by Jon Stallworthy (Oxford: Oxford University Press, 1984), 165.

11 I. A. Richards, *The Philosophy of Rhetoric* (Oxford: Oxford University Press, 1936).

12 The east end of the allée was replanted in the 1980s. This is Steen Høyer's observation.

13 The U.S. Soil Conservation Service, one of the most successful federal agencies, owes that success to a balance between local knowledge and expert advice.

14 For a classic essay on the subject, see Meinig, "The Beholding Eye: Ten Versions of the Same Scene," in *Ordinary Landscapes*.

15 John M. Hull, *Touching the Rock: An Experience of Blindness* (New York: Vintage, 1992), 29–30.

16 Watts, *Reading the Landscape of America*, v. See also her *Reading the Landscape of Europe*.

17 "What the Frog's Eye Tells the Frog's Brain," in Warren S. McCulloch, *Embodiments of Mind* (Cambridge: MIT Press, 1988), 231, 254.

18 See, for example, Griffin, *Animal Thinking*, von Frisch, *Animal Architecture*, Sebeok, *Sign and Its Masters*.

19 See, for example, Moshe Barasch, *Modern Theories of Art* (New York: New York University Press, 1990), and Charles Rosen and Henri Zerner, "Caspar David Friedrich and the Language of Landscape," in *Romanticism and Realism: The Mythology of Nineteenth Century Art* (New York: W. W. Norton, 1984).

20 Kathleen Morner and Ralph Rausch, *Dictionary of Literary Terms* (Lincolnwood, Ill.: National Textbook Company, 1991), 163.

21 William Cronon, "Authority, Tradition, and the Future of Disciplines: A Comment [On Beans]," *Yale Journal of Criticism* 5:2 (Spring 1992). See also Anderson, *Plants, Man, and Life*.

22 Cronon, *Nature's Metropolis*.

23 John McPhee, "Los Angeles Against the Mountains," in *Control of Nature*.

24 Riley, "Square to Road."

25 Andersson, "En trädgård efter fem år," 27.

26 Philadelphia Museum of Art.

27 Paul Klee, *The Thinking Eye: Notebooks of Paul Klee*, vol. 1, edited by Jürg Spiller (London: Lund Humphries, 1961), 63.

28 Andersson, "Karlsplatz," 17. My translation.

29 All are unpublished professional texts. Henrik Pøhlsgaard brought these texts to my attention and shared his experience and insights about their use and significance in Andersson's practice.

30 See Halprin, *RSVP Cycles*, and Halprin and Burns, *Taking Part*.

31 Eiseley, "Flow of the River," in *Immense Journey*, 15–27.

32 Maclean, *River Runs*, 92.

33 *Webster's New International Dictionary of the English Language*, unabridged 2d ed. (Springfield, Mass.: Merriam, 1955).

3 The Literature of Landscape

1 Revelation 12:7–9.

2 Adams, *Mont-Saint-Michel*.

3 Henry Decaens, Adrien Goetz, Gerard Baylis, Gerard Guiller, and Maylis Mayle, *L'ABCdaire du Mont-Saint-Michel* (Paris: Flammarion, 1996).

4 Pfeiffer, personal communication, March 2, 1995. The other two chapters, says Pfeiffer, are Taliesin North and Taliesin East (Wright's apartment in the Plaza Hotel in New York).

5 Wright, *Writings, 1930–1932*, 226.

6 Ackerman, *Villa*, 286, 12. See also Williams, *Country and the City*.

7 Cronon, "A Place for Stories."

8 Tom McArthur, ed., *Oxford Companion to the English Language* (Oxford: Oxford University Press, 1992), 343. An elegy can also mourn the passing of a way of life or express a general sense of mortality.

9 Steen Eiler Rasmussen, "Haven, det langsomme skuespil," in *Essays gennem mange aar* (Copenhagen: Gyldendal, 1968), 101–14.

10 Shakespeare, *As You Like It*, 2.7.139.

11 *SITE*, 28.

12 See Thompson, *Bryant Park.*

13 Olin, "Regionalism," 256.

14 Charles Bradley, "The Leopold Memorial Reserve," in Thomas Tanner, ed., *Aldo Leopold: The Man and His Legacy* (Ankeny, Iowa: Soil Conservation Society of America, 1987), 162.

15 Nina Leopold Bradley, quoted in ibid., 171.

16 This and other passages on Olmsted are adapted from Spirn, "Olmsted."

17 I employ the term *genre* both in its general sense—kind—and in its specific use in literature and art to refer to type of subject or performance and body of related conventions. This is akin both to Northrop Frye's idea of genre as corresponding to archetypal human responses and Barthes' and others' notion of genre as sets of conventions that change from one place and period to another. See Frye, *Anatomy of Criticism* (Princeton: Princeton University Press, 1957), and McArthur, *English Language,* 435.

18 Huth, *Nature and the American,* 151.

19 Jon Else, "Yosemite: The Fate of Heaven" (Sundance Institute and Yosemite Association, 1989), 58-min. video.

20 There were times when the court was too poor to pay for the rebuilding. Anne Walthall, personal communication.

21 Eliade, *Sacred and Profane.*

22 I am grateful to Shunsaku Miyagi for identifying the plant and its meaning.

23 Michelin, *Paris* (Clermont-Ferrand: Michelin, 1985), 174.

24 Attributed to Asplund by Sven-Ingvar Andersson, personal communication, May 21, 1990.

25 Sven-Ingvar Andersson, personal communication, June 4, 1990.

26 Lowenthal, *Past Is a Foreign Country,* 197.

27 Huizinga, *Homo Ludens,* 10.

28 The building is Gund Hall, home of Harvard University's Graduate School of Design, designed by the Australian architect John Andrews.

29 Alan Lukashok and Kevin Lynch, "Childhood Memories of the City," *Journal of the American Institute of Planners* 23:3 (Summer 1956), 146–52. Clare Cooper Marcus, "Environmental Autobiography," Working Paper 301 (Berkeley, 1979). I use Marcus's techniques in exercises with my students. See also Marcus, *House as Mirror of Self.*

30 Lukashok and Lynch, "Childhood Memories," 145.

31 Cranz, *Politics of Park Design.*

32 Sørensen, *Parkpolitik,* 54.

33 Sørensen, *Haver,* 140.

34 See Hurtwood, *Planning for Play.*

35 Lady Allen of Hurtwood and Susan Jellicoe, *The Things We See: Gardens* (Harmondsworth, Middlesex: Penguin Books, 1953), 46.

36 Halprin, *Freeways,* 17.

37 Ibid., 37.

38 Chang, *Lawrence Halprin,* 230. Angela Danadjieva was a principal designer on this project.

39 Material on rice cultivation from Richard D. Porcher, *A Teacher's Field Guide to the Natural History of the Bluff Plantation Wildlife Sanctuary* (New Orleans: Kathleen O'Brain Foundation, 1985).

40 *Middleton Place* (Charleston: Middleton Place Foundation, 1976), 26.

41 Ibid., 15.

42 George Perkins Marsh, *Man and Nature* (1865; repr. Cambridge: Harvard University Press, 1965), 35.

43   The Ramble at Central Park was planted to appear "wild," but it was only a small part of the park. William Robinson, an English acquaintance of Olmsted, published his book *The Wild Garden* in 1870. Olmsted was undoubtedly also aware of Martin Johnson Heade's contemporary paintings depicting marshes along Boston's North Shore (I am grateful to William Cronon and Neil Levine for this reference).

44   Olmsted, "Parks, Parkways," 253.

45   See, for example, Ashihara's description of Japanese space in *Hidden Order*.

46   Thayer, "Personal Dreams and Pagan Rituals," in Francis and Hester, eds., *Meaning of Gardens*, 194–97.

47   Wilhelm Miller, "The Prairie Spirit in Landscape Gardening," Circular no. 184 (Urbana: Agricultural Experiment Station, Department of Horticulture, University of Illinois, 1916).

48   Sun Xiaoxiang, personal communication.

49   This style was fashionable in Elizabethan prose; the term refers to Euphues, the principal character in a prose romance by John Lyly. See McArthur, *English Language*, 387–88.

50   And thus one gets books such as Margaret Drabble, *A Writer's Britain: Landscape in Literature* (New York: Thames and Hudson, 1987), that trace these reciprocal allusions.

51   Suzanne K. Langer, *Feeling and Form* (New York: Charles Scribner's Sons, 1953), 40; *Problems of Art* (New York: Charles Scribner's Sons, 1957), 25.

52   There is also significance in the plaza's location—the site of the house where William Penn granted the "Charter of Privileges" in 1701.

4 Elements of Landscape and Language

1   J. M. Moreno and W. C. Oechel, "A Simple Method for Estimating Fire Intensity after a Burn in California Chaparral," *Acta Oecologica/Oecologia Plantarum* 10:1 (1989). I am grateful to Michael Barbour for this reference.

2   Nita Lelyveld, "Desire for Scenic Beauty in California Leads to Disaster for Homeowners," *Philadelphia Inquirer*, March 9, 1998, 1, 8.

3   Stephen Davis, *The Hunter for All Seasons: An Aboriginal Perspective on the Natural Environ* (Northern Territory: Milingimbi School Literature Production Centre, 1984), 9.

4   Anthony F. Aveni, *Empires of Time* (New York: Basic Books, 1989), 73–75.

5   Halprin, *Freeways*, 23.

6   Ecclesiastes 1:7.

7   Yi-Fu Tuan, *The Hydrologic Cycle and the Wisdom of God: A Theme in Geoteleology* (Toronto: University of Toronto Press, 1968), 3–4.

8   Gould, *Time's Arrow, Time's Cycle*.

9   For Gaia theory, see James E. Lovelock, *Gaia* (New York: Oxford University Press, 1987); for challenge to the idea of harmony as nature's norm, see Botkin, *Discordant Harmonies*.

10   John M. Hull, *Touching the Rock: An Experience of Blindness* (New York: Vintage, 1992), 45.

11   James Steele, *Hassan Fathy* (London: Academy Editions, St. Martin's Press, 1988).

12   Joan Brigham, personal communication, April 6, 1997.

13   George Eliot, *Mill on the Floss* (1860; repr. London: Penguin Books, 1985), 94.

14   Andrews, *Living Materials*, 1.

15   Cooper, *Symbols*.

16   Walter L. Brenneman, "The Circle and the Cross: Loric and Sacred Space in the Holy Wells of Ireland," in Seamon and Mugerauer, *Dwelling*.

17   Krieger, "Up the Plastic Tree."

18   J. L. Reed, *Forests of France* (London: Faber and Faber, n.d.), 116–18.

19   Clay, *Close-Up*, on the significance of "breaks."

20   Lynch, "Environmental Adaptability," in *City Sense*.

21   Wallace Stevens, "Anecdote of the Jar," *Collected Poems* (New York: Knopf, 1991), 76.

22   Hull, *Touching the Rock*, 30–31.

23   Wright, *Writings, 1894–1930*, 117.

24   Ibid., 118.

25   T. S. Eliot, "Burnt Norton," from *Four Quartets*, in *The Complete Poems and Plays: 1909–1950* (New York: Harcourt, Brace, 1952).

26   Jensen, *Siftings*, 63; for discussion of Jensen's council rings, see also Engel, *Sacred Sands*, 200–01.

27   Munn, *Walbiri Iconography*.

28   Sutton et al., *Dreamings*.

29   Author's collection.

30   Addison, 1712, reproduced in Hunt and Willis, *Genius of Place*, 142.

31   Woodbridge, *Stourhead Landscape*.

32   Henry Hoare, in a letter to his nephew, quoted in ibid., 17.

33   Victor Pomare, quoted in Warner, *To Dwell Is to Garden*, 50.

34   Parts of this section are drawn from Spirn, "Uluru to Cooper's Place."

35   The term *performance* also acknowledges Halprin's *RSVP Cycles*. Kenneth Helphand referred me to Mayer Spivak's essay "Archetypal Place," *Architectural Forum* 140:3 (October 1973), 44–49. My performance spaces and Spivak's archetypal places differ, but there are important commonalities, especially in our emphasis on behavior patterns that generate spatial settings.

36   Appleton, *Experience of Landscape* and *Symbolism of Habitat*.

37   Norberg-Schulz, *Concept of Dwelling*. Lynch, *Image of the City*. Lynch's work has been particularly influential on the design and planning professions; this book is now in its twenty-third printing.

38   Alexander, *Pattern Language* and *Timeless Way*.

39   Alexander, *Multi-Service Centers*.

40   Dubos, *Man Adapting*, 9, and *So Human an Animal*, 70.

41   American Society of Landscape Architects Annual Meeting in Atlanta, 1978.

42   Jennifer Isaacs, *Arts of Dreaming*, 175–77.

43   Wright made numerous references in this vein, for example: "The land is the simplest form of architecture," in Brownell and Wright, *Architecture and Modern Life*, 17.

44   This text is adapted from a longer treatment of Wright's landscape design in Spirn, "Wright."

45   See Cronon, "Inconstant Unity," in Riley and Reed, *Frank Lloyd Wright*, 9–14.

46   See, for example, the traditional architecture of Japan, the work of Alvar Aalto, Adèle Naudé Santos, Glenn Murcutt, and Richard Le Plastrier.

47   Wright, *Writings, 1930–1932*, 246.

48   Repton, *Landscape Gardening*, 3, 69.

49   These associations are not far-fetched. Wright's Uncle Jenkin compared Tower Hill to a woman's breast in a sermon; see Graham, *Gospel of the Farm*. See also Biedermann, *Symbolism*, 100–02.

50   Wright described the symbolism of forms in "The Japanese Print," *Writings, 1894–1930*, 117, and he used a red square as his emblem. The hill garden, however, is merely a representation of fertility, for hilltops are not fertile here, the valley bottoms are. Mamah Borthwick Cheney was the wife of a client with whom Wright lived in Europe and built Taliesin; she was murdered at Taliesin in 1914.

51   Randall C. Henning, *At Taliesin* (Carbondale: Southern Illinois University Press, 1992), 68.

52 Wright, "Living in the Desert," 12.

53 Wright was strongly influenced by the gardens he saw during his visits to Japan. For a description of the principle of borrowed scenery (*shakkei*), see Itoh, *Space and Illusion*. For a description of the stroll garden, its relation to interior architectural space, and the concept of "movement-oriented architectural space," see Inoue, *Space in Japanese Architecture*.

54 Wright, "To Arizona," in *Writings, 1939–1949*, 34.

55 Brownell and Wright, *Architecture and Modern Life*, 277. The last chapter, a dialogue between Wright and Brownell, contains an extended reflection on the meaning of structure.

56 Wright, *Writings, 1894–1930*, 117.

57 Ibid.

58 Ibid.

59 Brownell and Wright, *Architecture and Modern Life*, 278–81. Wright used the big, blue Ming tea jar in the garden at Taliesin to illustrate his idea of structure as fusing "ideal" of function and purpose, process of formation, form and use.

60 Bruce Brooks Pfeiffer, personal communication, February 17, 1995. Apparently Wright worked these out in his head, then built directly; there are few drawings documenting these successive changes.

61 Brierly, personal communication, August 24, 1994.

62 Wright, *Writings, 1939–1949*, 33–36, and *Writings, 1931–1939*, 175–78.

63 Wright, *Living Voice*, 177.

5 SHAPING LANDSCAPE CONTEXT

1   T. S. Eliot, "Burnt Norton," *Four Quartets*, in *The Complete Poems and Plays: 1909–1950* (New York: Harcourt, Brace, 1952).

2   Gollwitzer, *Bäume*.

3   For a discussion of the development of these ideas, the changing paradigm, and the relation of both to prevailing political values, see Michael Barbour, "Ecological Fragmentation in the Fifties," in Cronon, *Uncommon Ground*.

4   For a charming description of this phenomenon, see Watts, "Watching the Islands Go By," in *Reading the Landscape of America*. For wonderful, detailed descriptions of river phenomena and their significance, see Twain, *Mississippi*.

5   Maclean, *River Runs*, 61–63.

6   Brown, *Occluded Front*, 22.

7   Count Giuseppe Panza di Biumo, "Artist of the Sky," in Brown, *Occluded Front*, 61–88.

8   Exodus 19:9.

9   The mountaineer Galen Rowell has photographed these and other phenomena of mountain light: Rowell, *Mountain Light*.

10 For a detailed description of the Roden Crater project, see Adcock, *James Turrell*.

11 Hill, *California Landscape*, 146.

12 Thomas, *Disney*, viii.

13 Halprin, *RSVP Cycles*, 58.

14 E. Hess, "A Tale of Two Memorials," *Art in America* 71 (April 1983).

15 Eliot, "The Dry Salvages," in *Four Quartets*.

16 Eiseley, *Immense Journey*, 20.

17 Ibid., 46.

18 Feld, *Sound and Sentiment*, 45.

19 Feld, liner notes to *Voices of the Rainforest* CD-ROM (Salem, Mass.: Rykodisc, 1991); *Sound and Sentiment.*

20 Feld, *Sound and Sentiment,* 23.

21 Rachel Carson, *Silent Spring* (Boston: Houghton, Mifflin, 1962), 2.

22 The institute has expanded, and the stand of trees is no more.

23 James Michener, *Centennial* (New York: Fawcett Crest, 1975), 47.

24 Psalms 23:2.

25 Hoskins, *Making of English Landscape;* Taylor, *Fields;* Cronon, *Changes in Land.*

26 Taylor, *Fields.*

27 Hoskins, *Making of English Landscape;* Taylor, *Fields,* 1975.

28 Cather, *My Ántonia,* 29.

29 Seddon, Conference on the Contribution of Landscape Planning to Environmental Protection, Hannover, Germany, June 6, 1990.

30 Panofsky, "Rolls-Royce Radiator."

31 Hayden, *Power of Place,* 9.

32 Robert Kennedy, quoted in Peter Medoff and Holly Sklar, *Streets of Hope* (Boston: South End Press, 1994), 245.

33 The drawings and text are online. See "Publications" at www.upenn.edu/wplp/sms.

34 Hidenobu Jinnai, "The Spatial Structure of Edo," in *Tokugawa Japan,* edited by Chie Nakane and Shinzaburo Oishi (Tokyo: University of Tokyo, 1990). I am grateful to Anne Walthall for bringing this essay to my attention.

35 Tax laws make it advantageous to keep some land in agriculture, for if you qualify for status as a farmer your taxes may be much lower than if you are merely holding land for development. Kazuhiko Takeuchi and Shunsaku Miyagi, personal communication, July 9, 1990.

36 Takamasa Miyazaki, personal communication.

6 Landscape Grammar

1 Bateson, *Ecology of Mind,* 154.

2 Bateson, *Mind and Nature,* 18.

3 David Crystal, *The Cambridge Encyclopedia of Language* (Cambridge: Cambridge University Press, 1987), 82.

4 Hippocrates, *Airs, Waters, and Places,* in *Hippocrates,* vol. 1, Loeb Classical Library, edited by T. E. Page (Cambridge: Harvard University Press, 1962), iii–vi; Aristotle, *Politics,* VII.xi.

5 The description of Priene is based on accounts in the following sources: Weigand and Schrader, *Priene;* R. E. Wycherley, *How the Greeks Built Cities* (Garden City, N.Y.: Anchor, 1962); and Crouch, *Water Management.*

6 See Schapiro's classic essay, "Style."

7 The description of scales is based on Morrison and Eames, *Powers of Ten.* The book was preceded by two animated film versions.

8 Andersson, "Brev fra hønsegård," my translation.

9 Ibid.

10 The treads are ca. twelve inches, the risers exactly one-half the tread, with a landing ca. thirty inches every twelve steps.

11 Attributed to Gunnar Asplund by Sven-Ingvar Andersson, personal communication, May 21, 1990.

12 William Weston told this to John deKoven Hill, who related the story to me. The grid gardens were planted ca. 1912.

13   Landscape architecture studio course at Harvard University, Spring 1985. For the subsequent de-
      velopment, see Peter Medoff and Holly Sklar, *Streets of Hope* (Boston: South End Press, 1994).
14   Hoskins, *English Landscape*, 20.
15   Arnheim, "Order and Complexity," 125.
16   Ibid., 123.
17   Lorraine Daston, personal communication, July 27, 1993.
18   Mukerji, *Territorial Ambitions*.
19   Schjetnan first told me of the traditional uses of these stones.
20   I am grateful to Mario Schjetnan for these examples.

7 PRAGMATICS OF LANDSCAPE EXPRESSION

1   *Spring*, by Pieter Breughel the Elder. Engraved by Petrus a Merica, 1570. Andersson was profes-
      sor of landscape architecture there until his retirement in 1995; now he devotes full time to his
      professional practice.
2   Andersson, "My Definition of My Profession This Year," paper at European Conference of Land-
      scape Architectural Schools, Ljubljana, Slovenia, August 1992, 3.
3   Andersson, "Brev fra hønsegård." Unless noted otherwise, quotations are from this article. The
      translations are mine.
4   These are references to two influential theorists and their books: Robert Venturi, *Complexity and
      Contradiction in Architecture* (New York: Museum of Modern Art, 1966); Norberg-Schulz, *Inten-
      tions in Architecture*.
5   Andersson, "Brev fra hønsegård."
6   Andersson has written about his garden, both explicitly and implicitly, in many essays; among
      those referred to here are "Trädgård efter fem år," "Brev fra hønsegård," and "Häckar och höns."
      For a complete list, see Spirn, "Texts, Landscapes, Life."
7   "Brev fra hønsegård," 581.
8   Adapted from T. S. Eliot and Northrop Frye.
9   These are all people he knew or wrote about. Steen Eiler Rasmussen was a Danish architect and
      historian, Sven Hermelin (1900–84), a Swedish landscape architect and one of Andersson's
      teachers, Frederik Magnus Piper (1746–1824), a Swedish architect who introduced the English
      landscape style into Sweden, Kazimir Malevich (1878–1935), a Russian painter, Geoffrey Jellicoe
      (1900–96) an English architect and landscape architect, and Kevin Lynch (1918–84), an Ameri-
      can urban designer and theorist.
10   Andersson and Høyer, *Sørensen*, 5.
11   For a description of these projects in the overall context of Boston and Olmsted's work, see
      Spirn, *Granite Garden* and "Constructing Nature." For a description of how basin and tidal gate
      were intended to work, see Olmsted's account of his dialogue with the city's engineer in a lecture
      to the Boston Society of Architects, "The Problem and Its Solution" in 1886. The handwritten
      notes for this lecture are in the Olmsted Papers at the Library of Congress. They were transcribed
      by Cynthia Zaitzevsky and reprinted in her doctoral dissertation, "Frederick Law Olmsted and
      the Boston Park System" (Harvard University, 1975), 295–306, and excerpted in her book of the
      same title (Cambridge: Harvard University Press, 1982). For a description of how the flood con-
      trol function worked, see E. W. Howe, "The Back Bay Park, Boston," a speech to the Boston So-
      ciety of Civil Engineers on March 16, 1881.
12   Zaitzevsky, *Olmsted*, 188.
13   Letter to F. L. Temple, March 15, 1886, Olmsted Papers, Library of Congress. Temple was the

landscape gardener Olmsted had hired to plant the Fens. Of the one hundred thousand plants, only thirty-five thousand survived, many of which were "nurse" plants actually intended to die. Of the plant species intended to predominate over time, 75–95 percent were dead. See also Zaitzevsky, *Olmsted*, 187–90.

14 Letter to Charles Eliot and John Charles Olmsted, October 28, 1893, Olmsted Papers, Library of Congress.

15 Rowe, *Design Thinking*, 15.

16 Olin, *Transforming the Common Place*.

17 Jellicoe, *Guelph Lectures*, 178.

18 Wright, *Writings, 1894–1930*, 124 (emphasis added).

19 Brownell and Wright, *Architecture and Modern Life*, 275.

20 Halprin, *RSVP Cycles*, 104.

21 See Laurie Olin's discussion of this point, which he elaborates in "Form, Meaning, and Expression."

22 Halprin, personal communication, August 16, 1989.

23 Bye, *Art into Landscape*, 155.

24 Françoise Fromonot, personal communication, May 13, 1993.

25 This is true not just for landscape authors. See, for example, descriptions of the essential roles visualization plays in engineering, science, and invention in McKim, *Visual Thinking*, or any of Tufte's books, such as *Envisioning Information*.

26 "What Is Design?" in Neuhart and Eames, *Eames Design*, 15.

27 For a more detailed description of this work, see John R. Clark, *The Sanibel Report* (Washington, D.C.: Conservation Foundation, 1976).

28 Randall Darwall and Fayette Watkis, "Shawl," eight-harness summer and winter twill weave handwoven of hand-dyed silk, wool, and cotton, dip-dyed warp, 100 by 24 inches, 1994. I have collected several sets of scarves, of different weaves, that are variations on a single warp. Darwall's fabrics are in the collection of the American Craft Museum. He exhibits each year at the leading American craft shows. See also Julie Dale, *Art to Wear* (Abbeville Press, 1986); Karen Searle, "The Scarves of Randall Darwall: The Consummate Cloth," *Ornament* 14:1 (Autumn 1990), 22–25, 63; Margo Mensing, "Randall Darwall: Infusing Function with Life," *Fiberarts* (March/April 1995), 40–44.

29 I described an early version of this approach of improvisation within a framework, likening it to jazz, in Spirn, "Poetics."

30 From 1987 to 1990, this work was funded by a grant from the J. N. Pew Charitable Trust, a collaboration between the Department of Landscape Architecture and Regional Planning at the University of Pennsylvania, the Organization and Management Group, and Philadelphia Green, an organization devoted to the promotion and support of community gardens and other local landscape projects that is part of the Pennsylvania Horticultural Society. Since 1991, it has been supported by grants from Penn's Center for Community Partnerships, the Philadelphia Urban Resources Partnership, the Kellogg Foundation, and the U.S. Department of Housing and Urban Development.

31 See Spirn, *West Philadelphia Landscape Plan*.

32 See Spirn and Marcucci, *Models of Success*.

33 See Spirn and Cameron, *Shaping the Block*, and Spirn, Cameron, and Pollio, *Vacant Land*.

34 See Spirn and Cheetham, *Digital Database*.

35 On the project's website at www.upenn.edu/wplp.

36 Pennsylvania Governor Tom Ridge featured this work as part of his Budget Address to the state legislature on February 3, 1998. The teacher Glenn Campbell, eighth grader Keith Sisco, and

seventh grader Oneil Hall presented the work via satellite, as part of the governor's speech, and received a standing ovation from the entire assembly.

37 Spirn and Pollio, *Garden Is a Town.*

38 Philadelphia City Planning Commission, the *Plan for West Philadelphia* (Philadelphia, 1994). There is a brief mention of the Mill Creek sewer collapse of 1961, in which more than one hundred homes were destroyed, but no indication of present or future problems related to the creek and sewer.

8 Poetics of Landscape

1 Definitions of figures and tropes discussed in this chapter are drawn from several sources, especially Tom McArthur, ed., *Oxford Companion to the English Language* (Oxford: Oxford University Press, 1992). Other sources are H. W. Fowler, *Modern English Usage* (Oxford: Oxford University Press, 1965); Wilson Follett, *Modern American Usage* (New York: Hill and Wang, 1966); Kathleen Morner and Ralph Rausch, *Dictionary of Literary Terms* (Lincolnwood, Ill.: National Textbook Company, 1991); and Edward P. J. Corbett, *Classical Rhetoric for the Modern Student* (Oxford: Oxford University Press, 1971).

2 Hogan, *Lawn*, 70.

3 Including Philip Johnson (who reportedly remains on the lawn advisory board for this purpose). Will Rieley, personal communication, April 17, 1989.

4 When the budget for the courtyard was cut, Schwartz had to change the design; she found the frogs in a garden supply store, where they were available in large quantities at low cost. Martha Schwartz, personal communication, December 13, 1993.

5 Cirlot, *Symbols*, 114–15. Cooper, *Symbols*, 72.

6 Emily Yoffe, "Silence of the Frogs," *New York Times Sunday Magazine*, December 13, 1992, 36–38, 64, 66, 76. See also "What the Frogs Are Telling Us," *New York Times*, March 6, 1994.

7 See Fuchs, *Richard Long*, and Brown, *Occluded Front.*

8 Jellicoe himself gave the walk this title; others, such as Michael Spens, refer to it as the "Magritte Walk."

9 Jellicoe, *Guelph Lectures*, 168.

10 Ibid., 149.

11 Al-Khalil, *Monument.*

12 Current preservation law does not permit transplanting the trees, which grow only in this place.

13 This was one of a series of sound compositions produced by six artists for particular sites in Parc de La Villette as part of a program called "Le chemin à l'oreille: Parcours sonores," May 30–October 31, 1992. The artist who composed this piece was Raoul de Pesters.

14 Alexander Pope, "An Epistle to Lord Birmingham," 1731, reprinted in Hunt and Willis, *Genius*, 213.

15 Palladio, *Architecture*, 41.

16 Candace Slater, *Trail of Miracles: Stories from a Pilgrimage in Northeast Brazil* (Berkeley: University of California Press, 1986), 5–6, 67–69.

17 See Olmsted, *Niagara.*

18 Andersson, "Principper for bevaring."

19 Andersson, "Tycho Brahes trädgård," *ale: Historisk tidskrift för Skåneland* (1992/2), 26–32; "Uraniborgs renässansträdgård: restaureringsprojektets förutsättningar och hypoteser," *Stencil* (1993/7), 13–20.

20 Opening speech at EPCOT, quoted in Holliss and Sibley, *Disney Studio*, 102. See also Walt Disney on planning for EPCOT, quoted in Thomas, *Disney*, 375.

21 Morner and Rausch, *Literary Terms*, 8.

22 McArthur, *English Language*, 653.

23 Sørensen, *Haver*, 165.

24 John 5:4.

25 Wilhelm Miller, "The Prairie Spirit in Landscape Gardening," Circular no. 184 (Urbana: Agricultural Experiment Station, Department of Horticulture, University of Illinois, 1916).

26 Jane Austen, *Pride and Prejudice* (New York: Signet Classics, 1961), 204.

27 John Bartlett, *Familiar Quotations* (Boston: Little, Brown, 1955), 110.

28 Loudon, *Suburban Gardener*, and Downing, *Landscape Gardening*.

29 Woodbridge, *Stourhead Landscape*, 19.

30 Janet Bord, *Mazes and Labyrinths of the World* (New York: E. P. Dutton, 1976), 141.

31 Quarles, *Emblems Divine and Moral, Together with Hieroglyphics of the Life of Man*, 1777, quoted in Bord, *Mazes and Labyrinths*, 7. Mazes are not always associated with confusion or difficulties; in the Italian Renaissance garden, for instance, they may refer to "order and human skill," Lazzaro, *Italian Garden*, 51–55.

32 Jellicoe, *Guelph Lectures*, 149.

33 Ibid., 172.

34 Cronon, *Uncommon Ground*, 59–66.

35 Anthony Hecht, "The Gardens of the Villa d'Este," *Hard Hours* (New York: Atheneum, 1967).

36 Quoted in Hunt and Willis, *Genius*, 213.

37 Van Valkenburgh, *Transforming the American Garden*, 16–19.

38 Linden-Ward, *Silent City*, 58.

39 Spens, *Jellicoe at Shute*, 55.

40 Thomas, *Disney*, 279.

41 Ibid., 264. These figures apply to Disneyland; the scale at Disney World is slightly different, the miniaturization more exaggerated from first to third storys.

42 See Corn and Horrigan, *Yesterday's Tomorrows*, and Adams, *Burle Marx*.

43 Walt Disney, speech at opening ceremonies for Disneyland, July 17, 1955, quoted in Holliss and Sibley, *Disney Studio*, 70.

44 Thomas, *Disney*, 280.

45 Ibid., 253.

46 Ibid., 289.

47 Leonard Shannon, *Disneyland: Dreams, Traditions, and Transitions* (Walt Disney Company, n.d.), 151.

48 Thomas, *Disney*, 281.

49 The frog pond has since been refurbished.

50 Quoted in Thomas, *Disney*, 387.

51 "The Comprehensive Design Plan for the White House: Desired Futures" (National Park Service, October 1993), 43

9 Polemical Landscapes

1 Reinhard Rürup, ed., *Topography of Terror* (Berlin: Arenhövel, 1991), 197.

2 Riley and Brown have addressed this topic in "Analogy and Authority: Beyond Chaos and Kudzu," *Landscape Journal* 14:1 (1995), 87–92.

3 Crowe, "Presidential Address," *Journal of the Institute of Landscape Architects* (November 1957), 4.

4 Quoted in Gröning and Wolschke-Bulmahn, "Mania for Native Plants," 123–24.

5 Quoted in ibid., 121.

6   Quoted in ibid., 122.

7   Tanya Barrientos, "Aliens Among Us," *Inquirer: Philadelphia Inquirer Magazine*, June 30, 1996.

8   For a balanced view of the conundrums, see John Rodman, "Restoring Nature: Natives and Ex-otics," in *In the Nature of Things*, edited by Jane Bennett and William Chaloupka (Minneapolis: University of Minesota Press, 1993).

9   Quoted by Brendan Gill in *Many Masks* (New York: Ballantine, 1987), 22. Another version, almost word for word, is transcribed from a tape of August 4, 1957, in Wright, *Living Voice*, 88. Wright told Mike Wallace the following in a television interview in 1957: "I've always considered myself deeply religious," said Wright. "Do you go to any specific church?" asked Wallace. Wright replied, "My church [pause], I put a capital 'N' on Nature and go there."

10   Letter from Wright to Lewis Mumford, January 7, 1929, University of Pennsylvania Library, Spe-cial Collections, Mumford Papers, folder 5477. Wright, *Living Voice*, 88. See also Spirn, "Wright."

11   See Thompson and Steiner, *Ecological Design*. The phrase *nonecological* is used in this volume by several authors with divergent views on the nature of ecological design whose essays reveal the pitfalls of appealing to "ecology" or "nature" for authority in landscape design.

12   See Max Weber's analysis of three forms of authority—traditional, legal-rational, and charis-matic—in *Economy and Society* (Berkeley: University of California Press, 1978).

13   Williams, "Ideas of Nature."

14   Arthur O. Lovejoy, "Meanings of 'Nature,'" in *A Documentary History of Primitivism and Other Ideas* (Baltimore: Johns Hopkins University Press, 1935).

15   Williams, *Keywords*, 219. Many essays and entire books have been written on the origins, history, use, and significance of the word *nature*. See, for example, Williams, "Ideas of Nature"; C. S. Lewis, "Nature," in *Studies in Words*; Lovejoy, "Meanings of 'Nature,'" and "Nature as Aesthetic Norm," in *Essays in the History of Ideas* (Baltimore, 1948); R. G. Collingwood, *The Idea of Nature* (London, 1945); Glacken, *Rhodian Shore*; Evernden, *Social Creation of Nature*; Cronon, *Uncom-mon Ground*.

16   See Worster, *Nature's Economy*; Botkin, *Discordant Harmonies*; Golley, *Ecosystem Concept*; and Gregg Mitman, *The State of Nature: Ecology, Community, and American Social Thought 1900–1950* (Chicago: University of Chicago Press, 1992).

17   Candace Slater, "Amazonia as Edenic Narrative," in Cronon, *Uncommon Ground*. Slater traces Edenic narratives as they relate to the biblical story of Genesis, but points out that such notions are not unique to the Judeo-Christian tradition. For a discussion of other religious traditions, see Poul Pedersen, "Nature, Religion, and Cultural Identity: The Religious Environmentalist Par-adigm," in *Asian Perceptions of Nature*, edited by Arne Kalland and Ole Bruun (Richmond, Sur-rey: Curzon, 1995).

18   ". . . a sermon which awakens the best in the human soul." Jensen, *Siftings*, 63. Edgar Tafel, *Ap-prentice to Genius* (New York: Dover, 1985), 152, and Cornelia Brierly, personal communication, August 24, 1994. Brierly was assigned to assist Jensen when he visited Taliesin.

19   Wright, *Writings 1930–1932*, 163.

20   Jensen, *Siftings*, 94.

21   Ibid., 23.

22   Ibid., 21.

23   Jensen was born of a Danish-speaking family in the Slesvig region, the contested border zone of northern Germany and southern Denmark. For perspectives on contemporary Danish and Ger-man ideas of nature and natural gardens, see Kenneth Olwig, "Historical Geography and the So-ciety/Nature Problematic: The Perspective of J. F. Schouw, George Perkins Marsh and E. Reclus," *Journal of Historical Geography* 6:1 (1980), and *Nature's Ideological Landscape*; Joachim

Wolschke-Bulmahn, "The Peculiar Garden: The Advent and Destruction of Modernism in German Garden Design," in *Masters of American Garden Design III: The Modern Garden in Europe and the United States,* edited by Rachel Karson (Proceedings of the Garden Conservancy Symposium, 1993). See also Frank Waugh, *The Natural Style in Landscape Gardening* (Boston: Richard G. Badger, 1917), for a North American perspective and Ruff, *Holland,* for an introduction to the work of Jacques Thijsse, J. Landwehr, and the Dutch *Heem* ("home") parks.

24 See Mitman, *State of Nature,* for a history of the Chicago school of ecology and the interplay between science and a social philosophy that stressed the value of cooperation over conflict.

25 For Jensen's relationship to these ideas, see Wolschke-Bulmahn, "The Peculiar Garden," and his review of Grese, *Jensen,* in *Journal of Garden History* 15 (1995), 54–55.

26 On the first day of class, I often ask students to define *nature.* Sometimes, at the end of the course I ask them to write a short paper defining *nature* once again. Their later answers are more articulate and reflective, but rarely change in substance from their first brief statement. I have concluded that ideas of nature are deeply held beliefs, closely tied to religious values, even for those who do not consider themselves religious. By the age of twenty-five, most students' ideas of nature seem set or at least not modified greatly by a single course on the subject (they range in age from twenty-two to fifty; most are in their mid to late twenties). While largely North American, approximately one-third have been from other parts of the world, including Europe, the Middle East, Africa, Asia, South America, and Australia. Of the North Americans, most grew up in the suburbs or in rural areas; a higher proportion of foreign students are from cities.

27 Ian McHarg, "Ecology and Design," in Thompson and Steiner, *Ecological Design,* 321.

28 One article included gratuitous, unfounded attacks, some from critics who chose to remain anonymous, such as: "The so-called Penn School led by McHarg produced a generation of landscape graduates who did not build." Daralice Boles, "The New American Landscape," *Progressive Architecture* (July 1989), 53. Statements such as these were retracted by the editors in a subsequent issue of the journal in response to letters to the editor.

29 Olin, "Form, Meaning, and Expression," 150.

30 Grese, *Jensen,* presents a useful comparison of the work of Olmsted and Jensen in this and other respects, but emphasizes similarities and does not probe their ideological differences.

31 The Ramble at Central Park was planted to appear wild, but it was only a small part of the park. William Robinson, an English acquaintance of Olmsted, published his book *The Wild Garden* in 1870. Olmsted was undoubtedly also aware of Martin Johnson Heade's contemporary paintings depicting marshes along Boston's North Shore.

32 Jensen, *Siftings,* 76.

33 Ibid., 77.

34 Olmsted, "Parks, Parkways and Pleasure Grounds," 253–54.

35 Jensen, *Siftings,* 83.

36 Ibid., 46.

37 Ibid., 35.

38 Ibid., 45.

39 Such views were common at the time, and Olmsted discussed them frequently in relation to his work. See, for example, *Niagara.*

40 Olmsted preferred to follow William Robinson's practice of mixing native and hardy exotic plants, described in *The Wild Garden* (1870). See Zaitzevsky, *Olmsted,* 196, for quotations of Olmsted's and Sargent's disagreement on this subject.

41 Olmsted, "General Plan for the Sanitary Improvement of Muddy River and for Completing a Continuous Promenade between Boston Common and Jamaica Pond" (Boston, 1881).

42   Robert Dorman, *Revolt of the Provinces: The Regionalist Movement in America* (Chapel Hill: University of North Carolina Press, 1993).

43   See Donald Scherer and Thomas Attig, eds., *Ethics and the Environment* (Englewood Cliffs: Prentice-Hall, 1983).

44   From the report for the West End Redevelopment Scheme, part of the Boston General Plan of 1950, reproduced on a slide in the Fisher Fine Arts Library, University of Pennsylvania.

45   Gans, *Urban Villagers*, 386.

46   Marc Fried, "Grieving for a Lost Home," in Leonard Duhl, ed., *The Urban Condition* (New York: Basic Books, 1963), 151–71.

47   Jacobs, *Death and Life*, 3.

48   See Walter Hood's documentation of the history of four small parks in Oakland, California, in *Urban Diaries*.

49   Olin, "Regionalism."

50   See Casey Blake, "An Atmosphere of Effrontery: Richard Serra, *Tilted Arc,* and the Crisis of Public Art," in *Power of Culture,* edited by Richard Wightman Fox and T. J. Jackson Lears (Chicago: University of Chicago Press, 1993).

51   Ibid., 253, 264.

52   Ibid.

53   The Vietnam Veterans Memorial, however, was built with private funds.

54.   Interview in Landecker, *Martha Schwartz*, 109.

55   Ibid., 149.

56   Schwartz, "Bagel Garden," 45–46. Schwartz, "Author-Designer Responds," *Landscape Architecture* (May 1980), 320. Daralice Boles, "New American Landscape," *Progressive Architecture* (July 1989).

57   Lasswell, *Signature of Power*, 7.

58   This description is from Mukerji, *Territorial Ambitions*, 46–48.

59   Lasswell, *Signature of Power*, 57.

60   Ibid.

61   A phrase used by Alexander Pope in "An Epistle to Lord Birmingham," 1731, repr. in Hunt and Willis, *Genius*, 213.

62   Dean MacCannell, *Empty Meeting Grounds* (London: Routledge, 1992), 81–82, cites numerous restrictions on house color and landscaping described in literature he received from Irvine's Chamber of Commerce: various covenants stipulate that houses must be painted with bland, earth tones. My rental agreement when I lived in Irvine in 1994 prohibited me from replacing the sheer, white curtains provided on all windows.

63   Italo Calvino, *Invisible Cities* (New York: Harcourt Brace Jovanovich, 1972), 165.

Sources

Sources acknowledge influential works, open the field to those interested in exploring it further, and reveal untrodden ground. This compilation is multidisciplinary, but is neither comprehensive nor exhaustive. It includes nonverbal sources not ordinarily cited in a bibliography, such as landscapes, maps, and photographs. As outlined above, the sources are divided into three major parts: landscapes, authors of landscape, and general references on reading and telling landscape. Primary sources—places themselves, materials consulted in archives, and interviews with landscape authors—are listed separately from secondary sources; landscapes, maps, photographs, and paintings studied in reproduction are under published sources. This selective list cites works of particular significance in shaping my ideas and others that will introduce readers to sources for further study of landscape as language. For more sources on specific topics, see the chapter notes.

LANDSCAPES

Nothing can replace direct encounter with the literature of landscape—places themselves, their sounds, smells, colors, textures, views, spatial sequences and relationships, feel of sun and wind. I am often familiar with a place I visit for the first time, have studied it in texts, plans, drawings, and photographs; yet I always discover the unforeseen and sometimes revise my views entirely after experiencing a place firsthand. Some places are disappointing (Salk Institute in La Jolla); others a delightful surprise (Villa Rotunda in Italy). Several telling differences between the work of "Capability" Brown and William Kent emerged only after visits to Bowood and Rousham in England. At the Villa Lante, I was unprepared for the significance of sound—lush, rhythmic, harmonic, melodic, symphonic sounds of waters gushing, roaring, rustling, spraying, splashing, dripping, resonating within manifold containers shaped to project, amplify, and even to silence. Fieldwork is essential to fluency in landscape language, and it shapes ideas. But experience alone is rarely sufficient to fully understand a place; depictions of places in maps, photographs, and paintings enable deeper readings, as do written guides. And one cannot visit every place; published sources are valuable substitutes to direct encounter, though not equivalents. It is best to be explicit about which landscapes one has read directly, and which one has experienced only through secondary sources.

Places: Fieldwork

The landscape sources listed below are organized alphabetically, by continent, country, and, in the United States, by state. The list is of places cited in the text or particularly influential in shaping my ideas. Since 1988, I have kept travel journals; transcribed into computer text in 1993, indexed by keywords, they were sources for refining key concepts as related to particular places. I have experienced some over many years. I have shaped others: community gardens in West Philadelphia and the Dorchester and Roxbury neighborhoods of Boston; the Toronto Central Waterfront; Woodlands, Texas; Sanibel Island, Florida. I have visited all types of biomes except tropical rain forest and arctic tundra, though not all continents or all great landscapes or works by all important authors. Many places I have not experienced directly are included among published sources.

Asia: Japan. 1990, by train from Osaka to Kyoto, Kobe, Ise, Toba, and Tokyo. Startling juxtapositions between traditional and new landscapes: in Osaka the Shitennoji temple district, the castle park, and the modern central city; in Tokyo, Asakusa, Shinjuku, Ginza, and the Meiji Shrine; in Kyoto, Gion, Tadao Ando's Time I, and the Kamo River, imperial villas of Katsura and Shugakuin, gardens in monasteries and temples (Saihoji, Ryoanji, Shisendo, Daitokuji). In Kobe, recently built landscapes: a floodplain park, a new town and winery behind the mountains, Port Island, newly built on fill, and Tadao Ando's Chapel at the Mt. Rokko Hotel.

Australia. 1987, from the tropical landscapes of Darwin and Kakadu National Park to the central desert of Uluru and Alice Springs, the new town of Yolara near Uluru, to Canberra and the new Parliament House, then to Sydney. 1988, Glenn Murcutt's house for Sydney Ball; Richard Le Plastrier's house in a palm grove. I walked the northern shore of Sydney Harbor, sailed its length, flew over it in a helicopter. At Melbourne, Werribee Farm sewage treatment facility.

Europe: Denmark. 1964–66, 1973, and frequent visits in 1990–95, based in Lejre, a settlement from ancient times, Roskilde, a provincial town, and Copenhagen, but with field trips throughout the country. The pattern of visits provided a perspective on landscape change, especially the transformations between 1966 and 1973, a time of prosperity: by 1973 bicycles were dramatically diminished, and cars and parking lots had proliferated. 1990–95, cemeteries and gardens by G. N. Brandt and dozens of C. Th. Sørensen's gardens, parks, amphitheaters, campuses, and housing projects.

Europe: Finland. 1990, Helsinki and a small island (Möland) in the Archipelago. The landscapes of the city parks, the harbor and its fort, the inland lakes surrounded by dark firs gave context to the work of Saarinen, Aalto, and the Sirens. The planned, manicured environment of Tapiola seemed bland in contrast to the vitality of another planned development, Kottby, built in the 1920s for workers.

Europe: France. 1978, Saint Malo, a town destroyed in the Second World War and reconstructed with new buildings and ramparts in old style, Dinan, a provincial town in Normandy, Mont-Saint-Michel, Chartres, and Paris. 1992–97, Paris, as advisor to the Organization for Economic Cooperation and Development, exploring traces of various times: from ancient Rome (Amphitheater Lutèce) to the Renaissance (Hotel Sully and Place des Vosges), the nineteenth-century city of Haussmann and Alphand (Père Lachaise, Buttes Chaumont, the boulevards), to more recent landscapes at La Défense, Parc de La Villette, and Parc Citröen. The Île-de-France, landscape compositions of André Le Nôtre at Vaux-le-Vicomte, Versailles, Chantilly, Sceaux and Claude Monet's garden at Giverny. 1996, Verdun, to see the First World War landscapes.

EUROPE: GERMANY. 1966, Heidelberg, the Rhine, Munich and Dachau, East Germany, and Berlin. 1983, Munich, the Englischer Garten, housing projects of the early twentieth century, then Stuttgart to see an urban landscape planned to funnel fresh cool air off the hillsides in order to reduce air pollution. 1990, Hannover and its Herrenhausen. 1993, the autobahns, across former East Germany to conference in Potsdam, the gardens at Sansoucci and ruins and reconstructions in Berlin. 1996, Trier and its Roman ruins en route to Verdun.

EUROPE: ITALY. 1988, Redipuglia, via Trieste, then the Veneto and Carlo Scarpa's Brione Cemetery, Palladio's Villa Rotundo, near Vicenza, and the Villa Barbara at Maser. 1996, Hadrian's Villa and Villa d'Este in Tivoli, Boboli Gardens, Villa Medici and others in Florence, Villa Lante and Bomarzzo north of Rome.

EUROPE: NETHERLANDS. 1978, Amsterdam and the polderlands, from the long, narrow fields of early examples to the vast new polders.

EUROPE: SLOVENIA. 1988, Ljubljana, the works of Joze Plecnik—bridges, lampposts, and other artifacts, the Slovene countryside.

EUROPE: SPAIN. 1983, Andalusia, from Málaga to Antequera, and several other white hilltowns. Granada, to trace the flow of water through the gardens of the Alhambra and Generalife.

EUROPE: SWEDEN. 1990–96, the medieval university town of Lund, the city of Malmö, and the countryside of Skåne, Sven-Ingvar Andersson's house and garden at Marnas, the beech forest nearby, Per Friberg's house and garden, Malmö Eastern Cemetery by Sigurd Lewerentz. 1990, with Andersson to the park he designed in Ronneby and to Stockholm, Lewerentz's and Gunnar Asplund's Forest Cemetery, the beach park of Holger Blom.

EUROPE: UNITED KINGDOM. 1973, walks in the Wye River Valley near Hereford, along public footpaths on the British Ordinance Survey maps. 1978, Scotland, Glasgow, Glencoe, the Great Glen, Glen Loy and Glen Roy, Edinburgh. 1983, Stonehenge, Avebury, and the Ridgeway, Port Sunlight and Joseph Paxton's People's Park in Birkenhead, then Liverpool and London to compare the inner-city landscapes to those of American cities. London's residential squares, Hyde Park, St. James Park, Regent Street, and Regent's Park, Camdentown Garden Center and Urban Farm (vacant land reclaimed). 1987, Avebury and the Ridgeway, the Vale of the White Horse, Glastonbury, Hampton Court, Claremont, Rousham, Bowood and its adventure playground, Blenheim, Longleat and its maze and safari park, Stourhead, Hestercombe, Sissinghurst, and Hidcote; at Bath, from Roman Baths to eighteenth- and nineteenth-century parks and residential developments by John Nash.

NORTH AMERICA: CANADA. 1975–76, fieldwork for a study of the environmental resources of Toronto's Central Waterfront; 1985 and 1991, the waterfront and Don River Valley revisited.

UNITED STATES:

ARIZONA. 1984, Phoenix and Taliesin West. 1990, Phoenix, canals and dams of the Salt River Project, gardens by Steve Martino and John Douglas, South Mountain. 1995 and 1996, living and working at Taliesin West for several weeks. 1996, the Sonoran desert around Phoenix, the high desert in the Flagstaff volcano field, Grand Canyon.

CALIFORNIA. 1976, Berkeley, San Francisco, Marin County, and Point Reyes. 1986, Plazas and parks in San Francisco, Donnell Garden, by Thomas Church, in Sonoma. 1989, San Diego, Torrey Pines, Salk Institute at La Jolla. 1990, with Lawrence Halprin to see places he designed: the garden for his parents-in-law, the community of Woodlake, the San Jose Freeway, a garden under construction. 1994, Irvine and the new "edge-city" landscapes of Orange County, Disneyland, the Crystal Cathedral, SWA Group's Fashion Island in Newport Beach and South Coast Plaza in Costa Mesa, Noguchi's California Scenario, also in Costa Mesa. I participated in Halprin's community workshops on the future of Laguna Creek Wilderness Park. Study trips with colleagues in residence at the Humanities Research Center: a day-long journey up the Los Angeles River from Long Beach to South Central, Watts, and Pasadena; field trips to Laguna Beach, San Diego's Sea World, and the desert near Palm Springs. 1995, Death Valley, its hillsides of brown, green, orange, and white, Sunset Crater, salt flats. 1996, UCLA, Brentwood, and Culver City, Orange County and Laguna Beach revisited.

COLORADO. 1976, Denver, to inventory natural resources and hazards, the Platte River and Red Rocks Amphitheater, foothills along the Front Range west of Denver and Boulder, Rocky Mountain National Park, Vail. 1985, Platte River Greenway, Confluence Park, Harvard Gulch, and Boulder Creek—Denver's innovative flood control and storm drainage system. 1986, Colorado Springs and Garden of the Gods. 1989, Denver, Red Rocks, and Foothills Highway revisited, Fort Collins and the foothills, the High Plains and Pawnee National Grassland. 1990, from Denver's edge-city office parks and Harlequin Plaza, west into the mountains via Kenosha Pass to South Park, Fairplay, and Beaver Creek.

CONNECTICUT. From 1947, northwestern Connecticut: New Preston, Washington, and the Shepaug River Valley. 1978, Carl Andre's Stone Field in Hartford.

DISTRICT OF COLUMBIA. August 23, 1963, from Constitution Avenue to the Reflecting Pool, Lincoln Memorial and "I have a dream": the March on Washington. 1981, projects of the National Park Service's Ecological Services Laboratory: the Mall, Constitution Gardens, George Washington Parkway, Rock Creek Parkway. 1986, 1990, 1996, Vietnam Veterans Memorial. 1994 and 1996, the gardens of Dumbarton Oaks. 1994, at the Woodrow Wilson Center, an office high up in the Smithsonian Castle's flag tower, with a view of the Washington Monument, Lincoln Memorial, and Arlington Cemetery prompted reflections on prospects and axes; daily walks on the Mall in 1995–96 emphasized effects of scale.

FLORIDA. 1975, Sanibel Island, fieldwork for a comprehensive plan included nocturnal field trips to tag alligators and observe baby sea turtles. 1989, Amelia Island to see the product of a plan produced by Wallace McHarg Roberts and Todd twenty years earlier. 1989 and 1990, Disney World, including a "back-stage" tour of the nurseries. 1991, University of Miami, Coral Gables, Vizcaya, Fairchild Gardens, and Matheson's Hammock.

KANSAS. 1991, from Kansas City up the Kansas River Valley to the Konza Prairie, then zigged and zagged across the Great Plains on routes aligned with the midwestern grid.

KENTUCKY. 1991, Lexington, limestone and Bluegrass Country, Gainesway Stables designed by A. E. Bye, Pleasant Hill Shaker Community.

MAINE. 1976–80, week-long stays along the coast of Maine from Camden to Mount Desert Island.

MASSACHUSETTS. 1965–69 and 1977–86, Cambridge, Harvard Square, Harvard Yard, and the Charles River were home landscapes. 1969, walked the length of Boston's Emerald Necklace: Fens, Riverway, Ward Pond, Jamaica Pond, Arnold Arboretum, Franklin Park. 1971–76, second-growth woods of Amherst and Quabbin in central Massachusetts. 1979 and 1980, experiments by Peter Walker and Martha Schwartz: field of Necco wafers at MIT, roof garden, Bagel Garden. 1980–91, beaches, marshes, and dunes, bogs and woods of Cape Cod. 1982–85, Cambridge's Mount Auburn Cemetery, Boston's Neponset River, Roxbury, and Dorchester were sites for studio courses and research; Boston Harbor Islands, Beacon Hill, Boston Common, the Public Garden, Back Bay were subjects of lectures. 1993, Cambridge, Splice Garden with Martha Schwartz. 1997, the Fens, Roxbury, and Dorchester revisited.

MINNESOTA. 1985–86, St. Paul for State Capitol Competition.

MISSOURI. 1986, Washington University and St. Louis, the Arch and the Mississippi River. 1991, Kansas City, George Kessler's Park System, the Paseo.

NEVADA. 1995, Las Vegas and the Strip, Mirage Volcano, Hoover Dam.

NEW HAMPSHIRE. 1987, Mount Washington and the White Mountains.

NEW MEXICO. 1989, Albuquerque, Santa Fe, and landscapes significant to Native Americans, ancient and modern: Chimayo, Taos Pueblo, Aztec Ruins, Mesa Verde (Colorado), Chaco Canyon, and Acoma Pueblo.

NEW JERSEY. 1971, Alloway, Salem, and the coastal plain of southern New Jersey, Island Beach State Park, the Pine Barrens.

NEW YORK. 1967–97, New York City, weekend and day trips to Manhattan and Brooklyn. 1973–74, fieldwork on Long Island for new residential developments at Eaton's Point and Gardiner's Cove. 1975, Buffalo and Niagara Falls. 1995–97, the Adirondacks and its camps.

NORTH CAROLINA. 1976, the Blue Ridge Parkway, all the way to Asheville and the Smoky Mountains, an experience of road design as a form of art and narrative.

OHIO. 1953–65, Cincinnati and Wyoming, a suburb in the Mill Creek Valley, were landscapes of childhood and adolescence. A tributary of the Mill Creek flowed a few blocks from my home; from hilltop to valley was an economic transect from wealthy to poor neighborhoods. 1989, Columbus and Indian mounds at Newark.

OREGON. 1975 and 1995, Portland and urban redevelopment of 1960s, including Halprin's fountains and Pettigrove Park, Pioneer Square.

PENNSYLVANIA. 1969–77 and, since 1986, Philadelphia. 1970–73, field trips in the Delaware River Basin were an introduction to landscape architecture at University of Pennsylvania. 1987–98, working in West Philadelphia and Mill Creek, living in Chestnut Hill, the drive down the Wissahickon Valley and along the banks of the Schuylkill River is a daily route. 1992, farm country around Lancaster with a Mennonite farmer and my Danish father. 1995, Gettysburg, where smooth slopes and green lawns contrast with the rough, rocky slopes of Civil War photographs. Every year since 1995, I have been introduced to new sections of the city by my students, who trace the evolution of a neighborhood over time as part of their classwork. The choice of neighborhood is theirs.

SOUTH CAROLINA. 1989, Charleston and two former rice plantations along the Ashley River: Middleton Place and Drayton Hall.

TEXAS. 1973, fieldwork in pine-oak forest north of Houston for the Woodlands, a new town; in 1991, the result was disappointing. 1991, downtown Houston, River Oaks, Buffalo Bayou, Memorial Park, and the low-lying Fourth Ward, an African-American neighborhood of small frame houses, seen against distant downtown towers. 1987, Dallas, Fountain Square, Robert Irwin's Portal Park Slice, and downtown plazas.

VIRGINIA. 1976, Skyline Drive to the Blue Ridge Parkway. 1985 and 1989, Monticello and the University of Virginia, Charlottesville. 1996, Arlington Cemetery, John F. Kennedy Memorial, and Robert F. Kennedy Memorial.

WASHINGTON. 1988 and 1995, Seattle, to see Freeway Park, Gas Works Park, and Bloedel Reserve. 1995, Mill Creek Canyon Park, a landscape designed by the artist Herbert Bayer for stormwater management.

WISCONSIN. 1994, University of Wisconsin at Madison and the Driftless Region, including Frank Lloyd Wright's Taliesin in Spring Green and the Wisconsin Dells. 1997, further fieldwork at Taliesin.

Places: Maps, Archives, and Museums

Maps, photographs, and paintings, though one or more steps removed from the places they depict, help decipher traces and places that might not otherwise be seen: past settlement, rocks underground, an entire region, a place one has never been, significant details of light, color, texture. Examples of those studied in the original are discussed below; others are listed under Places: Published Sources.

MAPS. Historic maps make it possible to trace certain kinds of landscape change over time. Using a soil map of Iowa County from 1910, for example, I was able to observe that Frank Lloyd Wright sited buildings and planted groves at Taliesin on erodible, rocky soils, leaving the more fertile soils for crops and pasture. (Lounsbury, Clarence, et al. *Soil Map: Wisconsin, Iowa County Sheet.* [Washington, D.C.: Bureau of Soils, U.S. Department of Agriculture, 1910]. Appended to Whitson et al., see Places: Published Sources.) Insurance atlases of the nineteenth and twentieth centuries, such as those published by G. W. Bromley, depict streets, sewers, streetcar lines, buildings and their materials, structure, occupancy, and use (and sometimes even owners' names). They are drawn at a much finer-grained scale (e.g., 1 inch = 100 feet; scales vary) and contain far more detail than most other historic maps, and they cover entire cities. I constructed an understanding of the evolution of Boston's Dudley Street neighborhood and Philadelphia's Mill Creek through studying successive atlases; such atlases are available for many American cities.

Contemporary maps published by the U.S. Geological Survey for many of the places I studied are not cited individually here. These maps of landforms, waterways, roads and trails, buildings, woods, fields, marshes, orchards reflect an extraordinary amount of information; overlaid, they reveal correlations among landscape features otherwise difficult to detect. Nor have I cited here other contemporary maps and aerial photographs of places which I consulted, such as those produced by federal and state agencies like the Soil

Conservation Service, the Wisconsin Geological and Natural History Survey, and the Colorado Geological Survey.

ARCHIVES: PHOTOGRAPHS. Photographic archives were another source of records for tracing landscape change. Photographs and newspaper articles from the Urban Archives at Temple University document successive cave-ins on and around Philadelphia's Mill Creek from the 1930s on. By assembling hundreds of photographs of Taliesin North, I was able to reconstruct the way the landscape changed from the late nineteenth century, before Frank Lloyd Wright built there, to the construction of his home in 1911, until his death in 1959. Gathering these photographs required searching several archives: the Wood Collection and the John Howe Collection at the State Historical Society of Wisconsin, Madison; the Frank Lloyd Wright Archives at Taliesin West, Scottsdale, Arizona.

MUSEUMS: PAINTINGS. Landscape paintings often distill significant qualities of particular places: clouds and light in seventeenth-century Dutch paintings; colors and forms of eroded slopes in the mountains and hills of New Mexico in Georgia O'Keeffe's work; effect of wind on leaves and light brushed by Johan Thomas Lundbye, the nineteenth-century Danish painter. Exhibitions of works by the same artist or on a single theme permit insights difficult to glean from individual works. For example, an exhibit of O'Keeffe's paintings at New York's Metropolitan Museum of Art in 1988 permitted the comparison of depictions of New York and New Mexico; another, at Louisiana Museum in Denmark in 1994, of Claude Monet's paintings of Giverny from 1880 to 1926 showed the development of both his gardens and vision. "The Golden Age of Danish Painting," a show at the Metropolitan Museum of Art in 1994, featured nineteenth-century Danish landscape paintings and highlighted typical features Danes still value.

Places: Published Sources

There is a wealth of published sources on landscapes of particular places. A brief selection, arranged here by continent, includes books on gardens and urban design, geography and geology, culture and politics, as expressed in landscape. For classic readings, see Watts, *Reading the Landscape of America*, on natural landscapes; Hoskins and J. B. Jackson on vernacular landscapes of England and the United States, respectively. For design and politics: in European landscapes, see Mukerji (Versailles), Cosgrove (Italy's Veneto), Pugh (Rousham), Olwig (Danish heath); in North America, see Rosenzweig and Blackmar (Central Park), Greiff (Independence National Park), Gans (Boston's West End), White (Columbia River).

Regional guides are useful tools for reading the landscape of a particular place. State Geological Surveys often produce excellent contemporary guides; see, for example, Chronic, *Prairie, Peak, and Plateau*. Among the best general introductions to the natural and cultural history of a region's landscape are geological and soil surveys from the early twentieth century, which often summarize history of land use; see Whitson's soil survey (1914) of the county in Wisconsin where Wright's Taliesin is located.

Certain fiction and poetry are guides to reading local landscapes; Twain's description of the Mississippi River, Cather's of the American prairie, Heaney's and Montague's of Ireland are examples of a long tradition rich in description of particular places and their dialects. Knowledge of literature is essential to reading other places; Hunt and Woodbridge read dialogues among literary and garden texts in English gardens. Dialects provide clues to reading local landscapes: Basso and Munn relate Apache and Walbiri languages, respectively, to the landscapes they inhabit; Stilgoe, *Shallow-water Dictionary*, describes "estuary English."

Most sources describe places in words; others depict in paintings and photographs. Corner and MacLean, in *Taking Measures across the American Landscape*, combine telling aerial photographs and graphic interpretations. In *American Country Woman*, Lange investigates the relationship between people and place on the ground. Photographs can show landscape change and past practices: see Helphand, *Colorado*; paired images of New Mexico's and Boston's past and present in Jackson, *The Essential Landscape*, and Campbell, *Cityscapes of Boston*; and nineteenth-century photographs in Adams, *Atget's Gardens*.

ASIA
Ashihara, Yoshinobu. *The Hidden Order: Tokyo through the Twentieth Century*. Tokyo: Kodansha International, 1989.

Inoue, Mitsuo. *Space in Japanese Architecture*. New York: Weatherhill, 1985.

Itoh, Teiji. *Space and Illusion in Japanese Garden*. New York: Weatherhill/Tankosha, 1973.

Keswick, Maggie. *The Chinese Garden*. New York: St. Martin's Press, 1986.

Kuck, Loraine. *The World of the Japanese Garden*. New York: John Weatherhill, 1980.

Moynihan, Elizabeth B. *Paradise as a Garden in Persia and Mughal India*. New York: George Braziller, 1979.

Siren, Osvald. *Gardens of China*. New York: The Ronald Press, 1949.

Wescoat, James L., Jr., and Joachim Wolschke-Bulmahn. *Mughal Gardens*. Washington, D.C.: Dumbarton Oaks, 1996.

AUSTRALIA
Bell, Diane. *Daughters of the Dreaming*. Melbourne, Australia: McPhee, Gribble/George Allen and Unwin, 1983.

Benterrak, Krim, Stephen Muecke, and Paddy Roe. *Reading the Country*. Fremantle, Australia: Fremantle Arts Center Press, 1983.

Berndt, Ronald, and Catherine H. Berndt. *The Speaking Land*. Australia: Penguin, 1989.

Breeden, Stanley, and Belinda Wright. *Kakadu*. Brookvale, Australia: Simon and Schuster, 1989.

Flood, Josephine. *Archaeology of the Dreamtime*. Sydney, Australia: 1988.

Isaacs, Jennifer. *Arts of the Dreaming*. Sydney, Australia: Lansdowne Press, 1984.

———, ed. *Australian Dreaming: 40,000 Years of Aboriginal History*. Sydney, Australia: Lansdowne Press, 1981.

Layton, Robert. *Uluru*. Canberra, Australia: Australian Institute of Aboriginal Studies, 1986.

Munn, Nancy. D. *Walbiri Iconography*. Chicago: University of Chicago Press, 1986.

Myers, Fred R. *Pintupi Country, Pintupi Self*. Washington, D.C.: Smithsonian Institution Press, 1986.

Seddon, George. *Swan River Landscapes*. Nedlands, Australia: University of Western Australia Press, 1970.

Sutton, Peter, et al. *Dreamings: The Art of Aboriginal Australia*. New York: George Braziller, 1988.

Taylor, Jennifer. *Australian Architecture Since 1960*. North Ryde, Australia: Law Book Company, 1986.

EUROPE
Adams, Henry. *Mont Saint Michel and Chartres*. New York: G. P. Putnam, 1980.

Adams, William Howard. *Atget's Gardens*. Garden City, N.Y.: Doubleday, 1979.

Andersson, Sven-Ingvar, and Annemarie Lund. *Landscape Art in Denmark*. Copenhagen: Arkitektens Forlag, 1990.

Bermingham, Ann. *Landscape and Ideology: The English Rustic Tradition, 1740–1860*. Berkeley:

University of California Press, 1986.

Burl, Aubrey. *Prehistoric Avebury*. New Haven: Yale University Press, 1979.

Cosgrove, Denis. *Palladian Landscape*. State College: Pennsylvania State Press, 1993.

Crouch, Dora P. *Water Management in Ancient Greek Cities*. New York: Oxford University Press, 1993.

Daniels, Stephen. *Fields of Vision*. Princeton: Princeton University Press, 1993.

Grabar, Oleg. *The Alhambra*. Cambridge: Harvard University Press, 1978.

Gröning, Gert, and Joachim Wolschke. "Some Notes on the Mania for Native Plants in Germany." *Landscape Journal* 11, no. 2 (Fall 1992).

Hansen, Martin A. *Dansk Vejr*. Copenhagen: Hasselbalch, 1953.

Heaney, Seamus. "The Sense of Place." In *Preoccupations: Selected Prose 1968–1978*. New York: Farrar, Straus, Giroux, 1980.

———. *Selected Poems 1966–1987*. New York: Farrar, Straus, and Giroux, 1990.

Hoskins, W. G. *The Making of the English Landscape*. Baltimore: Penguin Books, 1970.

Hunt, John Dixon. *The Figure in the Landscape: Poetry, Painting and Gardening during the Eighteenth Century*. Baltimore: Johns Hopkins University Press, 1976.

———. *Garden and Grove: The Italian Renaissance Garden in the English Imagination, 1600–1750*. Princeton: Princeton University Press, 1986.

———. *Gardens and the Picturesque*. Cambridge: MIT Press, 1992.

———, and Peter Willis, eds. *The Genius of Place: The English Landscape Garden 1620–1820*. New York: Harper and Row, 1975.

Jashemski, Wilhelmina. *The Gardens of Pompeii*. New Rochelle, N.Y.: Caratzas Brothers, 1979.

Lambert, Audrey M. *The Making of the Dutch Landscape*. New York: Seminar Press, 1971.

Lazzaro, Claudia. *The Italian Renaissance Garden*. New Haven: Yale University Press, 1990.

Lund, Annemarie. *Danish Landscape Architecture, 1000–1996*. Copenhagen: Arkitektens Forlag, 1997.

Monrad, Konrad. *Golden Age of Danish Painting*. New York: Hudson Hills Press, 1993.

Montague, John. *Selected Poems*. Winston-Salem, N.C.: Wake Forest University Press, 1991.

Mukerji, Chandra. *Territorial Ambitions and the Gardens of Versailles*. Cambridge: Cambridge University Press, 1997.

Olwig, Kenneth. *Nature's Ideological Landscape*. London: George Allen and Unwin, 1984.

Prieto-Moreno, Francisco. *Los Jardines de Granada*. Madrid: Grefol, 1983.

Pugh, Simon. *Garden-Nature-Language*. Manchester, U.K.: Manchester University Press, 1988.

Ruff, Alan. *Holland and the Ecological Landscape*. Stockport, U.K., 1979.

Shepherd, J. C., and G. A. Jellicoe. *Italian Gardens of the Renaissance*. Princeton: Princeton Architectural Press, 1986.

Stechow, Wolfgang. *Dutch Landscape Painting of the Seventeenth Century*. London: Phaidon Press, 1966.

Taylor, C. *Fields in the English Landscape*. London: J. M. Dent, 1975.

Varnedoe, Kirk. *Northern Light*. New Haven: Yale University Press, 1988.

Watts, May Theilgaard. *Reading the Landscape of Europe*. New York: Harper and Row, 1971.

Weigand, T., and H. Schrader. *Priene*. Berlin: G. Reimer, 1904.

Whittow, J. B. *Geology and Scenery in Scotland*. Middlesex, U.K.: Penguin Books, 1977.

Woodbridge, Kenneth. *The Stourhead Landscape*. N.p.: National Trust, 1986.

NORTH AMERICA

Adams, Robert. *From the Misssouri West*. New York: Aperture, 1980.

Banham, Reyner. *Los Angeles*. Harmondsworth, U.K.: Penguin, 1973.

Basso, Keith H. *Wisdom Sits in Places*. Albuquerque: University of New Mexico Press, 1996.

Beard, Richard. *Walt Disney's Epcot Center*. New York: Harry N. Abrams, 1982.

Beardsley, John. *Gardens of Revelation.* New York: Abbeville, 1995.

Campbell, Robert, and Peter Vanderwarker. *Cityscapes of Boston.* Boston: Houghton Mifflin, 1992.

Capasso, Nicholas J. "Vietnam Veterans Memorial." In *The Critical Edge,* edited by Tod A. Marder, 189–202. Cambridge: MIT Press, 1985.

Cather, Willa. *My Ántonia.* Boston: Houghton Mifflin, 1954.

Chronic, John, and Halka Chronic. *Prairie, Peak, and Plateau.* Colorado Geological Survey Bulletin 32. Denver: Colorado Geological Survey, 1972.

Conzen, Michael, ed. *The Making of the American Landscape.* Boston: Unwin Hyman, 1990.

Corner, James, and Alex S. MacLean. *Taking Measures Across the American Landscape.* New Haven: Yale University Press, 1996.

Creese, Walter L. *The Crowning of the American Landscape.* Princeton: Princeton University Press, 1985.

Cronon, William. *Changes in the Land.* New York: Hill and Wang, 1983.

———. *Nature's Metropolis.* New York: W. W. Norton, 1991.

Engel, J. Ronald. *Sacred Sands: The Struggle for Community in the Indiana Dunes.* Middletown, Conn.: Wesleyan University Press, 1983.

Findlay, John M. *Magic Lands: Western Cityscapes and American Culture after 1940.* Berkeley: University of California Press, 1992.

Francaviglia, Richard V. *The Mormon Landscape.* New York: AMS Press, 1978.

Gans, Herbert J. *The Urban Villagers,* updated and expanded edition. New York: Free Press, 1982.

Garnett, William. *Aerial Photographs.* Berkeley: University of California Press, 1994.

Garreau, Joel. *Edge City.* New York: Doubleday, 1991.

Greiff, Constance M. *Independence: The Creation of a National Park.* Philadelphia: University of Pennsylvania Press, 1987.

Gutheim, Frederick. *The Federal City.* Washington, D.C.: Smithsonian Institution Press, 1976.

Helphand, Kenneth. *Colorado: Visions of an American Landscape.* Niwot, Colo.: Roberts Rinehart, 1991.

Hill, Mary. *California Landscape.* Berkeley: University of California Press, 1984.

Hogan, Pendleton. *The Lawn: A Guide to Jefferson's University.* Charlottesville: University Press of Virginia, 1987.

Iseley, N. Jane, and William P. Baldwin. *Plantations of the Low Country: South Carolina 1697–1865.* Greensboro, N.C.: Legacy Publications, 1985.

Jackson, John Brinckerhoff. *The Essential Landscape: The New Mexico Photographic Survey.* Albuquerque: University of New Mexico Press, 1985.

———. *Landscape in Sight: Looking at America.* New Haven: Yale University Press, 1997.

Jackson, Kenneth. *Crabgrass Frontier: The Suburbanization of the United States.* Oxford: Oxford University Press, 1985.

Kreisman, Lawrence. *The Bloedel Reserve.* Bainbridge Island, Wash.: Bloedel Reserve; Arbor Fund, 1988.

Lange, Dorothea. *American Photographs.* San Francisco: Chronicle Books, 1994.

———. *Dorothea Lange Looks at the American Country Woman.* Fort Worth: Amon Carter Museum, 1967.

Linden-Ward, Blanche. *Silent City on a Hill: Landscapes of Memory and Boston's Mount Auburn Cemetery.* Columbus: Ohio State University Press, 1989.

Longstreth, Richard, ed. *The Mall in Washington 1791–1991.* Washington, D.C.: National Gallery of Art, 1991.

Lopes, Sal. *The Wall: Images and Offerings from the Vietnam Veterans Memorial.* New York: Collins, 1987.

MacLean, Alex S. *Look at the Land.* New York: Rizzoli, 1993.

McPhee, John. *The Control of Nature.* New York: Farrar, Straus, Giroux, 1989.

Meyerowitz, Joel. *Cape Light.* Boston: Little, Brown, 1985.

———. *St. Louis and the Arch.* Boston: New York Graphic Society, 1980.

Novack, Barbara. *Nature and Culture: American Landscape and Painting 1825–1875.* New York: Oxford University Press, 1981.

O'Malley, Therese, and Marc Treib. *Regional Garden Design in the United States.* Washington, D.C.: Dumbarton Oaks, 1995.

Riley, Robert B. "Square to the Road, Hogs to the East." *Places* 2:4, 72–79.

Rosenzweig, Robert, and Elizabeth Blackmar. *The Park and the People: A History of Central Park.* Ithaca: Cornell University Press, 1992.

Scruggs, Jan C., and Joel L. Swerdlow. *To Heal a Nation: Vietnam Veterans Memorial.* New York: Harper and Row, 1985.

Schafer, R. Murray, ed. *The Vancouver Soundscape.* Vancouver, B.C.: A.R.C. Publications, 1978.

Stilgoe, John R. *Common Landscape of America.* New Haven: Yale University Press, 1982.

———. *Shallow-water Dictionary: A Grounding in Estuary English.* Cambridge, Mass.: Exact Change, 1990.

———. *Alongshore.* New Haven: Yale University Press, 1994.

Streatfield, David C. *California Gardens.* New York: Abbeville Press, 1994.

Thomas, Frank, and Ollie Johnston. *Disney Animation.* New York: Abbeville Press, 1981.

Thompson, George F., ed. *Landscape in America.* Austin: University of Texas Press, 1995.

Thompson, J. William. *Bryant Park.* Washington, D.C: Spacemaker Press: 1997.

Twain, Mark. *Life on the Mississippi.* Library of America, 1982.

Van Dyke, John C. *The Desert.* Salt Lake City: Peregrine Smith, 1980.

Van Valkenburgh, Michael, curator. *Built Landscapes.* Brattleboro, Vt.: Brattleboro Museum and Art Center, 1984.

Warner, Sam Bass. *To Dwell Is to Garden: A History of Boston's Community Gardens.* Boston: Northeastern University Press, 1987.

———. *Streetcar Suburbs.* New York: Atheneum, 1976.

Watts, May Theilgaard. *Reading the Landscape of America.* New York: Collier Books, 1975.

Westmacott, Richard. *African-American Gardens and Yards in the Rural South.* Knoxville: University of Tennessee Press, 1992.

White, Minor, ed. *Paul Caponigro.* New York: Aperture, 1967.

White, Richard. *The Organic Machine.* New York: Straus and Giroux, 1995.

Whitson, A. R., et al. *Soil Survey of Iowa County, Wisconsin.* Madison: Wisconsin Geological and Natural History Survey, 1914.

Worster, Donald. *Under Western Skies.* New York: Oxford University Press, 1992.

MIDDLE EAST

Al Khalil, Samir. *The Monument.* Berkeley: University of California Press, 1991.

Holod, Renata, and Hasan-Uddin Khan. *The Contemporary Mosque.* New York: Rizzoli, 1997.

Petruccioli, Attilio, ed. *The Garden as a City; Environmental Design: Journal of the Islamic Environmental Design Research Centre.* Rome: Carucci Editore, 1984.

———. *The City as a Garden; Environmental Design: Journal of the Islamic Environmental Design Research Centre.* Rome: Carucci Editore, 1984.

Landscape Authors

Interviews

In interviews with landscape authors—artists, engineers, landscape architects, architects, farmers and gardeners—I inquired about their home landscapes, working methods, sources of inspiration. Discussions sustained over many years with Poul Henriksen, Ian McHarg, Glenn Murcutt, Lawrence Halprin, and Sven-Ingvar Andersson gave me an insight into relationships among their experiences, ideas, and practices. Discussions with A. E. Bye, Richard Haag, Richard Le Plastrier, Adèle Naudé Santos, Mario Schjetnan, and James Wines gave me an appreciation for the great differences in approaches to landscape composition. Interviews with Taliesin Fellows, who worked alongside Frank Lloyd Wright, made it possible to reconstruct the evolution of the Taliesins.

Landscape Authors: Drawings and Unpublished Writings

Landscape authors reveal their thinking in plans, diagrams, and sketches; notations provide clues to working methods (pragmatics) and intentions (poetics and polemics). Most designers make successive studies, embodying reasoned steps and intuitive leaps. Faint pencil guidelines on C. Th. Sørensen's plan drawings reveal the complex, carefully plotted geometries of his gardens. Frank Lloyd Wright wrote notes on site plans and perspective drawings about ideas and instructions to workers for what should be planted and built, and how. Notations often cannot be deciphered in reproduction and must be studied in the original. The early, messy drawings frequently convey an author's thinking best. In studying landscapes designed by Wright, for example, the studies drawn in the act of designing are more informative than rendered plans and perspectives intended for presentations to clients or for exhibition. Although "unfinished" drawings are rarely included in exhibitions or reproduced in publications, the most important may be kept by designers as records, then eventually preserved in an archive.

I studied drawings and papers in many public archives and private collections. The Frank Lloyd Wright Archives at Taliesin West is the single largest collection of Wright's drawn work and unpublished correspondence; I also consulted the smaller, but important, collection in the State Historical Society of Wisconsin and the Lewis Mumford Papers at the University of Pennsylvania for the Wright-Mumford correspondence. The graphic work of the Olmsted Office is housed at the Olmsted National Historical Site in Brookline, Massachusetts; the papers of Frederick Law Olmsted, Sr. are in the Library of Congress. Most of Sørensen's drawings are at the Royal Danish Academy of Fine Arts, where he was professor for many years. Lawrence Halprin's archives are at the University of Pennsylvania. Most contemporary landscape authors maintain a collection of their own drawings; I looked at those of Glenn Murcutt, Sven-Ingvar Andersson, Adèle Naudé Santos, Laurie Olin, and Anuradha Mathur, among others. For published journals, correspondence, and professional reports, see below.

Landscape Authors: Published Accounts of Own Work

Frederick Law Olmsted, Frank Lloyd Wright, C. Th. Sørensen, Geoffrey Jellicoe, Lawrence Halprin, and Laurie Olin, all great landscape authors, have written about their work, intentions, methods, and sources. Just as their drawings are windows into the way they think and shape landscape, so are their writings. Professional reports, from author to client, tell the official account of what landscape authors intend. Some classics are published: Alexander (*Oregon*), Eliot, Olmsted (*Niagara*, Fein). Most are uncollected by libraries, however, and are difficult to locate: see, for example, Center for Environmental Design and Wallace McHarg Roberts and Todd.

Alexander, Christopher. *A Pattern Language Which Generates Multi-service Centers*. Center for Environmental Structure, 1968.

———. *Oregon Experiment*. New York: Oxford University Press, 1975.

Andersson, Sven-Ingvar. "En trädgård efter fem år." *Hem i Sverige* (1965:1), 24–29.

———. "Brev fra min hønsegård." *Arkitekten* (1967), 579–83.

———. "Häckar och höns—min torparträdgård." *Landskap* (1976/8), 180–84.

———. "Karlsplatz—Resselpark: En park- og byfornyelsesopgave i Wien." *Landskap* (1979/1), 16–21.

———. "Principper for bevaring af gamle haver." *Fortidsvern* (1986/1), 112–21.

Baron, Robert C., ed. *The Garden and Farm Books of Thomas Jefferson*. Golden, Colo.: Fulcrum, 1987.

Brownwell, Baker, and Frank Lloyd Wright. *Architecture and Modern Life*. New York: Harper, 1937.

Bye, A. E. *Art into Landscape; Landscape into Art*. Mesa, Ariz.: PDA Publishers, 1983.

Center for Environmental Design. *Landscape Development Plan: University of Pennsylvania*. Philadelphia: Graduate School of Fine Arts, University of Pennsylvania, 1977.

Church, Thomas. *Gardens Are for People*. New York: McGraw-Hill, 1955.

Cleveland, H. W. S. *Landscape Architecture as Applied to the Wants of the West*. 1873. Reprint, Pittsburgh: University of Pittsburgh Press, 1965.

Downing, Andrew Jackson. *A Treatise on the Theory and Practice of Landscape Gardening*. 4th edition. New York: Orange Judd Agricultural Book Publisher, 1865.

Eliot, Charles. "Report of the Landscape Architect." In *Report of the Board Metropolitan Park Commissioners*. Boston: January 1893.

———. *Charles Eliot: Landscape Architect*. 1902. Reprint, Freeport, N.Y.: Books for Libraries Press, 1971.

Fathy, Hassan. *Architecture for the Poor*. Chicago: University of Chicago Press, 1973.

Fein, Albert, ed. *Landscape into Cityscape: Frederick Law Olmsted's Plans for a Greater New York City*. Ithaca: Cornell University Press, 1968.

Goldsworthy, Andy. *A Collaboration with Nature*. New York: Harry N. Abrams, 1990.

Graham, Thomas E., ed. *Agricultural Social Gospel: The Gospel of the Farm by Jenkin Lloyd Jones*. Lewiston, N.Y.: Edwin Mellen, 1986.

Halprin, Lawrence. *Freeways*. New York: Reinhold, 1966.

———. *The RSVP Cycles: Creative Processes in the Human Environment*. New York: George Braziller, 1969.

———. *Cities*. Cambridge: MIT Press, 1972.

———. *Notebooks: 1959–1971*. Cambridge: MIT Press, 1972.

———. *Take Part*. San Francisco: Lawrence Halprin and Associates, 1972.

———. *Sketchbook of Lawrence Halprin*. Tokyo: Process Architecture, 1981.

———. *Lawrence Halprin: Changing Places*. San Francisco: San Francisco Museum of Modern Art, 1986.

———. *The Franklin Delano Roosevelt Memorial*. San Francisco: Chronicle Books, 1997.

Halprin, Lawrence, and Jim Burns. *Taking Part: A Workshop Approach to Collective Creativity*. Cambridge: MIT Press, 1974.

Harrison, Helen Mayer, and Newton Harrison. *The Lagoon Cycle*. Ithaca: Cornell Office of University Publications, 1985.

Hood, Walter. *Urban Diaries.* Washington, D.C.: Spacemaker Press, 1997.

Jekyll, Gertrude. *A Gardener's Testament.* New York: Charles Scribner's Sons, 1937.

———. *Home and Garden.* Suffolk, U.K.: Antique Collectors' Club, 1982.

Jellicoe, Geoffrey A. *Studies in Landscape Design.* Volumes I–III. London: Oxford University Press, 1960, 1966, 1970.

———. *The Guelph Lectures on Landscape Design.* Guelph, Canada: University of Guelph, 1983.

———. *The Landscape of Civilization: As Experienced in the Moody Historical Gardens.* Sussex, U.K.: Garden Art Press, 1989.

———. "A Philosophy of Landscape." In *Architect's Yearbook* 1:1 (1945), 39–42.

Jensen, Jens. *Siftings, the Major Portion of the Clearing, and Collected Writings.* Chicago: Ralph Fletcher Seymour, 1956.

Irwin, Robert. *Being and Circumstance: Notes Toward a Conditional Art.* Larkspur Landing, Calif.: Lapis Press, 1985.

Kiley, Dan. *Landscape Design: Works of Dan Kiley.* Tokyo: Process Architecture, 1982.

Lassus, Bernard, and Stephen Bann, intro. and trans. "The Landscape Approach of Bernard Lassus." *Journal of Garden History* 3:2, 79–107.

Leopold, Aldo. *A Sand County Almanac.* New York: Bantam Books, 1966.

Loudon, J. C. *The Suburban Gardener and Villa Companion.* London: Printed for the author, 1838.

Lynch, Kevin. *Managing the Sense of a Region.* Boston: MIT Press, 1976.

Mathur, Anuradha. "Recovering Ground: The Shifting Landscape of Dacca." In *Landscape Transformed,* edited by Michael Spens. London: Academy Editions, 1996.

McHarg, Ian L. *Design with Nature.* Garden City: Doubleday, 1969.

———. *A Quest for Life.* New York: John Wiley and Sons, 1996.

Neuhart, John, Marilyn Neuhart, and Ray Eames, eds. *Eames Design.* New York: Abrams, 1989.

Olin, Laurie. "Regionalism and the Practice of Hanna/Olin, Ltd." In *Regional Garden Design in the United States,* edited by Therese O'Malley and Marc Trieb. Washington, D.C.: Dumbarton Oaks, 1995.

———. *Transforming the Common Place.* Princeton: Princeton Archtitectural Press, 1996.

Olmsted, Frederick Law. "Parks, Parkways and Pleasure Grounds." *Engineering Magazine* 9:2 (May 1895), 253–60.

———. *General Plan for the Improvement of the Niagara Reservation.* New York, 1887.

Olmsted, Frederick Law, Jr., and Theodora Kimball, eds. *Forty Years of Landscape Architecture.* Cambridge: MIT Press, 1973.

Palladio, Andrea. *Four Books on Architecture.* 1738. Reprint, New York: Dover, 1965.

Pollan, Michael. *Second Nature.* New York: Atlantic Monthly Press, 1991.

———. *A Place of My Own.* New York: Random House, 1997.

Repton, Humphrey. *Theory and Practice of Landscape Gardening.* Edited by John Nolen. Boston: Houghton Mifflin, 1907.

Robinson, William. *Wild Garden.* 1870. Reprint, London: J. Murray, 1903.

Schwartz, Martha. "Back Bay Bagel Garden." *Landscape Architecture* (January 1980), 43–46.

Sørenson, Carl Theodore. *Parkpolitik.* Copenhagen, 1931.

———. *Haver: Tanker og Arbejder.* Copenhagen: Christian Ejlers, 1975.

———. *Utypiske Haver til et Typehus: 39 Haveplaner.* Copenhagen: Christian Ejlers, 1984.

Spirn, Anne Whiston. *The West Philadelphia Landscape Plan: A Framework for Action.* Philadelphia: Graduate School of Fine Arts, University of Pennsylvania, 1991.

———, and Michele Pollio. *"This Garden Is a Town."* Philadelphia: Graduate School of Fine Arts, University of Pennsylvania, 1990.

———, and Daniel Marcucci. *Models of Success: Landscape Improvement and Community De-*

velopment. Philadelphia: Graduate School of Fine Arts, University of Pennsylvania, 1991.

———, and Mark Cameron. *Shaping the Block*. Philadelphia: Graduate School of Fine Arts, University of Pennsylvania, 1991.

———, Michele Pollio, and Mark Cameron. *Vacant Land: A Resource for Reshaping Urban Neighborhoods*. Philadelphia: Graduate School of Fine Arts, University of Pennsylvania, 1991.

———, and Robert Cheetham. *West Philadelphia Digital Database: Atlas and Guide*. Philadelphia: Graduate School of Fine Arts, University of Pennsylvania, 1996.

Unwin, Raymond. *Town Planning in Practice*. 2d edition. London: T. Fisher Unwin, 1911.

Walker, Peter. *Minimalist Gardens*. Washington, D.C.: Spacemaker Press, 1997.

Wallace, McHarg, Roberts, and Todd. *Amelia Island, Florida*. Philadelphia: Wallace, McHarg, Roberts, and Todd, 1972.

———. *Woodlands New Community: Site Planning Guidelines*. Philadelphia: Wallace, McHarg, Roberts, and Todd, 1973.

Wright, Frank Lloyd. "Living in the Desert: Part One—We Found Paradise." *Arizona Highways* (October 1940), 12–15.

———. *Frank Lloyd Wright: His Living Voice*. Edited by Bruce Brooks Pfeiffer. Fresno, Calif., 1987.

———. *Collected Writings, Volume 1: 1894–1930*. Edited by Bruce Brooks Pfeiffer. New York: Rizzoli, 1992.

———. *Collected Writings, Volume 2: 1930–1932*. Edited by Bruce Brooks Pfeiffer. New York: Rizzoli, 1992.

———. *Collected Writings, Volume 3: 1931–1939*. Edited by Bruce Brooks Pfeiffer. New York: Rizzoli, 1993.

———. *Collected Writings, Volume 4: 1939–1949*. Edited by Bruce Brooks Pfeiffer. New York: Rizzoli, 1994.

———. *Collected Writings, Volume 5: 1949–1959*. Edited by Bruce Brooks Pfeiffer. New York: Rizzoli, 1995.

Zion, Robert. *Robert Zion*. Tokyo: Process Architecture, 1991.

Landscape Authors: Secondary Sources

Books about modern designers are often written by other landscape authors and by architectural and landscape historians. Andersson's and Høyer's book on Sørensen, Fromonot's on Murcutt, Jewell's on Walker, De Long's on Wright, Ambasz's on Barragan are appraisals by members of a younger generation of designers.

Abrioux, Yves. *Ian Hamilton Finlay*. Edinburgh: Reaktion Books, 1985.

Adams, William Howard. *Jefferson's Monticello*. New York: Abbeville Press, 1983.

———. *Roberto Burle Marx*. New York: Museum of Modern Art, 1991.

Adcock, Craig. *James Turrell: The Art of Light and Space*. Berkeley: University of California Press, 1990.

Ahlin, Janne. *Sigurd Lewerentz: Architect*. Cambridge: MIT Press, 1987.

Ambasz, Emilio. *The Architecture of Luis Barragan*. New York: Museum of Modern Art, 1976.

Andersson, Sven-Ingvar, and Steen Høyer. *C. Th. Sørenson: Havekunster*. Copenhagen: Arkitektens Forlag, 1993.

Andrews, Richard. *James Turrell: Sensing Space*. Philadelphia: Institute for Contemporary Art, 1993.

Balmori, Diana, Diane Kostial Mcguire, and Eleanor M. McPeck. *Beatrix Farrand's American Landscapes: Her Gardens and Campuses*. Sagaponack, N.Y.: Sagapress, 1985.

Brown, Jane. *Gardens of a Golden Afternoon; The Story of a Partnership: Edwin Lutyens and*

Gertrude Jekyll. New York: Van Nostrand Reinhold, 1982.

———. *Vita's Other World: A Gardening Biography of Vita Sackville-West.* New York: Viking, 1985.

Brown, Julia, ed. *Occluded Front: James Turrell.* Larkspur Landing, Calif.: Lapis Press, 1985.

Burkhardt, François, Claude Eveno, and Boris Podrecca, eds. *Joze Plecnik, Architect: 1872–1957.* Cambridge: MIT Press, 1989.

Chang, Chin-Yu, ed. *Lawrence Halprin.* Tokyo: Process Architecture, 1978.

De Long, David, ed. *Frank Lloyd Wright: Designs for an American Landscape 1922–1932.* New York: Abrams, 1996.

Eaton, Leonard. *Landscape Artist in America: Life and Work of Jens Jensen.* Chicago: University of Chicago Press, 1964.

Frampton, Kenneth. *Tadao Ando.* New York: Museum of Modern Art, 1991.

Fromonot, Françoise. *Glenn Murcutt.* London: Thames and Hudson, 1995.

Fuchs, R. H. *Richard Long.* New York: Thames and Hudson, 1986.

Grese, Robert. *Jens Jensen.* Baltimore: Johns Hopkins, University Press, 1992.

Hargreaves. Tokyo: Process Architecture, 1996.

Helphand, Kenneth. "Shaping the Israeli Landscape." In *Shlomo Aronson.* Washington, D.C.: Spacemaker Press, 1998.

Hazlehurst, F. Hamilton. *Gardens of Illusion: The Genius of André Le Nostre.* Nashville: Vanderbilt University Press, 1980.

Hobbs, Robert. *Robert Smithson.* Ithaca: Cornell University Press, 1981.

Hodge, Brooke. *Design with the Land: Landscape Architecture of Michael Van Valkenburgh.* Princeton: Princeton Architectural Press, 1994.

Holliss, Richard, and Brian Sibley. *The Disney Studio Story.* New York: Crown, 1988.

Howett, Catherine, ed. *Abstracting the Landscape: The Artistry of Landscape Architect A. E. Bye.* University Park: Department of Landscape Architecture, Pennsylvania State University, 1990.

Høyer, Steen, ed. *Sven-Ingvar Andersson.* Copenhagen: Arkitektens Forlag, 1994.

Jewell, Linda, ed. *Peter Walker.* New York: Rizzoli, 1990.

Joyes, Claire. *Claude Monet: Life at Giverny.* New York: Vendome Press, 1985.

Landecker, Heidi, ed. *Martha Schwartz.* Washington, D.C.: Spacemaker Press, 1997.

Nichols, Frederick D., and Ralph E. Griswold. *Thomas Jefferson, Landscape Architect.* Charlottesville: University Press of Virginia, 1978.

Rasmussen, Steen Eiler, Frans Lassen, Lisbeth Hertel, and Sven-Ingvar Andersson. *Karen Blixen's Flowers.* Copenhagen: Christian Eilers, 1992.

Riley, Terence, and Peter Reed, eds. *Frank Lloyd Wright.* New York: Museum of Modern Art, 1994.

Simo, Melanie Louise. *Loudon and the Landscape.* New Haven: Yale University Press, 1988.

SITE. New York: Rizzoli, 1989.

Spens, Michael. *Gardens of the Mind: The Genius of Geoffrey Jellicoe.* England: Antique Collectors Club, 1992.

———. *Jellicoe at Shute.* London: Academy Editions. 1993.

———. *The Complete Landscape Designs and Gardens of Geoffrey Jellicoe.* London: Thames and Hudson, 1994.

Spirn, Anne Whiston. "Frank Lloyd Wright: Architect of Landscape." In *Frank Lloyd Wright: Designs for an American Landscape, 1922–1932,* edited by David De Long. New York: Abrams, 1996.

———. "Constructing Nature: The Legacy of Frederick Law Olmsted." In *Uncommon Ground,* edited by William Cronon. New York: W. W. Norton, 1995.

———. "Texts, Landscapes, Life." In *Sven-Ingvar Andersson,* edited by Steen Høyer. Copenhagen: Arkitektens Forlag, 1994.

Steele, James. *Hassan Fathy.* London: Academy Editions, St. Martin's Press, 1988.

Stephensen, Lulu Salto. *Tradition og Fornyelse: Dansk Havekunst: G. N. Brandt.* N.p.: Frangipani, 1993.

Tankard, Judith B., and Michael Van Valkenburgh. *Gertrude Jekyll: A Vision of Garden and Wood.* New York: Abrams, 1989.

Thomas, Bob. *Walt Disney.* New York: Pocket Books, 1980.

Treib, Marc, and Dorothée Imbert. *Garrett Eckbo.* Berkeley: University of California Press, 1997.

Zaitzevsky, Cynthia. *Frederick Law Olmsted and the Boston Park System.* Cambridge: Harvard University Press, 1983.

READING AND TELLING LANDSCAPE: GENERAL REFERENCES

Rare is the source which integrates interpretations of natural, vernacular, and designed landscapes, even in the case of particular places. One must turn to many different disciplines for a full reading: meteorology, geology, ecology, zoology, anthropology, geography, history, art history, architecture, landscape architecture, urban design, among others. This selective bibliography of general references, together with those on particular places (Landscapes) and individual authors (Landscape Authors), is representative of the contributions of these diverse perspectives to reading and telling landscape.

Minnaert, Bloom, Dunne and Leopold, Daubenmire, and Forman provide introductions to reading meteorological, geological, botanical, and zoological features. Meinig's collection of essays on reading vernacular landscapes includes an essay on "axioms" by Pierce Lewis. Clay's guide describes landscape patterns as clues to past and present phenomena. White's review essay, "American Environmental History," is a guide to a vast literature on reading landscape; Cronon's "Stories" is an exploration of landscape meaning and historical narrative. Preziosi applies semiotics to the built environment. Panofsky describes the iconography of art, and Geertz presents an approach to meaning informed by ethnography; Cosgrove and Daniels integrate these approaches. For the use of photography in interpreting cultural landscapes, see Collier and Collier. Poets, in their close reading and use of imagery, are guides to landscape language: Rich, Applewhite.

There are fewer references on telling landscape. Many probing studies of landscape expression are by landscape authors themselves—Alexander, Lynch, Olin (see also Landscape Authors for descriptions of their own work)—and by those, like Schon, who have observed practitioners at work. Lakoff and Johnson describe how human thought processes and verbal language reflect relationships between body and landscape; Donald reviews research on human evolution and language development in terms of interactions among body, mind, and environment. A complementary perspective on these relationships is provided by studies of animals; see Griffin, Sebeok, Dawkins, and Haraway.

The published literature on landscape has expanded rapidly since 1980. Historically, there is resurgent interest in gardens and landscape at times when the relationship between nature and humankind is being reexamined and redefined; this is such a time. For those readers who wish to follow future developments and delve more deeply into landscape studies, the following journals contain articles on specific topics and present reviews of new books: *Landscape Architecture* (1910–), *Landscape* (1951–), *Landscape and Urban Planning* (1974–), *Environmental History,* formerly *Environmental History Review* (1977–), *Studies in the History of Gardens and Designed Landscapes,* formerly *Journal of Garden History*

(1980–), *Landscape Journal* (1982–), *Places* (1983–), *Topos* (1992–).

Abram, David. *The Spell of the Sensuous*. New York: Vintage Books, 1996.

Ackerman, James. "The History of Design and the Design of History." *Via* 4 (1980), 19–28.

———. *The Villa*. Princeton: Princeton University Press, 1990.

Alexander, Christopher. *The Timeless Way of Building*. New York: Oxford University Press, 1977.

———. *A New Theory of Urban Design*. New York: Oxford University Press, 1987.

———, Sara Ishikawa, and Murray Silverstein. *A Pattern Language: Towns, Buildings, Construction*. New York: Oxford University Press, 1977.

Anderson, Edgar. *Landscape Papers*. Edited by Bob Callahan. Berkeley: Turtle Island Foundation, 1976.

Andrews, Oliver. *Living Materials: A Sculptor's Handbook*. Berkeley: University of California Press, 1983.

Appleton, Jay. *The Experience of Landscape*. London: John Wiley and Sons, 1975.

———. *The Symbolism of Habitat*. Seattle: University of Washington Press, 1990.

Applewhite, James. "The Near Landscape and the Far: Nature and Human Signification." In *Southern Literature and Literary Theory*, edited by Jefferson Humphries. Athens: University of Georgia Press, 1990.

Arnheim, Rudolf. "Order and Complexity in Landscape Design." In *Toward a Psychology of Art*, 123–35. Berkeley: University of California Press, 1966.

———. *Visual Thinking*. Berkeley: University of California Press, 1969.

———. *The Dynamics of Architectural Form*. Berkeley: University of California Press, 1977.

Bachelard, Gaston. *The Poetics of Space*. Translated by Maria Jolas. Boston: Beacon Press, 1969.

Baljon, Lodewijk. *Designing Parks*. Amsterdam: Architectura and Natura Press, 1992.

Bateson, Gregory. *Steps to an Ecology of Mind*. New York: Ballantine Books, 1972.

———. *Mind and Nature*. Toronto: Bantam Books, 1980.

———. *A Sacred Unity*. New York: Cornelia and Michael Bessie Book, 1991.

———, C. Wilder-Mott, and John H. Weakland, eds. *Rigor and Imagination*. New York: Praeger, 1981.

Beardsley, John. *Earthworks and Beyond*. New York: Abbeville Press, 1984.

Berger, John. *Ways of Seeing*. London: Penguin Books, 1977.

———. *About Looking*. New York: Pantheon Books, 1980.

———. *Sense of Sight*. New York: Random House, 1985.

Berger, John, and Jean Mohr. *Another Way of Telling*. New York: Random House, 1983.

Bickerton, Derek. *Language and Species*. Chicago: University of Chicago Press, 1990.

Biedermann, Hans. *Dictionary of Symbolism*. New York: Meridian, 1992.

Bloom, Arthur L. *The Surface of the Earth*. Englewood Cliffs: Prentice-Hall, 1969.

Botkin, Daniel B. *Discordant Harmonies: A New Ecology for the Twenty-first Century*. New York: Oxford University Press, 1990.

Bourassa, Steven C. *The Aesthetics of Landscape*. London: Belhaven Press, 1991.

Braudel, Fernand. *The Structures of Everyday Life*. New York: Harper and Row, 1979.

Carr, Stephen, Mark Francis, Leanne Rivlin, and Andrew M. Stone. *Public Space*. New York: Cambridge University Press, 1992.

Cirlot, J. E. *A Dictionary of Symbols*. Translated by Jack Sage. 2d edition. London: Routledge, 1971.

Clark, Kenneth. *Landscape into Art*. New York: Harper and Row, 1979.

Clay, Grady. *Close Up: How to Read the American City*. Chicago: University of Chicago Press, 1973.

Cobb, Edith. *Ecology of Imagination in Childhood*. New York: Columbia University Press, 1977.

Collier, John, Jr., and Malcolm Collier. *Visual Anthropology: Photography as a Research Method*. Albuquerque: University of New Mexico Press, 1986.

Cooper, J. C. *An Illustrated Encyclopedia of Traditional Symbols*. London: Thames and Hudson, 1978.

Cosgrove, Denis, and Stephen Daniels, eds. *The Iconography of Landscape*. Cambridge: Cambridge University Press, 1988.

Cranz, Galen. *The Politics of Park Design*. Cambridge: MIT Press, 1982.

Cronon, William. "A Place for Stories: Nature, History, and Narrative." *Journal of American History* 78:4 (March 1992).

———, ed. *Uncommon Ground: Rethinking the Human Place in Nature*. New York: W. W. Norton, 1995.

Crowe, Sylvia. *Tomorrow's Landscape*. London: Architectural Press, 1956.

———, ed. *Space for Living*. Amsterdam, 1961.

Cuff, Dana. *Architecture: The Story of Practice*. Cambridge: MIT Press, 1991.

Cutts, Simon, David Reason, Jonathon Williams, Lucius Burckhardt, Graeme Murray, John Bevis, and Thomas A. Clark. *The Unpainted Landscape*. London: Coracle Press, 1987.

Daubenmire, Rexford. *Plants and Environment*. New York: Wiley, 1959.

———. *Plant Communities*. New York: Harper and Row, 1968.

Dawkins, Marian. *Through Our Eyes Only?: The Search for Animal Consciousness*. Oxford: Freeman, 1993.

Dewey, John. *Art as Experience*. New York: Capricorn Books, 1958.

Donald, Merlin. *Origins of the Modern Mind*. Cambridge: Harvard University Press, 1991.

Dubos, René. *Man Adapting*. New Haven: Yale University Press, 1965.

———. *So Human an Animal*. New York: Charles Scribner's Sons, 1968.

Dunlop, Storm, and Francis Wilson. *Weather and Forecasting*. New York: Macmillan, 1987.

Dunne, Thomas, and Luna Leopold. *Water in Environmental Planning*. San Francisco: Freeman, 1978.

Eiseley, Loren. *Immense Journey*. New York: Vintage, 1957.

———. *The Firmament of Time*. New York: Atheneum, 1969.

Eliade, Mircea. *The Sacred and the Profane*. New York: Harcourt Brace Jovanovich, 1959.

Evernden, Neil. *The Social Creation of Nature*. Baltimore: Johns Hopkins University Press, 1992.

Fairbrother, Nan *The Nature of Landscape Design*. New York: Alfred A. Knopf, 1974.

Feld, Steven. *Sound and Sentiment: Birds, Weeping, Poetics, and Song in Kaluli Expression*. Philadelphia: University of Pennsylvania Press, 1982.

Ferguson, George. *Signs and Symbols in Christian Art*. New York: Oxford University Press, 1961.

Fitch, James Marston. *Historic Preservation: Curatorial Management of the Built World*. New York: McGraw-Hill, 1982.

———. *Land Mosaics: The Ecology of Landscapes and Regions*. Cambridge: Cambridge University Press, 1997.

Frampton, Kenneth. "Towards a Critical Regionalism." In *The Anti-aesthetic: Essays on Postmodern Culture*, edited by Hal Foster. Port Townsend, Wash.: Bay Press, 1983.

Francis, Mark, Lisa Cashdan, and Lynn Paxson. *Community Open Spaces*. Washington, D.C.: Island Press, 1984.

Francis, Mark, and Randolph T. Hester, eds. *The Meaning of Gardens*. Cambridge: MIT Press, 1990.

Gans, Herbert J. *People, Plans, and Policies*. New York: Columbia University Press, 1991.

Geertz, Clifford. *The Interpretation of Culture*. New York: Basic Books, 1973.

———. *Local Knowledge*. New York: Basic Books, 1983.

Gerster, Georg. *Below from Above*. New York: Abbeville, 1986.

Girouard, Marc. *Cities and People: A Social and Architectural History*. New Haven: Yale University Press, 1985.

Glacken, Clarence J. *Traces on the Rhodian Shore: Nature and Culture in Western Thought to the End of the Eighteenth Century*. Berkeley: University of California, 1976.

Glazer, Nathan, and Mark Lilla, eds. *The Public Face of Architecture: Civic Culture and Public Spaces*. New York: Free Press, 1987.

Gleick, James. *Chaos: Making a New Science*. New York: Viking Penquin, 1987.

Golley, Frank. *A History of the Ecosystem Concept in Ecology*. New Haven: Yale University Press, 1994.

Gollwitzer, Gerda. *Bäume: Bilder und Texte aus Drei Jahrtausenden*. Munich: Schuler Verlagsgesellschaft Herrsching, 1980.

Goody, Jack. *The Culture of Flowers*. Cambridge: Cambridge University Press, 1993.

Gothein, Marie Luise. *A History of Garden Art*. 2 volumes. 1928. Reprint, New York: Hacker Art Books, 1979.

Gould, Stephen Jay. *Time's Arrow, Time's Cycle*. Cambridge: Harvard University Press, 1987.

Greenbie, Barrie B. *Spaces: Dimensions of the Human Landscape*. New Haven: Yale University Press, 1981.

Griffin, David. *Animal Thinking*. New York: Van Nostrand Reinhold, 1974.

Hancocks, David. *Animals in Architecture*. New York: Praeger Publishers, 1971.

Haraway, Donna. *Primate Visions*. New York: Routledge, 1989.

Harrison, Richard Pogue. *Forests*. Chicago: University of Chicago Press, 1992.

Hart, John Fraser. *The Look of the Land*. Englewood Cliffs: Prentice-Hall, 1975.

Harvey, David. *The Urban Experience*. Baltimore: Johns Hopkins University Press, 1989.

Hayden, Dolores. *Seven American Utopias: The Architecture of Communitarian Socialism, 1790–1975*. Cambridge: MIT Press, 1976.

———. *The Power of Place: Urban Landscape as Public History*. Cambridge: MIT Press, 1995.

Heidegger, Martin. *Poetry, Language, Thought*. New York: Harper and Row, 1975.

Helphand, Kenneth. "Defiant Gardens." *Journal of Garden History* 17:2 (Summer 1997), 101–19.

Helphand, Kenneth, and Cynthia Girling. *Yard, Street, Park: The Design of Suburban Open Space*. New York: John Wiley, 1994.

Hester, Randolph T. *Neighborhood Space*. Stroudsberg, Penn.: Dowden, Hutchinson and Ross, 1975.

———. *Community Design Primer*. Mendocino, Calif.: Ridge Times, 1990.

Hiss, Tony. *The Experience of Place*. New York: Alfred A. Knopf, 1990.

Hough, Michael. *City Form and Natural Process*. New York: Van Nostrand Reinhold, 1984.

———. *Out of Place: Restoring Identity to the Regional Landscape*. New Haven: Yale University Press, 1990.

Huizinga, Johan. *Homo Ludens: A Study of the Play Element in Culture*. Boston: Beacon Press, 1955.

Hurtwood, Lady Allen of. *Planning for Play*. Cambridge: MIT Press, 1968.

Huth, Hans. *Nature and the American*. Lincoln: University of Nebraska Press, 1990.

Jackson, John Brinckerhoff. *The Necessity for Ruins*. Amherst: University of Massachusetts Press, 1980.

———. *Discovering the Vernacular Landscape*. New Haven: Yale University Press, 1984.

———. *A Sense of Place, A Sense of Time*. New Haven: Yale University Press, 1994.

Jacobs, Jane. *The Death and Life of Great American Cities*. New York: Random House, 1961.

Jellicoe, Geoffrey A., and Susan Jellicoe. *The Landscape of Man*. New York: Van Nostrand Reinhold, 1982.

———, Susan Jellicoe, Patrick Goode, and Michael Lancaster, eds. *The Oxford Companion to Gardens*. New York: Oxford University Press, 1986.

Johnson, Mark. *The Body in the Mind*. Chicago: University of Chicago Press, 1987.

Kaplan, Rachel, and Stephen Kaplan. *The Experience of Nature: A Psychological Perspective*. Cambridge: Cambridge University Press, 1989.

Kassler, Elizabeth B. *Modern Gardens and the Landscape*. New York: Museum of Modern Art, 1964.

Sources   307

Kepes, Gyorgy. *Language of Vision*. Chicago: Paul Theobald, 1944.

———, ed. *The New Landscape in Art and Science*. Chicago: Paul Theobald, 1967.

———, ed. *Arts of the Environment*. New York: George Braziller, 1972.

Knuijt, Martin, Hans Ophius, and Peter van Saane, eds. *Modern Park Design*. Amsterdam: Thoth, 1993.

Kostof, Spiro. *The City Shaped: Urban Patterns and Meanings through History*. Boston: Little, Brown, 1991.

Krieger, Martin. "Up the Plastic Tree." *Landscape Architecture* (July 1973), 349–60.

Lakoff, George. *Women, Fire and Dangerous Things: What Categories Reveal About the Mind*. Chicago: University of Chicago Press, 1987.

Lakoff, George, and Mark Johnson. *Metaphors We Live By*. Chicago: University of Chicago Press, 1980.

Lang, Jon. *Creating Architectural Theory*. New York: Van Nostrand Reinhold, 1987.

Lasswell, Harold D. *The Signature of Power*. New Brunswick, N.J.: Transaction Books, 1979.

Lawlor, Robert. *Sacred Geometry*. London: Thames and Hudson, 1982.

Leveson, David. *A Sense of the Earth*. New York: Anchor Press, 1982.

———. *Geology and the Urban Environment*. New York: Oxford University Press, 1980.

Linenthal, Edward Tabor, *Sacred Grounds: Americans and Their Battlefields*. Chicago: University of Illinois Press, 1991.

Lippard, Lucy R. *Overlay: Contemporary Art and the Art of Prehistory*. New York: Pantheon, 1983.

———. *The Lure of the Local*. New York: New Press, 1997.

Lobeck, Armin K. *Things Maps Don't Tell Us*. New York: Macmillan, 1956.

Lowenthal, David. *The Past Is a Foreign Country*. New York: Cambridge University Press, 1985.

Lyle, John T. *Design for Human Ecosystems*. New York: Van Nostrand Reinhold, 1985.

———. *Regenerative Design for Sustainable Development*. New York: John Wiley and Sons, 1994.

Lynch, Kevin. *Image of the City*. Cambridge: MIT Press, 1960.

———. *What Time Is This Place?* Cambridge: MIT Press, 1972.

———. *Theory of Good City Form*. Cambridge: MIT Press, 1981.

———. *City Sense and City Design: Writings and Projects of Kevin Lynch*. Cambridge: MIT Press, 1990.

———. *Wasting Away*. San Francisco: Sierra Club Books, 1990.

———, and Gary Hack. *Site Planning*. Cambridge: MIT Press, 1993.

Maclean, Norman. *A River Runs Through It*. Chicago: University of Chicago Press, 1976.

Mandelbrot, Benoit B. *The Fractal Geometry of Nature*. New York: W. H. Freeman, 1983.

Marcus, Clare Cooper. *House as a Mirror of Self*. Berkeley: Conari Press, 1995.

———, and Carolyn Francis, eds. *People Places*. New York: Van Nostrand Reinhold, 1990.

McHarg, Ian L. "An Ecological Method for Landscape Architecture." *Landscape Architecture* 57:2 (January 1967), 105–07.

McKim, Robert H. *Experiences in Visual Thinking*. Monterey, Calif.: Brooks/Cole, 1972.

Meinig, D. W., ed. *The Interpretation of Ordinary Landscapes*. New York: Oxford University Press, 1979.

Minnaert, M. G. J. *Light and Color in the Outdoors*. New York: Springer-Verlag, 1974.

Moore, Charles. *Water and Architecture*. New York: Harry Abrams, 1994.

———, William J. Mitchell, and William Turnbull, Jr. *The Poetics of Gardens*. Cambridge: MIT Press, 1988.

Morrish, William, and Catherine Brown. *Planning to Stay*. Minneapolis: Milkweed, 1994.

Morrison, Philip, Phylis Morrison, and the Office of Charles and Ray Eames. *Powers of Ten*. New York: Scientific American Books, 1982.

Norberg-Schulz, Christian. *Concept of Dwelling*. New York: Rizzoli, 1985.

———. *Existence, Space, and Architecture.* New York: Praeger, 1971.

———. *Intentions in Architecture.* Cambridge: MIT Press, 1965.

Oelschlaeger, Max. *The Idea of Wilderness.* New Haven: Yale University Press, 1991.

Olin, Laurie. "Form, Meaning, and Expression in Landscape Architecture." *Landscape Journal* 7:2 (1988), 149–68.

Olwig, Kenneth. "Recovering the Substantive Nature of Landscape." *Annals of the Association of American Geographers* 86:4 (December 1996), 630–53.

Panofsky, Erwin. *Meaning in the Visual Arts.* Garden City: Doubleday, 1955.

———. "Ideological Antecedents of the Rolls-Royce Radiator." *Proceedings of the American Philosophical Society* 107 (1963), 273–88.

Penning-Rowsell, Edmund C., and David Lowenthal, eds. *Landscape Meanings and Values.* London: Allen and Unwin, 1986.

Prest, John. *The Garden of Eden: The Botanic Garden and the Re-creation of Paradise.* New Haven: Yale University Press, 1981.

Preziosi, Donald. *The Semiotics of the Built Environment.* Bloomington: Indiana University Press, 1979.

———. *Architecture, Language, and Meaning.* The Hague: Mouton, 1979.

Rapoport, Amos. *The Meaning of the Built Environment.* Beverly Hills, Calif.: Sage Publications, 1982.

Relph, Edward. *Place and Placelessness.* London: Pion Limited, 1976.

———. *The Modern Urban Landscape.* Baltimore: Johns Hopkins University Press, 1987.

Rich, Adrienne. *The Dream of a Common Language.* W. W. Norton, 1978.

Rieber, Robert W., ed. *The Individual, Communication, and Society.* Cambridge: Cambridge University Press, 1989.

Riley, Robert. "From Sacred Grove to Disney World: The Search for Garden Meaning." *Landscape Journal* 7:2 (1988), 136–47.

Rothman, Hal. *Preserving Different Pasts: The American National Monuments.* Urbana: University of Illinois Press, 1989.

Rowe, Peter G. *Design Thinking.* Cambridge: MIT Press, 1987.

Rowell, Galen. *Mountain Light.* Sierra Club, 1986.

Rudofsky, Bernard. *Streets for People.* New York: Van Nostrand Reinhold, 1982.

Schaefer, Vincent J., and John A. Day. *A Field Guide to the Atmosphere.* Boston: Houghton Mifflin, 1981.

Schafer, R. Murray. *The Tuning of the World.* New York: Alfred A. Knopf, 1977.

Schama, Simon. *Landscape and Memory.* New York: Albert A. Knopf, 1995.

Schapiro, Meyer. "Style." In *Aesthetics Today,* edited by Morris Philipson, 81–113. Cleveland: World Publishing Company, 1961.

Schon, Donald A. *The Reflective Practitioner.* New York: Basic Books, 1983.

Seamon, David, and Robert Mugerauer, eds. *Dwelling, Place and Environment.* New York: Columbia University Press, 1985.

Sears, John F. *Sacred Places: American Tourist Attractions in the Nineteenth Century.* New York: Oxford University Press, 1989.

Sebeok, Thomas A. *The Sign and Its Masters.* Lanham, Md.: University Press of America, 1989.

Seddon, George. "Reflections: Words and Weeds: Some Notes on Language and Landscape." *Landscape Review* 2 (1995), 3–15.

Shepard, Paul. *Man in the Landscape.* College Station: Texas A&M University Press, 1991.

Shelton, John S. *Geology Illustrated.* San Francisco: W. H. Freeman, 1966.

Short, Lester L. *Lives of Birds.* New York: Henry Holt, 1993.

Sonfist, Alan, ed. *Art in the Land.* New York: E. P. Dutton, 1983.

Sørenson, Carl Theodore. *Europas Havekunst.* Copenhagen: G. E. C. Gads, 1959.

Sorkin, Michael, ed. *Variations on a Theme Park.* New York: Hill and Wang, 1992.

Spens, Michael. *Landscape Transformed.* London: Academy Editions, 1996.

Spirn, Anne Whiston. *The Granite Garden: Urban Nature and Human Design.* New York: Basic Books, 1984.

————. "Urban Nature and Human Design: Renewing the Great Tradition." *Journal of Planning Education and Research* 5:1 (Autumn 1985), 39–51.

————. "Landscape Planning and the City." *Landscape and Urban Planning* 13 (1986), 433–41.

————. "The Poetics of City and Nature: Toward a New Aesthetic for Urban Design." *Landscape Journal* 7:2 (Fall 1988), 108–26.

————, ed. *Nature, Form, and Meaning: A Special Issue. Landscape Journal* 7:2 (Fall 1988).

————. "From Uluru to Cooper's Place: Patterns in the Cultural Landscape." *Orion* 9:2 (Spring 1990), 32–39.

Strain, Priscilla, and Frederick Engle. *Looking at Earth.* Atlanta: Turner, 1992.

Summerson, John. *The Classical Language of Architecture.* Cambridge: MIT Press, 1963.

Symes, Michael. *A Glossary of Garden History.* Princes Risborough, Buckinghamshire: Shire, 1993.

Taylor, C. *The Archaeology of Gardens.* Aylesbury, U.K.: Shire Publications, 1983.

Thomas, Keith. *Man and the Natural World.* New York: Pantheon Books, 1983.

Thompson, George F., and Frederick R. Steiner, eds. *Ecological Design and Planning.* New York: John Wiley, 1997.

Treib, Marc, ed. *Modern Landscape Architecture.* Cambridge: MIT Press, 1993.

Tuan, Yi-Fu. *Topophilia.* Englewood Cliffs: Prentice-Hall, 1974.

————. *Space and Place.* Minneapolis: University of Minnesota Press, 1977.

Tufte, Edmund. *Envisioning Information.* Cheshire, Conn.: Graphics Press, 1990.

Turnbull, David. *Maps Are Territories.* Chicago: University of Chicago Press, 1989.

Van Valkenburgh, Michael, curator. *Transforming the American Garden: 12 New Landscape Designs.* Cambridge: Harvard University Graduate School of Design, 1986.

von Frisch, Karl. *Animal Architecture.* New York: Van Nostrand Reinhold, 1983.

Wagstaff, J. M., ed. *Landscape and Culture.* New York: Basil Blackwell, 1987.

Walker, Peter, and Melanie Simo. *Invisible Gardens: The Search for Modernism in the American Landscape.* Cambridge: MIT Press, 1994.

Walter, Eugene Victor. *Placeways.* Chapel Hill: University of North Carolina Press, 1988.

White, Richard. "American Environmental History: The Development of a New Historical Field." *Pacific Historical Review* 54 (1985).

————. "Environmental History, Ecology and Meaning." *Journal of American History* 76:4 (March 1990).

Whyte, William H. *The Social Life of Small Urban Spaces.* Washington, D.C.: Conservation Foundation, 1980.

Williams, Raymond. *The Country and the City.* New York: Oxford University Press, 1975.

————. "Ideas of Nature." In *Problems in Materialism and Culture.* London: Verso, 1980.

————. *Keywords.* New York: Oxford University Press, 1983.

Wines, James. *De-Architecture.* New York: Rizzoli, 1987.

Wolschke-Bulmahn, Joachim, ed. *Nature and Ideology: Natural Garden Design in the Twentieth Century.* Washington, D.C.: Dumbarton Oaks, 1997.

Worster, Donald. *Nature's Economy: The Roots of Ecology.* Garden City, N.Y.: Anchor Press/Doubleday, 1979.

Zevi, Bruno. *The Modern Language of Architecture.* Seattle: University of Washington Press, 1978.

Acknowledgments

This book entailed many journeys, actual and metaphorical, in familiar landscapes and foreign terrain: physiographic, cultural, and disciplinary. I have had excellent and generous companions and guides.

For friendship, for conversations about the language of landscape extending over hours, days, and years, and for their work, I owe a special debt to Glenn Murcutt, Sven-Ingvar Andersson, Charlotte Kahn, and Bill Cronon.

I have described aspects of the language of landscape in dozens of lectures since 1985. These occasions permitted me to test ideas with diverse audiences and landscapes, provoked valuable feedback, and prompted many people to show me places that supported, extended, or challenged the ideas. Without the people and institutions that sponsored these trips and the native guides who shared their local knowledge this would have been a very different book.

I formulated the idea of landscape as language in dialogue with landscapes and architects of Australia in 1988 and gave my first presentation on the topic in Sydney and Melbourne the following year. I would like to thank the School of Architecture at the University of Sydney for appointing me the first Ethel Chettle Distinguished Fellow in 1988 and for inviting me back in 1989. The Royal Australian Institute of Architects sponsored a trip across Australia in 1988, and the University of Melbourne and Royal Melbourne Institute of Technology made possible my visits to that city. Glenn Murcutt, Rick Le Plastrier, Jennifer Taylor, and Peter Johnson persuaded me that the language of landscape encompassed buildings. Michael Ewing, John Richardson, Peter Stutchbury, and Paul Pheleros showed me their work, and David Jones, George Seddon, Jim Sinatra, Peter Towson, Peter Webel, James Weirick, and David Yencken commented and took me to see particular places. Helen Armstrong provided home, friendship, and discussion.

A trip to Japan refined my ideas. I am grateful to the City Bureau of the Japanese Ministry of Construction, and to Director Kazuo Majima and Deputy-Director Isao Naitoh, for sponsoring my trip and for providing two extraordinary guides from their staff: Toshiaki Funabiki, in Tokyo and Osaka, and Ayumi Rai, my companion in Kyoto, Kobe, Ise, and Toba. Both guides responded to a constant stream of questions with patience, openness, and thoughtfulness. The City Planning Association of Japan gave additional support. In Tokyo, Yoshinobu Ashihara, Shigeru Itoh, Akihiko Tani, Kazuhiko Takeuchi, Shunsaku Miyagi, Toshio Oyama, Akira Kobayashi, and alumni of University of Pennsylvania, especially Keiko Takayama, were all very helpful. I would like to thank the cities of Kobe, Kyoto, Ise, and the Mie Prefecture for their generous hospitality, especially my hosts and guides: in Osaka, Yasuko Tsuji and Takeshi Okada; in Ise, Mitsuo Mizutani, Michihiro Okunishi, Sigehiro Got, and Hisashi Inagaki; in Mie, Yasumasa Masuda and Kazuto Ikemura; in Kyoto, Kunihiko Ibuki, Satashi Uemuru, Shun-ichi Uchida, Sen'ichi Oyama, Makoto Suganuma, and Hisako Maeda; in Kobe, Osamu Maki, Osamu Nishi, and Toshihiko Inamatsu.

For many visits to Scandinavia since 1990, I would like to thank the following: in Denmark, the Royal Danish Academy of Art, Royal Danish Agricultural Institute, University of Odense, and Århus University; in Sweden, the Swedish Agricultural University at Alnarp; in Finland, Helsinki Technical University. For sharing ideas and places, I am grateful to Sven-Ingvar Andersson, Thorbjörn Andersson, Annelise Bramsnæs, Per Friberg, Jan Gehl, Jan Gezelius, Pär Gustafsson, Peter Holst, Steen Høyer, Leif Johannesen, Bodil Kjær, Ib Asger Olsen, Ken Olwig, Sonja Poll, Jørgen Primdahl, Henrik Pøhlsgaard, Tom Simons, Preben Skaarup, and Gunnar Sorte. Tove and Poul Henriksen, Birgitte Henriksen, Carl-Erik and Birgit Birn Henriksen, Sanne and Hans Andersen have made Denmark my second home.

Meetings at the Organization for Economic Cooperation and Development provided the occasion for many trips to Paris since 1992, and Chris Brooks, Josef Konvitz, and Françoise Fromonot guided me to particular landscapes in France. Dusan Ogrin invited me to Ljubljana in 1988, showed me the countryside of Slovenia, and pointed me toward Redipuglia. Hans and Ulrike Kiemstedt were my guides in both Hannover and Berlin; the University of Hannover and the Verbund für Wissenschaftsgeschichte in Berlin sponsored those trips. Guido Ferrara and the Italian Society of Landscape Architects invited me to Florence and organized visits to landscapes there; Giorgio Galletti showed me lesser-known corners of the Boboli Gardens.

Phyllis Lambert and the Canadian Centre for Architecture and the U.S. Library of Congress supported my research on Frank Lloyd Wright and made possible several trips to Taliesin North in Wisconsin and Taliesin West in Arizona. Jack Holzhueter gave me insight into Wright's family background. Bruce Brooks Pfeiffer, John deKoven Hill, and Cornelia Brierly shared their memories and knowledge of life with Wright, and Penny Fowler, Oscar Muñoz, Margo Stipe, and Indira Berndtson made stays at the Taliesins productive and enjoyable.

For other field trips in North America, I would like to thank the following organizations and guides: Arizona State University, John Meunier, Frits Steiner, Steve Martino, John Douglas, Ruth Zimmerman, Sharon Southerland, Dennis Siewert; University of Virginia, Warren Byrd, Reuben Rainey, Will Rieley; University of New Mexico, Jane Thurber and Steve Schreiber; University of Oregon, Kenny Helphand, Robert Melnick, Anne Bettman; University of Washington, Anne Moudon; University of California Humanities Research Institute, Michael Barbour, Mike Davis, Susan Davis; University of California-Berkeley, Clare Cooper Marcus, Michael Laurie; University of California-Los Angeles, Kate Hayles; University of California-Davis, Mark Francis, Rob Thayer, Kerry Dawson; University of Wisconsin, Bill Cronon, Arnold Alanen; University of Georgia, Darrel Morrison, Catherine Howett; University of Miami; Washington University; the Society of Soil and Water Conservation for a trip to Lexington, Kentucky; University of Colorado-Boulder, Society of Landscape Ecology, International Pedestrian Conference, Women's League of Voters of Colorado Springs, Thorne Ecological Institute, and the Colorado Chapter of ASLA for successive visits to Colorado's Front Range; American Collegiate Schools of Architecture Teachers' Workshop at Cranbrook Academy of Art; Dallas Institute; Garden Clubs of Houston. From 1973 to 1977, Wallace McHarg Roberts and Todd sent me to Houston, Denver, Montauk, Wye Island, Sanibel, and Toronto for fieldwork. Adèle Naudé Santos and Vince Healey showed me landscapes in San Diego and La Jolla. Kenny Helphand and Robert Melnick took me on a tour of the Rocky Mountains west of Denver.

I am grateful to Richard Haag, John Lyle, Martha Schwartz, Peter Shepheard, and Ken

Wright for taking me to places they designed and to A. E. Bye, Carol Franklin, Laurie Olin, Leslie Sauer, Mario Schjetnan, Adèle Naudé Santos, Carl Steinitz, Peter Walker, and James Wines for discussing how they work. Talks, trips, and workshops with Lawrence Halprin stimulated, provoked, and inspired.

Charlotte Kahn introduced me to Boston's inner-city landscapes and community gardeners. Hayward Ford continued my education in Philadelphia, and Ira Harkavy recruited me to work with teachers and students in Sulzberger Middle School. Glenn Campbell and Zakiyyah Ali have given me insight into children, life, and community in Mill Creek. I have worked with many research assistants on the West Philadelphia Landscape Project over the past eleven years; John Berg, Mark Cameron, Robert Cheetham, Martin Knox, Dan Marcucci, Michele Pollio, Sam Spirn, and John Widrick all worked on the project for two or more years and contributed in crucial ways, as did W. Gary Smith. The National Endowment for the Arts sponsored my study of urban vacant lands in 1985, and the J. N. Pew Charitable Trust, U.S. Department of Housing and Urban Development, Philadelphia Urban Resources Partnership, the Kellogg Foundation, and University of Pennsylvania's Center for Community Partnerships have supported the West Philadelphia Landscape Project.

A Noyes Fellowship at the Bunting Institute in fall 1985 enabled me to reflect and write about the poetics of landscape. A sabbatical in 1990–91 permitted me to develop the language of landscape within the context of the West Philadelphia Landscape Project, and a project fellowship from the National Endowment for the Arts in 1991 provided support for landscape photographs. A fellowship at the University of California Humanities Research Institute in 1994 provided a lively forum of colleagues who raised new questions to address. A fellowship at the Woodrow Wilson International Center for Scholars in 1995–96 gave me the time and space to bring the manuscript to near completion.

Linda Seidel, Ian McHarg, Narendra Juneja, Bob Hanna, and Peter Shepheard were teachers whose influence was formative. I have learned much from my students, and many research assistants have helped gather material: George Batchelor, Victoria Hoffman, Elizabeth Lardner, Paul Rookwood, Bill Hartman, Sylvia Palms, Christine Min, Marc Kushner, and Kamni Gill. Cathy Ford and Amy Freitag helped with the bibliography. Ann Donaghy typed my journals from 1989 to 1994.

I thank the following for permission to adapt publications of mine to which they hold copyright: Canadian Center for Architecture for my essay on Frank Lloyd Wright, and William Cronon and W. W. Norton for my essay on Frederick Law Olmsted. For permission to quote from Anthony Hecht's poem "The Gardens of the Villa d'Este," in The Hard Hours, I am grateful to Knopf, and, for the right to reproduce illustrations, to Bruce Brooks Pfeiffer and the Frank Lloyd Wright Foundation for the plan of Ocatilla; Ed Grushesky and the Philadelphia Water Department for the photograph of the Mill Creek sewer; the University of Chicago Press for the Bedolina petroglyph from David Turnbull, Maps Are Territories (originally published in J. B. Harley and D. Woodward, eds., The History of Cartography, volume 1, Cartography in Prehistoric, Ancient, and Medieval Europe and the Mediterranean [University of Chicago Press]); Dorothy McLaughlin for the photograph of Taliesin. And to Dee Mullin, a special thanks for locating and reproducing the photograph of Lovejoy Fountain. For generously providing their photographs and drawings, I would like to thank Alex MacLean, Lawrence Halprin, Glenn Murcutt, Laurie Olin, Sven-Ingvar Andersson,

Sonja Poll, James Wines, Alan Ward, and Lewis Watts. With the exception of the Wolf Tree, my own photographs are all 35mm Kodachrome slides, transformed by Kodak into digital files on CD-ROMs and converted to black-and-white images in Adobe Photoshop. Sam Spirn and Charles Neer converted the preliminary low-resolution images; I produced the final high-resolution images after expert coaching by Sam Spirn and Chung Kim.

Sven-Ingvar Andersson, Bill Cronon, David DeLong, Susan Frey, Frank Golley, Kathryn Gleason, Donna Haraway, Kate Hayles, Catherine Howett, Tom and Agatha Hughes, Charlotte Kahn, Michael Katz, Clare Cooper Marcus, Darrel Morrison, Ken Olwig, Jenny Price, Reuben Rainey, Dan Rose, Mark Rose, Carl Steinitz, Jennifer Taylor, Sam Bass Warner, Richard White, and Joachim Wolschke-Bulmahn commented on early versions of various chapters. Takamasa Miyazaki, Chiharu Takenaka, Keichi Fujiwara, Kinya Muriyama, and Anne Walthall read and responded to my descriptions of Japanese culture and landscape. Dolores Hayden, Kenny Helphand, John Dixon Hunt, Paul Spirn, and Isabelle Whiston read the entire manuscript. I am grateful to all for their insights. Judy Metro's immediate, enthusiastic response to the manuscript spurred the final phase of writing, and Lawrence Kenney's deft editing brought it to closure; Mary Mayer ushered the book gracefully through design and production.

For eighteen years, Jeannette Hopkins has challenged me to find and sustain my own voice and dared me to take risks. She has listened, read, questioned, provoked, and inspired through twelve years and countless drafts. She complained that the book would never be finished if I didn't stop traveling to far-off places, then insisted that the journal texts belonged in the book and defended them from translation into academic prose. I owe her a profound debt as editor and friend.

Landscapes have the advantage over libraries and museums that families, even small children, are willing to take vacations in them. My husband, Paul, partner of more than half a lifetime, was an enthusiastic companion on many trips, sent me off on other travels, and never questioned why this book was taking so long to write. My son, Sam, has grown up with the book: he was five when I began; now seventeen, he has been my research assistant for several years. Growing, he led me to see freshly and to feel landscape again from a child's perspective. Hundreds of swim meets, baseball, soccer, and basketball games were occasions to meditate on movement, geometry, and sport and to realize that muscles have memory.

My mother and father taught me to see the world in terms of questions and stories that guide actions and to believe that what you do is who you are. My Danish mother and father affirmed common meanings and values even as they coached me in a new culture. Both sets of parents showed me how to read landscape and to belong to a place through caring for it. This book is dedicated to them.

Index

Boston *(continued)*
  Roxbury, 41, 96, 115–18, 207; and urban renewal, 63, 254; Riverway, 67, 90; Dudley Street neighborhood, 91–92, 179, 205, 207; Beacon Hill, 158; Redevelopment Authority, 207; Public Garden, 219, 237; and inner city decline, 257–58
Boston Urban Gardeners, 91
boundaries: rivers as, 33, 140; in Japan, 77; and territory, 118–19, 120
Bowood (England), 90, 203
Brandt, G. N.: Mariebjerg Cemetery, 110–11, 138, 264; and Andersson, 193, 195; and own garden, 198. *See also* Mariebjerg Cemetery
Brazil, 222
Brierly, Cornelia, 132
Brown, "Capability," 16, 90, 203, 252
Bryant Park (New York), 51
Bye, A. E., 203, 204

California, 78, 143, 238; Irvine, 86, 87, 233, 263; Newport Coast Road, 125; South Coast Plaza, 175; and paradox and irony, 233. *See also* Disneyland/Disney World; Laguna Canyon; Orange County, Calif.; Sea Ranch; Village Homes
Calvino, Italo, 265
Carson, Rachel, 149
cathedral, 58, 100
Cather, Willa, 159
cemetery, 59–63, 230, 235. *See also* Forest Cemetery; Mariebjerg Cemetery; Redipuglia
Central Park, 21, 24, 53–54, 197, 277n43; Bethesda Fountain, 126, 227
Chantilly (France), 90, 101–3, 182, 231
Chartres cathedral, 58
Chestnut Hill, Pa., 184–85
China: gardens in, 78, 233; Forbidden City, 106–7
Church, Thomas, 203, 252

Cicero, 31–32
Cincinnati, 5
circles: in landscape, 33, 104, 107, 108, 109–10; in architecture, 110
city plan, 106–7, 184–5; Greek, 169–70
cliché, 200, 229
climate, 89, 97, 156
climax, 223–24
clouds, 32, 33, 142–43, 200
Coastal Plain, 6, 184
Colorado, 157; Platte River, 43, 144; plains, 150–55, 156, 171; Fort Collins, 153. *See also* Denver
Columbus Park (Chicago), 250–51
community gardens, 7–8, 193; as landscape of community, 8, 72–75, 211; as expression of landscape, 22, 35–36, 73–75; and biblical allusion, 79–80; and land reclaimed, 115–18, 210–11. *See also* Aspen Farms
conceit, 228–29, 231
context: as shaper of landscape elements, 15, 17, 18–19, 86, 133; as woven fabric, 17, 160–61, 163–67; and anomalies, 18–19, 159–60; Latin word "contexere," 133; of Japan, 134–37, 163–67; and trees, 137–39; shaping, 138, 207–9; and rivers, 139–42; and clouds, 142–43; and mountains, 143–46; and humans, 146–48; and birds, 148–50; of Denver, 150–55; enduring v. ephemeral, 156–58; multiple, 168–69, 171; and scale, 171–74; design and deep context, 181–83, 184–86
contrast, 20, 219
Cooper's Place (Boston), 115–19, 121, 207
Copenhagen, 34, 230, 253–54
Courances (France), 261, 264
Cranz, Galen, 64
Cronon, William, 38–39, 49
Crouch, Doris, 169
Crowe, Sylvia, 246
culture, 95; and cultural blindness, 35, 114; local v. universal, 48–49, 75–77, 81, 195

Ferrand, Beatrix, 50
Finland, 96–97
Finlay, Ian Hamilton, 79, 201
fire, 86, 87, 89, 98, 99, 100
fishermen, 18, 24, 142
Ford, Hayward, 71–72, 215
forest, 36; at Chantilly, 102–3; in Japan, 136–37, 144; as communities, 139; at Bloedel Reserve, 259–62; urban, 271–72. *See also* trees
Forest Cemetery (Sweden), 121, 133, 180; Hill of Remembrance, 21, 61–62, 80, 125, 178; Woodland Chapel, 110
fountains, 64–65, 94, 126, 220, 227, 268; Tanner Fountain, 64, 98; at Parc André Citroën, 65, 199; at the Alhambra, 94, 144–45, 221, 226; Bethesda Fountain, 126, 227; Lovejoy Fountain, 145. *See also* Ira's fountain
framing, 130, 216, 218–19, 223
France: Regional Cultural Parks, 51; formal gardens in, 78, 90, 182, 228; river Rance, 141, 231, 265. *See also* Chantilly; Parc de Sceaux; Paris; Vaux-le-Vicomte; Versailles
Franklin Court (Philadelphia), 232, 234
Freeway Park (Seattle), 67
freeways, 67, 90
Friberg, Per, 201
Friedrich, Caspar David, on language of nature, 37
Fromonot, Françoise, 205
Frost, Robert, 125
Frye, Northrop, 195, 276n17
function: and art, 3, 256; and congruence with feeling and meaning, 80–81, 94, 169–70; and relation to form and feeling, 123; and deep context, 181; authority of, 244, 253–55, 256, 259

Gans, Herbert, 255
garden, 70–75; as "third nature," 32; as paradise, 33, 70, 248; experimental, 191–95, 201; and self-expression, 192–95; natural

garden movement, 246, 251. *See also* community gardens; *individual listings*
Gardner, Isabella Stewart, and courtyard garden, 235
Gasworks Park (Seattle), 262
gates, 77; and ritual passage, 55–56, 58, 222; and performance space, 117, 118–19, 121, 123, 125, 126; as context, 133
Geddes, Patrick, 196
genres, of landscape, 21, 54–55, 276n17; of worship, 55–57; of memory, 59–63; of play, 63–67; of movement, 67–68; of production, 68–70; of home and community, 70–77
geometry, 104–11, 216; and Le Nôtre, 102–3, 180, 182; fractal, 105–6; and F. L. Wright, 105, 109, 131, 181
Gettysburg, 50, 58–59
Ghost Parking Lot (Hamden, Conn.), 51, 52, 199
Gollwitzer, Gerda, 139
Gould, Stephen Jay, 95
Grand Canyon, 21
Great Plains, 150–55, 156, 171
grid, 102, 103, 110, 180–81; of American Midwest, 106, 153, 156–57; and city plans, 106–7, 169–70
Grundtvig, N. F. S., 28

Haag, Richard, 261, 262, 264
habitat, 16, 95, 119, 244; of tree, 17; forest as, 36
Hadrian's Villa (Italy), 175
Halprin, Lawrence, 16, 149, 196, 210, 215; and dialogue with clients, 42–43; and freeways, 67, 90; and fountains, 145, 147, 180, 195, 198–99; and directly shaping landscape, 202–3. *See also* Ira's Fountain; Lovejoy Fountain; Sea Ranch
Hargreaves, George, 228
Harlequin Plaza (Denver), 221, 226–27
Harrison, Helen, 245
Harrison, Newton, 245
Harvard University, 6, 7; Tanner Fountain,

64, 98; Graduate School of Design, 116, 238

Hayden, Dolores, 160–61, 264

Hecht, Anthony, 231

Heidegger, Martin, on concept of dwelling, 16

High Plains, 152

Hippocrates, on urban planning, 169

history, 48–49, 243

Hollis, Doug, 245

Hoskins, W. G., 179

Houston, 166, 228, 230

Hoyt, Burnham, 151

Huizinga, Johan, on places of play, 63

Hull, John, 36

humans: as shapers of landscape, 15, 17–18, 22–26, 156–58; and language of landscape, 22–23, 25–26; as trees, 139; as context, 146–48

Hunt, John Dixon, 32

Independence National Park (Philadelphia), 253, 263

International Style, 98, 182–83

Ira's Fountain (Portland, Ore.), 145, 146–47, 180, 198

irony, 31, 34, 229–33

Ise shrine (Japan), 55–58, 107, 234; and enduring impermanence, 56, 100; and nested enclosures, 56, 107, 180, 222

Italy, 55; gardens in, 18, 50, 78, 236; Villa d'Este, 18, 236; Villa Rotonda, 222; Villa Lante, 236. *See also* Redipuglia

Jacobs, Jane, 255

James, Henry, 80

James, William, 5, 265

Japan: as landscape of paradox, 50, 135–36, 230; subways, 68, 77, 166; houses, 75–77; cities, 76–77, 166–67; green light in, 81, 98–99, 135; and stroll garden, 125, 130, 279n55, 279n53; and influence on F. L. Wright, 127, 130, 278n50, 279n53; and deep context of landscape, 134–37; *tsubo*, 148; and integrating old and new, 163–67; rice fields, 166–67, 280n35; Yokohama railroad station, 225. *See also* Ise shrine; Ryoanji; Saihoji

Jefferson, Thomas, 21, 156, 194, 216, 252

Jekyll, Gertrude, 78

Jellicoe, Geoffrey, 195, 198, 219–20, 224, 229, 236

Jensen, Jens, 78, 109, 131, 248–49, 250–51

Johnson, Mark, 19

Kahn, Charlotte, 91

Kahn, Louis, 149, 163

Kansas City, Mo., 110, 125

Katsura (Kyoto), 99, 164, 218

Kennedy, Robert, 162

Kent, William, 90

Kentucky, 104, 110, 181

Kew, Royal Botanical Garden at, 225

Kiemstedt, Hans, 91

Klee, Paul, 39–40, 110, 196, 263

Kobe, 99, 136, 164

Kongenshus Memorial Park (Denmark), 28–31, 49, 50, 77, 121

Kyoto, 76, 98–99, 107, 135–36, 165–66; Shisendo, 39, 98–99, 164, 195; Shugakuin, 99, 137; Katsura, 99, 164, 218

Laguna Canyon, Calif., 86–87, 89, 98, 99

Laguna Canyon Wilderness Park, 42–43

Lakoff, George, 19

landscape: as language, 3, 8, 15–18, 20–21, 22–26; as dwelling, 15, 16; and early forms of writing, 15, 273n1; as text, 15–16, 35–37; word for, 16–17, 273n7; as shaping, 16–18, 24; vernacular, 17, 39, 49–50, 181–82, 202, 234; as manmade, 17–18, 24–25, 274n14; authors of, 17–18, 51–54; and scale, 18, 171–75; and anomaly, 18–19, 159–60, 224–2; and metaphor, 19–20, 27, 34, 200, 226–29; as rhetoric, 20–21; as expression of power, 20–21, 115, 158, 220, 257–59;

memorials, 49–50, 59–60; Kongenshus, 28–31; Verdun, 50, 59, 61, 62; as elegy, 50, 275n8; Leopold Memorial Reserve, 52–53; National French Resistance Memorial, 59. *See also* Forest Cemetery; Redipuglia; Vietnam Veterans Memorial

memory, 98–99, 138–39, 196; landscapes of, 50–51, 59–63, 196, 253

Messiaen, Olivier, 148

metaphor, 15, 19–20, 27, 34, 200, 217, 226–29

metonymy, 223, 227–28

Mexico City, 106, 183

Michener, James, 154

Middleton Place (South Carolina), 68–69

Mies van der Rohe, Ludwig, 195, 232

Mill Creek (Philadelphia): design for, 3, 7, 23, 42, 213–15; as sewer, 10–11, 161–62, 185–88, 212; and abandonment of inner city neighborhoods, 92, 161–63, 175, 187, 265; reimagining, 267–72. *See also* Aspen Farms; Sulzberger Middle School

Miller, Wilhelm, 78

Minnesota State Capitol, competition, 252–53, 259

Mishima, Yukio, 235

Mississippi River, 27, 37, 49, 142

Mohr, Jean, on language of lived experience, 25

Monet, Claude, 35, 39

Mont-Saint-Michel, 47–48, 49, 54, 56, 110, 223

Mont Valérien (Paris), 50, 59, 60

Morrison, Darrel, 197

Morrison, Philip, 172, 174

Morrison, Phylis, 172, 174

mountains, 77, 143–46; as sacred landscape, 20, 33, 143, 165; in Japan, 134–35, 165

Mount Auburn Cemetery (Cambridge, Mass.), 230, 235

Muir, John, 52, 55

Mumford, Lewis, 196

Murcutt, Glenn, 3, 125, 195; and use of landscape, 21, 43–45, 197, 200, 245; method of design, 43–45, 182, 202, 204–5, 206. *See also* Ball house; Bingie, Australia, house at

Muriyama, Kinya, 203

Mussolini, 20, 21, 59, 257

Nærum Garden Colony (Denmark): hedges at, 74–75, 222, 264; and Danish culture, 75, 158, 263; order and flexibility, 180, 193, 197

nature: cities as 3, 24, 156, 264–65; and shaping of landscape, 17–18; landscape as interpretation of, 24, 32; "native" nature, 31–32; and word for, 32, 273n7, 274n13; authority of, 244, 246–50, 259; and use of native species, 251; v. art, 252

Nazis, and political use of landscape, 17, 246, 249, 252

Netherlands, the, 158, 219

New York City, 158, 182–83, 232; Bryant Park, 51; Battery Park, 51–52, 224; Bronx River Parkway, 67, 90; Statue of Liberty, 218; Paley Park, 236; Jacob Javits Plaza, 255–56. *See also* Central Park

Niagara Falls, 53, 224, 262

Nicholson, Ben, 229

Noguchi, Isamu, 175

Norberg-Shulz, Christian, 122

Notre Dame cathedral, 58, 100

Nourlangie Rock (Australia), 124

Ocatilla (Arizona), 130, 180, 181

Ohio, 5, 205

Olin, Laurie, 51, 197, 250, 255

Olmsted, Frederick Law, 16, 196, 252; and wild landscape, 53–55, 70, 250, 277n43; Yosemite, 55, 70; Fens and Riverway, 70, 116, 196–97, 250–51, 281nn11,13; Niagara Falls, 224, 262. *See also* Fens and Riverway; Central Park

Oral Roberts University (Oklahoma), 220

Orange County, Calif., 42–43, 86, 87, 125, 175, 233, 263

order, 109, 179–81; and repeating events, 87–90; and F. L. Wright, 131–32, 180–81; and Mariebjerg Cemetery, 180, 193, 264; and Nærum, 180, 193, 264; and Marnas, 191–95; and framework for Mill Creek, 210–15. *See also* geometry

Osaka, 76, 165, 166; subway, 68; Shitennoji, 163

oxymoron, 230–32, 263

Palladio, Andrea, 222, 252

Palm Canyon, Calif., 88

Panofsky, Erwin, 160

paradox, 27, 229–33; at Kongenshus, 31; at Ryoanji, 50, 135; at Bloedel Reserve, 258, 259–62; cultivating, 262–65

parallelism, 218, 221, 223

Parc André Citroën (Paris), 64–65, 198

Parc de La Villette (Paris), 108, 200, 221, 222

Parc de Sceaux, 175–76, 182, 223

Paris, 224; Parc André Citroën, 64–65, 198; Place de Vosges, 97, 230; Champs-Élysées, 106; Parc de La Villette, 108, 200, 221, 222; plaza by La Grande Arche, 120; Arc de Triomphe, 125; Eiffel Tower, 227; and Haussmann, 257

parks, 78. *See also individual listings*

parkways, 67, 90

past: and landscape of memory, 50–51, 59–63, 253; erasing (Berlin), 63, 175, 240–44, 263; loss of through urban renewal, 63, 175, 263; re-creating, 243; authority of, 244, 250–53, 257; and tradition and invention in landscape, 263

paths: as metaphor, 20, 27; as landscape element, 22, 49, 84, 85, 102, 108–9; in sacred landscape, 27, 33, 111; as places of meeting and movement, 73–74, 119–21, 170; storied, 78–79, 114–15, 119, 259–60; at Uluru, 111, 114, 119; English footpaths, 119–20, 179; as performance space, 121; and form and meaning, 125, 178

Penn, William, 184

performance space, 121–26, 278n35; Uluru as, 111–14, 118–19; Stourhead as, 114–15, 118–19; Cooper's Place as, 115–19

performance zoning, 209

personification, 20, 228, 235

Pfeiffer, Bruce, 132

Philadelphia, 183–88; planning commission, 23, 163; water department, 23, 215; Welcome Park, 81; city plan, 81, 106, 197, 218, 222; seasons in, 175; Fairmount Park, 185, 189, 230; Franklin Court, 232, 234; Independence National Park, 253, 263; Redevelopment Authority, 254, 270. *See also* Mill Creek; Schuylkill River; West Philadelphia

Phoenix, 129, 159, 179

photography, 4, 5, 8

Piedmont, 6, 183–84

Pinchot, Gifford, 55

place: word for, 17; experience of, 80–81; identity of, 160–63, 182–82, 264

placement, 218, 223

planning, 8, 11, 23, 92, 166, 182, 208, 255

plants: succession of, 31, 35 223–24; communities of, 139, 181, 250; native v. foreign, 196, 246, 250, 251

play: landscapes of, 55, 63–67, 146–47; adventure playground, 65–66

Pliny, 39

Pøhlsgaard, Henrik, 201

Poll, Sonja, 108–9, 227

Pollan, Michael, 24

Pope, Alexander, 79, 222, 231

Poussin, Nicholas, 79, 235

Powelton/Summer-Winter Community Garden (Philadelphia), 74

power, expressed through landscape, 220, 257–59; at Redipuglia, 20–21, 257; in English landscape, 115, 158, 257; and stone, 133

prairie, 139, 152, 156, 157, 230; trees on, 139, 159, 219

Prairie School, 78

Westminster Community Garden (Philadelphia), 210–11, 213

West Philadelphia, 210–15, 254; West Philadelphia Landscape Project, 73, 211–12, 215; Powelton/Summer-Winter Community Garden, 74; Spruce Hill Garden, 74; Garden of Eatin', 79; Gethsemane, 79; Sulzberger Middle School, 96, 162, 163, 214, 271; and City Planning Commission plan, 163; Westminster Community Garden, 210–11, 213. *See also* Aspen Farms; Mill Creek

Whitman, Walt, 139

Widrick, John, 73, 123, 212, 215

wilderness: as chaos, 18, 24; as sacred ground, 18, 55; human impulse to control, 31; constructed by Olmsted, 53–54, 69–70

Williams, Raymond, 248

Williamsburg, Va., 50, 253

wind, 177–78; and Danish heath, 28, 34, 81; and Murcutt's designs, 44–45, 182, 200, 245; and Venturi effect, 183, 219

Wines, James, 51

wolf trees, 18–19, 77, 137, 138, 159

Wordsworth, William, 37, 79

worship, landscapes of, 47–48, 54, 55–58, 222, 229. *See also* sacred places

Worster, Donald, 49

Wright, Frank Lloyd, 16, 196; and an American style of architecture, 78; and use of geometric form, 105, 109, 131, 181; and land as architecture, 127–28, 130, 132, 278n43; and nature, 127, 198, 247, 248; Japanese influence on, 127, 278n50, 279n53; and abstraction, 128, 198, 248; prow garden, 129, 131, 178, 198; Ocatilla, 130, 180, 181; and structure, 131–32, 180–81, 279nn55,59; and experimentation, 132, 178, 201, 203–4; Johnson Compound, 181

Wright, Ken, 22, 245

Wye Valley, 119–20

yellowwood tree, 10–11, 22–23, 272

Yosemite, 21, 49, 53, 55, 70